THE RHETORIC OF THE PAGE

THE RHETORIC
OF THE PAGE

LAURIE MAGUIRE

OXFORD
UNIVERSITY PRESS

OXFORD
UNIVERSITY PRESS

Great Clarendon Street, Oxford, OX2 6DP,
United Kingdom

Oxford University Press is a department of the University of Oxford.
It furthers the University's objective of excellence in research, scholarship,
and education by publishing worldwide. Oxford is a registered trade mark of
Oxford University Press in the UK and in certain other countries

Published in the United States of America by Oxford University Press
198 Madison Avenue, New York, NY 10016, United States of America

British Library Cataloguing in Publication Data
Data available

Library of Congress Control Number: 2020930020

ISBN 978–0–19–886210–9

Printed and bound by
CPI Group (UK) Ltd, Croydon, CR0 4YY

For Dympna Callaghan

Is it that by its indefiniteness it shadows forth the heartless voids and immensities of the universe, and thus stabs us from behind with the thought of annihilation, when beholding the white depths of the milky way? Or is it, that as in essence whiteness is not so much a color as the visible absence of color, and at the same time the concrete of all colors; is it for these reasons that there is such a dumb blankness, full of meaning, in a wide landscape of snows—a colorless, all-color of atheism from which we shrink? And when we consider that other theory of the natural philosophers, that all other earthly hues—every stately or lovely emblazoning—the sweet tinges of sunset skies and woods; yea, and the gilded velvets of butterflies, and the butterfly cheeks of young girls; all these are but subtile deceits, not actually inherent in substances, but only laid on from without; so that all deified Nature absolutely paints like the harlot, whose allurements cover nothing but the charnel-house within; and when we proceed further, and consider that the mystical cosmetic which produces every one of her hues, the great principle of light, for ever remains white or colorless in itself, and if operating without medium upon matter, would touch all objects, even tulips and roses, with its own blank tinge—pondering all this, the palsied universe lies before us a leper; and like wilful travellers in Lapland, who refuse to wear colored and coloring glasses upon their eyes, so the wretched infidel gazes himself blind at the monumental white shroud that wraps all the prospect around him. And of all these things the Albino whale was the symbol. Wonder ye then at the fiery hunt?

Herman Melville, *Moby Dick*

'I have not speculated how to fill this space'
Randall McLeod, 'Obliterature'

Conventions

In old-spelling quotations I have silently regularized i/j and u/v, expanded contractions, corrected spacing and turned letters, and brought superscript letters down to the line. In dialogue from old-spelling plays I have added modernized speech prefixes and given character names in full; occasional exceptions to this occur when page layout is germane to the point being made. All through-line numbering (TLN) references to Shakespeare's plays are to *The First Folio: The Norton Facsimile*, ed. Charlton Hinman (New York: Norton, 1968). All modern-spelling Shakespeare quotations come from *The Riverside Shakespeare*, ed. G. Blakemore Evans and J. M. M. Tobin, 2nd edn (Boston, MA: Houghton Mifflin, 1997). Short Title Catalogue (STC) numbers are provided in the Works Cited, but I occasionally include them in the text and footnotes when discussing works that have several issues in a single year. Dates in parentheses are those of first publication; if there is a large gap between composition and publication, both dates are given.

Acknowledgements

This book ranges widely across texts, periods, disciplines, and languages; 'the fiery hunt' would not have been possible without those colleagues who shared their expertise when I ventured into their territory. To give specific examples of their generosity would turn these acknowledgements into a chapter, so in the list that follows I take my cue from Umberto Eco: he admires lists for eschewing saturation in favour of 'a poetics of the "etcetera"'. Given that this book is in part about the readerly pleasure of supplying what is missing, I hope that some of the same experience may attach to the undetailed contributions of those who appear here merely as names.

In the world of medieval studies I enjoyed assistance and stimulation from James Carley, David Carlson, Elisabeth Dutton, Mary Flannery, Simon Horobin, Hannah Ryley, Marion Turner, and Dan Wakelin.

The list of early modernists who helped me think by answering queries, volunteering information, discussing details, sending JPEGs, offering feedback, sharing unpublished work, and listening to lectures (formal and informal) is long: Sharon Achinstein, Mark Bland, Claire Bourne, Sophie Butler, Dympna Callaghan, A. E. B. Coldiron, Archie Cornish, Eleanor Decamp, José Pérez Díez, Sophie Duncan, Katherine Duncan-Jones, Derek Dunne, Saul Frampton, Indira Ghose, Margreta de Grazia, Zoë Hawkins, John Kerrigan, Andy Kesson, Chris Kyle, Hester Lees-Jeffries, Zachary Lesser, Raphael Lyne, Ben Morgan, Harry Newman, David Norbrook, Marion O'Connor, Will Poole, Lois Potter, Richard Proudfoot, Tom Roebuck, Jonathan Sawday, Philip Schwyzer, Jason Scott-Warren, Alison Shell, Bill Sherman, Cathy Shrank, Emma Smith, Clare Smout, Elisabetta Tarantino, Ramie Targoff, Kate Welch, R. S. White, Martin Wiggins, Alexandra Wingate, Gillian Woods, Daniel Yabut. The dedicatee has provided academic fellowship and camaraderie over many decades and it is a pleasure to pay tribute to her.

When I strayed into the eighteenth century I was lucky to have the help of Clare Bucknell, Jim McLaverty, John McTague, Abigail Williams, and Helen Williams.

I am hugely grateful to Robert Douglas-Fairhurst, Alexander Fyjis-Walker, and Adam Mars-Jones for alerting me to twentieth-century material and discussing it with me.

My local Oxford community has offered support in innumerable ways. I am grateful to Sharon Achinstein, Marta Arnaldi, Kate Bennett, Felicity Brown, Felix Budelmann, Colin Burrow, Ben Burton, Terence Cave, Juan-Carlos Condé, Archie Cornish, Robert Douglas-Fairhurst, Dennis Duncan, Sophie Duncan, Katherine Duncan-Jones, Nicola Gardini, Ben Higgins, Simon Horobin, Lorna Hutson, Paulina Kewes, Bethany Kidd, James McBain, Noel Mantock, Katie Mennis, Dianne Mitchell, Brian Moore, Ben Morgan, Joe Moshenska, Katie Murphy, David Norbrook, Sam Plumb, Hannah Ryley, Joe Sampson, Elizabeth Sandis, John Scholar, Richard Scholar, Charlotte Scott, Emma Smith, Adam Smyth, Robert Stagg, Tiffany Stern, Jane Stevenson, Elisabetta Tarantino, and Dan Wakelin.

I owe thanks to audiences in Cambridge, Canterbury, Exeter, Fribourg, London, Norwich, Oxford, and Stratford for the opportunity to try out ideas. An early version of Chapter 2 was given as a plenary paper at the 2011 Shakespeare Association of America meeting in Seattle. It was published in that early form in 2015 in *The Oxford Handbook of Embodiment*, edited by Valerie Traub. I am grateful to Oxford University Press for permission to include the revised version here.

In a book about reading, it is a pleasure to thank the librarians who brought me STC books in what felt like the rare-book equivalent of hotel room service. I was lucky to have a short-term fellowship at the Folger Shakespeare Library and two one-month residencies there. I am indebted to LuEllen DeHaven, Rosalind Larry, Camille Seerattan, and the late Betsy Walsh; Caroline Duroselle-Melish, Michael Witmore, and Georgianna Ziegler provided material and information that I would not otherwise have known about. Julie Swierczek enlightened me on the history of filming and digitizing rare books and Abbie Weinberg provided wonderful (and repeated) long-distance assistance when my sojourns on Capitol Hill came to an end.

In Oxford, the staff of the Weston Library Reading Room solved cataloguing problems, and allowed me access to items in storage and in exhibitions (I am especially grateful to Madeline Slaven and Sallyanne Gilchrist), and Richard Ovenden and Emma Stanford responded swiftly and generously to my queries about the technical aspects of digitizing. Sarah Wheale facilitated access to especially rare rare books and I am grateful to her for endless generosity of spirit.

I have been fortunate beyond all measure with two successive Fellow Librarians at Magdalèn College: Christine Ferdinand and Daryl Green. Christine also provided an apartment on Capitol Hill and Daryl identified material for me and shared his photographs. The Magdalen College Archivist, Robin Darwall-Smith, located Latin documents for me. Will Beharrell and Maggie Wainwright offered regular ancillary assistance, and the help given by Anne Chesher went above and beyond the call of duty.

This is also true of the assistance volunteered by the staff in the English Faculty Library. Because of Jocelyn English, Jen Gallagher, and Helen Scott (assisted by Emma Jambor and Stephanie Wales) I am now accustomed to ordering STC books at midnight and reading them at 9am. Even before I arrived at the Huntington Library, Stephen Tabor helped me enormously, as did Samuel Wylie. In the Ahmanson Reading Room I enjoyed superb assistance from Morex Arai, Stephanie Arias, Lisa Caprino, Mark Fletcher, and Katrina Sanchez. Julie Stoner at the Geography and Maps Division of the Library of Congress provided speedy digital help as did Lisa Lilliott at Harvard Law School Library.

For permission to reproduce images I record my thanks to Margaret Bartley at Bloomsbury Books; the President and Fellows of Magdalen College, Oxford; the Bodleian Library; the Folger Shakespeare Library; the British Library; the Library of Congress; the Ugly Duckling Presse; the Huntington Library, San Marino, CA; Penguin Random House; and CartoonStock.com. For permission to quote from Michael Donaghy's 'Liverpool', I thank Madeleine Paxman. For permission to quote from Don Paterson's 'On Going to Meet a Zen Master' and his '02:50: Newtyle', and from Tom Stoppard's *The Real Thing*, I am grateful to Faber and Faber. For permission to quote from George Saunders' *Lincoln in the Bardo*, from Kurt Vonnegut's *Breakfast of Champions*, and from Robert Graves' 'Leaving the Rest Unsaid', I thank Penguin Random House. For permission to quote from Susan Wheeler's *Meme*, I thank University of Iowa Press.

My appreciation to the British Library falls under two headings. My gratitude is due to the helpful and efficient staff in the Manuscript Reading Room and the Rare Books Reading Room. Many of them are anonymous to me, but I can identify, because of their help via email, Bill Emery, Jeff Kattenhorn, and Janet Portman. My second debt is to the Panizzi Council for their invitation to deliver the Panizzi lectures in 2018. The technical and human support provided by the British Library during the preparation of the lectures was exemplary; and it was visible, precisely because of its invisibility, to the audience, who commented on both the atmosphere and the organization. I single out especially Lucy Evans and Francisca Fuentes Rettig, who thoughtfully anticipated every need from the practical to the intellectual, before and after the lectures, both backstage and front of house. I am also grateful to David Pearson and to the late Chris Michaelides.

At Oxford University Press, I owe an immense debt to Ellie Collins, who encouraged this project from the beginning and whose commitment to it included, exceptionally, attending the lectures. Elizabeth Stone's copy-editing was exemplary. The two anonymous readers for Oxford University Press made generous and helpful suggestions and I am grateful to them for their feedback.

Finally, those who do not fit into categories (how could they?): Anne Maguire, Peter Friend, Patsy Doi Ra, and Susan Nyein Su Eain.

Contents

List of Illustrations

✽ THE ARGVMENT.

Introduction
The Arts of Ostentation

Learning to read...involves learning to read spatially.   (W. B. Worthen)

What sort of a place was the page in early modern England?
(Jason Scott-Warren)[1]

This is a book about blank space and blank spaces in early modern printed books. It's a story of the journey from incunabula to Google books, told through blanks and the signifiers of blanks: empty brackets, the *&c/etc./etcetera*, the asterisk. It is about typographical marks, readerly response, and editorial treatment. It is a book about the vestigial and the ghostly, the palimpsest and the trace, chronicling the ways in which the blank self-referentially invokes its own indeterminant existence and activates the reader's restorative critical instincts. It is about the semiotics of print and the social anthropology of reading. The book explores blank space as creator of both anxiety and of opportunity, looking at how readers respond to what is not there and how writers anticipate that response. Each chapter focuses on one typographical form of what is not there on the page but I begin here by using the loose omnipurpose term 'blank' for the phenomenon I will explore in varied, more specific, forms chapter by chapter.

---

[1] The epigraphs come from W. B. Worthen, 'The Imprint of Performance', in *Theorizing Practice: Redefining Theatre History*, ed. W. B. Worthen with Peter Holland (Basingstoke: Palgrave Macmillan, 2003), pp. 213–34 (p. 218) and Jason Scott-Warren, 'Reading Graffiti in the Early Modern Book', *Huntington Library Quarterly* 73:3 (2010), 363–81 (373).

The Rhetoric of the Page. Laurie Maguire, Oxford University Press (2020). © Laurie Maguire.
DOI: 10.1093/oso/9780198862109.001.0001

Approaching the Blank

In contemporary parlance, the concept of the blank is usually negative. To 'blank' or to 'blank out' is to be temporarily amnesiac; a 'blank stare' denotes incomprehension; to 'blank someone' is to ignore them. Failure to recall something or to solve a problem is characterized as 'drawing a blank'. This last phrase is Elizabethan in origin, derived from the ways that lotteries were conducted. Slips with purchasers' names were put in one pot; slips with the descriptions of the prizes to be won—and blank slips—were put in another. The lottery was 'drawn' by extracting one slip from each pot: winners drew slips with a named prize, losers drew a blank. When Elizabeth I's national lottery of 1567 was introduced to raise funds for harbour expansion and repair, with an enormous prize of £5000 (justifying the high cost of individual tickets at 10s each), it was advertised as 'A very rich Lotterie generall, without any Blanckes'.[2]

Elizabethan writers use the phrase 'drawing a blank' in contexts of chance and (mis)fortune. In a competitive discussion among four husbands about their wives' virtue in *The Rape of Lucrece* (1608), Thomas Heywood's Horatius says, pessimistically, 'I would put in for a lot, but 1000 to one I shall draw but a blancke' (F1r). The paper blank has an aural equivalent—silence—and blanks are often characterized as 'dumb': phrases such as 'driven to a dumb blank' or 'not caring what hee said to avoid a dumbe blanck' are common.[3] In Robert Abbot's *True Ancient Roman Catholic* (1611) we read: 'Here hee is blancke and can say nothing' (E2r). Receiving a rejection of his love suit in Heywood's *Fair Maid of the Exchange* (1607), Anthony loses control of several senses: 'strucke blancke, and blind, and mad withall' (G1r).

Today's technical terms or synonyms for the blank are similarly associated with lack: 'lacuna' (an unfilled space; in medical pathology it is a cavity); 'gap' or 'hiatus' (a break in continuity, an opening between two objects); 'omission' (a failure to fulfil or an act of exclusion). Lady Macbeth urges Banquo to the banquet: 'If he had been forgotten, / It had been as a gap in our great feast, / And all-thing unbecoming' (*Macbeth*, 3.1.11–13). The Chorus in *The Winter's*

---

[2] The printed advertisement comprises three pages: see Anon, *A Very Rich Lotterie Generall, without any Blanckes* (1567). Complications—mainly public distrust and the high cost of tickets—meant that the first draw was postponed for two years; the first lot was drawn in 1569. See John Ashton, *The History of Gambling in England* (London: Duckworth, 1898) and Gary Hicks, *Fate's Bookie: How the Lottery Shaped the World* (Stroud: History, 2009). For digital images of the British Library copy of the advertisement, see: http://www.bl.uk/learning/timeline/item102765.html.

[3] William Bishop, *A Disproof of D. Abbots Counterproofe* (1614), Pivv, Qiiv.

Tale apologizes for the 'gap' in time between Acts 3 and 4 (4.1.4–7) and Shakespeare's sonnet 77 moves from the 'vacant leaves' of line 3 to the 'waste blanks' of line 10.[4] Milton considers the 'unsightly gap' he worked hard to avoid at the beginning of his *History of Britain*.[5] 'Gap' is often used in phrases that indicate mental inferiority ('a gap in understanding').[6] The adjective formulaically associated today with omission is 'glaring'—a noun-adjective pairing in which the negative implications of 'omission' become overtly censorious; however, the oxymoron also introduces the concept of the visibility and legibility of omissions that will be the refrain of this book.

Even when the blank beckons positively, as in *tabula rasa*, its unwritten-ness inviting inscription in an optimistic forward gesture, the concept of lack or deletion is implicit. *Tabula rasa* translates into English as 'blank slate', used of an event or enterprise that is free from bias or predetermined outcomes, or, in epistemology, of the infant mind before it receives outside impressions. However, the Latin adjective foregrounds not the blank's potential but its loss; the *tabula* is *rasa*: scraped, erased. In *Merry Wives of Windsor*, Mistress Page proposes to 'scrape the figures [fantasies] out of [Ford's] brains' (4.2.216). The blank is the result of physical erasure, an effortful, almost violent, act of deletion, here transferred metaphorically to the tablet of Ford's jealous imagination.[7] In Jonson's *Bartholomew Fair* Quarlous facilitates a marriage by changing names in the marriage licence: 'I have a licence and all; it is but *razing* out one name and putting in another' (5.2.84–5, my emphasis).[8] In *Twelfth Night*, the history of Cesario's 'sister' is both pregnant with possibility—it is as yet untold—but consigned to oblivion precisely because it has not been narrated:

Duke: [W]hat's her history?
Viola: A blank. (2.4.109–10)

[4] Editors emend the quarto's 'blacks' to 'blanks', 'based on a plausible supposition that the manuscript used a contraction sign for "n"'. *Shakespeare's Sonnets*, ed. Katherine Duncan-Jones (London: Thomson Learning, 1997), 77.10n.

[5] John Milton, *The History of Britain* (1670), F1r (vol. II, 33).

[6] *OED n.*7 offers 'a breach or wide divergence in character or sympathies', citing E. A. Freeman, *History of the Norman Conquest* (1876), V. xxiv. 495: 'There was...a gap between him and the mass of his flock and Clergy'.

[7] The associations between Roman wax tablets and early modern mental faculties, and between early modern commonplace books, tables, and the brain, were recurrent metaphors in Elizabethan England. See Ann Moss, *Printed Commonplace-Books and the Structuring of Renaissance Thought* (Oxford: Clarendon Press, 1996).

[8] Ben Jonson, *Bartholomew Fair*, ed. Suzanne Gossett (Revels Student Editions; Manchester: Manchester University Press, 2000). *Razing* indicates erasure's roots in violent effort: it can be done with a razor or knife as we shall see in Chapter 1.

Writing about creativity, Montaigne describes the working practice of the philosopher Chrysippus, who 'intermingled not merely passages from other authors into his writings but entire books', and he cites approvingly the criticism of Apollodorus, who said that 'if you cut out [Chrysippus'] borrowings, his paper would remain blank'.[9] Here the blank is synonymous with unoriginality, lack of creativity, vacancy. The most neutral term involving a blank is 'blank verse' (*vers blanc* in French), which describes the early modern innovation of a regular metrical form whose lines do not rhyme. Initially used in the singular ('bombast out a blanke verse') it quickly became a generic term ('you talk in blank verse').[10]

In April 2019 the contributors to the BBC Radio 3 programme *The Verb* were challenged to explore the positive aspects of gaps.[11] The poet Ira Lightman played with line breaks and punned on '*agape*'. Discussing Shakespeare's fruitful ambiguities and uncertainties from stage directions to endings, Emma Smith coined the word 'gappiness', which she liked, she said, because it was only 'one letter away from happiness'.[12] Yoshiaki Tono, reviewing the modernist blank art of Robert Rauschenberg (whose work I explore in Chapter 1) invoked the concept of 'crossing-off'; as Sarah Roberts observes, he uses this term 'without negation or resistance',[13] an equivalent of the caesura in poetry or the rest symbol in music. In an analysis of long poems from Spenser to the Romantics, Balachandra Rajan claims the word 'unfinished' ('more malleable than fragment') and distinguishes it from the 'incomplete': the unfinished remains in dialogue with its own abruption and 'should not invite completion'.[14] Randall McLeod, studying censorship in John Donne's 'Elegy on his Mistress Going to Bed', coined the term 'Obliterature'.[15] Dean Colet anticipated him in

---

[9] 'On Educating Children', in Michel de Montaigne, *The Complete Essays*, ed. M. A. Screech (Harmondsworth: Penguin, 1991), pp. 163–99 (p. 165).

[10] Robert Greene, *A Groatsworth of Wit* (1592), F1v; Shakespeare, *As You Like It*, 4.1.31–2. See Margaret Tudeau-Clayton, '"The Lady Shall Say her Mind Freely": Shakespeare and the S/Pace of Blank Verse', in *Shakespeare and Space: Theatrical Explorations of the Spatial Paradigm*, ed. Ina Habermann and Michelle Witen (London: Palgrave Macmillan, 2016), pp. 79–102.

[11] 'Writing the Gap', 26 April 2019. See: <https://www.bbc.co.uk/programmes/m0004dtk>.

[12] For her exploration of gaps in Shakespeare's plays, see *This is Shakespeare* (Harmondsworth: Penguin/Random House, 2019).

[13] Yoshiaki Tono, 'From a Gulliver's Point of View', *Art in America* 48:2 (1960), 54–9; cited by Sarah Roberts, 'Erased de Kooning Drawing', *Rauschenberg Research Project*, July 2013, San Francisco Museum of Modern Art, <https://www.sfmoma.org/essay/erased-de-kooning-drawing/>.

[14] Balachandra Rajan, *The Form of the Unfinished: English Poetics from Spenser to Pound* (Princeton, NJ: Princeton University Press, 1985), pp. 6, 5. As will become clear, the forms of blank space I discuss do both. See also I. A. Richards, 'How Does a Poem Know When It is Finished?', in *Parts and Wholes*, ed. Daniel Lerner (Glencoe, IL: Free Press, 1963), pp. 163–74.

[15] Randall McLeod, 'Obliterature: Reading a Censored Text of Donne's "To his mistress going to bed"', *English Manuscript Studies* 12 (2005), 83–138.

the 1510s with 'blotterature'.[16] Attractive though these terms are, none describes the phenomenon I explore in this book in which typography cues us to engage with what is not there. And tempting though it is to apply the Chorus' injunction in *Henry V* to the topic of this book ('[p]iece out our imperfections with your thoughts'; Prologue 23), it would be inappropriate, for, although the blank is an absence requiring imaginative 'piecing out', my argument is that blanks are not seen as imperfections. We might think of blanks as a species of Carla Mazzio's *Inarticulate Renaissance*.[17] We associate the early modern with eloquence; even 'plain speech' is a form of rhetorical crafting. Mazzio looks at mumbling, verbal incoherence, dumbfoundedness (in secular and sacred contexts) as forms of literary innovation, and at the 'distinctly textual substrates of inarticulate speech', particularly in drama with its 'interplay of oral and textual forms' (p. 8). The textual blanks I examine give this concept a typographical focus.

Early modern typography is full of blanks—small localized units of text (a word, a phrase, an incomplete line) or larger units of blank space (lines, paragraphs, a page)—that invite readers to respond imaginatively to what is absent, interacting with typography to make meaning (which is, after all, simply a definition of reading). The heavy black pen deletions of the censor in Donne's 'Elegy' make the poem unreadable; Dean Colet's term was coined to indicate the difference in status between spiritual works (literature) and secular (blotterature); Tono's 'crossing off' is still a term of negation rather than opportunity, as is the prefix in Rajan's 'unfinished'.[18] *The Rhetoric of the Page* explores the positive, creative potential of the blank in printed texts. Although blank space in print lacks or awaits inscription (clearly, it has no writing on it), in typographical terms it is very much part of the text's composition in the print shop. Blanks are signalled typographically by white space or empty parentheses or asterisks or an *&c* or a dash or series of dashes;[19] all of these indications of emptiness have been as carefully composed in the compositor's stick with metal type as the letters on the page.

---

[16] On humanists' efforts to demarcate kinds of writing, see Daniel Wakelin, *Humanism, Reading, and English Literature 1430–1530* (Oxford: Oxford University Press, 2007), pp. 194–9 (Colet's statute for St Paul's, banishing 'blotterature', is quoted on p. 196), and Daniel J. Nodes, ed., *John Colet on the Ecclesiastical History of Dionysius*, Studies in Medieval and Reformation Traditions, 171:4: Texts and Sources (Leiden: Brill, 2013).

[17] Carla Mazzio, *The Inarticulate Renaissance* (Philadelphia: University of Pennsylvania Press, 2009).

[18] Rajan cites but does not pursue Barbara Herrnstein Smith's more positive term 'aperture' when she talks about 'unendings, indeterminables, indeterminacies'. Smith, *In the Margins of Discourse* (Chicago: University of Chicago Press, 1978), p. ix, cited by Rajan, *Form of the Unfinished*, p. 6.

[19] The em-dash is an early Jacobean development, popularized by Ben Jonson. See Henry R. Woudhuysen, 'The Dash—A Short but Quite Dramatic Account', paper delivered at 'The Jacobean Printed Book', Queen Mary College, University of London, September 2004.

It is the paradoxical nature of the blank from its composition to its readerly reception that provides the initial stimulus for each chapter in this book. I am interested in the way in which it is simultaneously something and nothing, the way in which it gestures to what was once there or might be there. For Barbara Freedman, 'blank spaces can express both anonymity and particularity, both an emptiness and a determined inclusiveness'.[20] In essay 54 'On Vainglory', Francis Bacon argues that 'Excusations, Cess[at]ions, Modesty it selfe well Governed, are but Arts of *Ostentation*'.[21] He is using ostentation in the neutral sense of display (Latin *ostentare*), although in an essay on vainglory some of the word's modern meaning of self-indulgence show. But Bacon's contrast is primarily binary, between what is absent (excused and ceased) and what is present (ostended, displayed). *The Rhetoric of the Page* explores the ways in which blanks are themselves arts of ostentation: never truly blank, they call attention to their own vacancy. This is also true of euphemistic forms of the blank such as nonce words (the early modern equivalent of today's 'whatchamacallit'). In *As You Like It* Touchstone addresses Jaques as 'good Master What ye call't' to avoid pronouncing his indecorous name (Jaques = jakes = toilet; 3.3.73). In *1 Edward IV* Heywood calls attention to contemporary politics by blanking out a topical name: 'Mistress Ferris or mistress-what-call-ye-her' (1.1.20–1).[22] Stephano's ineptitude is underlined with his reference to 'a what-sha'-call-'em doublet' in the quarto version of *Every Man in his Humour*.[23] The euphemistic blank works just like the other types of blank in this book as Gilbert and Sullivan's Lord High Executioner explains. His list of dispensable figures includes

Apologetic statesmen of a compromising kind,
Such as — What d'ye call him — Thing'em-bob, and likewise — Never-mind,
And 'St— 'st— 'st— and What's-his-name, and also You-know-who —
The task of filling up the blanks I'd rather leave to *you*.[24]

[20] Barbara Freedman, 'Shakespearean Chronology, Ideological Complicity, and Floating Texts: Something is Rotten in Windsor', *Shakespeare Quarterly* 45:2 (1994), 190–210 (210).

[21] Francis Bacon, *Essays* (1625), Rr3v.

[22] Richard Rowland's introduction explains the political relevance. See Thomas Heywood, *1 Edward IV*, ed. Richard Rowland (Revels; Manchester: Manchester University Press, 2005), pp. 37–9.

[23] Ben Jonson, *Every Man in his Humour*, ed. Robert S. Miola (Revels; Manchester: Manchester University Press, 2000), 1.2.17.

[24] *The Mikado* in W. S. Gilbert, *The Savoy Operas*, vol. I (London: Macmillan, 1957), p. 11.

Naming the Blank

George Lakoff's instruction not to think of an elephant has become the canonical example of how attempts to negate, cancel, or obliterate have the opposite effect. In Lakoff's elephant example, our cognitive faculties automatically supply the item they are invited to suppress.[25] Something similar happens when we encounter incompletion or deletion in literature: we speculate on the omission, we guess at the contents of the gap, we supply the continuation. Harry Newman analyses this in his study of a censored illustration—a female torso—in editions of Helkiah Crooke's *Microkosmographia* published between 1616 and 1651. The vulva has been erased, but the characters that label it remain. 'The negative space produced by the erasure', Newman concludes, produces 'greater interest in a part of the female body that becomes all the more provocative for its absence.'[26] The text's excisions are not confined to censorship. Crooke himself suggests that book 4 on the female reproductive system may be excised—an invitation to readers that 'provok[es] curiosity rather than inspiring modesty'.[27] We are haunted by what is not there, and the not-there-ness assumes a material presence. 'Haunting' is *le mot juste* as Hughes Mearns' popular Victorian rhyme 'Antigonish' conveys with its interplay between what is and is not there:

> Yesterday, upon the stair,
> I met a man who wasn't there.
> He wasn't there again today;
> I wish, I wish he'd go away.[28]

Mearns explained the rhyme's origin in a ghost rumour he encountered in Nova Scotia, and his lines express the spectral ontology of the blank, its

---

[25] George Lakoff, *Don't Think of an Elephant* (White River Junction, VT: Chelsea Green Publishing, 2004). Iago, Shakespeare's supreme cognitive psychologist, works on Othello in this way, prompting him to sexual suspicion by telling him not to think the worst of Cassio or Desdemona.

[26] Harry Newman, '"[P]rophane fidlers": Medical Paratexts and Indecent Readers in Early Modern England', in *Medical Paratexts from Medieval to Modern: Dissecting the Page*, ed. Hanna C. Tweed and Diane G. Scott (Basingstoke: Palgrave Macmillan, 2018), pp. 15–41 (pp. 19, 20). In some copies, readers have drawn in the missing vulva (p. 22).

[27] Newman, '"[P]rophane fidlers"', p. 27.

[28] Written in 1899, the poem was designed for a play performed in 1910; it was not published until 1922. The poem was frequently revised (by Mearns) and parodied (by others); it was also adapted as a song. See David McCord (ed.), *What Cheer* (Ann Arbor: University of Michigan Press, 1945).

Derridean absent presence—what Derrida would later punningly call 'hauntology'.[29]

Lara Prescott's first novel, *The Secrets We Kept* (2019) is a contemporary example of how a creative writer (simultaneously a creative reader) fills in blanks. In 2015 Prescott read recently declassified documents about 'the CIA's clandestine involvement in the Russian publication and dissemination of *Dr Zhivago*. The documents, with redacted names and blacked-out details, inspired her "to fill in the blanks with fiction" '.[30] Mark Haddon's novel, *The Porpoise* (2019) fills in the missing tale of Antiochus' daughter; what occupies only scene 1 of Shakespeare and Wilkins' *Pericles* becomes the emotional heart of his narrative. But these writerly responses are simply a variant of the reading process. For reader-reception theorists like Hans Jauss and Wolfgang Iser, literature is a system of gaps: it is about the relationship between what is present in the text and what is absent from it, and it is the reader's responsibility to fill the lacunae, providing continuity and connection (at the most basic level: plot, character). Reading 'trigger[s] synthesizing operations in the reader's mind';[31] it turns parts into wholes. This, in fact, is how all perception works. In night driving, the brain connects remarkably little visual input into a road, a bend, a hill. In audition, we do not hear every word addressed to us but use context to bridge the gaps; deafness is the state when the gaps become too large for meaning to be constructed. And reading is simply this instinctive desire to fill in gaps, writ large: 'to comprehend a text, we not only read it in the nominal sense of the word, we construct a meaning for it'.[32]

Print is associated with fixity and finality. However, as William Sherman observes in his study of endings, print is 'tolerant of incompletion'. He then rephrases his observation with an exhilarating incremental alternative: or

---

[29] Peter Holland quotes Mearns' poem in an article on the name Theseus in *Midsummer Night's Dream*, arguing that the classical name and its associations haunt the play. Although Shakespeare does not 'do' anything with the name, he does not need to: the mere presence of the name means we cannot ignore it. See Holland, 'Theseus' Shadows in *A Midsummer Night's Dream*', *Shakespeare Survey* 47 (1994), 139–51. For Derrida, see *Writing and Difference* (Chicago: University of Chicago Press, 1978), *Of Grammatology* (Baltimore, MD: Johns Hopkins, 2016), *Spectres of Marx* (London: Routledge, 1993).

[30] Allison Flood, 'First Novel Inspired by CIA's *Doctor Zhivago* Plan Nets $2m Book Deal', *Guardian*, 11 June 2018. Available at <https://www.theguardian.com/books/2018/jun/11/first-novel-doctor-zhivago-2m-lara-prescott-we-were-never-here>. The novel was published under the title, *The Secrets We Kept*.

[31] Wolfgang Iser, *How to Do Theory* (Oxford: Blackwell Publishing, 2006), p. 66.

[32] Merlin C. Wittrock, 'Reading Comprehension', in *Neuropsychological and Cognitive Processes in Reading*, ed. Francis J. Pirozzolo and Merlin C. Wittrock (Oxford: Oxford University Press, 1981), pp. 229–60 (p. 230).

'*uncomfortable with finality*'.[33] Indeterminacy and instability are visible at all stages of early modern texts. We might think of the marginal notes in George Gascoigne's *Poesies* (1575) which call attention to interpretive ambiguity: 'These thinges are mistical and not to bee understoode but by Thaucthor him selfe' (F1r) or Robert Greene's admission that his '*fiction called* A Maidens Dreame . . . *is Enigmaticall*'.[34] It is the positive opportunities afforded by eschewing completion and finality (of form or of content) that the blank embraces: it helps to create 'a halo of indefiniteness and to make the text pregnant with infinite suggestive possibilities'.[35] This is how Elena Ferrante describes her relationship with a particular form of blank—ellipses—noting the risky pleasure they offer, 'like stepping stones', and their variously suggestive powers: 'the mischief of saying and not saying'.[36] In *A Room of One's Own*, Virginia Woolf directs the reader to interpretation of her ellipsis: 'and the five dots here indicate five separate minutes of stupefaction, wonder and bewilderment'; of Woolf's *Orlando*, Alexandra Harris comments, 'we reach the end of a paragraph with a flirtatious dot-dot-dot'.[37] Henry James ended his novel *The Middle Years* with a period, changed by his editor to an ellipsis, 'as if to suggest a dying hand trailing across the page'.[38] Clearly, blanks of all kinds have 'meaning'. As the examples in this book show, the blank is not about suspension but about *extension*, the co-production of meaning between text and reader.

Early modern readers were accustomed to supplementing their reading process: they read allegorically, symbolically, typologically, morally, anagogically, analogically, politically, meditatively, rhetorically.[39] Thomas Nashe satirizes these habits when he complains that no one reads literally: he cannot write '*I pray how might I call you?*' without someone thinking he is referring to

---

[33] William H. Sherman, 'The Beginning of "The End": Terminal Paratext and the Birth of Print Culture', in *Renaissance Paratexts*, ed. Helen Smith and Louise Wilson (Cambridge: Cambridge University Press, 2011), pp. 65–87 (p. 85, emphasis original).

[34] George Gascoigne, *Poesies* (1575), F1r; Robert Greene, *A Maidens Dream upon the Death of the Right Honorable Sir Christopher Hatton, Knight, Late Lord Chancellor of England* (1591), A3v.

[35] Umberto Eco, *The Open Work* (Cambridge: Cambridge University Press, 1981), pp. 8–9.

[36] Elena Ferrante, 'Dialogue and Ellipsis', *Guardian*, 30 June 2018. See: <https://www.theguardian.com/lifeandstyle/2018/jun/30/elena-ferrante-dialogue-imposes-an-ellipsis>.

[37] Virginia Woolf, *A Room of One's Own and Three Guineas*, ed. Anna Snaith (World's Classics; Oxford: Oxford University Press, 2015), p. 32; Alexandra Harris, *Virginia Woolf* (London: Thames & Hudson, 2011), p. 100.

[38] Hannah Sullivan, *The Work of Revision* (Cambridge, MA: Harvard University Press, 2013), p. 92. For more on ellipsis as a specific form of blank, see Anne Toner, *Ellipsis in English Literature* (Cambridge: Cambridge University Press, 2015).

[39] Stephen Dobranski, *Readers and Authorship in Early Modern England* (Cambridge: Cambridge University Press, 2005), p. 23.

'one *Howe*, a Knave of that trade, that I never heard of before'.[40] Blank space capitalizes on this expected habit of supplementation. Throughout this book I move from the realm of typography to reader response via authors' awareness of the myriad signifying capacities of blank space. Each of the chapters begins with a typographical feature (the literal blank, the *&c*/etcetera, and the asterisk), then looks at the way this feature develops literary applications as the practical is pressed into the service of the creative by early modern writers and readers. Thus, all three chapters are interventions in the history of reading, that sub-speciality of the history of the book.

The Blank on Stage

If reading is an act of completion, so too is staging. Early modern texts do not just use stage directions to indicate stage business, they use typography. When one of the boys launches into a lengthy plot summary in the induction to Jonson's *Cynthia's Revels or The Fountain of Self-Love* (1601), we find this stage direction: 'At the breaches in this speech following, the other two Boyes interrupt him' (A2v). The breaches (breaks, gaps) are em-dashes (or rather, prototype em-dashes—broken fragments of the brass rules used to frame columns on the printed page):

> *By the way* Cupid *meetes with* Mercury, *(as that's a thing to be noted, take any of our Play-bookes without a* Cupid, *or a* Mercury *in it, and burne it for an Heretique in Poetry)* —— *Pray thee let me alone:* Mercurie, *he, (in the nature of a Conjurer) rayses up* Echo: *who weepes over her Love, or Daffodill* Narcissus, *a little; sings; cursses the Spring wherein the pretty foolish Gentleman melted himselfe away: and ther's an end of her* —— *Now, I am to enforme you, that* Cupid, *and* Mercury *do both become Pages.*   (A2v)

In George Wilkins' *The Miseries of Enforced Marriage* (1607), the adverb 'thus', followed by a colon and em-dash, is the page's spatial way of indicating pauses in dialogue occupied by stage business:

> For looke you Sir: the father according to the fashion, being sure you have a good living, and without Incumbrance, comes to you thus: —— takes you by the hand thus: —— wipes his long beard thus: —— or turns up his Muchacho thus: —— Walks some turne or two thus: —— to shew his comely Gravity thus: —— And having washt his foule mouth thus: —— at last breaks out thus. ——   (A3r)

---

[40] Thomas Nashe, 'A Private Epistle of the Author to the Printer', *Pierce Pennilesse, his Supplication to the Devil* (1592), ¶ 2v. I quote from STC 18372, published by John Busby; Nashe is commenting on responses to the first edition, published earlier the same year by Richard Jones (STC 18371).

In Ford's *The Lady's Trial* (1639) Fulgoso's whistling is twice signalled typographically by a dash (D2r). The compositor has right-justified and italicized the first stage direction ('*Whistles*') but the second 'whistles' has accidentally been left in roman type and incorporated in Fulgoso's speech (see Figure 0.1).

When, at the end of Middleton's *Chaste Maid in Cheapside* (c.1613, Q1630), Tim Yellowhammer's heiress-bride, with mountains in Wales, turns out to be a whore, Tim punningly resigns himself to a bodily substitute: 'And for my Mountaines, I'le mount upon ————' (K4r). Breaches in the playtext are filled by action on stage; indeed, breaches in the playtext *signify* action on stage. Both absence and the representation of absence, these typographical markers, like the blank generally, belong to a signifying system that embodies deferral and triggers desire for fulfilment in ways Saussure and Lacan have taught us to recognize.

Rhetoric

The title of this book, *The Rhetoric of the Page*, may need some explanation. It is prompted by the theatre historian W. B. Worthen, who says that we sometimes think that 'the rhetorical use of print' is long past.[41] His comment comes in an analysis of the way(s) modern drama negotiates the space of the page to indicate a text's 'fulfilment' in performance (his concept of 'filling out' the design of a play chimes with my argument in this book about the way the blank appeals to readers for fulfilment).[42] For Worthen, modernist poetry, with its use of white space, taught drama how to use typography (or, perhaps, it taught readers of drama how to read typography). He suggests, following Martin Esslin, that we know the length of a Pinter *Pause*, because of the amount of space around it.[43] With examples from George Bernard Shaw, Harold Pinter, David Greig, Caryl Churchill, Sarah Kane and others, Worthen shows how modern playwrights use punctuation marks and layout to score their text, and how (in the phrase which provides the epigraph to this chapter) 'learning to read...involves learning to read spatially, to account for the rhetoric of typographic space'.[44] For anyone familiar with early modern books, it is clear that 'learning to read' the pages of modern drama is a process of relearning.

---

[41] Worthen, 'Imprint', p. 227.
[42] The verbs 'fill out' and 'fulfill' appear in Worthen, 'Imprint', p. 213.
[43] Worthen, 'Imprint', p. 221.   [44] Worthen, 'Imprint', p. 218.

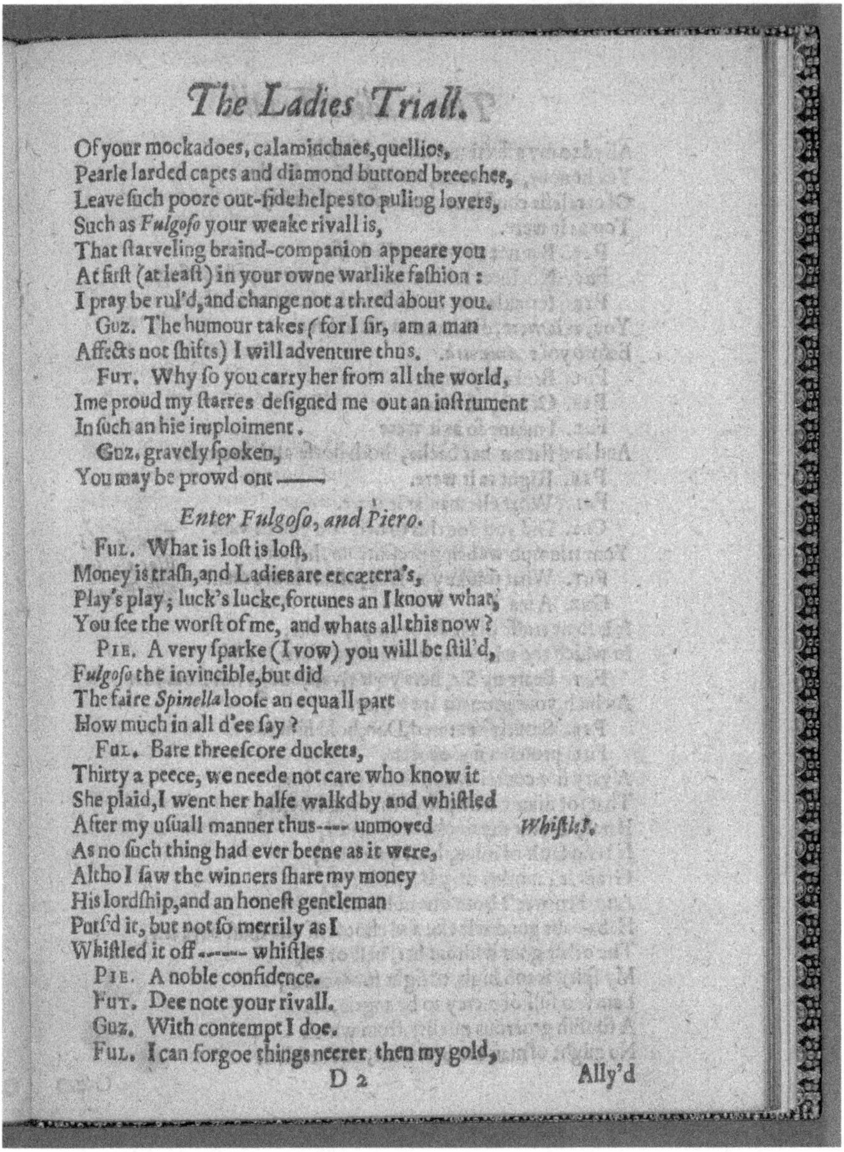

The Ladies Triall.

Of your mockadoes, calaminchaes, quellios,
Pearle larded capes and diamond buttond breeches,
Leave such poore out-side helpes to puling lovers,
Such as *Fulgoso* your weake rivall is,
That starveling braind-companion appeare you
At first (at least) in your owne warlike fashion :
I pray be rul'd, and change not a thred about you.
    Guz. The humour takes (for I sir, am a man
Affects not shifts) I will adventure thus.
    Fut. Why so you carry her from all the world,
Ime proud my starres designed me out an instrument
In such an hie imploiment.
    Guz. gravely spoken,
You may be prowd ont——

            Enter Fulgoso, and Piero.

    Ful. What is lost is lost,
Money is trash, and Ladies are et cætera's,
Play's play; luck's lucke, fortunes an I know what,
You see the worst of me, and whats all this now ?
    Pie. A very sparke (I vow) you will be stil'd,
Fulgoso the invincible, but did
The faire *Spinella* loose an equall part
How much in all d'ee say ?
    Ful. Bare threescore duckets,
Thirty a peece, we neede not care who know it
She plaid, I went her halfe walkd by and whistled
After my usuall manner thus—— unmoved   *Whistlet.*
As no such thing had ever beene as it were,
Altho I saw the winners share my money
His lordship, and an honest gentleman
Purs'd it, but not so merrily as I
Whistled it off ———— whistles
    Pie. A noble confidence.
    Fut. Dee note your rivall.
    Guz. With contempt I doe.
    Ful. I can forgoe things neerer then my gold,
                D 2   Ally'd

FIGURE 0.1 John Ford, *The Lady's Trial* (1639, STC 11161), D2r. Shelfmark 60703.
Courtesy of The Huntington Library, San Marino.

Print had left the cradle in the period that provides most of my examples
(the late sixteenth and early seventeenth centuries), but it was still in its
infancy—with all the experimental try-and-fail flexibility that infant learning
entails, in print as well as in person. Ways of presenting and promoting the
material text were under construction. Recent work by book historians has

shown this in a variety of ways. Claire Bourne's study of the pilcrow looks at the evolution of play layout, speech prefixes, paragraphization, and change of speaker in sixteenth-century drama; Tara Lyon chronicles the development of the two-part play; Tamara Atkin examines marketing strategies from title-page vocabulary to choice of typeface; Adam Hooks considers genre in the world of marketing, looking at the ways in which *Richard II* was published and promoted alongside *Venus and Adonis* as an Ovidian text.[45]

The early modern page is a visual unit as well as a textual unit and the relationship between layout and content is as productive for writers as it is for readers. This spatial interest in what Worthen calls the 'armature of print'[46] is evident in the vocabulary of current textual critics and book historians whose literary interests are inseparable from their visual interests. Bonnie Mak talks about the 'architecture of the page', a concept echoed by Claire Bourne when she invokes visual scaffolding ('the imperative to scaffold the text with . . . pilcrows and other symbols').[47] Adrian Johns considers typography a form of 'illustration', and Evelyn Tribble analyses the 'conversation between a text and its margins', the creative play 'made possible by the space of the page'.[48] A. E. B. Coldiron analyses *mise-en-page* in the world of early printing.[49] Jerome McGann reminds us that 'the reading eye is a scanning mechanism as

[45] See Claire M. L. Bourne, 'Dramatic Pilcrows', *Papers of the Bibliographical Society of America* 108: 4 (2014), 413–52; Tara L. Lyon, 'Richard Jones, *Tamburlaine the Great*, and the Making (and Remaking) of a Serial Play Collection in the 1590s', in *Christopher Marlowe, Theatrical Commerce and the Booktrade*, ed. Kirk Melnikoff and Roslyn Knutson (Cambridge: Cambridge University Press, 2018), pp. 149–63; Tamara Atkin, *Reading Drama in Tudor England* (London: Routledge, 2018); and Adam Hooks, *Selling Shakespeare: Biography, Bibliography, and the Booktrade* (Cambridge: Cambridge University Press, 2016). For similarly exciting recent work in this vein, see: Harry Newman, *Impressive Shakespeare: Identity, Authority and the Imprint in Shakespearean Drama* (London: Routledge, 2019); Rachel Stenner, *The Typographical Imaginary in Early Modern English Literature* (London: Routledge, 2019); Dennis Duncan and Adam Smyth (eds), *Book Parts* (Oxford: Oxford University Press, 2019); Adam Smyth, *Material Texts in Early Modern England* (Cambridge: Cambridge University Press, 2018); Kirk Melnikoff, *Elizabethan Publishing and the Makings of Literary Culture* (Toronto: University of Toronto Press, 2018); Abigail Williams, *The Social Life of Books: Reading Together in the 18th-Century Home* (New Haven, CT: Yale University Press, 2017); Cyndia Susan Clegg, *Shakespeare's Reading Audiences: Early Modern Books and Audience Interpretation* (Cambridge: Cambridge University Press, 2017); Jonathan P. Lamb, *Shakespeare in the Marketplace of Words* (Cambridge: Cambridge University Press, 2017); Claire M. L. Bourne, 'Making a Scene; or *Tamburlaine the Great* in Print', in *Christopher Marlowe*, ed. Melnikoff and Knutson, pp. 115–33; Toner, *Ellipsis*; and Scott-Warren, 'Reading Graffiti'.

[46] Worthen, 'Imprint', p. 224.

[47] Bonnie Mak, *How the Page Matters* (Toronto: University of Toronto Press, 2011), p. 5; Bourne, 'Dramatic Pilcrows', 449.

[48] Jerome McGann, *The Textual Condition* (Princeton, NJ: Princeton University Press, 1991), p. 113; Adrian Johns, *The Nature of the Book* (Chicago: University of Chicago Press, 1998), p. 434; Evelyn Tribble, *Margins and Marginality: The Printed Page in Early Modern England* (Charlottesville: University of Virginia Press, 1993), p. 1.

[49] A. E. B. Coldiron, *Printers without Borders* (Cambridge: Cambridge University Press, 2015).

well as a linear decoder'; for Margaret Jane Kidnie, 'readers construct meaning not just by *reading* a page but by *looking* at a page'.[50] For the new digital world of screen culture, Johannes Drucker coins the noun 'graphesis' in a book that 'looks at visual forms of knowledge production'.[51] Walter Ong has long been a champion of the way print 'situates words in space', a concept developed quirkily by Georges Perec in his essay 'On the Page' (see Figure 0.2).[52] So, by 'rhetoric of the page', I mean simply the persuasive effect of layout. *Mise-en-page* influences readers in the same way that rhetoric influences readers.

But I also mean rhetoric more literally. My large claim in this book is that Elizabethan concepts of rhetoric extended to the layout of the page. In classical oratory we are familiar with the rhetorical device of *occupatio* or *apophasis* (when a speaker brings up a subject by saying that s/he will not address it). As we have seen, this is what the blank does, strategically calling our attention to what is not there and thus accentuating rather than concealing. In his manual of rhetoric, *The Art of Poesie* (1589), George Puttenham observes how rhetoricians leave something out 'to the intent the reader should gesse at it' (Yiiir). In Francis Beaumont's *The Woman Hater* (1607), a character cultivates 'a bad hand' for the same reason: so that 'the Readers may take paines for it' (H4v). Blank space on the printed page functions in the same way, activating the reader's efforts to expand the vestigial. The blank is never (just) vacant: it is a *mark* of vacancy, what Dobranski calls 'a textual IOU'.[53] By apophatically calling attention to absent presence it encourages the reader to interact with the omission.

Varieties of Blank

Throughout this Introduction I have been using the term 'blank' in a capacious and generalized way to invoke a Protean phenomenon. Blanks come in many shapes and sizes. Henry Woudhuysen has studied blank pages at the beginning and ends of books, both in terms of economics (paper was expensive, the

---

[50] Margaret Jane Kidnie, 'The Staging of Shakespeare's Drama in Print Editions', in *Textual Performances*, ed. Lukas Erne and Margaret Jane Kidnie (Cambridge: Cambridge University Press, 2004), pp. 158–77 (p. 169, emphasis original).

[51] Johannes Drucker, *Graphesis* (Cambridge, MA: Harvard University Press, 2014).

[52] Walter Ong, *Orality and Literacy: The Technologizing of the Word* (London and New York: Methuen, 1982), p. 119; Georges Perec, *Species of Spaces and Other Pieces* (Harmondsworth: Penguin, 1974), p. 11.

[53] Dobranski, *Readers*, p. 144.

I write: I inhabit my sheet of paper, I invest it, I travel across it.

I incite *blanks*, *spaces* (jumps in the meaning: discontinuities, transitions, changes of key).

I write
in the
margin

I start a new

paragraph. I refer to a footnote[1]

I go to a new sheet of paper.

1. I am very fond of footnotes at the bottom of the page, even if I don't have anything in particular to clarify there.

FIGURE 0.2 Georges Perec, *Species of Spaces and Other Pieces* (Harmondsworth: Penguin, 1974), p. 11. By permission of Éditions Galilée and Penguin Random House.

'single most expensive item' in book production) and in terms of pragmatics ('the final blank served to stop damage to a book's vulnerable ending').[54] His essay analyses blank title-page versos in playtexts and the way in which they came to be occupied by prologues, dedications, or lists of roles. His study is bibliographical and historical, focusing on the development of one kind of blank, but like this book, he observes that 'the decision to leave paper unmarked may in itself convey some sort of meaning'[55]). Don McKenzie describes how he taught bibliography by giving his students a blank book (a 1930s printer's text-block)[56] to see how much they could infer from it. The answer was: a surprising amount. Format, weight, texture, the sewing of sections, compactness all enabled them 'to read between the (well, yes) non-existent lines of this non-existent text'.[57] David McKitterick looks at printing in fifteenth-century Ferrara, documenting the spaces left for illustrations that were never supplied.[58] Phillipa Hardman, Daniel Wakelin, and Susanna Fein study the same phenomenon in medieval English manuscripts.[59] Stephen Dobranski looks at incomplete poems and real or feigned literary omissions; Harry Newman analyses a censored illustration in a medical text; Barbara Freedman

---

[54] H. R. Woudhuysen, 'Early Play Texts: Forms and Formes', in *In Arden: Editing Shakespeare*, ed. Ann Thompson and Gordon McMullan (London: Thomson, 2003), pp. 48–64 (pp. 59, 51). Thomas Heywood's *1 If You Know Not Me, You Know Nobody* (1605) has been suspected of being a memorially reconstructed text although the stylistic problems are concentrated in scene 1 and scenes 20–3; damage (damp, wear) to the vulnerable outer leaves may have required these scenes to be replaced from some other source. Dekker and Webster's *Sir Thomas Wyatt* (1607) has similar stylistic problems confined to its opening scene, and, again, damage to the manuscript outer leaves may have necessitated a drastic remedial solution.

[55] Woudhuysen, 'Early Play Texts', p. 48.

[56] A text-block enables printers and publishers to make crucial calculations (about number of sheets, format, width of spine, etc.) before a book is printed; it is then used as a salesman's dummy for bookshops and book clubs. See D. F. McKenzie, *'What's Past is Prologue': The Bibliographical Society and History of the Book*, The Bibliographical Society Centenary Lecture, 14 July 1992 (Munslow: Hearthstone Publications, 1993).

[57] McKenzie, *'What's Past'*, p. 4.

[58] David McKitterick, 'What is the Use of Books without Pictures: Empty Spaces in Some Early Printed Books', *La Bibliofilia* 116:1–3 (2014), 67–82.

[59] See Phillipa Hardman, 'Reading the Spaces: Pictorial Intentions in the Thornton MSS, Lincoln Cathedral MS 91, and BL MS Add. 31042', *Medium Aevum* 63:2 (1994), 250–74, 'Windows into the Text: Unfilled Spaces in some Fifteenth-Century English Manuscripts', in *Texts and their Contexts, Papers from the Early Book Society*, ed. John Scattergood and Julia Boffey (Dublin: Four Courts Press, 1997), pp. 44–70, 'Interpreting the Incomplete Scheme of Illustration in Cambridge Corpus Christi College MS 61', *English Manuscript Studies* 6 (1977), 52–69; and Daniel Wakelin, 'When Scribes Won't Write: Gaps in Middle English Books', *Studies in the Age of Chaucer* 36 (2014), 249–78, *Scribal Correction and Literary Craft: English Manuscripts 1375–1510* (Cambridge: Cambridge University Press, 2014); Susanna Fein, *'Somer Soneday*: Kingship, Sainthood, and Fortune in Oxford, Bodleian Library, MS Laud Misc. 108', in *The Texts and Contexts of Oxford, Bodleian Library, MS Laud Misc.108: The Shaping of Vernacular Narrative*, ed. K. K. Bell and J. N. Couch (Leiden: Brill, 2010), pp. 275–97.

compares variants in Q and F *Merry Wives of Windsor*.[60] But all these critics agree that the different blanks they study 'enhance rather than diminish meaning', indeed that they 'provide special emphasis'.[61] Lisa Gitelman talks about 'elocutionary' blanks in nineteenth-century print: far from being silent, they are eloquent.[62]

The margin is a special category of blank, what George Bernard Shaw in the twentieth century referred to as 'rivers of white'.[63] Early modern margins invited occupation by the reader, an invitation that was regularly accepted. The Elizabethan playwright and pamphleteer, Thomas Nashe, owned a copy of John Leland's *Principum, ac illustrium aliquot & eruditorum in Anglia virorum* (1589) and used its margins for literary doodling (quotations from Marlowe's *Dr Faustus*, a Greek quotation from Epictetus, for instance).[64] Despite the high cost of paper, extravagantly wide margins were left by printers in botanical, pharmaceutical and medical books in evident anticipation of the owner's annotations (adjustments to medical recipes, records of personal experience, etc.). Shakespeare's Juliet is invited to read both the book of Count Paris's face and its margins:

> Read o'er the volume of young Paris's face, . . .
> And what obscur'd in this fair volume lies
> Find written in the margent of his eyes.   (*Romeo and Juliet*, 1.3.81–6)

Lucrece, an inexperienced reader, '[c]ould pick no meaning from [Tarquin's] parling looks, / Nor read the subtle shining secrecies, / Writ in the glassy margents of such books' (*Rape of Lucrece*, 100–2). The early modern margin supplemented the text with printed glosses (the 'sidenote' is an embryonic form of what later comes to be the footnote) or manuscript glosses provided by the reader's annotative practice. Either way, the annotated margin invites the reader to cross what William Slights, in a book-length study of early modern marginalia, calls, in terms similar to Shaw, 'the void of white space'.[65] The

---

[60] Dobranski, *Readers*; Newman, '"[P]rophane fidlers"'; Freedman, 'Shakespearean Chronology'.

[61] Dobranski, *Readers*, pp. 2, 5.

[62] Lisa Gitelman, *Paper Knowledge: Towards a Media History of Documents* (Durham, NC: Duke University Press, 2014), p. 28.

[63] G. B. Shaw 'Letter to Ellen Terry, 5th January 1898', in *Ellen Terry and Bernard Shaw: A Correspondence*, ed. Christopher St. John (London: Reindhardt & Evans, 1949).

[64] Nashe's copy is in the Folger Shakespeare Library. Nashe rotated the book 90° to enable him to write longitudinally in the margins, a not uncommon practice. Such 'vertical' writing (it looks vertical when the book is reoriented for reading) can be seen in many readers' annotations.

[65] William W. E. Slights, *Managing Readers: Printed Marginalia in English Renaissance Books* (Ann Arbor: University of Michigan Press, 2001), p. 22.

voluminous white space of the margins, so ably explored by Slights, is not my concern here, nor is the 'compositors' fat' (effortless print jobs such as blank pages) explored by Woudhuysen, nor the unfinished or interrupted works analysed by Dobranski as evidence of increasing authorial authority in the early modern period. My interest lies in excised words or lines in texts, in marks of suspension and interruption (such as '&c') and in the stand-in for what is excised (the asterisk). I am interested in rhetorical techniques of breaking-off and the relationship between rhetoric and the world of print.

Each chapter of this book looks at the development of normative practices we now take typographically for granted. Chapter 1 is about literal blank space in early modern texts: missing words, empty brackets, censored lines; it looks at blank space in an era in which the blank did not yet prompt readerly unease, suspicion of error, or the need for reassurance (as in our 'this page intention-ally left blank'). Chapter 2 investigates the '*etcetera*', '*et cetera*', '*etc.*', or '&c', the sign of breaking-off or interruption. Today *&c/etcetera* functions solely as an abbreviation, indicating the continuation of properties in a list, but in the early modern period that was only one of several meanings and uses it had. Chapter 3 explores the development of the asterisk from its use in nascent systems of annotation (marginal comments and footnotes) to its employment as a substitute for offensive vocabulary. In my final chapter I look at the way the typographical features I analyse take on a rich metaphoric life beyond the world of print. Thinking about representation then prompts the extension of my enquiry to the layout of dramatic texts.

Literary Blanks

I have mentioned that I am also interested in the blank conceptually: in par-ticular, in the many overt or implicit invitations to the reader to fill in gaps. The Elizabethan mindset was attuned to gaps, and lacunae were often used thematically. Shakespeare's *Venus and Adonis* is a poem of 1194 lines, written in 199 six-line stanzas. One additional stanza would have rounded up these num-bers nicely, giving the reader a poem of 1200 lines in 200 stanzas. Given Shakespeare's fluency, it is hard not to see a deliberate connection between the foreshortened numerical sequence and the poem's subject matter. In a poem about frustrated desire, neither the female protagonist nor the poetic form reach the desired end. Aphra Behn is similarly technically playful with a sexual subject in 'The Disappointment' (1680).[66] This 'imperfect enjoyment' poem (a poem about premature ejaculation) takes the form of fourteen 12-line verses which rhyme *abba cdcd ee* or *abba cddc ee*. The affinities with sonnet form are obvious: each verse is a truncated sonnet. The poem reaches the desired end of the Elizabethan sonnet—the climactic rhyming couplet—but by missing out the third quatrain, it does so prematurely. The couplet comes too soon.[67]

Sex is an obvious topic for writers to manipulate blanks and we also see this in plot terms. Gordon Braden finds a gap at the heart of Marlowe's epyllion *Hero and Leander* and tries to work out when the couple have sex (and how often);[68] a similar question has long preoccupied critics of *Othello*. John Marston teases readers with sexual suggestions in his erotic epyllion, *The Metamorphosis of Pygmalion's Image* (1598), where, instead of giving them wanton, Ovidian description, he appeals to their imagination (what male readers would like to do with their mistresses is exactly what Pygmalion did with his). He leaves a gap in the narrative but apophatically and meiotically tells us what he is not telling us: 'What he would doe, the self same action / Was not neglected by Pigmalion'.[69] Donne's mistress in 'The Flea' clearly answers him in the gaps between the verses so that each new verse is a response to her response. Although the woman is not given a voice, the reader works out her replies by the poet's counters to them. Because we infer the content of the gaps, a poetic monologue by a man becomes a dialogue between a man and a woman.

The gap can be as effective in spiritual writing as it is in erotic poems. George Herbert's 'Church Monuments' is a heavily enjambed pentameter poem in four verses of six lines each; John Drury points out that 'most strikingly, [the enjambement] happens over the gaps between the verses, giving the whole thing the continuous and inevitable flow of time's "ever-rolling

---

[66] The poem was first published as Rochester's in his *Poems on Several Occasions* (1680).

[67] The relationship between verse form and content is often invoked in early modern poetry. In *The Fruits of War* (in *Poesies*, 1575), Gascoigne explains that 'the verse is roughe. And good reason, sithence it treateth of roughe matters' (G8v). Adam Smyth contemplates the final Marprelate pamphlet of 1589, 'produced by an amateur printer, probably on the run while fleeing the authorities, with an irregular left margin, eccentric spacing and uneven inking: a *mise-en-page* that performed the dramatic contexts of its production' (*Material Texts*, p. 2).

[68] Gordon Braden, 'Hero and Leander in Bed (and the Morning After)', *English Literary Renaissance* 45:2 (2015), 205–30.

[69] *The Metamorphosis of Pygmalion's Image* in *Elizabethan Minor Epics*, ed. Elizabeth Story Donno (London: Routledge/Kegan Paul, 1963), stanza 36 (p. 251).

stream" '.[70] Given that there are only five sentences in the entire poem, the combination of long sentences and enjambement does indeed give continuity and inevitability of flow. But as the enjambed lines hold hands across the verse breaks, they create a *trompe l'oreille* in which the pause between stanzas forces a shift from one meaning to another. When stanza 1 ends 'Therefore I gladly trust', the pause makes the verb intransitive (not inappropriate in a religious poem); however, when it receives its object at the start of stanza 2 ('my body to this school') we recalibrate. Stanza 3 ends 'thou shalt grow fat', which readers might reasonably assume to have somatic reference; but when the line connects with stanza 4, it becomes metaphoric: 'and wanton in thy cravings'. In a poem about resignification (tomb inscriptions denote mortality not dynastic pride) and about severing ('These laugh at Jet and Marble put for signs, / To sever the good fellowship of dust, / And spoil the meeting'), the verse form illustrates both. The gaps between the verses 'spoil the meeting'. What Herbert does between stanzas, many poets do between lines, taking advantage of the pause enforced by the white space of line breaks, as we see in Matthew Arnold's *Dover Beach*:

> Ah, love let us be true
> To one another.[71]

What seems a general ethical plea narrows to a focus on the relationship.

One of the most famous descriptive passages in Shakespeare, Enobarbus' description of Cleopatra, has a gap at its centre. Enobarbus is able to describe everything around Cleopatra, and influenced by her, in sumptuous and erotic detail. The winds that fan her are lovesick; the water on which she floats is amorous; but for the fact that nature itself abhors gaps, the air would have gone to gaze on Cleopatra. But Enobarbus is unable to describe Cleopatra's actual person: 'For her own person, / It beggar'd all description' (*Antony and Cleopatra*, 2.2.197–8). The gap can become part of a poem's thematic structure even more extensively as in Raleigh's 'Ocean to Cynthia'. One of the most remarkable gap poems of the period, it not only contains lacunae but is itself about a hiatus: its subject is the rupture in Raleigh's relationship with Elizabeth

---

[70] John Drury, *Music at Midnight: The Life and Poetry of George Herbert* (London: Allen Lane, 2013), p. 36.

[71] Mathew Arnold, *New Poems* (London: Macmillan, 1867), p. 113. For white space round Edmund Spenser's stanzas in *The Faerie Queene* see Theresa Krier, 'Time Lords: Rhythm and Interval in Spenser's Stanzaic Narrative', *Spenser Studies* 21 (2007), 1–9.

and is structured round images of blank spaces.[72] Charlotte Scott finds a similar pattern in *Romeo and Juliet*, where childhood 'is the absence that fills up the room; the "thing" that the lovers are denied both in hindsight and in the action of the drama'.[73] This is part of her argument that childhood in Shakespeare is 'an idea "more honoured in the breach than in the observance"'—we notice it because it is not there.[74] The gap has a similar generalized presence in the background countries of Nashe's picaresque *Unfortunate Traveller* where Alexander Leggatt says 'Italy is the first location that is allowed to be something other than a blank background.'[75] In 1897 Virginia Woolf recorded in her diary the death of her beloved stepsister, Stella, describing the event as 'impossible to write of'. The next day's diary entry is blank; for Hannah Sullivan 'the blankness enacts the trope of incapacity visually, as a gap on the page'.[76] I do not mean to suggest that anything can be or become a metaphorical gap—non-narrated sex or descriptions, absent childhood, vague locations, grief. But I do think that the literal gap in printed texts cues readerly awareness of other kinds of literary absences and I will pick up some of these examples in Chapter 1.[77] The way that early modern printed texts use typography to signal beyond the text is the starting premise for each chapter in this book (a typographical location of reader-response theory). Each chapter then extends the investigation into the literary realm. Dobranski interprets 'omissions' (gaps in printed texts) as examples of increased authorial, and readerly, authority, with readers 'witness[ing] firsthand an author's poetic development';[78] I am interested in how authors capitalized on readers' tolerance of incompletion to create meaning, gaining mileage from what Adam Smyth calls 'the overlapping cultures of the bibliographical and the literary', what E. A. Levenston calls 'graphicology', and what Juliet Fleming (following Derrida) calls 'cultural

---

[72] Walter Raleigh, *The Poems of Sir Walter Ralegh*, ed. Agnes M. C. Latham (Cambridge, MA: Harvard University Press, 1951). Jonathan Sawday explores this further in *Print, Space, and Void* (in progress).

[73] Charlotte Scott, *The Child in Shakespeare* (Oxford: Oxford University Press, 2019), p. 73.

[74] Scott, *Child in Shakespeare*, p. 73.

[75] Alexander Leggatt, 'Artistic Coherence in *The Unfortunate Traveller*', *Studies in English Literature, 1500–1900* 14:1 (1974), 31–46 (43).

[76] Sullivan, *Work of Revision*, p. 221.

[77] For a book-length exploration of this topic, see Nicola Gardini, *Lacuna: Saggio sul non detto* (Turin: Einaudi, 2014).

[78] Dobranski, *Readers*, p. 8.

graphology'.[79] Literal representation (typography) and literary representation (fictionality) go hand in hand.

Although I am chiefly concerned with typography as visual rhetoric, the topic is vital to a study of editing: editorial attitude and editorial treatment. This is where this book differs, crucially, from Dobranski's or Sawday's studies of the blank (with which this book shares similar departure points) and from the work of the book historians mentioned (with which this book shares an interest in reader response). By historicizing blank space from the medieval scriptorium to the current (digital) day, I trace the history of editing blanks. Sometimes the questions about editing are gathered in a specific section, as in Chapter 1; sometimes they are interspersed, as in Chapter 2; but they are never far from the surface, for, as William Sherman notes, 'it may not be going too far to suggest that every piece of punctuation poses something of a textual crux'.[80]

*

This book began life as the Panizzi lectures, delivered at the British Library in November and December 2018. The lectures were 'bespoke' for the British Library, designed with their audience and their wonderful audiovisual facilities in mind. The lectures have been altered for publication in several ways. The range of material means that what in lectures was, of necessity, a one-sentence summary of medieval scribes or Italian censorship can now be fleshed out with detail; and although the book has many illustrations, the narrative structure has been changed to reduce the dependence on images that was a feature of the lectures. There has been no attempt to preserve the oral format of the original lectures.[81] This has meant both sacrifices and gains. The crispness of the lectures was enabled by glancing summaries of material that now receives extended treatment or provision of details; but because book history often derives its story and its authority from a wide range of material, exploring the contextual details for all the items runs the risk of each chapter initially reading as a list or anthology before reaching its interpretive pay-off. Each

---

[79] Smyth, *Material Texts*, p. 16; E. A. Levenston, *The Stuff of Literature: Physical Aspects of Texts and their Relation to Literary Meaning* (Albany: State University of New York Press, 1992); Juliet Fleming, *Cultural Graphology* (Chicago: University of Chicago Press, 2016).

[80] William H. Sherman, 'Early Modern Punctuation and Modern Editions: Shakespeare's Serial Colon', in *The Book in History, the Book as History: New Intersections of the Material Text*, ed. Heidi Brayman Hackel, Jesse M. Lander, and Zachary Lesser (New Haven, CT: Yale University Press, 2016), pp. 303–23 (p. 309).

[81] However, on each occasion I enjoyed discussion and subsequent correspondence with audience members, and the informal nature of these interactions is reflected in footnotes.

chapter moves from the specific to the general, from the textual to the theoretical, developing larger questions about representation and editing, and about the ways in which writers manipulate readers' awareness that they are holding a book. The different typographical ways of representing blanks— white space, the *&c/etcetera*, the asterisk—call attention both to the irreducible facticity of the book and to the act of reading, for 'nothing is more calculated to remind a reader he is reading than the deliberate foregrounding of graphic form'.[82] Let us now look at the ways in which one specific subgenre of graphic form—white space, a literal blank—contributes to this reminder.

---

[82] Levenston, *Stuff of Literature*, p. 119.

This page intentionally left blank

'This Page Intentionally Left Blank';
or, the Apophatic Page

A book is a sequence of spaces... The most beautiful and perfect book
in the world is a book with only blank pages.   (Ulises Carrión)

It makes me nervous to see three quarters of a page and no *writing* on it.
                                    (Tom Stoppard, *The Real Thing*)[1]

Introduction

At first glance, blank space in early modern printed texts seems too
straightforward a concept to require definition. Thomas Hood's 1592
description of terrestrial and celestial globes explains the obvious: 'the
surface... is to be understood as a blancke having nothing inscribed in it, yet
fit to receive any inscription'.[2] Thomas Cooper offered the same explanation in
a sermon of 1580: 'a blanke, wherein nothing is written'.[3] This is the way
Othello understands the chaste white space of his wife's body: 'Was this fair
paper, this most goodly book, made to write whore upon?' (4. 2.71–2) and the
resonantly named Blanche in Shakespeare's *King John* is thematically depicted
as a blank page awaiting masculine inscription by marriage.[4] Such associations
stem logically from the word's etymology in French *blanc* (white), giving us
items such as blancmange (literally 'eat white'), the opaque white custard-jelly
introduced in the Middle Ages as a savoury mixture of chicken and cream,

---

[1] The epigraphs come from Ulises Carrión, 'The New Art of Making Books', reprinted in Joan
Lyons (ed.), *Artists' Books: A Critical Anthology and Sourcebook* (Rochester, NY: Visual Studies Workshop
Press/Peregrine Smith Books, 1985), pp. 16–27 (p. 23); Tom Stoppard, *The Real Thing* (London: Faber
and Faber, 1984), 1.4.87–8, p. 40.

[2] Thomas Hood, *The Use of Both the Globes* (1592), B2v.

[3] Thomas Cooper, *Certain Sermons* (1580), R2v.

[4] For *King John* see Jean E. Howard and Phyllis Rackin, *Engendering a Nation: Shakespeare's Histories*
(London: Routledge, 1997).

The Rhetoric of the Page. Laurie Maguire, Oxford University Press (2020). © Laurie Maguire.
DOI: 10.1093/oso/9780198862109.001.0001

only later becoming a sweetmeat. The hyphenated entry in Henry Cockerham's *English Dictionary* (1623) makes the etymon clear—'Blanke-manger. A Custard' (C1r)—as does Francis Bacon's recommendation of '*Blanck-Manger*' as food for invalids; Edmund Coate's dictionary defines the verb 'blank' in a non-culinary context: 'to make white'.[5]

The poet Simon Armitage draws a distinction between poetry and prose as printed forms: 'Prose fills up a page. Once that page is full, it fills up the next one. Poetry stakes out a position on a page.'[6] In one sense, his distinction between two genres, poetry and prose, is correct (if one thinks in poetic terms, as we would expect Armitage to do, blank space is just as important as words in poetry). But the picture changes if one thinks about the history of the book—whether in terms of early modern book history or indeed about the history of the book across centuries. For, as we saw in the Introduction, early modern writing also 'stakes out a position' on the page, that is, makes rhetorical use of the page. Nowhere is this more obvious than in the use of blank space. From the reader's perspective, early modern blanks conform to Armitage's description of modern poetry's white 'oxygenated spaces, ventilated cavities where the mind's vapour trail overshoots and imagination undergoes millimetres of freefall'. They invite imaginative occupation, playing a conceptual game of hide and seek. In this chapter I want to think about how readers interact with and interpret blank space and blank spaces on the early modern page. My destination is the way in which practical typography came to be seen as creative opportunity, for writers as well as readers, and how modern editorial treatment elides that creativity; but before I reach that stage it will be necessary to look at the interactive reader generally.

Part I: Filling In

The Interactive Reader

The transition to print meant that readers were accustomed to books being hand-finished. Gaps were left by printers for rubrication, or for Greek letters

---

[5] Francis Bacon, *Sylva Sylvarum* (1627), C3v; Edmund Coate, *The English Schoolmaster* (1630), k3r.

[6] Simon Armitage, 'Mind the Gap: Omission, Negation and "a final revelation of horrible Nothingness—"', lecture delivered at Oxford University, 8 April 2016. Available at <http://podcasts.ox.ac.uk/series/poetry-simon-armitage>.

FIGURE 1.1 Terence, *Works* (1476), A5v. Shelfmark INC T59. Used by permission of the Folger Shakespeare Library.

and phrases, as in Terence's *Andria* (1476), where we see decorative majuscules provided by hand (see Figure 1.1).[7] This hand-finishing was done in the printing house so did not invite the reader to be an artist; my point is simply that readers were already attuned to the concept of the supplement. We can see this especially in those cases where the hand-finishing was left incomplete. In Figure 1.2, blank space is left in two consecutive lines for Greek letters; the gap in the first line was never filled in.[8] Thus, readers experienced gaps in their reading experience, gaps that they may or may not have rectified by filling in the omissions.

Peter Stallybrass reminds us that one of the most frequent things Elizabethan printers did was print blank documents—licences, receipts, ledgers, plague bills, visitation articles—just as today's consumers can buy blank tenancy agreements or wills, till receipts, blank stationery personalized with printed addresses, greetings cards, and postcards.[9] Derek Dunne has developed Stallybrass's work

---

[7] Terence, *Works* (1476), A5v.   [8] Terence, *Works* (1476), A6r.

[9] Peter Stallybrass, '"Little Jobs": Broadsides and the Printing Revolution', in *Agent of Change: Print Culture Studies after Elizabeth L. Eisenstein*, ed. Sabrina Alcorn Baron, Eric N. Lindquist, and Eleanor F. Shevlin (Amherst: University of Massachusetts Press, 2007), pp. 315–41. See also Henry R. Woudhuysen, *Sir Philip Sidney and the Circulation of Manuscripts 1558–1640* (Oxford: Clarendon Press, 1996), p. 20. Stallybrass points out that the printing of blank material complicates the concept of reader: these items have not readers but *users*. It is notable how often one slips into the business vocabulary of 'end user' when looking at blanks in print history. See William Sherman, *Used Books: Marking Readers in Renaissance England* (Philadelphia: University of Pennsylvania Press, 2008), p. xiii; his title puns on the concept. We see this repeatedly in criticism: William Worthen asks 'is the form of the printed book an adequate *delivery system* for plays? Is it a delivery system at all?' ('The Imprint of Performance', in *Theorizing Practice: Redefining Theatre History*, ed. W. B. Worthen with Peter Holland (Basingstoke: Palgrave Macmillan, 2003), pp. 213–34 (p. 213, my emphasis)); Jason Scott-Warren discusses early modern books as '*vehicles* for many kinds of life-writing' in 'Reading Graffiti

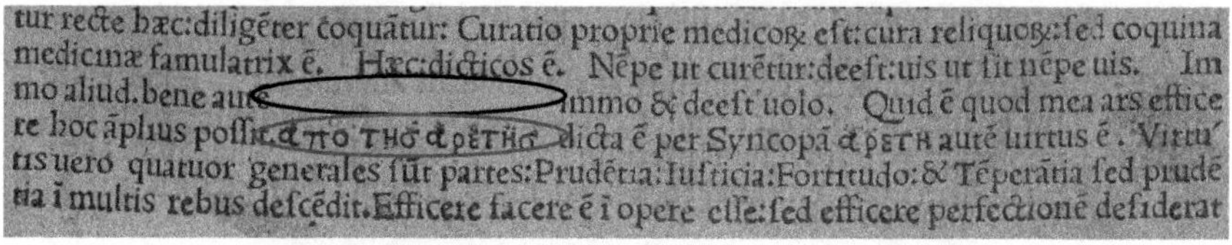
tur recte hæc:diligẽter coquãtur: Curatio proprie medicoꝝ est:cura reliquoꝝ:sed coquina
medicinæ famulatrix ẽ. Hæc:dicticos ẽ. Nẽpe ut curẽtur:deest:uis ut sit nẽpe uis. Im
mo aliud.bene au[…]mmo & deest uolo. Quid ẽ quod mea ars effice
re hoc ãplius possit.ἀπὸ τῆς ἀρετῆς dicta ẽ per Syncopã ἀρετη autẽ uirtus ẽ. Virtu
tis uero quatuor generales sũt partes:Prudẽtia:Iusticia:Fortitudo:& Tẽperãtia sed prudẽ
tia ĩ multis rebus descẽdit.Efficere facere ẽ ĩ opere esse:sed efficere perfectionẽ desiderat

FIGURE 1.2 Terence, *Works* (1476), A6r. Shelfmark INC T59. Used by permission of the Folger Shakespeare Library.

in a study of licences and warrants.[10] Elizabethan literature abounds with references to such blanks, as Dunne has documented. In Thomas Tomkis' *Albumazar* (1615), Trinculo commissions 'blank [...] / *Mittimusses* [warrants for arrest] Printed in readinesse' (C4v); Shakespeare's Richard II raises taxes through 'blank charters' (1.4.48). In *Merry Wives of Windsor* the eponymous wives receive identical love letters from Falstaff; Mistress Ford speculates that Falstaff 'hath a thousand of these letters, writ with blank space for different names' (2.1.74–6).[11] The spendthrift in Cooke's *Greene's Tu Quoque* (1614) is brought a bond by a 'Master *Blanke*' (D4r) and in Middleton's *The Widow* a character has 'blank warrants of all dispositions' (1.1.67) for the names of malefactors, and 'four blank warrants' are discovered in Act 4.[12] The textually alert Jonson canon repeatedly references blank printed documents.[13] A printed folio commonplace book from 1585 handsomely illustrates blank printing: John Foxe's *Pandectae Locorum* (1585) runs to over 1500 pages, all blank except for thematic headings at the top of pages ('abstinence', 'temperance'), inviting the owner to fill up the blank folios with extracts on the relevant themes.[14]

in the Early Modern Book', *Huntington Library Quarterly* 73:3 (2010), 363–81 (380, my emphasis). Fred Schurink discusses 'goal-oriented' readers and 'pragmatic readers' (as well as the 'great Variety of Readers') in 'Manuscript Commonplace Books, Literature, and Reading in Early Modern England', *Huntington Library Quarterly* 73:3 (2010), 453–69.

[10] Derek Dunne, 'Rogues' Licence: Counterfeiting Authority in Early Modern England', *Shakespeare Studies* 45 (2017), 137–43.

[11] For a discussion of printing concepts in *Merry Wives of Windsor*, see Elizabeth Pittenger, 'Dispatch Quickly: The Mechanical Reproduction of Pages', *Shakespeare Quarterly* 42:4 (1991), 389–408.

[12] *The Widow* in Thomas Middleton, *Collected Works*, ed. Gary Taylor and John Lavagnino (Oxford: Clarendon Press, 2007). All references are to this edition and are included parenthetically in my text.

[13] See *Epicoene*: 'Where is the writing? I will seal to it, that, or to a blank, and write thine own conditions' (5.4.175–6); *The Devil is an Ass*: 'To publications; ha' your deed drawn presently. / And leave a blank to put in your feoffees' (3.5.59–60). Ben Jonson, *Epicoene*, ed. R. V. Holdsworth (New Mermaids; London: Ernest Benn Ltd, 1979); *The Devil is an Ass and Other Plays*, ed. M. J. Kidnie (Oxford: Oxford University Press, 2000).

[14] The full title is *Pandectae Locorum Communium Praecipua Rerum Capita et Titulos Ordine Alphabetico Complectentes*. For studies of commonplace books see Ann Moss, *Printed Commonplace-Books and the*

(Other pages—blank pages with empty boxed headings—act as continuation sheets or expect readers to supply themes of their own.) Print invites the interactive reader, what Tamara Atkin in a recent study identifies as the effortful reader or the reader as completer, engaged in a process of 'performative reading'.[15] Readers interact at all stages of book ownership: they illustrate their books or commission illustrations; they assemble and order books in thematic collections; they disassemble and reorder them; they bind them.[16] They don't just buy a book as a finished object and read it.

Medieval Scribes

It is possible to draw an arc from the medieval scriptorium to the digital book, although attitudes to, and anxieties about, blank space are not constant across the centuries or across media. Studies of medieval scribes by critics such as Phillipa Hardman and Daniel Wakelin have done much to illuminate our understanding of scribal attitudes, readers' attitudes, and patrons' attitudes to gaps and blanks.[17] Wakelin shows how scribes copied blanks from their exemplars; they themselves created blanks when they could not decipher a word, read an unusual spelling, recognize a classical name, or when their exemplar

Structuring of Renaissance Thought (Oxford: Clarendon Press, 1996), Zachary Lesser and Peter Stallybrass, 'The First Literary *Hamlet* and the Commonplacing of Professional Plays', *Shakespeare Quarterly* 59:4 (2008), 371–420; Schurink, 'Manuscript Commonplace Books'; Laura Estill, 'Commonplacing Readers', in *Shakespeare and Textual Studies*, ed. M. J. Kidnie and Sonia Massai (Cambridge: Cambridge University Press, 2015), pp. 149–62; Laura Estill, *Dramatic Extracts in Seventeenth-Century English Manuscripts: Watching, Reading, Changing Plays* (Newark: University of Delaware Press, 2015). See also the database curated by Laura Estill and Beatrice Montedoro, DEx: A Database of Dramatic Extracts, available at: <https://dex.itercommunity.org/>.

[15] Atkin, *Reading Drama in Tudor England* (London: Routledge, 2018), p. 178.

[16] See Jeffrey Todd Knight, *Bound to Read: Compilations, Collections, and the Making of Renaissance Literature* (Philadelphia: University of Pennsylvania Press, 2013).

[17] See Phillipa Hardman, 'Reading the Spaces: Pictorial Intentions in the Thornton MSS, Lincoln Cathedral MS 91, and BL MS Add. 31042', *Medium Aevum* 63:2 (1994), 250–74, 'Lydgate's "Life of our Lady": A Text in Transition', *Medium Ævum* 65:2 (1996), 248–68, 'Windows into the Text: Unfilled Spaces in some Fifteenth-Century English Manuscripts', in *Texts and their Contexts, Papers from the Early Book Society*, ed. John Scattergood and Julia Boffey (Dublin: Four Courts Press, 1997), pp. 44–70, 'Interpreting the Incomplete Scheme of Illustration in Cambridge Corpus Christi College MS 61', *English Manuscript Studies* 6 (1977), 52–69; Daniel Wakelin, 'When Scribes Won't Write: Gaps in Middle English Books', *Studies in the Age of Chaucer* 36 (2014), 249–78, 'William Worcester Writes a History of his Reading', *New Medieval Literatures* 7 (2005), 53–71, *Scribal Correction and Literary Craft: English Manuscripts 1375–1510* (Cambridge: Cambridge University Press, 2014). See also Susanna Fein, '*Somer Soneday*: Kingship, Sainthood, and Fortune in Oxford, Bodleian Library, MS Laud Misc. 108', in *The Texts and Contexts of Oxford, Bodleian Library, MS Laud Misc.108: The Shaping of Vernacular Narrative*, ed. K. K. Bell and J. N. Couch (Leiden: Brill, 2010), pp. 275–97.

did not make sense because it was faulty. Sometimes they began a word, writing one or more letters, and then abandoned it. Their blanks range from the length of a word through a square for a large initial to a half-page for an illustration. In almost all cases it is clear that they intended to fill in the space later, often leaving small marks in the margin (e.g. a cross) as location markers.[18] But frequently the spaces were left unfilled, leading critics to speculate not only on readers' tolerance levels for gaps in the manuscripts they commissioned and read but whether there was ever any intention to fill these gaps. If, for instance, the purpose of an illustration is to call attention to the part of the text it accompanies, might not the same purpose be served by a blank space? This is Phillipa Hardman's question about empty space for never-supplied illustrations; her question explores the paradox familiar to us from the Introduction in which the blank acts as pointer rather than concealer.[19] Daniel Wakelin explores a similar paradox with missing words, suggesting that the gaps showcase the scribe's conscientious care rather than any lack of it; they demonstrate to the reader the high quality of the manuscript s/he possesses.[20] It is worth exploring these examples in more detail.

Hardman's work introduces a new hybrid category of manuscript: one where illustrations were intended but never supplied.[21] What do we call this category, given that it is neither illustrated nor unillustrated? Hardman finds these liminal specimens in several places and genres: a prose *Life of Alexander* with ten box-shaped blanks for illustrations; an extract from *Cursor Mundi* (the 'Life of Mary and Jesus') with nine box-shaped blank spaces (unlike the *Life of Alexander*, this manuscript has been 'prepared for the reader's use...with numerous rubricated chapter headings'[22]); Lydgate's *Life of Our Lady* with ten spaces for pictures; a *Northern Passion* with a blank space of fourteen lines; and a devotional lyric on the Passion. All of Hardman's blanks are substantial squares with no rubric or source to indicate what should fill the spaces—and there is no one-size-fits-all explanation for her examples. The *Life of Alexander* was awaiting illustrations. The scribe may have been copying from an exemplar that was itself unillustrated; or he may have been making independent

---

[18] Wakelin, 'When Scribes Won't Write', *passim*.   [19] Hardman, 'Reading the Spaces', 258.

[20] Wakelin, 'When Scribes Won't Write', 258, 277.

[21] David McKitterick explores this phenomenon in fifteenth-century books printed in Ferrara. See 'What is the Use of Books without Pictures: Empty Spaces in Some Early Printed Books', *La Bibliofilia* 116:1–3 (2014), 67–82.

[22] Hardman, 'Reading the Spaces', 257.

artistic decisions with only his close reading to guide him (the blanks are left, as Hardman shows, at narrative moments that cumulatively tell a simple political story of imperial conquest rather than a moral story).

The *Cursor Mundi* explanation is slightly different. Although one critic thinks its blanks were left for illustrations to be added later, possibly to be copied from an exemplar that was illustrated, Hardman queries whether 'there ever was a real intention to provide rubricated initials in the spaces'. Her speculation is linked to manuscript status: she suggests that blanks may have been an option in inexpensive or non-professional manuscripts and that 'prerubrication came to be seen as an acceptable convention in itself'.[23] She sees the space left for illustrations as an 'opportunity offered to the reader, prompted by the blank space, to visualise the incident'.[24]

Readers with artistic ability may have extended the invitation to visualize into the realm of the practical: the Bodleian copy of Lydgate's *Life of Our Lady* has its first four drawings inexpertly filled in. Hardman's final examples concern gaps introduced by scribes for an illustration of the crucifixion to encourage meditation. When one scribe introduces a textual emendation (revising 'the cross' to 'this cross') related to his blank ('no doubt intended for an illustration of this scene') we can see this scribe's thought processes in action.[25]

Daniel Wakelin's analysis of gaps (from one word to entire lines) in fifty-two medieval manuscripts further shows scribes' thinking processes. His argument, like Hardman's, concludes with a conceptual paradox: gaps are effortful; they show us not careless scribes but careful. Wakelin's research transfers helpfully to the print world, where the medieval scribe's gap-creation in the face of material he cannot decipher or understand is paralleled in the work of Elizabethan compositors. Book II, canto X, verse 24 of Spenser's *Faerie Queene* includes complex Welsh-language vocabulary:

> How oft that day did sad *Brunchildis* see
> The greene shield dyde in dolorous vermell?
> That not *Scuith guiridh* he mote seeme to bee,
> But rather *y Scuith gogh*, signe of sad crueltee. (X8v)[26]

---

[23] Hardman, 'Reading the Spaces', 258.   [24] Hardman, 'Reading the Spaces', 259.
[25] Hardman, 'Reading the Spaces', 265–6.
[26] '*Scuith*' is noted in the Errata list as an error for '*Seuith*'.

This is the reading of the 1590 edition in the Huntington Library (STC 23081a). But another copy of the 1590 edition (now in the British Library; STC 23081) presents the last two lines of this verse as follows:

> That not   he mote seeme to bee,
> But

Clearly, the compositor was baffled by what he saw in his manuscript copy and, rather than guess, left a gap. The correct readings were inserted during stop-press corrections.

Wakelin's study raises important questions, and not just about our modern assumptions about quality (gaps in medieval manuscripts are evidence of scribes' refusal 'to do a job badly').[27] Scribes, it seems, are anxious about unfinished texts such as *The Canterbury Tales*, where they distinguish the author's incompletion from their own; they are 'wary of their exemplars',[28] querying the words they are employed to copy; they do not lightly introduce gaps into their own copies; they complete their work in stages, revisiting and filling in gaps; they are aware of the 'visual distraction' of blank space;[29] they also have a Barthesian awareness of the difference between 'work' and 'text', between the text as physical copy ('work') and the text as 'language'.[30] So medieval scribes and their readers tolerated gaps as a necessity and embraced them as an opportunity; they were aware of imperfect texts as material artefact and perfect texts as immaterial ideal.

We see a similar negotiation of boundaries in the numerous early modern errata lists which apologize for printers' errors and invite the forgiving reader to rectify the listed oversights.

Errata Lists

Situated either at the start of a book or at the end, these lists address the reader directly in imperatives, as in a translation of Paracelsus' *How to Cure the French*

---

[27] Wakelin, 'When Scribes Won't Write', 276.

[28] Wakelin, 'When Scribes Won't Write', 269.

[29] Wakelin, 'When Scribes Won't Write', 276.

[30] Although Barthes' distinction seems counterintuitive to textual critics, for whom a text is a physical object rather than Barthesian discourse, it makes etymological sense as Barthes invokes the concept of woven cloth to describe language; consequently, 'while the work is held in the hand, the text is held in language: it exists only as discourse.... In other words, the Text is experienced only in an activity, a production. It follows that the Text cannot stop, at the end of a library shelf, for example'. Roland Barthes, 'From Work to Text', in *Textual Strategies: Perspectives in Post-Structuralist Criticism*, Josué V. Harari (Ithaca, NY: Cornell University Press, 1979), pp. 73–91 (p. 75).

Pox (1590): '[p]age 2, line 3, put out the first and', '[p]age 8, line 25, for Bernagie read Borrage' (H4v). The errata list in this medical book is followed by a very modern warning to the reader, advising against trying the remedies at home without first seeking medical advice. Clearly readers of this text were expected to have two kinds of active response to it.

Eschewing the traditional imperative, the errata list at the end of *The Countess of Pembroke's Ivychurch* (1591), puts its request more into entreaty than command:

> B.29. He that will, may for those verses,
> *Ile soone charme thy cheeke, this secreate lately I learned*
> *Of Beldame* Sagane, *for an yvory combe that I gave her.*
> Reade these,
> *Ile soone charme thy cheeke: this charme did* Aresia *teach mee, For myne yvory horne, with gold all briefly adorned.*[31]

Errata lists vary in length from a few lines to an entire page but it is clear that they are meant to be illustrative rather than comprehensive. Addressing readers at the beginning of *The Muses' Elizium* (1630), Michael Drayton entreats them to correct the volume's errors, '*[s]ome of which faults (I dare not say all) I have heereunder set downe*'. After the errata list he explains further, '*I onley shew you these few, for brevity sake, that in your Reading you may correct the like, which I am afraid are many more then these*' (A4r). The reader has an even more complicated proofreading task as Drayton qualifies his errata list with the note that, because there have been stop-press corrections, the last item on the list does not apply to all copies: '*this last fault is not through all the Impression*' (A4r).

Readers also corrected texts even when there was no errata list instructing them to do so. John Day's *Isle of Gulls* (1606) misprinted 'lover' as 'lord', making nonsense of the satiric line 'I think a lover cannot be sav'd for hee is of all religions' (B4v). The readers of the Bodleian Library copy (STC 6413) and the Carl Pforzheimer Library copy (STC 6412) both use their common sense to correct the line. An invitation to hear 'a worthie Jest' in Gascoigne's *Glass of Government* (1575, STC 11643a, British Library copy) seems a puzzling paradox. The reader of the Folger Shakespeare Library copy has made it more logical by pasting the adjective 'merrye' over his text (A3v). Characters are frequently confused in the printed texts of Elizabethan plays—for example, Robert

---

[31] Abraham Fraunce, *The Countess of Pembroke's Ivychurch* (1591), M4r. The difference between the two readings is so vast that one is inclined to suspect revision rather than erratum. The compositor may have misinterpreted the signs for deletion and insertion in his MS copy.

Greene's *Friar Bacon and Friar Bungay* (1594) and Henry Chettle's *Hoffman* (*c*.1601–2, Q1631)—but attentive readers have made the appropriate emendations: 'Bungay' for 'Bacon' in the former (with an elegant attempt to match the typeface) and 'my brother' for 'your brother' in the latter.[32] Wear and tear on paper rendered words illegible in two lines of Ben Jonson's *Epicoene*; the words have been supplied by a dutiful reader: 'chastest' and 'must'.[33] But sometimes blanks remain unfilled as in the blank banderoles in the *Interlude of Youth* (*c*.1554?, printed 1557): Charity and Youth are identified but three other characters remain anonymous (British Library copy, C 34 b.24).

Supplementation and Omission

Once a reader has improved a text by correcting errors, why stop there? A cropped marginal note is supplied in John Davies of Hereford's *Continued Inquisition against Paper-Persecutors* (1625).[34] The dedicatee to Spenser's pastoral elegy on the death of Sir Philip Sidney, the Countess of Essex, is identified as 'Fraunces' in the Folger copy (B1r).[35] Diligent readers often supply indices: to the poems of John Donne or to Sidney's *Arcadia* (this index runs to eight folio pages).[36] The indexer of Donne also adds titles to each poem throughout the volume, a necessary prefatory act to indexing. One bibliographically aware early modern reader observes that his 1611 edition of Spenser's *Shepherd's Calendar* is not the first edition, noting that it was first printed by William Ponsonbie in 1579.[37] Readers' marginal notes indicate their talents as literary critics—the reader of Spenser's *Faerie Queene* now in the Folger noted, for instance, a simile's affiliations to Senecan tragedy and identified the 'shepheard of the ocean' in *Colin Clout's Come Home Again* as Walter Raleigh.[38] 'Simile' is one of the most frequent marginal notes and although this might seem to us a

---

[32] Greene, *Friar Bacon and Friar Bungay* (1594), D2v, British Library copy: C.34.*c*.37; Chettle, *Hoffman* (1631), D1v, British Library copy: 644.b.11.

[33] Ben Jonson, *Works* (1616, STC 14752), Bbb1v, Folger Shakespeare Library. There were two different issues of this folio, STC 14751 and STC 14752; the Folger has eleven copies of STC 14751 (some of which have manuscript markings) but only one copy of STC 14752.

[34] *A Continued Inquisition against Paper-Persecutors* appended to *A Scourge for Paper-Persecutors* (1625), A1v, British Library copy. For more on this marginal note, see Chapter 3.

[35] 'Astrophel' in *Colin Clout's Come Home Again* [and other minor works] bound in with *The Faerie Queene* (1590, STC 23083.8, Folger Shakespeare Library copy 1), B1r.

[36] John Donne, *Poems* (1633, STC 7045, Folger Shakespeare Library copy 2); Philip Sidney, *Arcadia* (1593, STC 22540, Folger Shakespeare Library copy).

[37] *Shepherd's Calendar* (1611, STC 23093.5, title page). The edition, at the Folger Shakespeare Library, is bound with *The Faerie Queene*.

[38] STC 23083.9: 'Sen Trag' on N1r and identification of Raleigh on A3r.

self-evident or superfluous observation, it indicates a reader engaged in purposively rhetorical reading, someone who is noting figurative language for their own subsequent use. Daniel Wakelin has observed identical instances in medieval readers of Chaucer, and Fred Schurink has noted the extraction of similes from texts into Edward Pudsey's commonplace book.[39]

Theatrically sensitive readers added missing stage directions. A reader of Jonson's *Poetaster* supplied necessary exits ('*Exit*', '*Exeunt*').[40] A reader of the 1622 Quarto of *Othello* inserts a crucial direction in Act 3, scene 3: 'lets falle her / napkine' [i.e. she drops her handkerchief] (H1v); at the end of this same scene s/he balances the quarto's 'Iago kneeles' with 'Othello kneeles' four lines earlier (H3v).[41] This reader's eye for key theatrical moments is again in evidence in 4.1 with the marginal addition 'he strikes her' (K2v) and a clarification of Roderigo's 'o.o.o' at 5.1 with the marginal note: 'gives up ghost' (L4r);[42] his/her final inserted stage direction comes in 5.2 with 'Iago strikes his wife with a sworde' (M4r). (This is a very attentive reader whose other annotations will be examined in detail in Chapter 3.)

Attribution is a frequent addition on title pages, whether from knowledge or guesswork. The owner of the anonymous *How to Choose a Good Wife from a Bad* (1602), adds 'written by Joshua Cooke'.[43] In Cotgrave's *Treasury of Wit and Language* (1655), a commonplace-book-style printed collection of poetic extracts, the extracts are unattributed but a contemporary hand adds authorship attributions to many of the quotations.[44]

It is abundantly clear that readers were accustomed to interacting with what is not there. This then extends beyond the local and typographical. Richard Jones, the publisher of Thomas Nashe's *Pierce Pennilesse* (1592), calls attention to Nashe's 'unwonted beginning without Epistle, Proeme, or Dedication', explaining that because these prolegomena are distributed throughout the volume, rather than gathered at the start, the reader must hunt for them:

---

[39] Schurink, 'Manuscript Commonplace Books', 468.

[40] Ben Jonson, *Works* (1616, STC 14752), Aa4r, Folger Shakespeare Library copy.

[41] STC 69337, Huntington Library copy.

[42] The 1623 folio removes the triple 'o', as do most modern editors, following F. Although the phrase is used colloquially today, the phrase 'gives up ghost' is biblical (John 19:30, Matthew 27:50), describing the crucifixion; in the early modern period 'ghost' still had its meaning of 'spirit'. John Davies of Hereford uses the phrase in the manuscript marginal annotations to his printed poem *The Holy Rood* (1609, STC 6330) when he summarizes Christ's crucifixion: 'Gives up ghost' (G2r). This copy is in the Folger Shakespeare Library.

[43] STC 5594, British Library copy (B.M. C. 34, b.53).

[44] Wing C6368. See Peter Stallybrass and Roger Chartier, 'Reading and Authorship: The Circulation of Shakespeare 1590–1619', in *A Concise Companion to Shakespeare and the Text*, ed. Andrew Murphy (Oxford: Blackwell, 2007), pp. 35–56.

'al which he hath inserted conceitedly in the matter: but Ile be no blab to tell you in what place. Bestow the looking, and I doubt not, but you shall find Dedication, Epistle, & Proeme to your liking' (STC 18371, A2r). In his preface to *The Pageant of Popes* (1574), John Bale's translator explains

> because of the sodaine finishing of this worke in ye printers hande, I am forced in this Preface to leave out many matters which I thought to have uttered.... At this time therefore this onelye I have to request of thee (gentle Reader) till God shal giue me better oportunitye to finishe that order which I purposed in publishing this booke, to marke as thou readest how the manner of these Prelates do agree to the description of Antichrist.   (*b4v)

In his *Collection of the History of England* (1618) Samuel Daniel apologizes for the fact that his work lacks a dedication, preface, and '*all the Complements of a Booke*', and so the reader must be content 'to be payd by peeces' (A3r). George Turberville's *Book of Hunting/Art of Venery* (1575), a translation and adaptation of a French original, tells us he has left out 'unseemely verses' because they are only fit for 'lascivious mindes' but if we want to read them we can consult the original French (I6v).

More soberly, a rape trial omits material out of modesty. *A Brief Description of the Notorious Life of John Lamb* (1628) explains, 'There are certain passages which are upon the Records which for Modestie sake are here omitted' (C2v). In the world of prose fiction, both George Gascoigne and Thomas Nashe indicate omissions in rape actions, creating a blank in the narrative. Describing the rape of Elinor in *The Adventures of Master F.J.* (1573), Gascoigne's sentence trails off with 'and &c'.[45] Forcing his sexual attentions on Elinor, F. J. 'bare hir up with such a violence against the bolster, that before shee could prepare the warde [assume a defensive position], he thrust hir through both hands, *and &c.* wher by the Dame swoning for feare, was constreyned (for a time) to abandon hir body to the enemies curtesie' (I4r, my emphasis). I will examine this moment in detail in Chapter 2, but here I note that the '&c' stands in not just for a sexual word but for a larger sexual narrative, cued by the conjunction 'and'. In the episode in which Heraclide is raped in *The Unfortunate Traveller* (1594), Nashe, more prosaically, invites the reader simply to '[c]onjecture the rest' (K4v). Thus, from translation and adaptation to testimony and fiction, texts are framed in such a way as to extend beyond themselves, with narrative and typographical blanks creating a readerly mindset in which supplementation is expected.

---

[45] This is included in *A Hundreth Sundrie Flowres Bound Up in One Small Poesie* (1573, STC 11635).

Literary Adoption/Adaptation

From the typographical to the literary: I am interested throughout this book in the ways in which typographical features with practical functions—white space, the '&c', the asterisk—and textual conventions such as errata lists—start to have creative, literary, and ludic possibilities. John Taylor the Water Poet adapts the convention of the errata list in a prefatory twenty-six-line poem which asks his readers for a blanket pardon:

> Then in your reading mend each mis-plac'd letter,
> And by your judgement make bad words sound better.
> Where you may hurt, heale; where you can afflict,
> There helpe and cure, or else be not too strict.
> Look through your fingers, wink, connive at mee,
> And (as you meet with faults) see, and not see.   (Works (1630), A4v)

There is much to comment on in this poem—the medical imagery of the correcting reader as textual healer, the paradoxical presentation of performative reading as seeing and not seeing, for example—but at stake here is the way that a typographical convention, the errata list, has been converted into literary form. We also see this in one of the Marprelate tracts, 'written against Puritans'. It provides an errata list which riffs on printers' faults and Puritans' faults, itemizing the latter in the familiar print-shop language of the former: material textual faults are developed into faults of belief and behaviour.[46] Abraham Fraunce's errata list at the end of *The Countess of Pembroke's Ivychurch* (1591), introduces one emendation with an explanation that drily exploits the ironic congruence of the error and its cause: 'In most part of the impression, by too much haste, *hastneth* went foorth, insteede of, *hasteneth*.' (Here we see the Elizabethan poetic concern with acoustic form since this erratum affects scansion not sense; M4r.) The quarto of Dekker's *Satiromastix* (1602) pursues an extended analogy between the way a play conventionally begins in the theatre (with three trumpet calls) and the way a play conventionally begins in print (with an errata list):

> In steed of the Trumpets sounding thrice, before the Play begin: it shall not be amisse (for him that will read) first to beholde this short Comedy of Errors, and where the greatest enter, to give them in stead of a hisse, a gentle correction.
>
> (A4v)

---

[46] *An Epitome of the First Book . . . written against Puritans* (1588), G1v. The pamphlet is likely authored by Thomas Nashe.

Adam Smyth offers further examples of playful uses of errata-list conventions, suggesting that the errata list becomes 'less about actually correcting' than 'a rhetorical set piece'.[47] He pursues the literary relationships readers and authors had with error, invoking analogies with metaphor and poetry ('notes of errata sometimes do what poets like to do: they yolk together unlike things') and suggesting that the overlap between print-shop conventions and literary writing may be due to the 'striking number of authors who worked and even lived in print shops'.[48] As typographical corrections become literary fodder, paratext loses its practical raison d'être, becoming part of literary form.

Seneca reassures Jasper Heywood, in an extended verse preface to Heywood's translation of Seneca's *Thyestes* (1560), 'learned men shall soone discerne / thy fautes from his [the printer's], and saye, / Loe here the Printer dooth him wrong'(❧1v).[49] There is a division here between printer and author and between printed text and reader (as Tamara Atkin writes, 'where print corrupts, readers might correct'). But a correcting reader becomes a writer, just as a careless compositor becomes a literary prompt for parody. Boundaries, in other words, become blurred.[50]

Personalization

Blanks are often left in a text for the user to personalize references. I say 'user' (picking up the vocabulary of footnote 9) since this is particularly true of dramatic texts. John Rastell's interlude, *The Nature of the Four Elements* (c.1510–20) concludes with a song. The printed text, unsure of the musical preferences or abilities of the theatre companies who might buy the play, provides convenient blank staves, allowing any purchasers to insert their own musical notation (E4v and E7r). The medieval *N-Town Plays* indicate by the title we give them (N = *nomen*) the topical (literally) potential of the blank, where blanks allow the theatre company to personalize the location on tour. The MS promises a

---

[47] *Material Texts in Early Modern England* (Cambridge: Cambridge University Press, 2018), p. 98. He further explores the errata list's 'potential for satirical wit' in 'Errata Lists', in Dennis Duncan and Adam Smyth (eds), *Book Parts* (Oxford: Oxford University Press, 2019), pp. 251–62 (p. 256).

[48] Smyth, *Material Texts*, pp. 84, 101–2. Thomas Nashe, Gabriel Harvey, Henry Chettle, Anthony Munday, William Baldwin, and John Dee all lodged with printers at some stage.

[49] For a discussion of Heywood's relationship with the printer Richard Tottel, see Atkin, *Reading Drama*, pp. 88–9 and 116–18.

[50] Adam Smyth is consistently stimulating on overlaps in all the categories he discusses in *Material Texts*: for instance, a correcting reader turns a printed book into a print-manuscript hybrid and cutting up a text is a means of writing.

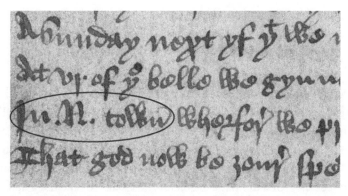

FIGURE 1.3 *N-Town Plays*, fol. 9, II. 525–9. © The British Library Board. British Library MS Cotton Vespasian D VIII.

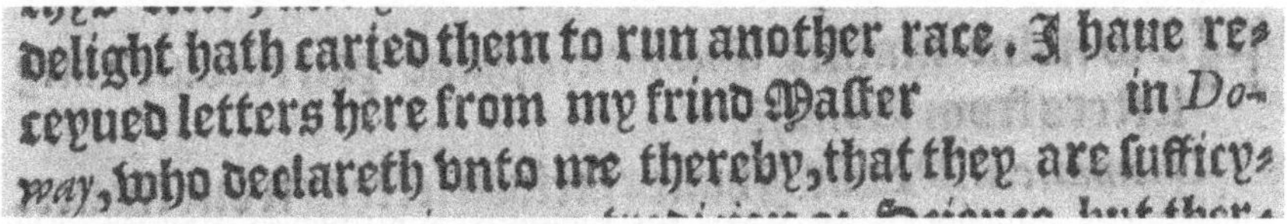

delight hath caried them to run another race, I haue re=
cepued letters here from my frind Master   in Do=
way, who declareth vnto me thereby, that they are sufficy=

FIGURE 1.4 George Gascoigne, *The Glass of Government* (1575, STC 11643a), L3r. Shelfmark 81918. Courtesy of The Huntington Library, San Marino.

performance 'A Sunday next.../ At six of the belle.../ In N. town' (Banns, lines 525–27) (see Figure 1.3). Similarly, the Banns that introduce *The Castle of Perseverance* leave blanks in the announcer's speeches where a place name should be: 'At...on the green.../...Ye manly men of..., ther Crist save you all!'[51] (I represent the blanks by ellipses although the scribe uses an idiosyncratic mark to indicate the blank.) In Gascoigne's *Glass of Government* (1575), a human-ist dialogue, the fill-in-your-own-name opportunity is indicated by a blank (see Figure 1.4).

Whether Gascoigne's play was performed, or designed for performance, is a moot point. It presents itself as a playtext. The title page announces the play's genre as 'a tragicall Comedie'; the text has a cast list explaining characters and their relationship; it is full of stage directions that are attentive to movement:

> *They adresse their talke to the Schoolemaister*   (Aii^v)
> *The Ladies passe by, with a reverence to the gentlemen*   (Ei^v)

[51] Folger Shakespeare Library MS. V.a. 354, f. 155v.

> *Pandarina interrupteth her* (Eiv^v)
> *The youngmen kneele down* (Iiii^v)
> *He departeth, as the Skoolmaster cometh in* (Iiv^r)
> *He delivereth him the letter* (Li^r)[52]

Nonetheless, the sheer number of such stage directions, and their detail, including intentionality—'*Philosarchus taketh her by the hand to comfort her*' (E4v, my underlining)—might equally argue against this text being designed as a play since stage directions in such quantity are unusual in early modern drama.[53]

The play is unlike drama in other respects. Gnomaticus has unusually lengthy speeches for a dramatic character: he speaks for six and a half pages in Act 2 (from signatures Civ^r to Diii^v) and for over two pages in Act 4 (Iiv^v to Ki^v). The text is presented to the reader as a moral treatise, with hortatory marginalia ('Love God.', Biii^r; 'Trust in God.', Biv^r) and marginal references to biblical source texts ('Gen. 17', 'Num. 14', Biv^r). When the students in the play compose homework verses, their rhetorical topics are noted in the margin. Elsewhere the margins offer moral summaries ('Murmurers disobedient seldome prove wel', Iii^r) or extra-dramatic commentary ('A fine excuse', Fiii^v).[54] The publisher clearly saw the dialogue as a didactic treatise rather than a drama, identifying and explaining the 'sentences' on which 'this work is compiled', and tabulating them numerically in eight groups at the start of the book (Aiv^r).[55]

---

[52] Given the volume and detail of the stage directions, it is hard to know what prompted Christopher Gaggero's comment that 'the play rarely invokes the space of the stage. Its massed entries give little sense of movement, and *there are no other stage directions*'. See Christopher Gaggero, 'Pleasure Unreconciled to Virtue: George Gascoigne and Didactic Drama', in *Tudor Drama before Shakespeare, 1485–1590*, ed. Lloyd Kermode, Jason Scott-Warren, and Martine van Elk (Basingstoke: Palgrave Macmillan, 2004), pp. 167–94 (p. 183, my emphasis).

[53] However, this text was printed at a time when dramatic conventions had not yet been standardized.

[54] Gascoigne's *Supposes* (in *A Hundreth Sundrie Flowres*) frequently uses this kind of phrasing in the margins to comment on the various 'supposes' the play and its characters present.

[55] Gaggero uses these presentational quiddities to argue that the play asks to be read 'as a book of duties' ('Pleasure Unreconciled', 187). Tamara Atkin uses them, along with other features such as the title-page designation of 'tragicall Comedie', as part of her argument that publishers are experimenting with ways of presenting drama in printed form (*Reading Drama*, pp. 35, 73, 130).

Other arguments against the play-as-drama are less clear cut. Gascoigne frequently inhabits the fiction rather than visualizing a stage. Characters 'depart to their howses' (Cii^v), for instance, rather than 'exeunt'. The phrasing is clearly the author's, as the dialogue here concludes with Pandarina suggesting 'let us depart', followed by the stage direction, and so the influence of the dialogue on the direction is clear. 'Depart' is not unusual in academic drama; see Terence's *Andria*, trans. Maurice Kyffin (1588): 'Simo departeth and Davus stayeth still' (Gii^r). But although Gascoigne regularly uses '*departeth*' for '*exit*' in this text, he equally often uses '*cometh in*' and '*goeth out*'. The distancing locution to explain the location—'The Comedie to be presented as it were in Antwerpe' (Aii^v)—seems

Gaggero is adamant that the play 'was never performed and, as I see it, was never intended to be'.[56] Linda Salomon, on the other hand, views it as a closet drama.[57] The blank space for the name of Gnomaticus' friend in Douai may help adjudicate between these two positions. Gascoigne could simply have invented a name for the purposes of his fiction; instead, he left a blank for someone to fill.[58] The blank invites a local, topical, relevant insertion and while this is potentially an invitation to the reader to insert a name silently in his study, it is more logically an opportunity for a performer. The performer could be a student, of any age, at home, in school, or at university; and the 'performance' need be no more than the text read aloud in company. In other words, this text looks more like a closet drama than a didactic treatise.

Names and Initials

Since early modern title pages frequently identify authors only by initials (what Lisa Gitelman calls 'nominal blanks'[59]), they perform the textual tease associated with the blank. In the eighteenth century, initials provided only a faint disguise as Jonathan Swift noted: 'We are careful never to print a man's name out at length, but, as I do, that of Mr. St——le, although everybody alive knows who I mean'. As Gitelman comments, citing this passage from Swift, 'The same public knowledge that made [eighteenth-century] names supposedly unprintable made them known to all. . . . The author gets to pretend or perform discretion within an elaborate game of "I know you know I know you know".'[60] In early modern texts the disguise may have been equally apparent. Both John Florio (in *World of Words*, 1598) and Thomas Nashe (in *Nashe's Lenten Stuffe*, 1599) make a great deal of 'this H.S', with whom each had a literary quarrel. H. S. had previously criticized Florio, and in his dedicatory epistle

curiously literal, given that all drama is presented 'as it were', but this phrasing, with its stress on representation, is paralleled in Gascoigne's translation of *Jocasta*: 'The Tragedie Represented in *Thebes*' (*Jocasta* in *A Hundreth Sundrie Flowres*, Kiiᵛ). These examples are witness to the embryonic and uncertain identity of drama in print rather than evidence of dramatic or non-dramatic origin or intention.

[56] Gaggero, 'Pleasure Unreconciled', 173.

[57] Linda Bradley Salomon, 'A Face in *The Glasse*: Gascoigne's *Glasse of Government* Re-Examined', *Studies in Philology* 71 (1974), 47–71 (47).

[58] I am assuming that the blank is not the result of censorship (Gascoigne having satirically supplied an anti-Catholic reference), although this remains a possibility.

[59] Lisa Gitelman, *Paper Knowledge: Toward a Media History of Documents* (Durham, NC: Duke University Press, 2014), p. 27.

[60] Gitelman, *Paper Knowledge*, p. 27.

to the *World of Words*, Florio inveighs against him with all the force humanist copia can command:

> [M]*y quarrell is to a tooth-lesse dog, that hateth where he cannot hurt, and would faine bite, when he hath no teeth. His name is* H. S. *Doe not take it for the Romane* H.S. *for he is not of so much worth, unlesse it be as* H S *is twice as much and a halfe as halfe an As. But value him how you will, I am sure he highly valueth himselfe. This fellow, this* H. S. *reading (for I would you should knowe he is a reader and a writer too) under my last epistle to the reader* I. F. *made as familiar a word of* F. *as if I had bin his brother. . . . . And might not a man, that can do as much as you (that is, reade) finde as much matter out of* H. S. *as you did out of* I. F? *As for example* H. S. *why may it not stand as well for* Haeres Stultitiae, *as for* Homo Simplex? *or for* Hara Suillina, *as for* Hostis Studiosorum? *or for* Hircus Satiricus, *as well as for any of them? And this in Latine, besides* Hedera Seguace, Harpia Subata, Humore Superbo, Hipocrito Simulatore *in Italian. And in English world without end.* Huffe Snuffe, Horse Stealer, Hob Sowter, Hugh Sot, Humphrey Swineshead, Hodge Sowgelder. *Now Master* H. S. *if this doe gaule you, forbeare kicking hereafter, and in the meane time you may make you a plaister of your dride Marjoram.*   (A5v)

It is hard to know which form of copia merits the greater admiration: Florio's rhetorical flow or the printer's apparently inexhaustible stock of majuscule H and S. Besides such varied onomastic expansion, Nashe's inventiveness seems unusually tame. He addresses his fictitious patron '*Lustie Humfrey*' insultingly, with his invective against H. S. confined to one unflattering comparison in an appositive phrase: '*Most courteous unlearned lover of Poetry, and yet a Poet thy selfe, of no lesse price then H. S., that in honour of Maid-marrion gives sweete Margera[m] for his Empresse . . .*' (A2r).

The relation of the lines in Florio and Nashe to 'H. S.' (probably Hugh Sanford, secretary to the Countess of Pembroke) is complex. McKerrow observes that 'behind these allusions there seems to be a rather interesting literary quarrel' but because it has more to do with Florio than Nashe he concludes that his notes must 'pass it over'.[61] A brief summary of the quarrel would need to note the following: the dedicatory lines immediately before this quotation in Nashe allude to the title page of the 1593 edition of Philip Sidney's *Countess of Pembroke's Arcadia*; the first edition of Sidney's *Arcadia* was unauthorized (1590, STC 22539a) and the publisher explains that the chapter divisions were devised by someone else, an editor ('*over-seer of the print*'), who also chose and distributed Sidney's eclogues (A4v). The official second edition of 1593 (STC 22540) was edited by the Countess' secretary, Hugh Sanford, who made it

---

[61] Thomas Nashe, *The Works of Thomas Nashe*, vol. IV, ed. R. B. McKerrow (London: Sidgwick and Jackson, 1910), p. 375.

clear that the Countess had been unhappy with the liberties taken in the first edition (it was '*disfigured*' and '*blemished*', ¶4r), and 'the editor—almost certainly John Florio—gets a flea in his ear for his meddlesome additions to Sidney's original'.[62] The 'maid Marion' and 'Empress' allusions in the Nashe quotation just given refer to the Countess of Pembroke. Sidney's sonnet sequence, *Astrophil and Stella*, had also 'gathered much corruption' in 'being spred abroade' but Thomas Newman, the publisher of STC 22536 (1591), explains that he has been 'very carefull in the Printing of it'. By this he seems to mean not (or not just) typesetting but something we would recognize as editing: 'I have used their helpe and advice in correcting & restoring it to its first dignitie, that I knowe were of skill and experience in those matters' (Aii^v). Newman's letter is followed by a preface by Thomas Nashe, and this is presumably why Nicholl concludes that Nashe was one of these editors, if not *the* editor.[63] The Florio and Nashe allusions of 1598–9 seem to reflect simmering resentment against H. S., a quarrel that would have been well known in London literary circles. Sanford's initials provide no disguise, nor are they meant to.[64]

Initials can be misinterpreted, of course. In 1573 George Gascoigne published a prose novella (the rape narrative mentioned), *The Adventures of Master F. J.*, in an anthology, *A Hundreth Sundrie Flowres*. The volume contained Gascoigne's poems (the hundred flowers of the title), two plays, and this prose novella. Developing the garden imagery of the title, the printer's prefatory epistle to the volume talks about preferences for different kinds of flowers: as we smell different flowers until we find one we like best, so the reader may pass from 'good morall lessons clerkly handled' in Gascoigne's translation of Euripides to his comic 'conceit closely conveyed' in his translation of Ariosto to 'the better understanding' of 'the unlawfull affections of a lover' in *The Adventures of Master F. J.* ('whome the reader may name Freeman Jones'; Aii^v–Aiii^r). Gascoigne implicitly notes here the readerly instinct to expand cryptic initials to a name. There is no evidence that the initials were misread in a nefarious way or that they were designed to traduce a known person, but it is clear that the narrative was interpreted as a roman-à-clef. The second edition of 1575 (*Poesies*, STC 11636) notes that 'sundrie wanton speeches and lascivious phrases'

---

[62] Charles Nicholl, *A Cup of News: The Life of Thomas Nashe* (London: Routledge and Kegan Paul, 1984), p. 84.

[63] Nicholl, *A Cup of News*, p. 84.

[64] J. B. Steane believes that the identification of H. S. in Nashe as Hugh Sanford is far from secure. Thomas Nashe, *The Unfortunate Traveller and Other Works*, ed. J. B. Steane (Harmondsworth: Penguin, 1971), p. 372.

in the first edition were 'doubtfully construed and (therefore) scandalous' and so Gascoigne revised the text (¶iir). One of the revisions is the expansion of 'F. J.' to 'Ferdinando Jeronimi', with the story now advertised as a 'pleasant Fable...translated out of the Italian riding tales of *Bartello*' (Nir). Paul Salzman believes Gascoigne when he complains that readers misinterpreted his fiction as alluding to real events: 'his thin disguise of it as a translation would seem to support his assertion, as a true scandal would only be averted by the complete excision of the narrative'.[65]

The most familiar example of Gitelman's 'nominal blanks' are title pages, where authors are often identified only by initials. 'W. S.' appears on the title pages of *Locrine* (1595), *Thomas, Lord Cromwell* (1602), *The Puritan, or the Widow of Watling Street* (1607), and *A Funeral Elegy in Memory of Master William Peter* (1612).[66] Early modern readers sometimes expanded initials or supplied names where none existed but the infrequency with which they did this suggests that our evaluative need to identify authorship is a recent concern. John Donne's *Poems* first reached print in 1633 in a book whose title page advertised 'Poems by J. D. with Elegies on the Author's Death'. As Stephen Dobranski points out, the volume is more interested in telling us that the author is dead than it is in telling us who he is.[67] However, an image of the author at the start of the volume, and elegies in memory of 'Dr Donne' at the end, mean that the information is easy to uncover.[68] Tamara Atkin negotiates this balancing act between obscured identity and authorial agency when she analyses the initials 'A. N.' (Alexander Neville) on a translation of *Oedipus* (1563). The initials 'construct an intimate coterie of readers, easily able to decode the riddle of the author's identity'[69] at the same time as unsettling our modern assumptions that knowing this identity will lead to deeper textual understanding.[70] In an observation that takes us back to the Introduction, where I noted that blank space is the product of typesetting just as much as is the composition of words, Marcy North reminds us that authorial identification and anonymity often occupy 'the same typographical mark on a page'. They are not binaries or opposites.[71]

---

[65] Paul Salzman (ed.), *An Anthology of Elizabethan Prose Fiction* (Oxford: Oxford University Press, 1987), p. xiii.

[66] On the title pages of Shakespeare's apocryphal drama, see Peter Kirwan, *Shakespeare and the Idea of Apocrypha: Negotiating the Boundaries of the Dramatic Canon* (Cambridge: Cambridge University Press, 2015).

[67] Stephen B. Dobranski, *Readers and Authorship in Early Modern England* (Cambridge: Cambridge University Press, 2005), p. 124.

[68] Dobranski, *Readers and Authorship*, pp. 123–33.   [69] Atkin, *Reading Drama*, p. 123.

[70] Atkin, *Reading Drama*, p. 124.

[71] Marcy L. North, *The Anonymous Renaissance: Cultures of Discretion in Tudor-Stuart England* (Chicago: University of Chicago Press, 2003), p. 74.

Censorship

By far the largest category of blanks that tempt curious readers to supply lacunae are those that result from censorship (external censorship or self-censorship) and usually relate to insults or obscenity. Expurgated oaths are easy to supply: '*By (- - -)* '*tis good*' (Jonson, *Cynthia's Revels*) or 'By (   ) but I do' (Marston, *The Dutch Courtesan*).[72] John Donne's satires II and IV appear in the first printed edition of his *Poems* (1633) with nine lines about religious and sexual matters deleted (six in satire II, three in satire IV); the deletions are indicated by a series of long dashes separated by blank spaces (see Figure 1.5).

The censored lines are supplied by hand in several copies. In copy 2 in the Folger Shakespeare Library a seventeenth-century reader has filled in some of the blanks.[73] Did he seek out manuscripts to find the missing material? Did he use context to guess the missing content? We may infer the latter as he managed to supply 'dildoes' in satire II, for instance, but drew a blank (literally) at the 'litany' (see Figure 1.6).[74] However, elsewhere he was able to supply runs

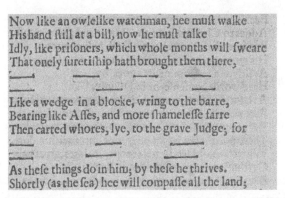

FIGURE 1.5 Satire II in John Donne, *Poems* (1633, STC 7045), Vv1v. Shelfmark Vet. A2 e.363. By permission of the Bodleian Libraries, University of Oxford.

---

[72] Ben Jonson, *Cynthia's Revels* in *Works* (1616), Z3r; John Marston, *The Dutch Courtesan* (1605), F2r.

[73] The early modern owner of the copy in Harvard University Library has a 100 per cent success rate in supplying the missing words and lines. Of the nine copies in Oxford college libraries, three contain insertions in an early modern hand (Corpus Christi, St John's College, Worcester; however, in this last the annotator was unable to supply 'litany'). The insertions in the New College copy are in a later hand. The copies in All Souls, Balliol, Brasenose, Christchurch, and Wadham remain blank, as do the three copies in the Bodleian Library.

[74] These are lines 33–4 in *Donne: Poetical Works*, ed. Herbert Grierson (London: Oxford University Press, 1973).

> The meate was mine, th'excrement is his owne:
> But these do mee no harme, nor they which use
> To out-doe ———; and out-usure Jewes;
> To out-drinke the sea, to out-sweate the ———
> Who with sinnes of all kindes as familiar bee
> As Confessors; and for whose sinfull sake

FIGURE 1.6 Satire II in John Donne, *Poems* (1633, STC 7045), Vv1v. Shelfmark STC 7045 copy 2. Used by permission of the Folger Shakespeare Library.

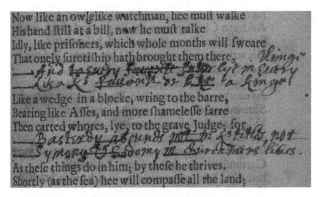

FIGURE 1.7 Satire II in John Donne, *Poems* (1633, STC 7045), Vv2r. Shelfmark STC 7045 copy 2. Used by permission of the Folger Shakespeare Library.

of lines, which cannot be the result of guesswork (see Figure 1.7). Since his insertions agree with those of the annotator of the Harvard copy, it seems that both readers had access to an unexpurgated version of these poems. And whether guesswork or research, in both cases the effect of the blank spaces on the reader of satire II is the same: they turn an 'already waggish poem into a bawdy guessing game'.[75]

The poet and dramatist John Marston is a Donne-style satirist. In *The Malcontent* (1604, STC 17479), the titular malcontent, Malevole enters 'from the publick place of much dissimulation' (B1v). The ensuing appositive or parenthetical phrase which would clarify this cryptic utterance has been removed, leaving a blank line, as in this image from STC 17481 (Folger copy 2): Figure 1.8. But the offensive epithet escaped in some editions, from which we

---

[75] Dobranski, *Readers and Authorship*, p. 142.

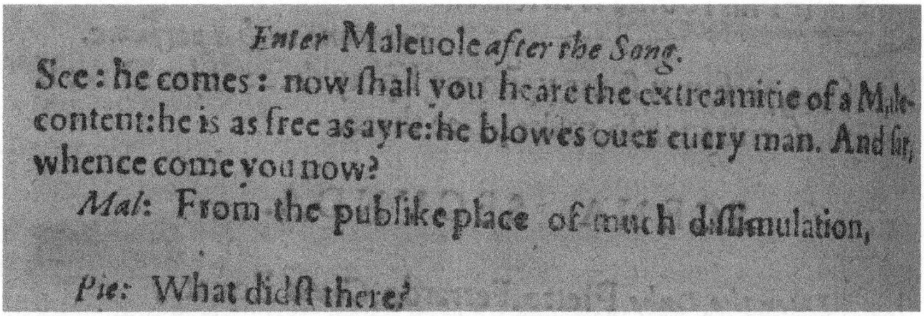
Enter Maleuole *after the Song.*
See: he comes: now ſhall you heare the extreamitie of a Male-
content: he is as free as ayre: he blowes ouer euery man. And ſir,
whence come you now?
Mal: From the publike place of much diſſimulation,
Pie: What didſt there?

Figure 1.8 John Marston, *The Malcontent* (1604, STC 17481), B1v. Shelfmark STC 17481, copy 2. Used by permission of the Folger Shakespeare Library.

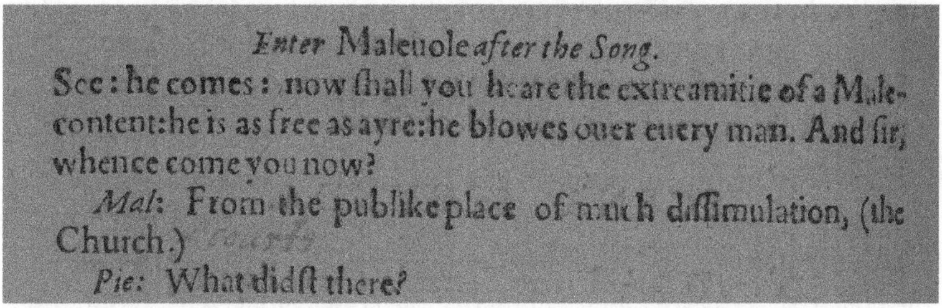
Enter Maleuole *after the Song.*
See: he comes: now ſhall you heare the extreamitie of a Male-
content: he is as free as ayre: he blowes ouer euery man. And ſir,
whence come you now?
Mal: From the publike place of much diſſimulation, (the
Church.) Courts
Pie: What didſt there?

Figure 1.9 John Marston, *The Malcontent* (1604, STC 17481), B1v. Shelfmark STC 17481, copy 1. Used by permission of the Folger Shakespeare Library.

learn that this censored place is '(the Church)'. However, as we can see from the faint ink mark in Figure 1.9, a reader inscribed his copy of the unexpurgated line with a logical alternative: 'the Courts'.

Continental printers and their readers show the same pattern of censorship and ingenuity in supplementation. Petrarch's *Canzoniere*, over three hundred poems written across several decades in the fourteenth century, are famous for the poet's love for Laura. But the sonnets cover many other subjects: poetry itself ('Laura' puns on 'laurel'), religion, politics, mutability, glory. During Petrarch's lifetime, Pope Clement V had moved the papal court from Rome to Avignon—the so-called Babylonian exile or Babylon on the Rhone (1309–77);[76] Petrarch lived and worked in Avignon for several years. Sonnets 106–8, the 'Babylonian sonnets', as well as material in Petrarch's *Liber sine Nomine*, criticize the avarice, corruption, ambition, spectacle, luxury, and practice of simony for

[76] It was designed as a temporary relocation but lasted for a further six papacies. Clement V was French and his election had been engineered by King Philip IV of France.

which the papal court had become known (Petrarch would say that his criticism was of individuals, not of the pope himself).[77] Two centuries after Petrarch's death, three of the sonnets fell foul of the Italian censor.[78] Pope Paul IV (1555–9) placed Petrarch's anti-papal material (which included not only the three sonnets but passages from *Liber sine Nomine*) on an Index of proscribed books in 1559. In 1595, Pope Clement VIII (1592–1605) took further issue with the Babylonian sonnets—not, as it happens, because of their papal criticism but because of their potential use as propaganda by Protestants.[79] From 1559 until 1722 the sonnets were 'deleted from editions of the *Canzoniere* printed in Catholic countries'.[80] Subsequent printings present them only as a series of sonnet numbers, followed by blank space, although the printer calls attention to the gaps as editorially deliberate rather than accidental with the heading '*Qui mancano tre Sonetti*' ('Here are missing three sonnets') and the numbers 106, 107, and 108. Perhaps the printer strategically supplied the numbers of the missing sonnets so that an enterprising reader could seek them out and copy them into the gaps, as early modern readers of the copies at the Folger Shakespeare Library and Yale's Beinecke Library have done (see Figure 1.10).[81]

The manuscript inscription on the title page of the 1586 Venetian edition at the Folger Shakespeare Library notes that the book belonged to 'WSlingisbie', bought in Sienna on 12 May 1593 for 2s 4d. It was probably Slingsby who filled in the missing sonnets (the handwriting and ink are the same). An owner of the 1595 Venetian edition now at the Beinecke also wrote in the missing sonnets but added a defiant note: 'Questi Sonetti copiata da̶ sono proibite, e li proibe Clemente ne 1596' ('these sonnet copies are prohibited, and Pope Clement prohibited them in 1596').[82]

---

[77] See 106: Famme del ciel [Flames from heaven]; 107: Fontana di dolore [Font of sorrows]; 108: De l'Empia Babilonia [Unholy Babylon].

[78] The sonnets are sometimes numbered 136–8.

[79] His fears were well founded. For an account of Petrarch's usefulness to Protestant polemicists, see Robert Coogan, 'Petrarch's *Liber sine Nomine* and a Vision of Rome in the Reformation', *Renaissance and Reformation* 19:1 (1983), 1–12. Petrarch's *Works* have a strong printing history in 'Protestant centres like Lyons, Geneva, Basel, Strasbourg, and Cologne, a further indication of their reception in the Renaissance' (7).

[80] Coogan, 'Petrarch's *Liber*', 8. In the Basle edition of Petrarch's *Works* (1581) in Magdalen College Library, Oxford, the sonnets are printed in their entirety in an unbroken sequence, as the last items in the volume (pp. 149ff.; new pagination begins after page 1132).

[81] The Folger edition is: *Il Petrarca, con nuove spositione* (Venice, 1586). The Beinecke editions are: *Il Petrarca, con l'esposizione d'Alessandro Velutello* (Venice, 1552) and *Il Petrarca, con nuove spositione* (Venice, 1595).

[82] S/he or his/her source offered a variant reading of sonnet 108, replacing 'l'empia' with 'l'aura'—perhaps a deliberate pun, perhaps a misreading.

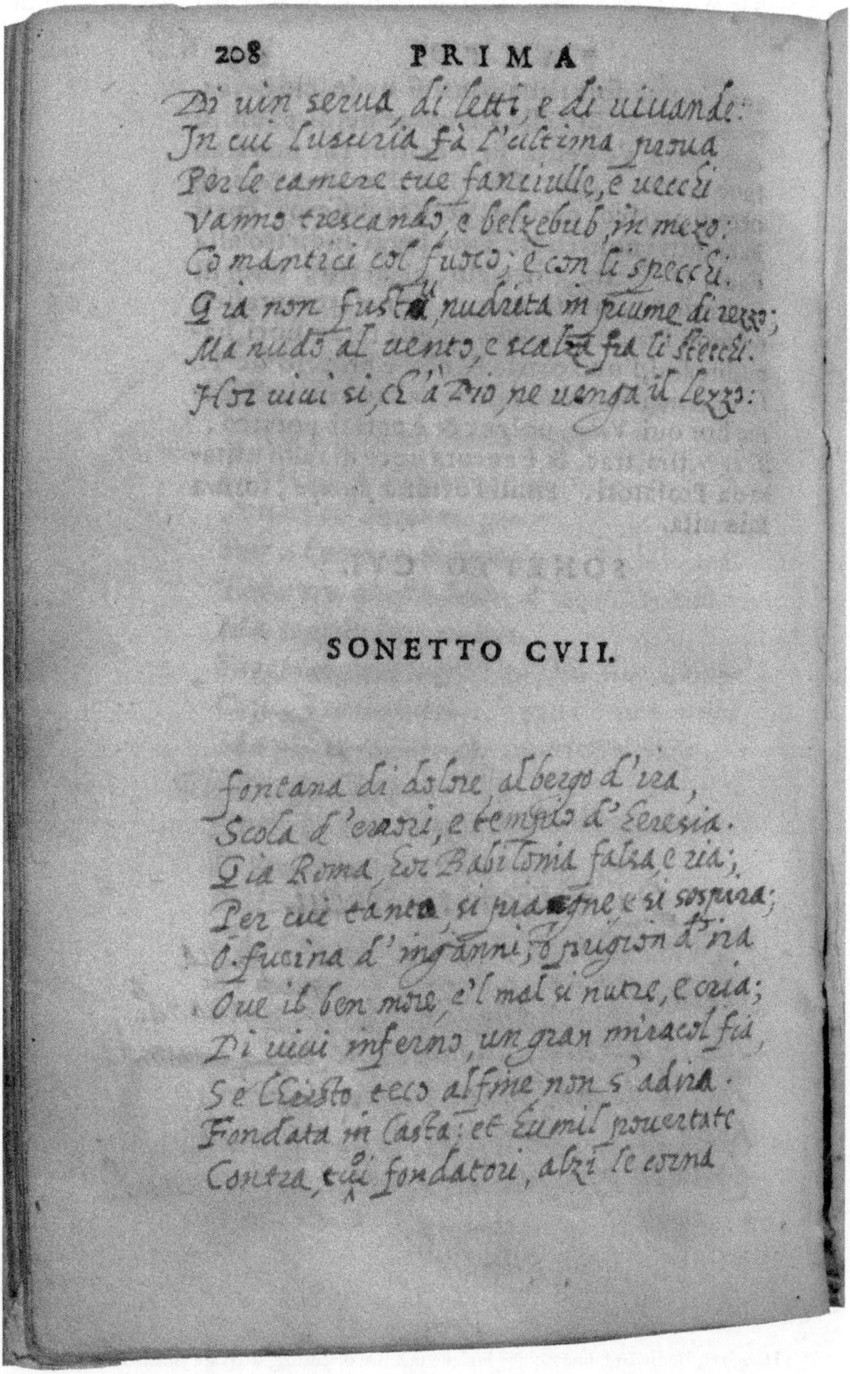

208   PRIMA

Di uin serua, di letti, e di uiuande:
In cui lusuria fà l'ultima prua
Per le camere tue fanciulle, e uecchi
Vanno trescando, e belzebub in mezo:
Cō mantici col fuoco, e con li specchi.
Gia non fustù nudrita in piume di rezzo;
Ma nuda al uento, e scalza fra li stecchi.
Hor uiui si, ch'à Dio ne uenga il lezzo:

SONETTO CVII.

Fontana di dolore, albergo d'ira,
Scola d'errori, e tempio d'heresia.
Gia Roma, hor Babilonia falsa e ria;
Per cui tanto si piagne e si sospira;
O fucina d'inganni, ò prigion d'ira
Oue il ben more, e'l mal si nutre, e cria;
Di uiui inferno, un gran miracol fia,
Se Christo teco alfine non s'adira.
Fondata in Casta, et humil pouertate
Contra, tui fondatori, alzi le corna

FIGURE 1.10 Petrarch, *Il Petrarca, con nuove spositione* (Venice, 1586), V7v. Shelfmark 193-192q. Used by permission of the Folger Shakespeare Library.

Readers who already owned earlier editions of Petrarch responded to the ban with various degrees of compliance. A copy of the Venetian edition of 1547 was bound as a presentation copy for Clement VIII. Perhaps for this reason it has quires S and T1 removed, demonstrable evidence that Clement's ban had been irreversibly acted upon.[83] An owner of the 1552 Venetian edition now in the Beinecke Library scored out each sonnet line by line with heavy horizontal lines in black ink (and adding multiple diagonal lines of deletion over the whole of the first sonnet for good measure, a process abandoned for the next two sonnets, probably because it was otiose or too time-consuming). Another owner of the 1552 edition, now at Louisiana State University, also drew black pen lines through each printed line; the lines are so thick and heavy that the ink has eaten through the paper. Deletion becomes mutilation. A copy of the 1560 edition now in the University of New Mexico shows a reader responding to censorship with a more benign deletion mark (one that is common in authorial manuscripts): a large X through the cancelled material. This marks the material for deletion while leaving it completely legible. Discussing readers' responses to censorship, Michael Taylor observes the paradox that is recurrent in discussions of the blank: here 'censorship seems to have done nothing more than draw attention to the controversy, like a blinking neon sign saying READ ME!'[84]

Some anti-Catholic blanks, however, are unrecoverable. The Bodleian Library copy of John Rastell's *Calisto and Melibea* (*c*.1525) contains—or rather, contained—a joke about a friar. The punchline has been cut out (literally—it was removed with a razor), leaving us only the joke's set-up and reaction:

> What frere quod he [?] wilt thou nedes know qud I [?] then
> It is the f
> O quod he what a lode hath that woman
> To bere hym   (Av^r)

The cut has the obvious unfortunate effect of removing a line of dialogue on the verso page.[85]

---

[83] This edition was offered for sale by Sokol Books, UK, in 2016. See the description in the sale catalogue at <http://sokol.co.uk/petrarca-francesco-4/print/>.

[84] Michael Taylor, '"X" Marks the Spot: Petrarch's Censored Sonnets', blog post, 26 September 2016. Available at: <https://libguides.unm.edu/blog/x-marks-the-spot-petrarch-s-censored-sonnets>. See University of New Mexico Special Collections PQ4476.B60. Cf. Dunstan Roberts' study of prayer-book censorship where forbidden material was crossed out with heavy ink or scratched off with a knife. 'The Expurgation of Traditional Prayer Books (*c*.1535–1600)', *Reformation* 15 (2010), 23–49.

[85] STC 20721, Bodleian Library copy. For the practice of cutting texts see Adam Smyth, *Material Texts*, ch. 1 (pp. 17–54). Smyth explores cutting both as a form of editing and of writing.

In Act 1 scene 1 of Chettle's *Hoffman* (*c*.1600, Q1631) a one-line insult has been removed and a lengthy gap printed instead:

> thou   organ of the soule   (B3v)

The note in the Penguin edition reads '*Thou*: followed by a long space, perhaps indicating the setting-copy was damaged or illegible.'[86] The suggested explanation takes us back to the world of the medieval scriptorium where gaps are indications of careful workmanship rather than negligence; however, the context (a reference to the soul) and the vocative (which seems to lead to an insult) means that censorship or self-censorship may be a stronger possibility.

In Dekker's *Patient Grissil* (1603), an insult has been removed and it is difficult to work out what it might have been from the context: 'the corporation cannot be (   )' (H2v). Here the gap is emphasized by the empty brackets.[87] In Beaumont's *The Woman Hater* (1607), the line 'some hope to find fit matter to *feede his* ——— *mallice* on' (A2r) makes sense as it is; however, one cannot help but wonder whether the long horizontal rule was designed to indicate a deleted adjective rather than a dramatic pause.

Paper

Readers were not the only ones to fill in blanks. Paper was expensive so, in a household, books were often adopted by other members of the family, who used the blank pages for new purposes. An account book could end up as a diary or vice versa. The most famous example in Elizabethan theatre history is the account book known as *Philip Henslowe's Diary*. The book in which Henslowe recorded his theatre receipts and expenses was originally owned by his brother, who used part of it for his forestry accounts in Sussex. Sometime before 1591 London theatre manager Philip acquired the book, opened it at the back, inverted it, and started keeping accounts for his South Bank theatres. The compiler of a Jacobean commonplace book inverted his own book to provide an alphabetized selection of Erasmus' proverbs. Robert Sidney's son inherited his father's commonplace book although he did not know which of

---

[86] Henry Chettle, *The Tragedy of Hoffman*, in *Five Revenge Tragedies*, ed. Emma Smith (Harmondsworth: Penguin, 2012), 1.1.191n, p. 251.

[87] On the development of parentheses and the uses of empty brackets, see John Lennard, *'But I Digress': The Exploitation of Parentheses in English Printed Verse* (Oxford: Oxford University Press, 1991).

his relatives had been the previous owner ('some Learned man').[88] The commonplace book of Lady Anne Southwell (1573–1636) in which she drafted poetry and copied out quotations was later used for accounts by other members of her family.[89]

Diarists and accounts managers were not the only ones to know the value of paper. Printers and publishers saw the advertising opportunities afforded by blank space in texts going through their presses. The printer of the 1652 edition of Shakespeare's *Merchant of Venice* for William Leake (1652) had a blank half-page beneath the dramatis personae on A1v and divided it into two columns to advertise other books '*Printed and solde by* William Leake'. The following year, the space following the epilogue to Thomas Middleton's *The Changeling* (1653) was similarly used to advertise '*PLAYES newly Printed*' and '*PLAYES in the Press*', followed by the one-line addition (perhaps an afterthought), 'Also, The *Spanish Gypsies*' (I3v) (see Figure 1.11).

Authors too took the opportunity to fill up blank space. Thomas Churchyard's *Musical Consort of Heavenly Harmonie* (1595) concludes with two printer's ornaments, between which is sandwiched an extraordinary piece of advertising: 'My next Booke comes out shortlie: dedicated to my Honorable woorthy friende, master Henrie Brooke, sonne and heire to the noble Lord Cobham' (G4v). Clearly, it is not Churchyard's book that is being advertised (we are not told its title or subject matter) so much as the noble dedicatee, who thus reaps the benefit of not one but two acknowledgements of his patronage. King James VI's *Phoenix* ends with a 'Sonnet of the *Authour*' followed by FINIS then adds two pages of source material which are there simply to take advantage of the blank pages at the end of the folio volume, as James himself explains: 'I HAVE INSERT [= inserted] FOR THE FILLING OUT OF THIR [= these] VACAND PAGEIS THE VERIE wordis of *Plinius* upon the *Phoenix*, as followis'.[90] Michael Drayton's epic chorographical history, *Poly-Olbion* (1622) follows each historical episode with notes ('Illustrations') written by John Selden. On one occasion the printer overestimated the amount of space that the notes would require. Selden then provided a genealogical table of Welsh kings 'not so much for intellectual

[88] See Schurink, 'Manuscript Commonplace Books'. He describes the Jacobean commonplace book on 460–3 and the Sidneys' commonplace book on 457–9.

[89] Folger Shakespeare Library MS V.b.198. See Peter Beal, 'Anne, Lady Southwell', in *Catalogue of English Literary Manuscripts, 1450–1700*. Available at: <http://www.celm-ms.org.uk/introductions/SouthwellAnneLady.html>.

[90] In *Essays of a Prentice in the Divine Art of Poesie* (1584), P4r.

EPILOGUE.

Alſ. ALL *we can doe, to Comfort one another,*
To ſtay a Brothers ſorrow, for a Brother;
To Dry a Child, from the kinde Fathers eyes
Is to no purpoſe, it rather multiplies :
Your only ſmiles have power to cauſe re-live
The Dead agen, or in their Rooms to give
Brother a new Brother, Father a Child ;
If theſe appear, All griefs are reconcil'd.

Exeunt omnes.

FINIS:

PLAYES newly Printed.

THe *Wild-gooſe-Chaſe,* a Comedy; written by *Francis Beamont* and *John Fletcher,* Gent'.
The *Widdow,* a Comedy; written by *Ben: Johnſon, John Fletcher,* and *Thomas Midleton,* Gent'.

PLAYES in the Preſs.

FIve *Playes* written by Mr *James Shirley,* being All of his that were Acted at the *Black-Fryers :* Together with the *Court-Secret,* written by the ſame Author, but never yet Acted.

Alſo, The *Spaniſh Gypſies.*

FIGURE I.II Thomas Middleton, *The Changeling* (1653, Wing M1980), I3v. Shelfmark K-D 293 (3). Courtesy of The Huntington Library, San Marino.

reasons as for filling what would otherwise be blank pages'.[91] The anonymous author (perhaps authors, given the text's use of the plural pronoun in the quotation that follows) of *A Continuation of More News from the Palatinate* (1622) concludes his narrative then adds this explanatory paragraph: 'Because the Printer shewed us a blancke page at the end, we therefore have filled it up with forraine relations which are nothing to the continuation of our discourse' (C3r).[92] This confession of irrelevance is followed by a page of up-to-date military information and then 'FINIS' in larger font (C3v). One sees in all these examples an extended equivalent of the aesthetic habit, in manuscript and print, of right-justifying lines by inserting an ornamental flourish (~ or =) to avoid a ragged margin. Blanks appear unsightly (see Figure 1.12).

More practical reasons underlie Hieronymus Braunschweig's use of blank space at the foot of a page of his surgical textbook, the folio volume *A Noble Experience of the Virtuous Handiwork of Surgery* (1525). This book is designed with densely printed double columns in black letter. There is one exception: a quarter-page at the foot of the right-hand column on B3r—blank of text but filled with asterisms (three asterisks arranged in a triangular shape). If we turn the page, we see why: the verso contains a large diagram, occupying more than half the page in length and a little over one column in width. Forcing a page break left a blank; and the blank had to be attractively filled.

---

[91] Angus Vine, *In Defiance of Time: Antiquarian Writing in Early Modern England* (Oxford: Oxford University Press, 2010), p. 186.

[92] Authors were clearly often involved in the printing process. Several authors lodged with printers short term while their books were going through the press. Printers often comment on the inconvenient absence of the author during printing (the printer of the first edition of Nashe's *Pierce Pennilesse* (1592, STC 18371) is 'bold' to publish 'in the Authour's absence' (A2r); Nashe himself writes an epistle to the second edition of the same year, explaining that he is in the country to escape the plague (STC 18372); Marston's absence while his *Works* (1633) were being printed is noted). Johannes Sturm tells us that the printer would not allow him as many diagrams as he wanted (*A Rich Storehouse or Treasurie for Nobility*, 1570, E1v); Michael Drayton says he was not consulted about font size (*The Legend of Great Cromwell*, 1607) and as a result he has converted what should have been marginal notes aligned with the poem's stanzas into an explanatory preface (A2v); John Selden says he was not given enough time to provide the notes while Drayton's *Poly-Olbion* (1622) was going through the press (A3v). (On the identification of Selden as the author of the notes, see Chapter 3.) Helkiah Crooke read proofs of *Mikrocosmographia*, and the second edition was the result of the printer asking him to revise and expand the book (*Mikrocosmographia*, 1631, §3v–§4r). George Chapman complains that the notes to his *Memorable Masque* (1613) are not in the right places because the printer never sent him proofs until he had passed the relevant speeches (a1v). Thomas Heywood, the writer of the preface to John Cooke's *Greene's Tu Quoque* (1614), said he was in the print shop while the play was being printed so wrote a prefatory epistle (A2r). All of these comments (and complaints) indicate a close relationship between writers and the printing house, at least once the presses began to roll.

> ho w be it that the asset afterwarde yet it is felony &
> Wiht out the kynges charter maketh mecyon of rape
> it aupleth hym nought.statutū inde Westm scōi.Au ⊜
> no.rrrii.
> ⦗There be also felons that contrpuyth takynge ⓐ⊜robberye
> Wape of mennes goodes as roberye and thefte rob ⊜
> berye is Where a man lyeth by the kiges hygh Wape
> to market⟨Towne in Woodes diches oʒ in ony other
> secrete places Where by they comen foʒth by and rob
> beth theym/ how be it that he taketh aWape but the
> value of a peny oʒ lesse it is felony foʒ the mallapeṟ⊜
> nesse of the dede & Ieonerdue that a man is in' of hys

Figure 1.12 Anthony Fitzherbert, *The Book of Justices of Peace* ([1505], STC 14862), A6r. Shelfmark Tanner 209 (3). By permission of the Bodleian Libraries, University of Oxford.

However, this habit may originate in manuscript culture's concern for security rather than appearance. Blanks 'mean' different things in manuscript where they leave the writer vulnerable: insertions by others provide opportunity for forgery. Hence the elaborate signature flourishes designed to occupy blank space.[93]

Part II: Leaving Out

Imperfect and Unfinished: Desunt Nonnulla

The readerly acceptance of gaps and blanks perhaps goes some way towards explaining the early modern propensity to publish unfinished works: two of the classical texts most revered in the early modern period, Ovid's *Metamorphoses* and Virgil's *Aeneid*, were themselves unfinished.[94] Milton's *Poems 1645* contain his juvenilium, 'The Passion', whose inconclusion is explained with the editorial note: '*This Subject the Author finding to be above the yeers he had, when he*

---

[93] On manuscript blanks see Jonathan Gibson, 'Significant Space in Manuscript Letters', *The Seventeenth Century* 12:1 (1997), 1–10. I am grateful to Dianne Mitchell for sharing her prodigious knowledge of manuscripts with me and for several generous conversations on this topic. On the paradoxical use of blank space in letters as an indicator of status, see Jonathan Sawday, *Print, Space, and Void* (in progress).

[94] Dobranski, *Readers and Authorship*, p. 4.

wrote it, and nothing satisfi'd with what was begun, left it unfinisht' (B2r). John
Donne's 'To the Countess of Bedford' explains at the beginning that the poem
was '*[b]egun in France but never perfected*' [perfected = completed] and ends with
'*[d]esunt caetera*' (*Poems* (1633), P4r). The 1598 edition of Marlowe's *Hero and
Leander* ends with '*[d]esunt nonnulla*', an explanatory tag provided by the
publisher Edward Blount that has been responsible for the view that the poem
is artistically incomplete (interrupted by Marlowe's death).[95] Variants of the
'*desunt caetera/desunt nonnulla*' are frequent. Robert Herrick's 'The Apparition
of his Mistress' in *Hesperides* ('The Country Life', 1648) begins with the headnote '*[d]esunt nonnulla—*' and ends '*[c]aetera desunt*' (Q4v–R2r); John Donne's
'Resurrection' warns '*imperfect*' at the beginning (almost as part of the title:
Resurrection, imperfect) '*[d]esunt caetera*' at the end (Y1r–v). Abraham Cowley's
book-length *Poem on the Late Civil War* (1679) ends with a comma—'Since
Luther's noise wak'd the *Lethargick Earth,*'—and the explanation '*The Author
went no further*' (E4v). A pastoral in Francis Davison's *Poems* (1621) has the
headnote '*The beginning and end of this Eglogue are wanting*' (N4v). Ben Jonson
embarked on a play about *Mortimer's Fall* (the material represented in Marlowe's
Edward II) but according to the 1641 folio *Works* the play was 'left unfinished'
(Qq4v).[96] However, a variant state of the folio expands this to the more romantic narrative that characterizes texts such as Marlowe's *Hero and Leander*: 'Hee
dy'd, and left it unfinished' (Qq4v, my emphasis).[97]

[95] The poem was published in 1598, five years after Marlowe's death; a continuation by George
Chapman, published the same year, with four additional sestiads, cemented the view that the poem is
unfinished: its title page reads, 'Hero and Leander: begun by Christopher Marloe; and finished by
George Chapman'. The jury is still out on whether the poem is incomplete, although persuasive cases
have been made for it as an aesthetic unity based on Marlowe's trademark controlled anti-climax. See
Gordon Braden, *The Classics and English Renaissance Poetry: Three Case Studies* (New Haven, CT: Yale
University Press, 1978); *Hero and Leander: A Facsimile of the First Edition, London, 1598*, ed. Louis Martz
(Washington, DC: Folger Shakespeare Library, 1972); and W. L. Godshalk, '*Hero and Leander*: The
Sense of an Ending', in '*A Poet and a Filthy Play-Maker': New Essays on Christopher Marlowe*, ed. Kenneth
Friedenreich, Constance B. Kuriyama, and Roma Gill (New York: AMS Press, 1988), pp. 293–314. For
several critics, incompletion is a thematic point of the poem, and its form embodies its theme.
Georgia E. Brown describes it as 'a poem that avoids conclusions' ('Marlowe's Poems and Classicism',
in *The Cambridge Companion to Christopher Marlowe*, ed. Patrick Cheney (Cambridge: Cambridge
University Press, 2004), pp. 106–26 (p. 116)) and Danielle Clarke analyses its 'open-endedness (formal,
generic, and stylistic)' ('Marlowe's Poetic Form', in *Christopher Marlowe in Context*, ed. Emily C. Bartels
and Emma Smith (Cambridge: Cambridge University Press, 2013), pp. 57–67 (p. 59)).
[96] The title page has the date 'M.DC.XL'. I quote from the copy of STC 14754 in the Oxford
Bodleian English Faculty Library.
[97] See *Mortimer, His Fall*, ed. Karen Britland, in *The Cambridge Edition of the Works of Ben Jonson*, vol.
VII, ed. David Bevington, Martin Butler, and Ian Donaldson (Cambridge: Cambridge University
Press, 2012), textual note, p. 416. I quote here from the Early English Books Online (EEBO) copy,

George Gascoigne's MS *Grief of Joy: Certain Elegies* ends with two '&c's ('And sundry greeves, that &c &c') followed by the explanatory note, '[l]*eft unperfect for feare of horsmen*'. The fact that this MS is a presentation copy to the Queen indicates that there is nothing cavalier about printing or presenting unfinished works.[98] Francis Bacon's *New Atlantis* (1628) is advertised on its title page as 'A Worke unfinished', a fact of which we are reminded at the end: '*The rest was not Perfected*' (Z5v). Sir John Davies's *Orchestra* (1596) in *Nosce Teipsum* (1622) similarly has the title-page description '*Not finished*'. We can see this poem petering out in stages. Close to the end, an insertion after stanza 126 in larger font tells us, '*Here are wanting some Stanzaes describing Queene* Elizabeth. / Then follow these' (L2r). 'These' are stanzas 127 to 131, but stanza 132 begins (and ends): 'So &c. &c. * * *' and is followed immediately by the errata list.[99] Sir Philip Sidney's *Arcadia* (1590) ends mid-sentence, without any concluding punctuation: 'Whereat ashamed (as never having done anything so much before in his life)' (Zz8v). The frequency of incompletion puts the otherwise odd proclamation of Gascoigne's *Poesies* (1575) in context. The 207-stanza poem 'Dulce Bellum Inexpertis' ends with 'FINIS', then an envoi followed by FINIS; then, after Gascoigne's signature epigraph ('Tam Marti quàm Mercurio') we encounter the advertising assurance that the poem is 'Corected, perfected, and finished' (kviii^r). The anonymous author of *A Collection of the Contents of all the Chapters Contained in the Bible* (1605) provides summaries of biblical books—but sometimes he doesn't, 'as by the blanck places appeareth' (G1r). He advertises the chapters which have 'no contents'; the second page of the Proverbs of Solomon (G1v) is reproduced in Figure 1.13.

Richard Jones, the printer of Christopher Marlowe's *Tamburlaine* (1590), turns omission into an advertising strategy and a mark of intellectual prestige:

> I have (purposely) omitted and left out some fond and frivolous Jestures, digress-ing (and in my poore opinion) far unmeet for the matter, which I thought, might seeme more tedious unto the wise, than any way els to be regarded, though (happly) they have bene of some vaine co[n]ceited fondlings greatly gaped at, what times they were shewed upon the stage in their graced deformities: never-theles now, to be mixtured in print with such matter of worth, it wuld prooue a great disgrace to so honorable & stately a historie.   (A2r–v)

which cites its sources as the Folger Shakespeare Library, British Library, and Harvard University Library.

[98]   British Library Royal MS 18 A LXI.

[99]   See William H. Sherman, 'The Beginning of "The End": Terminal Paratext and the Birth of Print Culture', in *Renaissance Paratexts*, ed. Helen Smith and Louise Wilson (Cambridge: Cambridge University Press, 2014), pp. 65–88. For more on Davies' *Orchestra*, see Sawday, *Print, Space, and Void*.

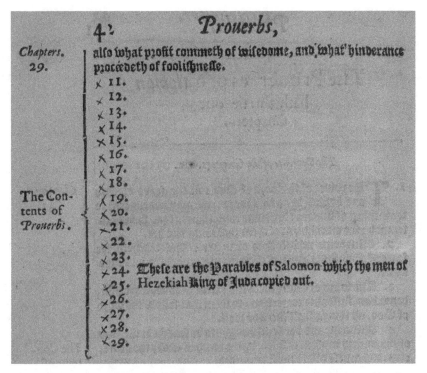

FIGURE 1.13 Anon, *A Collection of the Contents of all the Chapters Contained in the Bible* (1605, STC 3020.5), G1v. Shelfmark 5556.5. Used by permission of the Folger Shakespeare Library.

Other stationers go further, with prefaces where authors or publishers point out that although the book is not finished, they will only print what they have got so far. The preface to *Pierce Pennilesse* (1592, STC 18372) explains that Nashe is in the country and so the prefatory epistle summarizes what the reader is missing ('certayne Epistles to Orators and Poets, to insert to the later end: As namely, to the Ghost of *Machevill*, of *Tully*, of *Ovid*, of *Roscius*, of *Pace* the Duke of Norfolks Jester; and lastly, to the Ghost of *Robert Greene*'; π2r). *The Terrors of the Night* (1594) ends with Nashe saying, 'I shut up my Treatise abruptly.' Aposiopesis works at the level of the text as well as the utterance, as we see when Edmund Spenser breaks off abruptly at the end of his *Epithalamion*:

> Song made in lieu of many ornaments,
> With which my love should duly have been decked,
> Which cutting off through hasty accidents,
> You would not stay your due time to expect,
> But promised both to recompense,

Be unto her a goodly ornament
And for short time an endless monument.[100]

The editor comments, 'The short stanza may indicate that the poem itself has been cut short by hasty accidents. The poem is both an eternal monument and a fragmentary casualty'.[101]

Don Paterson's collection of poems, *God's Gift to Women* (1977) ends enigmatically, *Arcadia*-fashion, with an incomplete subordinate clause and an incomplete parenthesis, filling up the blank of 'this white page' but creating further blanks:

> *Of this white page, ask no more sense*
> *than of the skies (though you may believe*
> *The rain His tears, the wind his grief,*
> *the snow His shredded evidence*[102]

Robert Graves' poem, 'Leaving the Rest Unsaid', equates death with typographical features of termination. The two are combined in adjective–noun pairings as the poet objects to 'testamentary appendices' and 'graveyard indices'. The poem begins with '*Finis*' and concludes:

> So now, my solemn ones, leaving the rest unsaid,
> Rising in air as on a gander's wing
> At a careless comma,[103]

But the comma is careless only in the sense of being free from care. The last verse is a carefully constructed sequence of grammatical subordination and dependence, building up to the absent main clause. As Edward A. Levenston notes, the grammatical subject of the missing clause is clear: 'I'. Consequently, 'the spirit of the poet hovers grammatically above the page, forever present by inference, though banished from life and from print'.[104] For Hugh Haughton, this poem is 'thoroughly complete, though it is all about incompletion'.[105]

---

[100] 'Epithalamion' ll. 427–33 in Edmund Spenser, *Spenser: The Shorter Poems*, ed. Richard McCabe (Harmondsworth and New York: Penguin, 1999), p. 449.

[101] Spenser, *Shorter Poems*, p. 705.

[102] Don Paterson, *God's Gift to Women* (London: Faber and Faber, 1977). According to Simon Armitage, the sentence is completed in the boilerplate of a later volume of Paterson's poetry; Armitage, 'Mind the Gap' (see footnote 6 for podcast details).

[103] Robert Graves, *Poems Selected by Himself* (Harmondsworth: Penguin, 1957), p. 198.

[104] Edward A. Levenston, *The Stuff of Literature: Physical Aspects of Texts and their Relation to Literary Meaning* (Albany: State University of New York Press, 1992), p. 86.

[105] Hugh Haughton, 'Xanadu and Porlock: Thoughts on Composition and Interruption', in *The Book of Interruptions*, ed. David Hillman and Adam Phillips (Oxford and Bern: Peter Lang, 2007), pp. 27–43 (p. 37).

Modernism loved to play with incompletion (as we shall see in the section 'The fascination of the blank'); the most celebrated example is probably the end of *Finnegans Wake* where the apparently incomplete last sentence ('Our way to love a last a love a long the') is completed by the novel's uncapitalized first sentence:

> riverrun, past Eve and Adam's, from swerve of shore to bend of bay, brings us by a commodus vicus of recirculation back to Howth Castle and Environs.[106]

The image of swerving, bending, and recirculating is captured by the novel's circular structure—a kind of prose ouroboros. Robert Graves is similarly Joycean, reprinting 'Leaving the Rest Unsaid' as the final poem in every new edition of his *Collected Poems* from 1952.[107]

Gaps across Media

So far I have mentioned only creative works: poems, plays, novellas. But historical reference works such as Thomas Fuller's *The Worthies of England* (1662) also feature gaps and blanks. Writing about Shakespeare, Fuller leaves a blank for the date of the poet's death: 'He died anno Domini 16....' (Q3v). This looks like a research problem familiar to academics: we can recognize that stage of writing where we have not yet finished checking details, intend to go back and fill in the blanks, but sometimes forget.[108] In Fuller, however, this is not an oversight but an editorial policy. He apologizes in the preface for the many blanks in his book because, he says,

> I had rather my Reader should arise hungry from my Book, than surfeited therewith; rather uninformed than misinformed thereby; rather ignorant of what he desireth, than having a falsehood, or (at the best) a conjecture for a truth obtruded upon him.
>
> Indeed, I humbly conceive that vacuity which is hateful in nature, may be helpful in History.   (I2v)

---

[106] James Joyce, *Finnegans Wake*, ed. Robert-Jan Henkes, Erik Bindervoet, Finn Fordham, and Jeri Johnson (Oxford: Oxford University Press, 2012), pp. 628, 3.

[107] Levenston, *Stuff of Literature*, p. 86. For a brilliant discussion of modernism's deliberate creation of incomplete forms through revision and excision, see Hannah Sullivan, *The Work of Revision* (Cambridge, MA: University of Harvard Press, 2013), ch. 3.

[108] Philip Henslowe's *Diary* frequently records payments for play titles that are left blank. Some of the blanks were later filled in; most were not.

Fuller makes a case for blanks, gaps, hiatuses as appropriate to history. In fact, the blank is not genre-specific.

As Stephen Dobranski reminds us, sculpture has the concept of the *non finito* where it functions as testimony to the sculptor's imagination: a vision that could not be executed.[109] Blanks also occur in cartography: the Dutch cartographer Joan or Johannes Blaeu (1596–1673) was a pioneer of map-making (alone; with his father, Willem; and with his brother, Cornelis). His *Nova et Accuratissima Totius Terrarum Orbis Tabula* ('New and most accurate map of the whole world') was first published in the first volume of his *Atlas Maior* (Amsterdam, 1662; 11 volumes). The double hemisphere format allows artistic space for allegorical figures (the figure of Apollo—the Sun god—at the top of the map is an early incorporation of heliocentric theory).[110] Blaeu depicts beautifully the geographic knowledge of the time (California is shown as an island, for instance). But he also depicts the *lack* of knowledge of the time, using blank space to do so: the solid lines that outline the coasts of America and Australia stop, leaving a gap, at the north-west coast of America and the south coast of Australia—areas that had not yet been charted.[111] The Portuguese pilot Diogo Ribeiro had done the same over a century before in 1525.[112] Like Wakelin's medieval scribes, it would be irresponsible of the cartographer to fill in what he does not know (see Figure 1.14).

Stephen Harrison's description of the architectural constructions for James I's coronation also privileges the blank over technical details. A lavish affair (unsurprisingly), the coronation included speeches written by the city's heavyweight dramatists such as Ben Jonson and Thomas Middleton. These 'speeches of Gratulation' by allegorical figures in six pageants took place at various city stations in specially constructed 'pegme' (moveable theatrical structures), which took the form of large triumphal arches. Stephen Harrison, the architect and joiner, is credited on the 1604 title page of a printed volume which contains the speeches, descriptions of the structures, and Harrison's architectural designs: *The Arches of Triumph* (1604; the book contains twenty pages with seven plates).

---

[109] Dobranski, *Readers and Authorship*, p. 9.
[110] Jerry Brotton, *A History of the World in Twelve Maps* (London: Allen & Unwin, 2012), p. 262; Rodney W. Shirley, *The Mapping of the World: Early Printed World Maps, 1472–1700* (Riverside, CA: Early World Press, 2001). For a discussion of Blaeu, see Brotton, *History*, pp. 260–93.
[111] I am grateful to Jane Stevenson for bringing this map to my attention.
[112] Brotton, *History*, pp. 207–8.

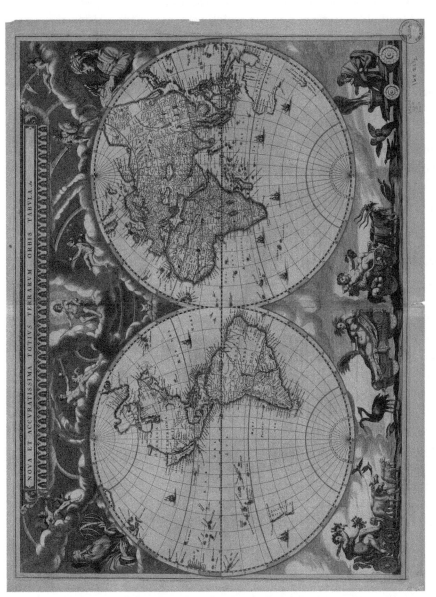

FIGURE I.14 Joan Blaeu, *Nova et Accuratissima Totius Terrarium Orbis Tabula* from the *Atlas Maior* (1664 edition). Courtesy of the Library of Congress Geography and Map Division, DC.

Harrison gives elaborate illustrations of the arches but the accompanying descriptions omit the measurements, for reasons which he explains:

> in all the descriptions, where mention is to bee made of *Heights*, *Breadths*, or any other Commensurable proportions, you shall find them left thus—with a blancke, because we wish you rather to apply them to the Scale your selfe, then by setting them downe, to call either your skill or judgement in question.
>
> ('The Device called Londinium', C1r)

Prima facie, it is an odd explanation, although in the context of this book, a familiar one: blanks allow the reader to fill in what they imagine. Providing measurements requires us to have technical skills to apply them accurately; Harrison would rather we imagined our own scale. (We might note also his technical vocabulary. He uses 'blancke' to describe the dash (in fact, a long rule): punctuation marks are called 'blanks' because they stand in for absent text.) On the next page, when he describes the 'Italians' pegme', he begins:

> It tooke up the whole breadth of *Gracious-streete* (on which it stood) being——foote: the height of it was——foote. The lower parte of this *Building*, was a large square, garnished with foure great *Corinthia Columnes*: In the midst of which square, was cut out a faire and a Spacious hie gate, Arched, being——foote in the *Perpendicular-line*, and——in the *Ground-line*. (D1r)

Authorial Uses of Gaps

This tolerance of blanks in all media leads to three things. The first is an alibi authors can hide behind. Ben Jonson's verse 'epistle to Elizabeth, the Countess of Rutland' offers an example of diplomatic self-censorship, with its disingenuous conclusion '*[t]he rest is lost*'. Elizabeth (1585–1612) was the only surviving daughter of Sir Philip Sidney; she married Roger Manners, 5th Earl of Rutland, in 1599. Manners participated in the abortive Essex Rebellion of that year and was subsequently exiled from court. This 1600 poem to the Countess (the first of three written to her by Jonson) was presented to her on New Year's Day 1600.[113] The poem ends with an encomium of Philip Sidney and a wish that Elizabeth may continue his line by bearing a son. However, the version published in Jonson's *Works* (1616) concludes as follows:

> But high, and noble matter, such as flies
> From braines entranc'd, and fill'd with extasies;

113 Ian Donaldson, *Ben Jonson: A Life* (Oxford: Oxford University Press, 2011), p. 146.

> Moodes, which the god-like SYDNEY oft did prove,
> And your brave friend, and mine so well did love.
> Who wheresoere he be........
> *The rest is lost.*
>   (*The Forest* XII in Jonson, *Works* 1616, Aaaa4r)

In fact, the rest is far from lost: it is in two MSS.[114] What we have in the printed folio is a strategic blank. The wish that the Countess bear a son that had been the conclusion in the poem's first publication was now sensitively omitted by Jonson because of the Earl's impotence.[115] Sir John Davies' description of his *Orchestra* as '*Not finished*' (as mentioned) is similarly disingenuous; the poem was finished and published in 1596. The 1622 reprint deliberately creates lacunae, cutting out the concluding references to a friendship that had since fractured, then blaming incompletion rather than revision for the gaps.[116]

The second is a creative use of blank space and omission. Thomas Nashe plays 'a typographical prank' with the sly insertion of a space in *Have With You to Saffron Walden* (1596). This changes the Cambridge barber-surgeon Richard Lichfield from 'a notable' benefactor into 'a not able' benefactor.[117]

The third is a deliberate writing towards the readerly capacity for gap-filling, not just typographically but conceptually. Consider Dr Faustus' self-deception in his opening soliloquy when he fails to complete biblical quotations: ' "The reward of sin is death". That's hard' (1.1.41).[118] This is his justification for renouncing divinity and turning to black magic. But every member of the audience would know how to complete the quotation: 'the wages of sin are death *but the gift of God is eternal life*' (Romans 6:23, my emphasis). Faustus repeats the tactic immediately with a second incomplete biblical quotation. Quoting 1 John 1:8–9, 'If we say that we have no sin,/We deceive ourselves and there is no truth in us', he concludes 'Why then belike we must sin and so consequently die' (1.1.42–7). But the quotation he has truncated continues, 'If we acknowledge our sins, he is faithful and just to forgive us our

---

[114] British Library Harley MS 4064 and Oxford Bodleian Rawlinson poetry MS 31. See Dobranski, *Readers and Authorship*, pp. 97–101.

[115] Dobranski disputes the suggestion of tactical omission, situating the poem's truncation in the context of the folio's assertion of Jonson's authority (*Readers and Authorship*, pp. 99–101).

[116] For extended discussion of the personal quarrel that led to these excisions, see Sawday, *Print, Space, and Void*.

[117] Nicholl, *A Cup of News*, p. 233.

[118] Christopher Marlowe, *Dr Faustus A- and B-Texts*, ed. David Bevington and Eric Rasmussen (Revels; Manchester: Manchester University Press, 1993). I quote from the A-text.

sins and to cleanse us from all unrighteousness'.[119] The audience's sceptical response to Faustus is dependent on their recognizing that he has 'rigged his syllogism by neglecting to quote in full the source of its two premises'.[120]

The most familiar example of the literary blank is Shakespeare's sonnet 126. This sonnet concludes the sequence addressed to the young man and rehearses one of the familiar concerns of the first 126 sonnets: the power of time over beauty. It begins optimistically, complimenting the young man's growth, before warning him of the paradox that time, responsible for his development, will ultimately destroy him. In an accountancy image we read in the conclud-ing lines: 'Her audit, though delayed, answered must be, / And her quietus [final settlement] is to render [surrender] thee'.

So far, so familiar. But in formal terms, sonnet 126 is an unusual sonnet: it is in rhymed couplets throughout rather than the typical Shakespearean form of *abab*, *cdcd*, *efef*, *gg*; it has only twelve lines; and where the final couplet should be, Shakespeare or his printer (George Eld) or publisher (Thomas Thorpe) has inserted two pairs of italic parentheses, bracketing the empty lines. The two sets of empty brackets might be designed to indicate the absence of a final couplet, drawing the reader's attention to missing material, as we have seen the blank so often does (G. Blakemore Evans notes the possibility that the pub-lisher removed the lines because they revealed the identity of the young man[121]). Or they could be more evocatively symbolic, indicating both the shape of a crescent moon and a sickle,[122] or a grave 'and thus the oblivion that comes with death',[123] or the hourglass which will consume the youth's hours.[124] Or they could gesture to the emptiness of the gaping grave which awaits the youth or the failure to couple(t) or the endlessness of the youth's post-mortem existence or the wordlessness that is the inevitable conclusion of time's 'rendering' him, or they could indicate that the 'poet's verse is incomplete and

---

[119] The sequence is the same in both A- and B-texts.

[120] Marlowe, *Dr Faustus A- and B-Texts*, p. 16.

[121] William Shakespeare, *Sonnets*, ed. G. Blakemore Evans with a new introduction by Stephen Orgel (Cambridge: Cambridge University Press, 2006).

[122] William Shakespeare, *The Complete Sonnets and Poems*, ed. Colin Burrow (Oxford: Oxford University Press, 2002), p. 632.

[123] William Shakespeare, *The Complete Poems of Shakespeare*, ed. Cathy Shrank and Raphael Lyne (London: Routledge, 2018), p. 554.

[124] Don Paterson rejects this suggestion because the brackets are not represented as ( ) but look 'like two spare tyres on a fat lad': Don Paterson, *Reading Shakespeare's Sonnets* (London: Faber and Faber, 2010), p. 378.

so is the youth's life'.[125] Helen Vendler characterizes the parentheses as 'eloquently silent' (reminding us of Lisa Gitelman's description of 'elocutionary' blanks). Vendler retains the empty brackets in her edition (not all editors do) because they 'emphasize the reader's desire for a couplet and the grim fact of its lack. Inside the parentheses there lies, so to speak, the mute effigy of the rendered youth'.[126]

The first line of Spenser's *Faerie Queene* puns on his own filling in of the blank—'a gentle knight was pricking on the plain' (1. spurring his horse across the field; 2. inscribing on a blank piece of paper).[127] The poem contains half a dozen Virgilian half-lines which Richard Danson Brown sees as deliberate attempts to 'turn poetic shortfall to artistic advantage'.[128] These 'ruptures' indicate Spenser's mimetic amazement at what he is representing—and at times unable to represent—as his 'unfinished edge hovers into semantically uncertain space on the white page'.[129]

Ben Jonson toys with the convention of the dramatis personae list at the start of *Every Man Out* (1600). He provides one-paragraph descriptions of each character before reaching the character of Mitis, who '*[i]s a Person of no* Action, *and therefore wee have* REASON *to afford him no* Character' (A3r). Consequently, his paragraph is empty. Francis Davison's *Poems* (1621) contain a sequence of thirty-four two-line 'lots' (aphoristic mottoes) that were drawn from a 'Lottery presented before the late Queenes Ma*jesty at the Lord Chancelors house*. 1601.' Typical of the fortune-cookie-style lots are:

> 10. *A Lace.*
> Give her the Lace that loves to be straightlac'd,
> So Fortunes little gift, is aptly plac'd.
> 11. *A paire of Knives.*
> Fortune doth give these paire of Knives to you,
> To cut the thred of love if't be not true.
>
> (D6v)

---

[125] William Shakespeare, *Shakespeare's Sonnets*, ed. Katherine Duncan-Jones (Arden 3; London: Thomas Nelson, 1997), p. 126.

[126] Helen Vendler, *The Art of Shakespeare's Sonnets* (Cambridge, MA: Harvard University Press, 1997), p. 538. Katherine Duncan-Jones' edition (Shakespeare, *Shakespeare's Sonnets*, ed. Duncan-Jones), published the same year as Vendler's, also retained the brackets. These two are the first modernized editions to do so.

[127] Edmund Spenser, *The Faerie Queene*, ed. A. C. Hamilton (London: Longman, 1977), Book I, canto I, line 1.

[128] Richard Danson Brown, ' "And dearest love": Virgilian Half-Lines in Spenser's *Faerie Queene*', *Proceedings of the Virgil Society* 29 (2018), 49–74 (64).

[129] Brown, ' "And dearest love" ', 63, 66.

The final six lots play with the idea of the blank (number 29: '*A Nutmeg with a blanke Parchment in it*') and the final five are each titled '*Blanke*' with appropriately punning contents. Device 33, for instance, proclaims:

> Nothing's your Lot, that's more then can be told,
> For nothing is more precious then gold.   (D8r)

Literary manipulations of 'nothing' and its related terms have a long history from Odysseus' successful blinding of, and escape from, the Cyclops ('It's Nobody's treachery', screams Polyphemus[130]) through the anonymous play *Nobody and Somebody* (*c.*1592, Q1606) whose Prologue announces 'A subject, of no subject, we present, / for No-body, is Nothing: / Who of nothing can something make?' (A2v) to the tragic outcome of Cordelia's one-word response in *King Lear*. Literary nothings and typographical blanks are related.

The Comic Pay-Off

The localized gap—the missing word—comes into its own in comic punchlines, where we are expected to supply the missing word. This is usually straightforward: often the missing word rhymes, often it is rude. Marston's *Malcontent* (1604, STC 17481) contains a sequence about national stereotypes:

> *Malevole*: The Dutchman for a drunkard.
> *Maquerelle*: The Dane for golden locks:
> *Malevole*: The Irishman for Usquebath.
> *Maquerelle*: The Frenchman for the (   ) (H1r)

Clearly, the missing word must rhyme with 'locks': pox.

Like Marston, John Taylor the Water Poet leaves rhymes incomplete with a blank parenthesis:

> This Gentleman accounts it no great wrong,
> Amidst thy praise, to say thy eares be long:
> His meaning my construction much surpasses,
> I wot not what he meanes, except an (.)[131]

(We can supply 'ass's'.)

---

[130] Homer, *The Odyssey* trans. E. V. Rieu, rev. D. C. H. Rieu (Harmondsworth: Penguin Books, 1991), p. 136.
[131] John Taylor the water-poet, *Works* (1630), Gg3r.

> T'interpret this, I need to goe to Schoole,
> I wot not what he meanes, except a ( ) .   (Gg2v)

(We can supply 'fool'.)

> But much I feare, thy booke in print will staine,
> Because thou art not di'd a (   ) in graine.   (Gg2r)

(We can supply 'fool' or 'knave'—probably the latter: although both are traditional phrases, 'a knave in grain' is more frequent in early modern books than 'a fool in grain'.)

In *A Scourge for Paper Persecutors* (1625) by John Davies of Hereford, personified blank paper complains:

> Then to recount the volumes hugely written,
> Where I lye soild as I were all be-(   )

(We supply 'shitten'.) (B1r)

Unlike the other categories of blank I have cited so far, this category is not occupied by flexible meanings but fixed: there is obviously only one 'right' answer. The verbal occupation that is being invited is already predetermined. We see this in the epilogue to Chapman's *All Fools* (1605) where the last two lines read:

> *We can but bring you meate, and set you stooles,*
> *And to our best cheere say, you all are welcome.*[132]

The comedy comes from the deliberate bathos of not filling in the gap with what was expected.

A coarse joke in Ben Jonson's *Poetaster* (1602), 'my very spermaceti, and my very city of—', relies on the dash (and us) to complete Albius' chiastic pun. The Q layout offers help, underlining the sperm-city joke by dividing 'spermaceti' into two words: 'my *Sperma Cete*, & my verry Citty of—' (C2r). By the time the text was reprinted in the folio *Works* of 1616, this bawdy balancing act has been typographically downgraded to a single word: '*spermaceti*' (Aa6r).

The Blank Page Writes Back

I move now to writers' ludic use of blanks. The prize exhibit here, predictably, is Laurence Sterne's eighteenth-century novel *Tristram Shandy*. Faced

---

[132] George Chapman, *All Fools* (1605), K1v.

with the task of describing the beautiful Widow Wadman, Sterne gives the reader a blank page and invites us to fill it in:

> Call for pen and ink – here's paper ready to your hand. – Sit down, Sir, paint her to your own mind – as like your mistress as you can – as unlike your wife as your conscience will let you –[133]

If the Widow Wadman is indisputably beautiful, as soon as Sterne provides details he renders her beauty disputable. He has used this tactic earlier in the novel when he presents a black page for Yorick's death. Ostensibly a tribute, a textual representation of mourning, this black page, like the later blank page, is actually a failure of language (and an implicit acknowledgement of that failure). What can one say when a Yorick dies? It has already been said, in *Hamlet*.

Sterne's use of blank space was anticipated by Thomas Nashe in his long pamphlet, *Have With You to Saffron Walden* (1596), Nashe's last salvo in the four-year literary quarrel with Gabriel Harvey. Saffron Walden was Harvey's hometown; hence the title means something like 'Go back to Saffron Walden' and the pamphlet is a long series of creative vituperation against Harvey. At one stage Nashe's invective takes a break and he hands the baton to us. The printed text provides a rectangular blank space, beautifully framed (B3v), and Nashe explains, 'Purposely that space I left, that as manie as I shall perswade they [the Harvey brothers] are *Pachecoes*, *Poldavisses*, and *Dringles*, may set their hands to their definitive sentence, and with the Clearke helpe to crye *Amen*, to their eternall unhandsomming' (B4r). In other words, we are to fill it up with our own insults (see Figure 1.15).

Nashe in turn was anticipated by the Frenchman, Bernard André, a chronicler at Henry VII's court. André was born *c.*1450 in Toulouse, studied law, became an Augustinian friar, and met Henry Tudor when Henry was on the Continent between 1471 and 1485. Daniel Hobbins suggests that it was André's ability to recite Latin poetry that brought him to Henry's attention.[134] André

---

[133] Laurence Sterne, *The Life and Opinions of Tristram Shandy*, 9 vols (London, 1759–67), vol. VI, pp. 450–1. Critics regularly comment on the novel's relationship to art. Peter de Voogd notes the visual qualities of Sterne's writing, 'both in the highly pictorial descriptions of characters and scenes and in the allusions to artists and contemporary aesthetic theory. [...] Commentators on his narrative technique regularly note his distinctive use of the indescribability trope ("words cannot paint...") and the visual imperative, and it is striking how frequently the reader is urged to "behold" or "observe", to "picture" or "see" a scene'. See Peter de Voogd, 'Sterne and Visual Culture', in *The Cambridge Companion to Laurence Sterne*, ed. Thomas Keymer (Cambridge: Cambridge University Press, 2009), pp. 110–59 (p. 145) and cf. W. B. Gerard, *Laurence Sterne and the Visual Imagination* (Aldershot: Ashgate, 2006).

[134] Bernard André, *The Life of Henry VII*, trans. and intro. Daniel Hobbins (New York: Italica Press, 2011), p. xiii. See also David R. Carlson, 'André, Bernard (c.1450–1522)', in *Oxford Dictionary of National Biography*. Available at: <http://www.oxforddnb.com/view/article/513>.

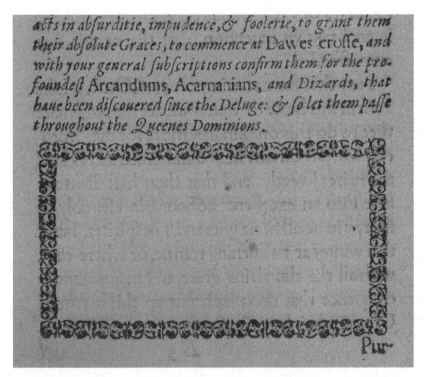

FIGURE 1.15 Thomas Nashe, *Have With You to Saffron Walden* (1596, STC 18369), B3v.
Shelfmark STC 18369. Used by permission of the Folger Shakespeare Library.

was brought to court, received financial gifts, the informal title of poet laureate,
and then, in 1496, the position of tutor to Prince Arthur.[135] He began his Latin
Life of Henry VII in the summer of 1500 but abandoned it after the death of
Prince Arthur in 1502.[136]

In his biography, André leaves blanks for various factual items such as details
of Henry's nativity (perhaps astrological details). The blanks are of varying
lengths—half a line for a phrase, a few centimetres for some missing information. But these blanks simply *are*—André does not call attention to them.
There is one blank that is extraordinarily different. When he comes to describe
the triumphant, epic Battle of Bosworth, André leaves us 1½ blank pages, and
explains he is leaving us white space to imagine it: 'inalbo relinquo' (fols
161r–162r, Hobbins p. 29). There is a complication in that André was blind,
perhaps from birth, and often draws attention to his inability to describe fully
events which he had not seen (he does say here that he did not witness the

<hr>

[135] André, *Life*, ed. Hobbins, pp. xiii–xiv.
[136] I discuss the MS in more detail in Part III of this chapter.

battle; maybe he was intending to interview an eyewitness). But nowhere else does he offer a paragraph of apology ('Auctoris excusatio') and leave blank pages. He is dealing with the indescribable, and realizes, like Sterne and Nashe, that the blank is more effective than descriptive representation. Harrison invoked the same principle when he declined to provide measurements of James' coronation pegme, preferring that we imagine the scale.

Virginia Woolf also realized this in her novel, *Orlando*, when she presented the wittiest man of the early 1700s, Alexander Pope:

> ....the little gentleman said.
> He said next,
> He said finally.
> Here, it cannot be denied, was true wit, true wisdom, true profundity.
> The company was thrown into complete disarray. One such saying was bad enough; but three, one after another, on the same evening! No society could survive it.
> 'Mr Pope', said old Lady R, ... You are pleased to be witty.[137]

John Davies of Hereford uses blank space as metaphor and extended conceit. His *A Continued Inquisition against Paper-Persecutors*, appended to *A Scourge for Paper Persecutors* (1625), is a poem written by an anthropomorphized piece of paper complaining about the rubbish with which writers fill its blanks. This poem, written by a blank page about blank pages, is itself full of teasing local blanks:

> Th'Impostors that these *Trumperies* doe utter,
> Are A, B, C, D, E, F, G, and (-------)   (A4r)

The missing word is probably 'Butter'—the stationer, Nathaniel Butter, who is also satirized by Jonson in *The Staple of News* (performed 1625, Q1631). Davies' poem is famous for providing a name check of Elizabethan authors (scurrilous Nashe, wanton Ovidian Shakespeare) but it is also an embryonic work of philosophy about the beauty of white paper, not a million miles away from Ulises Carrión in the twentieth century in one of the epigraphs at the

---

[137] Virginia Woolf, *Orlando: A Biography*, ed. Michael H. Whitworth (Oxford: Oxford University Press, 2015) p. 118. Woolf's footnote adds that 'these sayings are too well known to require repetition and can be found in Pope's published works'. For Woolf's minor reworking of this passage, see Virginia Woolf, *Orlando: The Original Holograph Draft*, transcribed and ed. Stuart Nelson Clarke (London: S. N. Clarke, 1993).

start of this chapter: 'the most beautiful and perfect book in the world is a book with only blank pages'.

A contemporary variant of Nashe and Sterne occurs in chapter 4 of Pieter and Rita Boogaart's *A272: An Ode to a Road*.[138] This charming and inventive book fully understands the rhetoric of the page. *A272* is a guide to the countryside, villages, history, art and architecture, literary associations, famous people, oddities, and points of interest to the north and south of this ninety-mile road between the north and south downs, from Hampshire to East Sussex. The road happens to run almost horizontally east to west and the layout of each double spread is typographically coordinated with the layout of the landscape. In the middle of each double spread, large rectangular blocks of text provide the main narrative; around the north, south, east, and west margins are smaller blocks of text in different fonts and type size, providing additional information on everything from slab stone material to politics. The reader navigates the page the way the traveller navigates the landscape: horizontal text above the main block introduces sites up to six or seven miles north of the road; horizontal text at the bottom of each spread covers sites up to six or seven miles south of the road. The vertical margins to the left and right contain notes: poems, anecdotes, biographies, explanations, technicalities, associations, etymologies, parallels. (The technical coordination by the printing press or its computer programme is extraordinary, as it is possible to read the book horizontally from one central section to the next: the prose content within each central section continues onto the following page, and this is often true of the side notes as well.) One of the many witty touches is seen in the county maps on the front and back endpapers: as well as having the usual coloured wavy lines for A and B roads, motorways, Roman roads, railways, and so on, the maps contain an additional pink line for chapter breaks. In quasi-Joycean fashion, *A272* itself has 272 pages: the textual and the cartographic map onto each other.[139]

Each double spread is lavishly illustrated with up to five colour photographs but also with diagrams, cross-sections, and maps. There is one exception, on pages 106–107, devoted to Cowdray Park. At the foot of the page, we learn of the manor house in West Dean built in 1804, bought by Willie James in 1891,

---

[138] Pieter and Rita Boogaart, *A272: An Ode to a Road*, 4th rev. edn (2000; London: Pallas Athene, 2013). I am grateful to the editor, Alexander Fyjis-Walker, for bringing this book to my attention (and for sending me a copy) after the Panizzi lecture on blank spaces.

[139] For the relationship between material text and literary content in the 1922 first edition of *Ulysses* (e.g. 366 pages, the number of days in the leap year 1904), see Sullivan, *The Work of Revision*, p. 157.

now West Dean College, a residential school for artists, run by a foundation established by Willie's son Edward. One of the portraits of Edward James painted by René Magritte in 1937 is called *La Reproduction Interdite* ('Reproduction forbidden'). It is a portrait *manqué*: we see the back of James' head as he looks into a mirror but what we see reflected is the back of his head. In the same year Magritte had painted *The Pleasure Principle*, a portrait of James seated at his desk, wearing a smart suit and tie, but with a lightbulb for a head. The two portraits of James are blanks, surrealist-style (with surrealism's artistic gestures to the subconscious and the treasures hidden in the mind, as the Freudian title *The Pleasure Principle* makes clear).

Edward James was a millionaire of Anglo-American descent (Henry James was a distant cousin; Edward VII was his godfather) who supported and collected surrealist art. An admirer and friend of Salvador Dalí and a promoter of Joan Miró and Leonora Carrington, for a short time in 1936–8 he was closely involved with Magritte (who vainly hoped that he had found a new long-term patron). In 1937 James commissioned Magritte to provide three paintings for his house in Wimpole Street; Magritte provided two portraits of James and a revision of his earlier *On a Threshold of a Dream*.[140]

A reader of *A272* might expect one of the portraits of Edward James to accompany the text that describes his manor house; instead we are given a beautifully framed box filled only with a description of *La Reproduction Interdite* and an explanation of why the painting has not been reproduced (the usual prosaic reason: prohibitive copyright costs. We are given details of the costs in relation to those of other reproduction rights in the book). The blank is thus triple: the page contains a portrait frame that lacks a portrait, instead describing a portrait that fails to reflect its subject; and the portrait frame is filled with text explaining the forbidding cost of reproducing a portrait titled *Forbidden Reproduction*. The tone of the narrative is factual and regretful rather than satirical but one can see the line of descent from Nashe's framed blank space to this.

Blanks in Dramatic Manuscripts

Orlando Furioso

I return now to the world of drama. Early modern play manuscripts and associated documents (such as play records in *Henslowe's Diary* or the manuscript 'Part' of Orlando in Robert Greene's play *Orlando Furioso*) are full of blanks.

---

[140] See <http://www.mattesonart.com/friends-of-magritte-edward-james.aspx>.

Orlando Furioso was published in quarto in 1594 but was written in the early 1590s. The role of Orlando in the published version does not match the role in the manuscript Part and it is clear that the play was abridged, revised, or adapted at some stage. In *The Defence of Cony Catching* (Stationers' Register, 1592) Greene is accused of having sold the play twice, once to the Queen's Men and then again, when they were on tour, to the Admiral's Men (C3r-v). Edward Alleyn was the star actor of the Admiral's Men, for whom he had played Tamburlaine—a role that must have led naturally to the ranting madness of Orlando at the centre of Greene's play—and it is for Alleyn that the scribe prepared the Part (it has corrections in Alleyn's hand).

Alleyn's manuscript role of Orlando is the only surviving Elizabethan actor's 'Part' or 'side'. Now in Dulwich College (the college which Alleyn founded), the Part comprises eleven strips, ranging in completeness from one line to an entire strip, that were once pasted together; the original total was probably fourteen strips.[141] The scribe who prepared Alleyn's Part left gaps when he could not read a word or phrase in his copy but he rarely left enough space for the missing material. This suggests something about the source— presumably the scribe was not reading from a written source as this would have given him the length of the word he missed out. Was he preparing the cue script from dictation? Alleyn regularly filled in the gaps with what looks like intelligent guesswork but sometimes he was unable to fill in the gaps.

Many of the scribe's missing words or phrases are classical and mythological references, which tells us something about his education and knowledge: he could not work out the correct mythological name from the context. He left gaps for names such as Ate (l. 62), Flora (l. 10; Alleyn inserted 'Clora' but the 1594 Q prints 'Flora'), and Mnemosyne (l. 315; later inserted as 'neymoseney' by Alleyn).[142] He seems to have no problem with Latin but does not under-stand Italian: he left a gap in the middle of a line in Italian that was never filled in (l. 95). He also left a gap for the unusual 'Galaxsia' in line 243 (later filled in by Alleyn), for the straightforward words 'child' and 'twins' at the beginning

---

[141] See R. A. Foakes, 'The "Part" of Orlando in Robert Greene's play *Orlando Furioso*'. Available at: <https://www.henslowe-alleyn.org.uk/essays/orlando.html>. I cite the Part from W. W. Greg's Malone Society parallel-text edition of the Part and the Quarto: *Two Elizabethan Stage Abridgements: The Battle of Alcazar and Orlando Furioso* (Oxford: Oxford University Press, 1922).

[142] This parallels Wakelin's medieval scribes who left gaps for words of foreign derivation and for foreign and classical names (seventeen such gaps in one copy of *The Canterbury Tales* out of a total of thirty-one). Wakelin notes a pattern in the treatment of classical names: the scribe recognized well-known names such as Aristotle but not obscure ones ('When Scribes Won't Write', 266).

and end of line 269, and for the adjective 'crimson' at line 239 (all were later filled in by Alleyn).

Sometimes the scribe left gaps which he himself was later able to supply: 'poel' at line 265 or the word 'rising' in line 231. The last three letters are too crowded for the available space, showing the scribe underestimated the necessary gap size; when he later discovered the correct reading, it had to be squeezed in.[143] Sometimes the scribe left entire lines blank: the one-line blank at line 208 was later filled in by Alleyn ('inconstant, base injurious and untrue'), but the blank beginning of line 50 was never completed.

The gaps may tell us about the original or about the scribe's circumstances. The manuscript has a run of blanks with four gaps in five lines at 315–19. (Each gap was later filled in by Alleyn. The missing words or phrases are: 'neymoseney', 'and entertained', 'Tyms', 'meloweth'.) If the scribe was copying from a manuscript, was the handwriting suddenly less legible? Or if he was copying by ear from dictation, was tiredness here making him slower or less attentive?

Despite the variety in these examples, or perhaps because of it, we can recognize the scribal attitude to illegibility and incomprehension highlighted by Daniel Wakelin, where gaps are evidence of medieval scribes' care rather than carelessness. The Orlando scribe was not prepared to guess, or to write what he did not recognize, or to create nonsense. He was conscientious in reviewing his work, going back over the missing material and filling in gaps (from whatever source). He was a professional, doing a professional job.

Blanks in MSS can also tell us about the circumstances (or complexity) of composition and collaboration—as we see in another dramatic manuscript, this time of a whole play, prepared about the same time as the Orlando Part.

John of Bordeaux

The manuscript play *John of Bordeaux*, also by Robert Greene, is a sequel to Greene's popular comedy of 1589, *Friar Bacon and Friar Bungay*; the manuscript, now in Alnwick Castle (MS 507), was clearly prepared or annotated sometime in the early 1590s (it contains the name of an actor, John Holland).[144] The manuscript never reached print or, if it did, the edition has not survived.

---

[143] In fact, his inserted reading is probably not the correct one because, as Greg notes, it is nonsense (*Two Elizabethan*, p. 170). Wakelin finds wrongly sized gaps in the medieval scribal manuscripts he studied, observing that 'invisible mending is difficult to do' ('When Scribes Won't Write', 271).

[144] John Holland may have been a member of Strange's Men in 1590–1; see E. K. Chambers, *The Elizabethan Stage*, vol. II (Oxford: Clarendon Press), p. 324. His name appears later in the 1590s in the playhouse 'plot' of *2 Seven Deadly Sins*, which names many actors from the Chamberlain's Men.

The manuscript contains three hands—that of the scribe, S, who prepared the text, with annotations by two others, hands A and B. Annotator B seems to be concerned with stage directions for sound. Annotator A deals with props, stage business, sounds, speech prefixes, and entrances; he corrects the lining of one misaligned speech prefix at line 64; he adds many omitted speech prefixes and corrects all of the errors in which Rossacler (son of John of Bordeaux) is named in dialogue instead of Ferdinand (son of the Emperor Frederick).[145] He brings those speech prefixes camouflaged by S's continuous lineation into the margin and he encloses one of S's stage directions in a box to make it more prominent. He supplies entrances, and highlights those already given. It is A who adds the name of John Holland, which occurs on four occasions (at 466–7, 593, 678–9, and 1071). The final scene is damaged and incomplete, and the last folio contains six fragmentary lines with no indication of where they belong.[146] One scene is missing or was improvised; it exists only as an introductory stage direction: 'Enter the seane of the whiper' (1058).

The verse is often continuously lined, misleadingly looking like prose, and the text itself is relatively short (when relined it runs to about 1500 lines). In the twentieth century Harry Hoppe suggested that the text might be a memorial reconstruction, although the available evidence suggests that it is more likely to be an abridgement.[147]

Towards the end of the manuscript, the scribe left a gap for a two-line speech: 'her john of Burdaox speckes' (l. 1119, fol. 11v), followed by a short gap, indicating his expectation that the lacuna would be filled. Earlier, on the same folio, a twelve-line gap for a speech by Bordeaux ('her john of Burdiox speackes his specth'; line 1089) was subsequently filled in by Henry Chettle (the scribe did not leave him quite enough room: Chettle's writing becomes cramped as he approaches the end of the available space).[148] One can understand that speciality speeches might be outsourced (Thomas Dekker testified that he had written a speech in the last act of the lost play *Keep the Widow*

---

[145]   He misses the error at line 697 in which 'fredrick'/'ferdinand' are confused. Line numbers come from the edition prepared for the Malone Society: Robert Greene, *John of Bordeaux*, ed. W. L. Renwick (Oxford: Oxford University Press, 1936).

[146]   For an analysis of what is lost, see Waldo F. McNeir, 'Robert Greene and *John of Bordeaux*', *Publications of the Modern Language Association* 66 (1951), 540–3.

[147]   Harry R. Hoppe, '*John of Bordeaux*: A Bad Quarto that Never Reached Print', *Studies in Honor of A. H. R. Fairchild, University of Missouri Studies* 21 (1946), 119–32; Laurie E. Maguire, *Shakespearean Suspect Texts: The 'Bad' Quartos and their Contexts* (Cambridge: Cambridge University Press, 1996), pp. 266–8.

[148]   This is in contrast to his large, free, and bold hand in his additions to *Sir Thomas More* (BL MS Harley 7368, fol. 6).

Waking 'for the boy who had murdered his mother'; presumably this was a repentance speech).[149] But it is less easy to explain the blank left by the *Bordeaux* scribe—a blank that was never filled in—for the two lines.

These gaps both illuminate and complicate the evidence that the *John of Bordeaux* manuscript was being prepared from dictation. The primary evidence used to support dictation is four occurrences of dittography at the foot/top of folios 3r; 3v/4r; 6v/7r; 8r/8v.

> We can almost hear the scribe admonishing the reporter, 'hold on a moment' as his pen scribbles the last line of the page before he turns the leaf as he reaches for another sheet. And then, when the new page is ready, the reporter, in order to regain momentum, retraces his path and repeats his last words before going on with the rest of the speech.[150]

The speech contains one *currente calamo* alteration ('young fferdinand' becomes 'proud fferdinand' (l. 1091) and the last three lines are marked for deletion. Was Chettle composing as he wrote, rather than copying? The couplet at lines 1097–8 has a terminative ring: 'But a disguise shall maske me from their hate/to free my Rosaline Ile tempt my fate.' It is then followed unexpectedly by a second contrastive conjunction which introduces the three lines marked for deletion ('But Burdeaux thou art poore, and povertie / can get no cloake, no covert, no disguise / great hearts in want may purpose not effect'). However, the final aphorism is also conclusive and the contrast between sartorial and ontological disguise is profound.

Dictation may perhaps explain why the scribe did not leave enough room for the missing material; it does not explain why the material was missing in the first place. If an abridgement was being prepared, the assumption is that it was being prepared from a full text (a copy prepared for performance?), not from one that had lacunae (an authorial draft?). The presence of Chettle affects dating (little is known of his dramatic activities before 1598). The nature of the *Bordeaux* manuscript is puzzling and the blanks may be key to solving the puzzle.

Sir Thomas More

Scott McMillin used blanks in the manuscript play of *Sir Thomas More* to solve a long-standing puzzle: was the play ever performed?

Sir Thomas More dramatizes two key events of recent history: the 'evil May Day' riots of 1517 and More's refusal to subscribe to Henry VIII's divorce

---

[149] E. K. Chambers, *William Shakespeare: A Study of Facts and Problems*, vol. I (Oxford: Clarendon Press, 1930), p. 211.
[150] Hoppe, '*John of Bordeaux*', 125.

articles in 1532 (conflated in the play with his refusal to subscribe to the Act of Succession in 1534). The play links the two by having More talk the rioters into obedience in the first half while himself refusing obedience to his King in the second half.[151] The manuscript is one of the most complicated Elizabethan dramatic manuscripts extant. It contains seven hands, one of which is that of the Master of the Revels, Edmund Tilney, who requested revisions so extensive that many scholars believe the play can never have been performed. The manuscript has been revised, although not in ways that comply with the censors' requests. The revisions, with pasted-on slips and inserted leaves, make the manuscript so difficult to follow that it is hard to imagine it ever reached Tilney in this form, and the way the manuscript was treated for conservation in the nineteenth century, when the leaves were separated and tracing paper glued on to some of them, has made it even more difficult to follow and read. Looking at the manuscript and at the censor's instructions, one can see why one might conclude the play had been abandoned. To make the play politically acceptable, Tilney asked the playing company to omit everything that is dramatic about the play's opening sequence and theatrically interesting about the subject matter.

John Jowett's edition of the play steers us through the sequence of compositional activities. The original play was written by Anthony Munday and Henry Chettle; it was then censored by Tilney; an unknown playhouse scribe coordinated revisions by Chettle and three additional authors: Thomas Dekker, Thomas Heywood, and Shakespeare. Jowett places the play's composition in the late Elizabethan period, c.1600 (plays about Henry VIII's reign were coming into companies' repertoires then) and the revision in 1603–4 (although Jowett feels 'more secure' in his suggested date for the revision than for the original composition).[152]

When Scott McMillin examined the manuscript's quiddities with his theatrical eye, he concluded that this complex manuscript was being prepared for performance. Part of his evidence came from a blank half-page in Addition IV (folios 12r–13v), which, in the initial composition, had scene viii ending mid-page; scene viii was 'progressively lengthened' by Hand C before receiving a

---

[151] See Gillian Woods, '"Strange Discourse": The Controversial Subject of Sir Thomas More', *Renaissance Drama* 39 (2011), 3–35.

[152] Anthony Munday and Henry Chettle, revised by Henry Chettle, Thomas Dekker, Thomas Heywood, and William Shakespeare, *Sir Thomas More*, ed. John Jowett (Arden; London: A. & C. Black, 2011). Prior to this edition, received opinion was that the play was composed in the early 1590s.

thirty-line extension from Hand E, who thus filled up the blank half-page.[153]
C wrote an entrance direction for a Messenger at lines 203–4, clearly heralding
a new scene (the Messenger's scene eventually takes place in Addition V); C
then crossed it out and continued the dialogue between Erasmus and Faulkner.
Eight lines later he wrote 'exit' and then deleted it, again extending the dialogue between Erasmus and Faulkner. The remaining half-page was blank
until E's further extension of the scene. W. W. Greg and the New Bibliographers
had drawn the (extraordinary) conclusion that Hand E wrote to fill up the
space. One is reminded of Tom Stoppard's sardonic playwright Henry in *The
Real Thing* in the second epigraph to this chapter: 'It makes me nervous to see
three-quarters of a page and no *writing* on it'. McMillin pointed out that
dramatists don't write to fill up space; they write to extend time. Extending
time in a play means only one thing: it enables a costume change. Therefore,
McMillin concluded, this play manuscript was performed or being prepared
for performance: 'Hands C and E discovered reasons to lengthen the scene's
conclusion as they worked. The purposes behind this bit of patching concern
the casting and staging of the play'.[154] Rarely can a textual blank have been put
to such good deductive use (see Figure 1.16).

The Fascination of the Blank

Throughout this chapter I have been exploring the conceptual game of hide-
and-seek that the blank plays, whether in censored omissions, topical omissions, comically incomplete lines, or abruptly incomplete works. Blanks are
never truly blank because they always call attention to what is not there. The
paradox also applies when we provide a line reassuring the reader 'this page
intentionally left blank'. As the page snail from Andy Griffiths' children's book
Just Stupid! reminds us with its metatextual speech bubble, 'This page would
be blank if I were not here telling you it were blank'.[155]

That paradoxical space, the cusp between what is not there and what is
imagined, is fascinating to audiences in all media. One thinks of the crowds at
the Louvre in 1911 when the *Mona Lisa* was stolen: the public queued to see the
blank space on the wall where the *Mona Lisa* had been. A newspaper photograph from the time shows the evocative wall with its four sturdy nails

---

[153] Scott McMillin, *The Elizabethan Theatre and the Book of Sir Thomas More* (Ithaca, NY: Cornell University Press, 1987), p. 27.
[154] McMillin, *Elizabethan Theatre*, p. 27.
[155] Andy Griffiths, *Just Stupid!* (New York: Scholastic Printing, 1999).

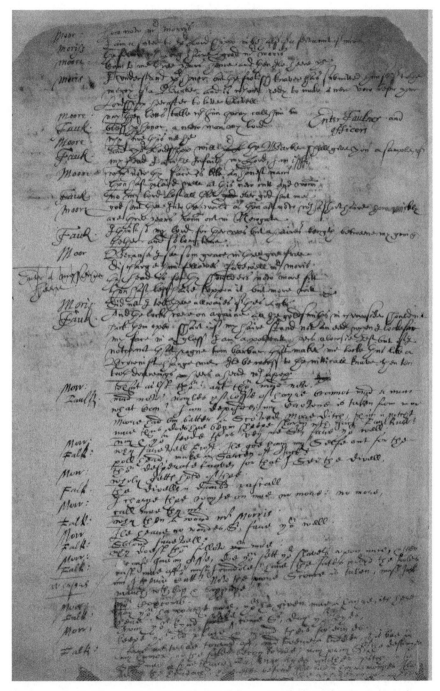

Figure 1.16 *Sir Thomas More*, Addition IV, fol. 13v. © The British Library Board. British Library MS Harley 7368.

supporting what is no longer there. At the centre of Lewis Carroll's 'Hunting of the Snark' is a blank map; the quest in *Kung Fu Panda* leads to a blank scroll.

Modernist art pioneered the blank canvas: Kazimir Malevich's *White on White* (1918) or Robert Rauschenberg's series of *White Paintings* (1951). A gallery label from New York's Museum of Modern Art 2013 exhibition on 'Inventing Abstraction 1910–1925' explained the innovation of Malevich's *White on White*:

> Malevich pushed the limits of abstraction to an unprecedented degree. Reducing pictorial means to their bare minimum, he not only dispensed with the illusion of depth and volume but also rid painting of its seemingly last essential attribute, color. What remains is a geometric figure, barely differentiated from a slightly warmer white ground and given the illusion of movement by its skewed and off-center position. [...] Malevich expressed his exhilaration in 1919: 'I have overcome the lining of the colored sky.... Swim in the white free abyss, infinity is before you'.[156]

Malevich's vocabulary here recalls Simon Armitage's description of the reader's encounter with white marginal space in poetry, the 'ventilated cavities where the mind's vapour trail overshoots and imagination undergoes millimetres of freefall'.[157] In the same lecture from which this quotation is taken, Armitage revealed that he felt himself, as a poet, to have more in common with the visual artist or graphic novelist than with other kinds of writer. In fact, the forms overlap, as this chapter has attempted to illustrate: the early modern page is an art form as well as a text.

We can see the creative appeal of the blank in other examples from the world of art. Robert Rauschenberg's series of *White Paintings* (1951) offered vertical rectangles of white (five panels in units of one, two, three, four, and seven abutting rectangles). Rauschenberg's aim was 'to create a painting that looked untouched by human hands, as though it had simply arrived in the world fully formed and absolutely pure'.[158] The paintings were exercises in objective looking, a principle taught by Rauschenberg's tutor at Black Mountain College in North Carolina, Josef Albers. As Matthew Collings wrote in 2016, reviewing the Rauschenberg exhibition at Tate Modern, 'Albers taught objectivity and Rauschenberg added vitality. The irreverence is lovely'.[159] Some saw Rauschenberg's irreverence as a swindle. Yasmina Reza's

---

[156] See <https://www.moma.org/interactives/exhibitions/2012/inventingabstraction/?work=146>.
[157] See footnote 6 for podcast details.
[158] See <https://www.sfmoma.org/artwork/98.308.A-C>.
[159] Matthew Collings, 'Out on a Whim', *Evening Standard*, 29 November 2016, pp. 42–3 (p. 43).

1994 play, *Art*, dramatizes the sceptical responses a blank canvas can prompt: a long-standing friendship is fractured when one man spends a fortune on a work of art that turns out to be 'only' a white canvas.[160]

There is no better artistic example of the paradox of the blank than Rauschenberg's *Erased de Kooning Drawing* (1953), a work that asks whether art can be produced through removal rather than inscription. Rauschenberg persuaded the Dutch artist Willem de Kooning to part with a drawing which he promised to erase (de Kooning agreed reluctantly); Rauschenberg painstakingly erased it over two months, using different kinds of rubbers. Traces of the erased drawing are barely perceptible on the blank page.

The narrative is inevitably more complex than this simple summary conveys. Rauschenberg had initially erased one of his own drawings but was dissatisfied with the result. For the erasure to signify, he needed a respected artist, one whose work was widely recognized as 'art'. (But, he later said, not just any well-known artist: erasing a Rembrandt would be vandalism.[161]) De Kooning understood the concept; in fact, later conservation work on the Rauschenberg revealed an incomplete graphite drawing by de Kooning on the reverse, thus authenticating the absent original. A mat, an inscription by Jasper Johns, and a thin gilded wooden frame all form part of the composition. These elements are often overlooked but, as Sarah Roberts explains, they combine to present the artwork as 'a religious reliquary, which depends on an ornate presentation and associated narrative to create an aura of significance around the remains it houses'.[162] Her reference to religious remains activates the concept of absent presence associated with all stages of thanatological loss, from the casket to the shrine, and links it to the blank.

In his *Erased Erased de Kooning Drawing* Geraint Edwards explores what acts of erasure mean in the world of Photoshop. His 104-page 'poem' records the computer data log of the nine hours and thirty-three minutes (in five sessions) it took Edwards to complete his digital erasure, which he characterizes as an exploration of truth retreating from 'our retinal environment'.[163] His *Blank Canvas (Conceptual Monochrome)*, a series of seven grey-and-white chequerboard

---

[160] Yasmina Reza, *Art*, trans. Christopher Hampton (London: Faber and Faber, 1996).

[161] Leo Steinberg, *Encounters with Rauschenberg* (Houston: Menil Foundation, 2000), p. 18. Steinberg also notes that de Kooning's work itself frequently relied on erasure and blurred lines. This is why digitally enhanced infrared images of the paper make it impossible to distinguish between Rauschenberg's erasure and any made previously by de Kooning.

[162] Sarah Roberts, 'White Painting'. Available at: <https://www.sfmoma.org/essay/white-painting-three-panel/>.

[163] See <http://geraintedwards.com/?page_id=638>.

works ('although they are not monochromes in the sense of being rendered in a single colour, they represent the same depiction of emptiness, or blankness, and so for this reason they are best seen as conceptual monochromes'), contemplates the meaning of blank digital space:

> Rauschenberg himself said that a canvas is never empty. Is a blank photoshop canvas more distracting than a physical blank canvas? If I start with a physical blank canvas, and I add digital absence, what must have been there was a digital presence.... If the purpose of painting these canvases is in order to represent nothingness, I cannot create nothingness by adding to it. So I must be erasing something. What is it that I am erasing?[164]

Rauschenberg's equivalent in the world of music is John Cage. Indeed, the two men became friends in 1952 when both were at Black Mountain College, and in 1953 Rauschenberg settled close to Cage in New York City. Cage acknowledged the direct influence of Rauschenberg on his silent symphony, *4'33"*, which premiered in 1952. The three movements are each labelled 'Tacet' and the score contains a note which explains:

> The title of this work is the total length in minutes and seconds of its performance. At Woodstock, New York, August 29, 1952...the three parts were 33", 2'40" and 1'20". It was performed by David Tudor, pianist, who indicated the beginnings of parts by closing, the endings by opening the keyboard lid. However, the work may be performed by any instrumentalist or combination of instrumentalists and last any length of time.

Silence is both something one can hear (as our cliché, 'audible silence', acknowledges) and something that one can perform (one definition of received pronunciation, with its clipped precise articulation, is the practice of speaking the gaps between words). Silence works in relation to sound, just as a textual blank is defined by what is either side of it. Cage's point is that silence makes one acoustically aware of other sounds: like the printed gap, silence is never truly empty. The meditative opportunities offered by the acoustic blank are seen in Remembrance Day's poignant two-minute silence—designed to be filled with memories and gratitude—or the silent space in the bidding prayers of Anglican services where worshippers offer up names of their own.[165]

Cage was influenced not only by Rauschenberg but by Zen principles (he wrote a poem about nothingness that featured on the gallery walls at the first

---

[164] See <http://geraintedwards.com/?page_id=164>.

[165] Cf. Carla Mazzio, *The Inarticulate Renaissance: Language Trouble in an Age of Eloquence* (Philadelphia: University of Pennsylvania Press, 2009).

exhibition of Rauschenberg's *White Paintings*). Don Paterson depicts the meditative, acoustic blank in a poem representing the silence of Buddhist philosophy. Paterson gives us only the title of a poem that is a blank page:

On Going to Meet a Zen Master in the Kyushu Mountains and Not Finding Him

The poem is about absence as failure ('not finding him') and absence as perfection (a Zen '*master*', my emphasis).

If modernist art transferred blanks to canvas, the modernist poet Basil Bunting played wittily with the *desunt nonnulla* formula. 'Attis: or Something Missing' (1931) concerns the loss of Attis' testicles. The poem concludes:

> What mournful stave, what bellow shakes the grove?
> O, it is Attis grieving for his testicles.
>   Attis his embleme:
>   *Nonnulla deest.*[166]

Shakespeare's *Twelfth Night* invokes absence when the cross-dressed Viola, exhorted to show masculine courage, confesses '[a] little thing would make me tell them how much I lack of a man' (3.4.302–3). It is easy to see this as Freudian lack (which it partly is) but the play's consistent topos is that of the blank: moved by Cesario's description of his 'sister', Orsino queries 'What's her history?' to be met by the haunting answer, 'A blank' (2.4.109–10). Forbidding Cesario to talk of Orsino, Olivia says, 'For him, I think not on him. For his thoughts, / Would they were blanks rather than fill'd with me' (3.1.103–4).

Michael Donaghy's poem 'Liverpool', with its combination of art erased, typographical indications of absence (the blank space in parenthetical brackets), visible traces, the play between what is and is not there, what does and does not exist (St Valentine, St Christopher, the tattoo, lost but lingering love), and readerly curiosity, brings together all the elements of this chapter.

> *Liverpool*
> Ever been tattooed? It takes a whim of iron,
> takes sweating in the antiseptic-stinking parlour,
> nothing to read but motorcycle magazines
> before the blood-sopped cotton, and, of course, the needle,
> all for—at best—some Chinese dragon.
>
> But mostly they do hearts,

---

[166] Basil Bunting, 'Attis: Or, Something Missing', in *Collected Poems*, 2nd edn (Oxford: Oxford University Press, 1978), pp. 8–13 (p. 13).

hearts skewered, blurry, spurting like the Sacred Heart
on the arms of bikers and sailors.
Even in prison they get by with biro ink and broken glass,
carving hearts into their arms and shoulders.
But women's are more intimate. They hide theirs,
under shirts and jeans, in order to bestow them.

Like Tracy, who confessed she'd had hers done
one legless weekend with her ex.
Heart. Arrow. Even the bastard's initials, R.J.L.
somewhere where it hurt, she said,
and when I asked her where, snapped 'Liverpool'.
Wherever it was, she'd had it sliced away
leaving a scar, she said, pink and glassy
but small, and better than having his mark on her,
that self-same mark of Valentinus,
who was flayed for love, but who never
—so the cardinals now say—existed.
Desanctified, apocryphal, like Christopher,
like the scar you never showed me, Trace,
your ( ), your ex, your 'Liverpool'.

Still, when I unwrap the odd anonymous note
I let myself believe that it's from you.[167]

This is a poem about Tracy (Trace)/the trace; about how occurrences (whether a tattoo or a love affair) leave marks; about the impossibility of removing a tattoo or extricating oneself without leaving a scar; about how things continue to exist when they have been denied, removed, or rejected (St Valentine, tattoos, relationships); about how we want to know what is behind the blank, beneath the mark of erasure; about how we insert the meaning we want into the blank (romantic hope into an anonymous note). This poem shows that the blank is always *sous rature*, a trace, an invitation, a site of opportunity.

Part III: Editing

Editing the Blank

As we have seen, blanks come in all shapes and sizes. The edited blank does not. When modern editions represent texts with blanks, a one-size-fits-all

---

[167] Michael Donaghy, 'Liverpool', in Michael Donaghy, *Errata* (Oxford: Oxford University Press, 1973), p. 23.

model is in operation—that is, if the edition even acknowledges the blank (readers of several editions of Shakespeare's sonnets would have no idea that sonnet 126 ends with empty parentheses). This editorial tendency to reduce or eliminate blanks has a long history. Let us revisit some of the texts mentioned in this chapter and look at how their editors have treated blanks.

Bernard André, *The Life of Henry VII*

Bernard André's *Life of Henry VII*, written at the start of the sixteenth century, has, as we have seen, a variety of gaps—over thirty-five in number. The first gap occurs sixteen pages into the manuscript (fol. 134r, p. 9) with a gap of a few lines for the hour at which Henry VII was born (see Figure 1.17).[168] Presumably the missing material is astrological rather than simply numerical. (The gap is now filled by the ink stamp of the British Museum.)

A gap of a few centimetres is left for details of Henry's education (fol. 134v) and there are numerous other short and long gaps that await material or expansion (e.g. 139v, 148r, 150v, 156v, 157v), where the contents cannot be confidently inferred from context. The gaps are numerous until folio 171r, then become fewer in number.

Sometimes gaps are left for technical information such as names: 'A port in Wales which was called []' (157v, p. 26; a half-line is left vacant), 'buried with every due respect in []' (164r, p. 31; an entire line, minus the one word 'in' is left), 'at last [] was sent across' (186r, p. 45; an entire line is left), 'this embassy included the distinguished []' (197r, p. 52; a two-centimetre gap is left which allows two lines). Sometimes grammar indicates that the material requires continuation, as on folio 147r (p. 19) where a sentence ends with a conjunction and a gap: 'he drew near him and' ('et', followed by a four-centimetre gap).

The manuscript is of interest for several reasons. It is part biography, part hagiography (p. xxii). It is political, genealogical, symbolic, and classical; it is humanist in learning, and personal in structure: a linear narrative is cross-cut with episodes as André remembered them ('as events present themselves to the imagination and the memory with no connection or order, so I set them down', p. 16; 'although I know that the events do not follow in proper order...', p. 41). This memoir structure, where events occur with a Proustian association, leads to a narrative that is structurally comfortable with pauses, omissions and interruptions. On page 17 André tells us 'I cannot check the

---

[168] When discussing gaps, I cite both the British Library manuscript folio and the page number in Daniel Hobbins' translation (André, *Life*, ed. Hobbins). When discussing literary matters I quote only from Hobbins.

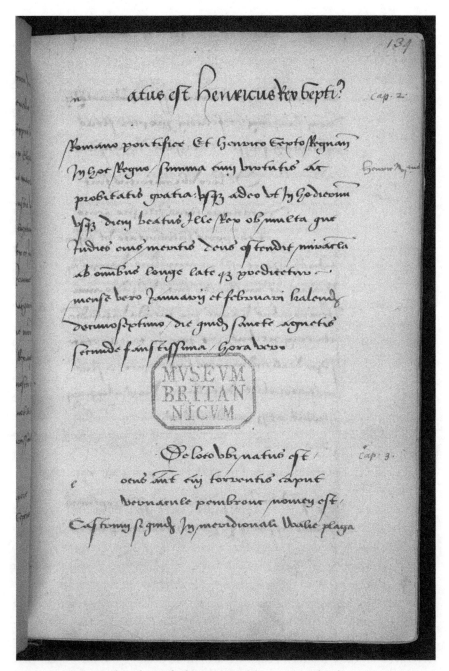

FIGURE 1.17 Bernard André, *Life of Henry VII*, fol. 134r. British Library MS Cotton Domitian A XVIII. © The British Library Board.

tears when I rehearse in my innermost mind the savage, fierce and cruel acts visited upon that man [Henry VI]. I might be allowed then to pause a moment in my enterprise to cry out with great proof of sorrow'. The pause is not a lacuna but an interruption to the historical flow with a prayer about unjust treatment of the godly. Then: 'let us now turn back to the good king himself' (p. 18). Later, when Prince Arthur is born, André tells us that 'in celebration of his birthday, I wrote a poem of 100 verses that I have omitted here because of its length. But here is its beginning:' (p. 37).[169] The 'beginning' comprises a lengthy thirty-five verses on four folios, after which we are reminded that 'other verses follow' (176r, p. 38). André then reflects on the optimism expressed in the missing verses, which was dashed by the prince's subsequent death, so his poetic silence ('my tongue cleaves to my palate'; p. 38) is not inappropriate. He recalls himself to his historical narrative: 'but lest I neglect the course of history, I shall proceed and leave others to write of the display, cheer, and magnificent splendour of his baptism' (p. 38).

The manuscript was intended for presentation to Henry VII, but this cannot be the presentation copy; indeed it seems that André abandoned his task. (The narrative does not reach its anticipated destination, concluding only with the rebellion of Perkin Warbeck.) The numerous gaps are intended as temporary, with André himself drawing attention to his need to fill them: 'until I am provided with a fuller knowledge of this affair, here too I shall pass over the remaining space' (fol. 220, p. 66; a half-page is left blank).

Sometimes the allusions to gaps invoke an ineffability topos: 'Restrain your foot here too, O Muse. Where are you rushing, O rash one? For you are not equal to the task of describing and immortalizing such great matters' (p. 32). Sometimes they are because of references to André's ignorance or his blindness: 'I ask the reader here to forgive me if I do not run through the train of events and explain all the stormy battles of those times. For I was not present then, nor have I heard anything previously myself' (p. 16); 'I certainly had no reporter or reviewer of the events as I was writing these words, as I wanted at first, to provide me with the substance of the things to be written' (p. 16).

Despite the narrative comfort with gaps, André intended to fill in missing factual material, as mentioned above. Not for him Fuller's principle of whetting the reader's appetite. On folio 167r (p. 33) he writes 'when I am more certain about these matters, I shall write in more detail. I also leave space here for this purpose'. More than half the page is left blank. On the next page he

---

[169] David Carlson is sceptical of this assertion, noting that the verses have a self-contained elegance. See David R. Carlson, 'King Arthur and Court Poems for the Birth of Arthur Tudor in 1486', *Humanistica Lovaniensia* 36 (1987), 147–83 (156); he provides an edition of the Latin poem on 167–8.

writes 'likewise I have deliberately passed by these matters until I have learned from others the exact details of each event' (fol. 167v, p. 33). Half a blank page follows, resuming with one line at the foot. Speed described André's *Life* as a work 'full of wide breaches and unfinished'.[170]

The manuscript was edited by James Gairdner in 1858 as part of the Rolls series. His edition is of the Latin text. Throughout, he uses asterisks to record omissions. Gairdner has a sliding scale of asterisk for representation. He indicates half-lines with three or four asterisks that occupy the equivalent space of the manuscript blanks:

*   *   *   *   opinionis errore, libidine[171]

Or:

His ultro citroque protractis   *   *   *[172]

For longer gaps, he uses a full line of asterisks with a footnote recording a 'blank in the manuscript', but does not indicate the length of the blank.

The asterisk was the nineteenth-century way of indicating omissions, even when the lines of asterisks occupy as much space as the missing lines of text and thus render the omission eye-catchingly nugatory. For example, writing in *The Retrospective Review* for 1828, an anonymous reviewer of Nashe's play *Summer's Last Will and Testament* quotes a long speech by Winter.[173] The speech occupies over four pages of the review, and is introduced by the reviewer with apologetic acknowledgement ('though long, we are tempted to quote it').[174] Towards the end, he omits four lines but indicates their omission as follows:

> Naso, that could speak nothing but pure verse,
> And, had more weight than words to utter it,
> And words as choice as ever poet had.

[Then he inserts four lines of indented asterisks]

> You that be wise, and ever mean to thrive,
> O study not these toys we sluggards use.

The lines of asterisk occupy as much space as the omitted lines of text.[175]

---

[170] Quoted by James Gairdner in the introduction to his Latin edition of André, included in *The Chronicles and Memorials of Great Britain and Ireland during the Middle Ages*, ed. James Gairdner (London: Longman, Brown, Green, 1858), p. xviii. André's text occupies pp. 3–76.

[171] *Chronicles and Memorials*, ed. Gairdner, p. 15.

[172] *Chronicles and Memorials*, ed. Gairdner, p. 16.

[173] Anon, 'Review', *The Retrospective Review* 2 (1828), 1–22.   [174] Anon, 'Review', 7.

[175] It is an injudicious cut as two of the missing lines introduce a quotation from Ovid's *Amores*, given in Latin in the next two lines and then translated into English in the following two. The reviewer retains the translation but omits its introduction.

In Gairdner's edition of André, blank half-pages are given one line of asterisks.[176] Two lines of asterisks stand in for blanks of a page or more. Thus, on his page 32, the passage of 'auctoris excusatio', we are given two lines of asterisks at the foot of the page, before the text resumes at the top of page 33 and a footnote explains: 'a page and a half left blank after these words'. All the asterisked lines receive a footnote: 'a blank here in manuscript';[177] 'a blank here in manuscript'; 'a blank here in the manuscript for the name';[178] (the change in footnote format is because Gairdner has supplied the name of Catherine Gordon (the wife given to Perkin Warbeck) in square brackets). Despite this apparent editorial consistency, unexplained variants occur (as on page 71 when two lines of asterisks are given although the footnote records that 'about half a page is left blank after these words').

Unlike Nashe or Sterne, André's blanks were not designed as artistic features but as temporary lack, so worrying about how editors represent them may seem otiose. Furthermore, depicting blanks is not easy (I have had difficulty in describing them in this section). But there is a difference between narrative description of the blank, as in this chapter, and editorial representation. The varying lengths of the gaps seem important: important in inferring content, important in understanding André's desiderata, important in following his process of composition/dictation.

When Daniel Hobbins translated and edited André in the twenty-first century, his edition adopted the notation of ellipses within angled brackets to indicate blanks. (This is also standard practice in Malone Society editions of manuscript plays.) But although his footnotes note the varied length of the manuscript's blank, it is clear that they function primarily to reassure the reader that the blank spaces 'belong to the text, and no text is missing'.[179] Hobbins is not interested in the blanks *qua* blanks. His footnotes provide occasional commentary on the nature of the blanks—for instance, he notes when they 'seem to have a specific purpose, such as providing for missing names, or when they are particularly long'[180] (Gairdner did the same) but the edition offers a uniform reading experience in which all blanks are indicated by the same five-character-length notation (ellipses within angled brackets). Furthermore, this same notation is also used for material present in the

---

[176] *Chronicles and Memorials*, ed. Gairdner.   [177] *Chronicles and Memorials*, ed. Gairdner, p. 69.

[178] *Chronicles and Memorials*, ed. Gairdner, p. 70.   [179] André, *Life*, ed. Hobbins, p. xl.

[180] André, *Life*, ed. Hobbins, p. xl.

manuscript but illegible or defective, as on page 57 (note 157) where [...] indicates that 'the next few words in the manuscript appear corrupt'.

John Manly and Helen Rickert's collation of Chaucer manuscripts is similarly levelling, depicting all blanks in manuscripts as 'space'.[181] Of 156 occurrences of 'space', fifty-nine are for complete lines of verse, and gaps at ends of verse lines are recorded 'as "om" without signalling that space is left'.[182]

Editing Medieval Drama and Poetry

Medieval and early sixteenth-century dramatic manuscript and printed texts often lack substantial material (the Tudor Facsimile Texts indicate this with a page noting, for example, 'A lacuna occurs here in the original: one leaf, sig. Eiii, is missing').[183] Editing *Mankind* in 2009, Doug Bruster and Eric Rasmussen record a missing leaf after line 70.[184] They deal with it in three ways. The dramatic text itself indicates the lacuna by ellipses after Mercy's speech prefix, then follows a boxed paragraph which explains that the manuscript is missing about seventy lines (see Figure 1.18). Finally, a footnote summarizes inferred action so that the reading experience can proceed continuously, at least in terms of plot understanding.

Editors deal with a different kind of gap at the centre of the *Pearl* poem. The poem appears in British Library manuscript Cotton Nero A. X. (along with *Cleanness*, *Patience*, and *Sir Gawain and the Green Knight*). It has 101 twelve-line stanzas, arranged in groups of five, with one group of six. The heavily alliterated poem has an *abababbcbc* rhyme scheme. It is this rhyme scheme that enables easy detection of a missing line in group VIII. E. V. Gordon inserted a line of five widely spaced dots:

> 'Cortaysé', quod I, 'I leve,
> And charyté grete, be yow among,
> Bot my speche þat yow ne greve,
>
> .   .   .   .   .
>
> þyself in heven over hyȝ þou heve,
> To make þe quen þat watȝ so ȝonge.   (ll.469–74)[185]

[181] John Manly and Helen Rickert, *The Text of the Canterbury Tales: Studied on the Basis of all Known Manuscripts* (Chicago: University of Chicago Press, c.1940), vols V–VIII.

[182] Wakelin, 'When Scribes Won't Write', 256, 255.

[183] *The Trial of Treasure (1567)* (London: T. C. & E. C. Jack, 1908).

[184] Anon, *Everyman and Mankind*, ed. Douglas Bruster and Eric Rasmussen (Arden; London: A. & C. Black, 2009).

[185] Anon, *Pearl*, ed. E. V. Gordon (Oxford: Clarendon Press, 1974).

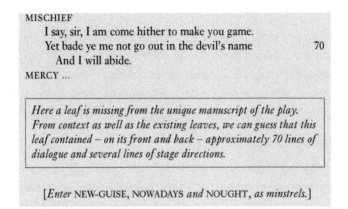

MISCHIEF
   I say, sir, I am come hither to make you game.
   Yet bade ye me not go out in the devil's name   70
     And I will abide.
MERCY ...

*Here a leaf is missing from the unique manuscript of the play.
From context as well as the existing leaves, we can guess that this
leaf contained – on its front and back – approximately 70 lines of
dialogue and several lines of stage directions.*

[*Enter* NEW-GUISE, NOWADAYS *and* NOUGHT, *as minstrels.*]

FIGURE 1.18 *Mankind* in *Everyman and Mankind*, ed. Douglas Bruster and Eric
Rasmussen (Arden; London: Methuen, 2009), p. 95. Courtesy of Bloomsbury Books.

The manuscript (fol. 45r) gives no indication of a missing line: there is no
gap, no marginal prompt. The scribe was clearly not alerted by his rhyme
scheme. This is not one of Wakelin's conscientious scribes paying attention to
sense and logic.

In a poem so symbolic, much has been made of numerical symbolism. The
twelve-line stanzas are associated with the twelve foundational tiers of the
New Jerusalem; the poem is designed to have 1212 lines.[186] The reiterated symbols of loss provide a different kind of pattern, from the absent pearl at the
heart of the poem to the lost vision at the end via the absence of language to
describe experiences or landscapes.[187] Simon Armitage sees the missing line as
a textual equivalent of the poem's other losses.[188]

A translation by the contemporary poet Jane Draycott emends the source
silently by giving a twelve-line stanza.[189] Simon Armitage's translation follows
the original more closely. The hardback edition offers a parallel text and indicates the lacuna with a blank line and a left-justified asterisk directing the
reader to a footnote: '*Line missing in original manuscript.'[190] Victor Watts
supplies a conjectural line in both Middle English and modern English;

---

[186] For further examples of numerical significance, see *Pearl*, ed. Sarah Stanbury (Kalamazoo, MI:
Medieval Institute Publications, Western Michigan University, 2001), p. 5.

[187] See, for just one example of the many critics who write on this topic, Ann Chalmers Watts,
'*Pearl*, Inexpressibility, and Poems of Human Loss', *Publications of the Modern Language Association* 99:1
(1984), 26–40.

[188] Armitage, 'Mind the Gap'.

[189] Jane Draycott, *Pearl*, introduced by Bernard O'Donoghue (Manchester: Carcanet Press, 2011).

[190] Simon Armitage, *Pearl: A New Verse Translation* (New York: Liveright/W. W. Norton, 2016),
p. 67. The UK paperback edition (London: Faber and Faber, 2016) does not include the Middle

William Vantuono gives a line of ellipses in Middle English but provides a conjectural line in square brackets in his translation.[191] As in E. V. Gordon's edition, these three poets number the missing line. This has the obvious benefit of rectifying the poem's total line count (now enabling even division by the number of stanzas). But it also gives the missing line a textual—numerical—presence, making it materially present although absent of content.

Shakespeare, Sonnet 126

It was 1997 before a modernized edition of Shakespeare's sonnets included the two empty brackets at the end of sonnet 126. In that year, both Katherine Duncan-Jones and Helen Vendler retained the 1609 typography, with extended discussion of its potential interpretive meanings (see my section 'Gaps across Media').[192] The pages of the 1609 quarto of Shakespeare's sonnets are very bare in comparison to continental humanist editions of Italian sonnets, which surround their poems with interpretive material. Critics have long noted the unmediated nature of the experience of reading Shakespeare's sonnets, beginning with the title page which advertises 'Shakespeare's Sonnets' (as opposed to 'Sonnets by William Shakespeare'). If the quarto presentation is deliberately innovative rather than simply unorthodox, all the more reason to retain its empty brackets.

All editors before Duncan-Jones and Vendler had declined to include the brackets on the grounds that they were accidentals. (New Bibliography had divided textual features into 'substantive'—features to do with authorial meaning—and 'accidental'—typographic choices made by compositors in the printing house, such as punctuation, which have no relation to the author and which the editor is therefore under no obligation to retain.) John Kerrigan, following this standard editorial rationale, omits the brackets from his edition 'not without regret'.[193] His headnote then offers a beautiful interpretation of the formal and thematic advantage of including them:

> What they usefully point up in Q is a sense of poetic shortfall, as though the recoiling, inconclusive quality of earlier sonnet couplets...had been concentrated in a single poem, consisting entirely of such rhymed endings, which

English text, does not have line numbers, and presents the missing line differently: it prints a line of dots with a right-justified asterisk keyed to the footnote explanation.

[191] *Pearl*, trans. Victor Watts (London: Enitharmon Press, 2005); *Pearl*, ed. William Vantuono (1995; Notre Dame, IN: University of Notre Dame Press, 2007).

[192] Vendler, *The Art*; Shakespeare, *Shakespeare's Sonnets*, ed. Duncan-Jones.

[193] William Shakespeare, *Sonnets*, ed. John Kerrigan (Harmondsworth: Penguin, 1986), p. 350.

> 'rounded off' the sub-sequence (was a couplet conclusion to the meta-poem) without solving by aesthetic means the problems it addressed.[194]

This one-sentence critique perfectly analyses the relation between absence (concluding couplet) and presence (six couplets), between form (couplets rather than quatrains) and typography (parentheses). Colin Burrow does something similar even more simply: 'As a part of the typographical effect of Q they should certainly be retained: they highlight the frustrated expectations created by the poem's form'.[195] What Burrow calls 'typographical effect', I am calling the 'rhetoric of the page'.

Digitizing the Blank

Obviously, one does not expect to be able to search for blanks digitally on EEBO (Early English Books Online). But one might expect EEBO to be able to represent a blank in its transcription page. We recall Gascoigne's *Glass of Government* (1575) with its blank for personalized insertion of a name (L3r) (see Figure 1.19) which EEBO transcribes misleadingly as follows:

> vayne delight hath caried them to run another race. I haue re|ceyued letters here from my frind Master in *Do|way*, who deelareth vnto me thereby, that they are sufficy|ently able to conceiue any tradicion or Science,

If you search for 'my frind' or 'Master' or 'Doway', the hits page gives no indication that there is a gap. Not until you click on 'view document image' do you see the photographic evidence.[196]

Empty brackets fare a bit better on EEBO because, as units of typography, the brackets are transcribed—but the length of the gap between them is not

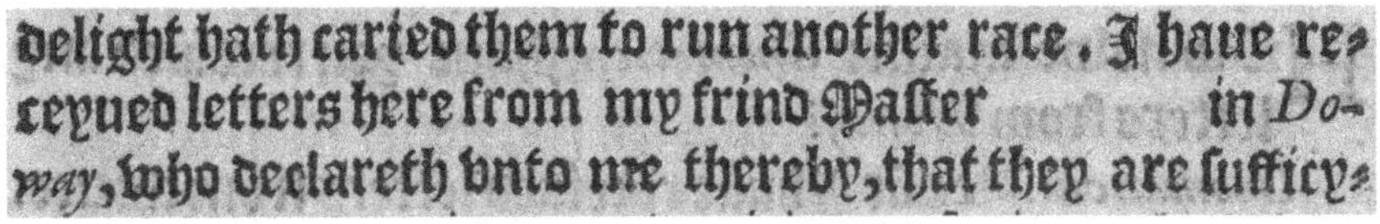
delight hath caried them to run another race. I haue re-
ceyued letters here from my frind Master in *Do-*
way, who declareth vnto me thereby, that they are sufficy-

Figure 1.19 George Gascoigne, *The Glass of Government* (1575, STC 11643a), L3r. Shelfmark 81918. Courtesy of The Huntington Library, San Marino.

[194] Shakespeare, *Sonnets*, ed. Kerrigan, pp. 350–1.

[195] Shakespeare, *Sonnets*, ed. Burrow, p. 632.

[196] In *Hoffman* (Q1631), EEBO similarly gives no indication of the blank space before 'organ of the soule'. As we have seen, the note in the Penguin edition reads '*Thou*: followed by a long space'. The editor interprets the space—'perhaps indicating the setting-copy was damaged or illegible'—but does not try to quantify its length (Chettle, *Hoffman*, in *Five Revenge Tragedies*, 1.1.191n., p. 251).

indicated accurately. In *Patient Grissil* 'cannot be ( )' on EEBO is a gap of two characters at most, as opposed to the printed text's 1.6cm (H2v). Greek letters do best of all: although EEBO does not represent them, it responsibly indicates 'undefined span, non-Latin alphabet'.

EEBO transcribers are not the only ones guilty of misrepresenting gaps: one Elizabethan compositor overlooked a gap in his manuscript copy. In *The Wit of a Woman* (1604), Rinaldo disguises himself as a painter in order to woo Isabella. Asked for his profession and his name, he replies (see Figure 1.20):

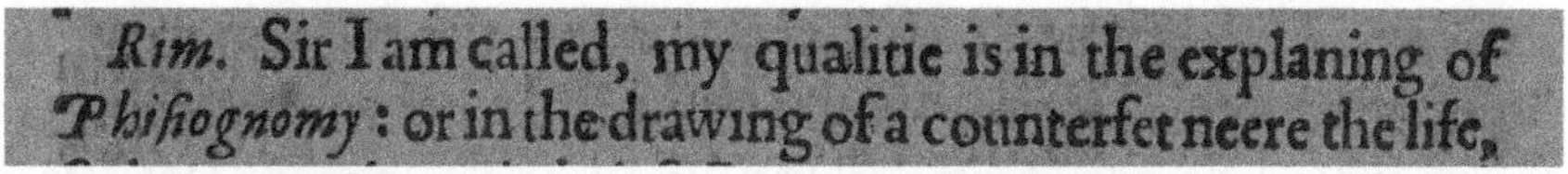

Rim. Sir I am called, my qualitie is in the explaning of *Phisiognomy*: or in the drawing of a counterfet neere the life,

FIGURE 1.20 Anon, *The Wit of a Woman* (1604, STC 25868), E1v. Shelfmark STC 25868. Used by permission of the Folger Shakespeare Library.

The play is confused in terms of plot and nomenclature and Martin Wiggins thinks the underlying copy was an 'early or abandoned authorial draft'. The blank for Rinaldo's disguise name may await the author's final decision, or it may indicate a topical opportunity for the players (especially if, as Wiggins suspects, the play has academic auspices), but in either case the compositor's presentation does not help matters for the reader.[197]

Those undertaking digitization projects in rare-book libraries have to formulate a policy on reproducing blank pages. This has not been as straightforward as it might seem and is related to the evolution of library photographic services.[198] What is today called 'Imaging' tended previously to be called 'Photographic Services'. Photographic Services existed primarily to support publication: of academic books, library exhibition catalogues, advertising posters, fundraising materials. Publication-standard photography was expensive and time-consuming so, inevitably, it focused on single images and on artistry. Its aim was aesthetic not archival. For archival images, the medium was microfilm, whose quality was such that if blanks were filmed, no researcher

---

[197] Martin Wiggins with Catherine Richardson, *British Drama 1533–1642: A Catalogue*, vol. V: *1603–1608* (Oxford: Oxford University Press, 2015), #1438, pp. 135–8 (p. 135).

[198] I am grateful to Julie Swierczek, Associate Librarian for Collection Description and Imaging at the Folger Shakespeare Library, for her detailed and helpful responses to my enquiries about Folger policy and history. The material in these paragraphs is indebted to her narrative about time lines and development at the Folger, a story that is paralleled in other institutions. I give her job title in full here as it encapsulates the evolution of the role.

could do anything useful with them (chain lines and watermarks were not visible). At the Folger Shakespeare Library, microfilming practice was to capture a blank verso facing a printed recto, but for a sequence of blank pages, only first and last pages would be captured plus an image of a card that read '16 blank pages omitted'. Julie Swierczek likens the logic of microfilm practice to photocopying attitudes: why would anyone photocopy blank pages in a book?

But imaging—as opposed to fine-art photography—also had a role in rare-book libraries where its home was not in Photographic Services but in the Conservation Lab. Just as today's bibliographers are interested in the material text as object, the purpose of imaging in the lab was to document the material object before, during, and after conservation treatment. Aesthetics had no role (rulers and colour targets were deliberately left in the images). This 'naked truth' approach had important non-academic benefits, such as when insurance claims were made or books lent to another library, so here, obviously, documenting the entire material object, including blank pages and damaged pages, was crucial.

Current imaging practice and policy in most rare-book libraries is thus a confluence of three separate tributary streams with three different approaches: fine-art photography for publication, imaging for conservation, and microfilming with its attitudes inherited from photocopying. At the Folger Shakespeare Library, Imaging is now part of the Collections division: just as cataloguing describes items in the collection (verbally), so does imaging (visually). It is thus unlikely that blanks will be excluded by any library in twenty-first-century digitization projects.

The evolution of digitization at the Bodleian Library over the last quarter-century is similar and the Bodleian now operates a cover-to-cover approach. However, since its digitization projects tend to be funded by grants, costed on the basis of number of images, a balancing act is necessary. Blanks that are foliated (i.e. part of the original composition) are digitized; those inserted in later rebindings may be omitted. (In practice, that decision, taken during a specific project to digitize Hebrew manuscripts, has never needed to be acted on.) The Bodleian also captures stub folios when possible (see, for example, <https://digital.bodleian.ox.ac.uk/inquire/p/8acd6189-a6b4-4b9b-a289-db152df6957b>).[199]

---

[199] Stubs can be difficult to photograph: one stub that was not photographed individually is visible in the gutter of the subsequent recto image:<https://digital.bodleian.ox.ac.uk/inquire/p/30da75f2-cc09-40d6-b5bc-baa91629993c>. Stubs and blank leaves photographed during the Bodleian's 'Early Manuscripts at Oxford Project' (digitized 1996–8) can be seen in MS Junius 11: <https://digital.bodleian.ox.ac.uk/inquire/p/3640b80d-bc20-4c7e-accf-d0ba234b4a67>. For comparison with current

The Editorial Gloss

Gaps in the text usually lead to gaps in understanding; but gaps in understanding can be caused by other textual problems (corruption) or simply by historical distance (we do not recognize allusions in Thomas Nashe for instance). G. K. Hunter uses the obelisk (†) in his modernized edition of Marston's *Malcontent* to frame lines or phrases that resist editorial explanation:

> † shue, should exemplary punishment†   (1.3.148)[200]

Hunter's footnote explains that he follows the reading of the 'only authoritative text' but marks it 'with an obelus to indicate my inability to emend into sense' (1.3.147–8n). At 2.3.17 the obelisked line is footnoted as follows: 'the Qq reading has been followed, though meaningless, since no convincing emendation has been proposed or comes to mind' (2.3.17n). Similar footnotes confessing editorial frustration and inability call attention to interpretive gaps even when the phrase itself makes grammatical sense:

> Quidlibet in Quodlibet 'which ever in what ever'. Some legal joke may be suspected here but I don't know what it may be.   (5.5.38n)

In a satirically allusive author such as Thomas Nashe, such confessions of editorial helplessness are frequent. The editions of both R. B. McKerrow and J. B. Steane are replete with 'meaning unknown', 'meaning uncertain', 'further meaning untraced', 'this seems to make no sense', 'reference unknown', 'untraced allusion', 'unknown', 'unidentified'.[201] Editing and annotation are a process of dealing with gaps. These glossarial notes, like the physical blank space we investigated at the start of this chapter, call attention to the interpretive gaps. Consequently, the notes invite us to ponder the problem, to try to supply what the editor could not. In these digital days the temptation to use databases to supply what McKerrow's wide reading could not is very strong. However, in all instances where I have keyed in McKerrow's 'unknown' Nashe phrases in EEBO, I have been no more successful than he was a hundred years ago.

I have been suggesting that there are interpretive losses when an editor removes blank space. André's missing information is different from, but

---

practice, see <https://hab.bodleian.ox.ac.uk/en/blog/blog-post-6/>. Any omissions from photographic capture are recorded in the metadata. I am grateful to Bodley's Librarian, Richard Ovenden, and to Emma Stanford, Bodley's Digital Curator, for detailed information and correspondence about the history of digitizing at the Bodleian.

[200] John Marston, *The Malcontent*, ed. George K. Hunter (Revels; Manchester: Manchester University Press, 1999).

[201] These phrases come from Steane's edition of *The Unfortunate Traveller* where sometimes Steane is quoting McKerrow.

related to, his references to his blindness or the indescribability of state occa-sions. *Pearl*'s missing line is a textual absence in a poem about emotional loss. My final example of editorial elision comes from George Peele's narrative poem, *The Tale of Troy*, where we see how the editorial closing up of gaps closes down meaning.

Editing George Peele, *The Tale of Troy*

Peele had a long and palimpsestic relationship with this poem (1589). He prob-ably wrote it while an undergraduate at Oxford between 1572 and 1579.[202] The poem was first published in 1589 but its composition predates its publication by several years, for in the dedicatory epistle Peele refers to it as '*an olde Poeme of myne owne*' (A2r). References in published poems of the late sixteenth cen-tury frequently point out the interval between composition and publication, often apologizing for inconsistencies or change of style but doing nothing about revising or updating. George Gascoigne draws our attention to the gap in time when he was composing his elegy 'The Complaint of Philomene' and consequently, to the different styles in the poem. He does nothing to smooth over the joins, leaving us with a poetic dislocation in form, which he points out without apology or embarrassment: '*thus my very good L. may se[e]*', he writes to his patron, '*how coblerlike I have clouted a new patch to an olde sole, begin-ning this co[m]plainte of* Philomene, *in Aprill, 1562. continuing it a little furder in Aprill. 1575 and now, thus finished this thirde day of Aprill. 1576*'.[203]

Peele subsequently revised *The Tale of Troy*. The revision probably occurred around 1596 when Peele sent the poem as a gift (which is to say: a literary beg-ging letter) to Lord Burghley, the Lord Chancellor. Burghley filed Peele's poem and accompanying letters 'with others from cranks and crackpots'.[204] Peele died later in 1596 but in 1604 a revised version was published (presumably the revisions for the Burghley refurbishment) in a tiny presentation volume (one and a half inches high) of which only one copy is extant, now in private hands.[205] Lines from the poem also appear in Peele's earlier court pastoral, *The Arraignment of Paris* (1584). Thus, if *The Tale of Troy* was written when he was at college, Peele recycled lines from the poem into the play. A. H. Bullen

---

[202] George Peele, *The Life and Minor Works of George Peele*, ed. D. H. Horne (New Haven, CT: Yale University Press, 1952).

[203] George Gascoigne, *The Steel Glass* (1576), Qvr.

[204] Peele, *The Life and Minor Works*, p. 108.

[205] The book was sold to a private bidder in the Houghton sale at Christie's of London on 11/12 June 1980, lot 362, for £14,000.

edited the poem in the nineteenth century; he collated both the 1589 and 1604 texts. In the following extract I quote from the 1589 text; where variants between the two printed versions are relevant, I quote both versions separately, relying on Bullen's representation of the 1604 text.

Until the final lines the poem consistently stresses Helen's love of Paris. She gazes on him, studies his face, is inflamed with love. Although she is torn between right and wrong, love 'will be no better rulde' (1604: 'will not be over-ruled') and so she 'armes her boldlie to this great amis' (B2v). The couple are 'lovers' (B2v); Helen's willing flight constitutes marital treason.

But the final paragraph offers an alternative reading of Helen's departure for Troy and a bathetically tentative ending.

> My Author sayes, to honour Helens name, [1604: in favor of her name]
> That through the worlde hath beene belide by Fame:
> Howe when the King her pheere [husband] was absent thence,
> A tale that well may lessen her offence,
> Sir Paris tooke the Towne by Armes and skill,
> And carried her to Troy [1604: And carried Helen thence] against her will.
> Whom whether afterward she lov'd or no,
> I cannot tell, but may imagine so.   (C3r)

Bullen's edition misrepresents the poem, or its compositor, in a crucial way. In Bullen, these final eight lines follow on as a continuous part of the poem. In the 1589 edition they are distinguished typographically: they are italic to the poem's roman, they begin with a large woodcut majuscule M which forces the indentation of the second line (as happens at the beginning of the poem with the factotum initial) and they are separated by four lines of white space. The Elizabethan compositor has intentionally differentiated the lines, setting them off from the rest of the poem, and the blank space is a crucial part of that typographical differentiation.

The content of the last eight lines invites such typographical treatment. Peele has already left Helen's narrative behind and taken us on to Aeneas and Italy; the return to Helen's story in these eight lines is abrupt and unexpected. It functions as a coda, and this coda is extraordinary for three interpretive moments. One is the alternative beginning to Helen's story in which Paris 'carried her to Troy [1604: Helen thence] against her will' (C3r). Another is the introduction of moral commentary in the form of hesitant exculpation—'A tale that well may lessen her offence' (my underlining). The third is the attempt at emotional imagining—did Helen love her abductor?—accompanied by a recognition that we cannot answer that question ('I cannot tell') and then an inability to accept that inconclusiveness as an answer for, despite the conclusive feel of the two iambs which begin the final pentameter ('*I cannot tell*'), the line trails off into the vague and conjectural '*but may imagine so*'. Why may he imagine so (given that he proffers no evidence)? Could he not equally imagine the opposite? Why voice the possibility of abduction now when, earlier in the poem, extended passages made Helen's love clear, called it a revolt against Menelaus, and smoothed it over with the jaunty couplet, 'And for her hart was from her body hent [snatched], / To Troy this *Helen* with her Lover went' (B2v). Even as Peele tries to conclude his poem, he opens it out again, admitting the possibility of an alternative scenario, and ending with an after-story that runs counter to the preceding lines not only in narrative content but in tone—the tentative nature of the second scenario with its emotional hypotheses undoes the confident tone in which the body of the poem blames Helen. The majuscule M, the italics, and the spatial gulf of blank space all indicate the separate nature of this second story. To edit out the blank space is to undo a crucial part of the poem's meaning.

Conclusion

When Google books reassures us that 'this page intentionally left blank' it signals our unease with blank space: a blank in the text must be an error. In origin this reassuring *vacat* page was designed to protect readers from the potentially damaging effects of printing errors—in legal documents or in exam papers, for instance. Blanks are regularly seen as a problem, as in a recent example from the *International New York Times*: the newspaper's Thai edition had a blank front page on 1 December 2015 because of self-censorship (anticipating an adverse response from the Thai government, the Bangkok office removed a negative story about the economic situation in Thailand). So alarming are blank spaces to us that this story made headline news in the US *New York Times* (2 December 2015) and was covered by the UK broadsheets. Roger Chartier and Peter Stallybrass are disquieted by Bernice Kliman's edition of *The Three-Text Hamlet* because 'a lot of the first quarto in this edition is blank space'; blank space conditions us to think that something is amiss.[206] The Google books example at the start of this paragraph comes from a novel. Our need for reassurance about blank space in works of fiction is now so standard that it can

---

[206]   Stallybrass and Chartier, 'Reading and Authorship', p. 35.

be parodied, as in Demetri Martin's *This is a Book* (2011), which contains the announcement 'This page unintentionally left blank'.[207]

But reading with early modern eyes—looking at the history of the *page* as well as the history of the book—reveals the rapid evolution of blanks in all their forms, from a typographical shorthand to a ludic creativity. This creativity continues in twenty-first-century printed forms. Jen Bervin's *Nets* (2004) has a palimpsestic typographical relation to Shakespeare's sonnets. The full title is THE SONNETS OF WILLIAM SHAKESPEARE. Small haiku-style poems are made by bleaching out each of Shakespeare's sonnets, leaving only a few words in black type. (For Sonnet 12 see Figure 1.21.)

Like Armitage, Bervin stresses the importance of poetry's blank spaces: 'When we write poems, the history of poetry is with us, pre-inscribed in the white of the page'.[208] By stripping Shakespeare's sonnets 'bare to the "nets"', she foregrounds poetry's blank spaces, both metaphorically and literally.

Jerome Rothenberg's edited collection, *Technicians of the Sacred*, highlights concrete poetry.[209] Unsurprisingly, many of the poems play with typographical form, as in Acoma Pueblo's foregrounding of the forward slash: 'they / we [...] were / are [...] we / they'.[210] Samuel Mercer's *The Fragments* contains more ellipses than words.[211] Armand Schwerner combines ellipses with lines of plus-signs (from 'The Tablets');[212] his notes explain that he was seeking 'ways out of closure' and that he enjoyed 'put[ting] in holes'.[213] Seneca Nation's 'Old Man's Beaver Blessing Song' contains sixty-six words and eighty-three asterisks. Rothenberg's notes to Mercer's *The Fragments* explain that 'Time & chance have worked on the materials, not only to corrode but to create new structures: as if "process" itself had turned poet, to leave its imprints on the work'.[214] This is an excellent description of Bervin's *Nets* or Austin Kleon's *Newspaper Blackout*. Kleon makes poems by blacking out newspapers.[215] The result is a contemporary variant of imagist poetry. In an appendix he offers advice on how to create a newspaper blackout poem: do not read the

---

[207] Demetri Martin, *This is a Book* (London: Penguin, 2011), n.p. [p. 134].

[208] See <http://www.jenbervin.com/images/nets/about.html>.

[209] Jerome Rothenberg (ed.), *Technicians of the Sacred*, 3rd edn (Los Angeles: University of California Press, 2017).

[210] Rothenberg (ed.), *Technicians of the Sacred*, p. 396, my ellipses.

[211] Rothenberg (ed.), *Technicians of the Sacred*, p. 37.

[212] Rothenberg (ed.), *Technicians of the Sacred*, p. 471.

[213] Rothenberg (ed.), *Technicians of the Sacred*, p. 472.

[214] Rothenberg (ed.), *Technicians of the Sacred*, p. 470.

[215] Austin Kleon, *Newspaper Blackout* (New York: Harper Perennial, 2010), p. 159.

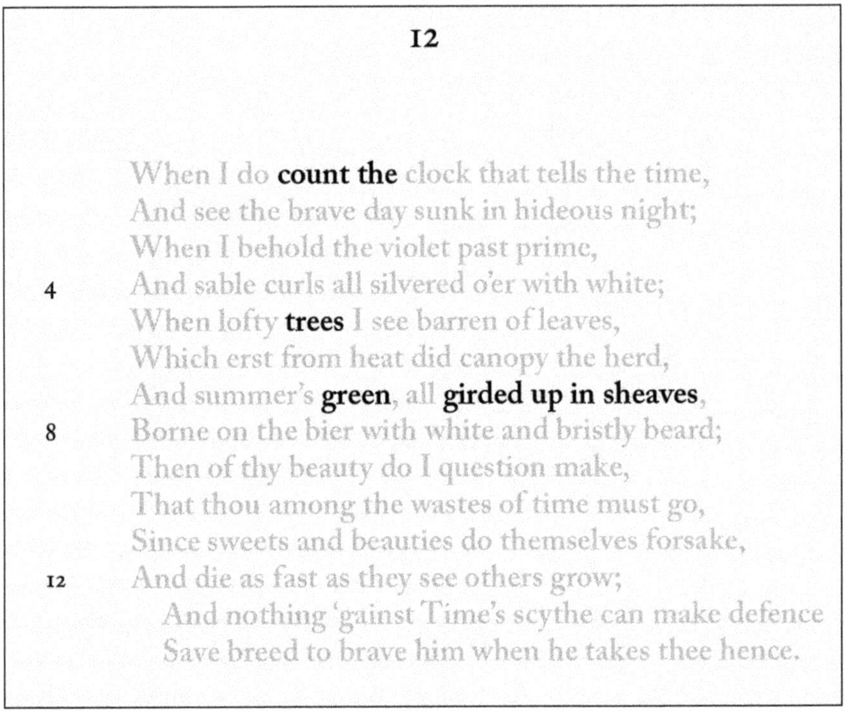

12

When I do **count the** clock that tells the time,
And see the brave day sunk in hideous night;
When I behold the violet past prime,
4   And sable curls all silvered o'er with white;
When lofty **trees** I see barren of leaves,
Which erst from heat did canopy the herd,
And summer's **green**, all **girded up in sheaves**,
8   Borne on the bier with white and bristly beard;
Then of thy beauty do I question make,
That thou among the wastes of time must go,
Since sweets and beauties do themselves forsake,
12   And die as fast as they see others grow;
      And nothing 'gainst Time's scythe can make defence
      Save breed to brave him when he takes thee hence.

FIGURE 1.21 Jen Bervin, *Nets* (Berkeley, CA: Ugly Duckling Presse, 2004). Courtesy of Ugly Duckling Presse.

newspaper article because narrative then eclipses the images. 'You want to begin by looking for a word, or a combination of words, that forms an image in your head. [...] You want an *anchor*—a place to start'.[216] The book's final section includes poems by readers of his work, submitted to an online competition, with Kleon's analysis of his readers' innovations, such as Alison Conlon's geometric shapes round her words,[217] or Stephanie Cheng's 'snaking white trails in between the words' which not only create a pattern on the page but 'slow down your reading experience'.[218] Of his Sumero-Akkadian tablets Rothenberg continues: 'But the workers who pieced such scraps together have left their marks too: not only dots as here, but brackets, parentheses, numbers & open spaces. So something else appears: a value, a new form [...] as a Greek statue that has lost its colors'.[219] In this insight he could equally be describing the compositors of early modern texts, whose marks give a value and create a

---

[216] Kleon, *Newspaper Blackout*, p. 159, emphasis original.
[217] Kleon, *Newspaper Blackout*, pp. 164–5.   [218] Kleon, *Newspaper Blackout*, p. 168.
[219] Kleon, *Newspaper Blackout*, p. 470.

new form. Jonathan Safran Foer's *Tree of Codes* (2010) takes writing into the world of sculpture. Taking a novel by the Polish writer Bruno Schultz, he cut out words and quite literally carved out a new novel form.[220]

Keri Smith's children's books—*Finish This Book, Wreck This Journal, This Is Not A Book*[221]—return us to the start of this chapter with its focus on books that get completed by the reader. This completion can be focused on one word: *etcetera* or its abbreviation *&c*. The way in which this mark gives 'a value' and the way in which it invites the reader to fill its ambiguous blankness is the subject of Chapter 2.

---

[220] Jonathan Safran Foer, *Tree of Codes* (London: Visual Editions, 2010).
[221] Keri Smith, *Finish This Book* (London: Penguin, 2011), *Wreck This Journal* (London: Penguin, 2013), *This Is Not a Book* (London: Penguin, 2011).

&c

Et Cetera/Etcetera/&c; or,
the Aposiopetic Page

& cetera was no word of art for a foole.   (Robert Greene)[1]

Introduction

In *The Defense of Coney Catching* (1592), Robert Greene tells a 'pleasant Tale how a holy brother Conny-catcht for a Wife' (C4v). Claiming to be heir to a fortune, this coney-catching wooer schools an accomplice to confirm the claim. In an interview with the prospective father-in-law, the accomplice attests that the wooer was 'the sonne and heire of one Maister &c. dwelling in Cheshire, at the Manor of &c.' (C4v–D1r). Greene's two uses of '&c' are not designed to indicate or conceal a real person, nor is the reader meant to fill in a customized name (as in the N-town manuscript in Chapter 1); rather '&c' indicates the improvisatory ability of the accomplice.

The '&c' in the lyrics that accompany the musical notation in John Rastell's Tudor interlude, *The Nature of the Four Elements* (?1520), has a different function. Signatures E5r to E6v contain three pages of musical notation, with three staves per page. Printed below the first stave is the lyric that accompanies it: 'Tyme to pas with goodly sport our spryte[s] to[o]' (E5r). It is a three-part song (each stave is in a different clef) and the next two staves on the page repeat the musical notation with minor variations for different voices. The first line of the lyric is repeated below each stave in abbreviated form: 'Tyme to pas &c'. The '&c' is obviously an instruction that all singers sing the same words, despite their different musical parts. An owner of the British Library copy actually followed the implied instruction to continue by writing in the omitted words: 'wyth goodly sport our spryte[s] to'. Presumably he was a

[1] Robert Greene, *Farewell to Folly* (1591), B4r.

The Rhetoric of the Page. Laurie Maguire, Oxford University Press (2020). © Laurie Maguire.
DOI: 10.1093/oso/9780198862109.001.0001

singer, or a coordinator of singers, and wanted to be able to follow the line of music without having to raise his eyes to the full line of printed lyric at the top of the page.[2]

The Rastell example uses '&c' in the way we do today: to indicate continuation. A Victorian-style manual, Justin Brenan's *Composition and Punctuation*, devotes considerable space to '&c', advising authors to 'Avoid the frequent &c. as your great enemy to improvement in writing. If you depend upon this crutch, your composition will always be lame. This is the most prominent mark of a poor, vulgar, and ignorant writer'.[3] Brenan castigates the '&c' as a 'miserable substitute for plain expression' which authors resort to only because they are unable to be precise.[4] His example of a prose passage before and after his editorial improvements supports his point, with its pedantic exaggeration of *etcetera*'s faults. For Brenan and his authors, as for us today, '&c' is simply an abbreviation, indicating that we should continue by supplying material that can be inferred.

But abbreviation is only one of many uses of *etcetera* available to the early modern writer, as the example from Greene's pamphlet suggests. As a noun and a verb, early modern *etcetera* can represent the body (sexual parts and activities, or physical functions such as urination or defecation) and the bawdy; it works both as a coy euphemism and as its opposite, a nudge-nudge, wink-wink metonymy. As a punctuation mark, it can indicate omission: a mark of things that cannot be said, or have been said previously but are now omitted or censored, or are interrupted and uncompleted. As such, it works as a forerunner of the punctuation mark that indicates silence or interruption—the dash. As a rhetorical term it can refer to silence or the form of breaking off known rhetorically as aposiopesis. As an abbreviation it functions, as it does today, to indicate the continuation of properties in a list; and when that list occurs in stage directions or in an actor's Part, *etcetera* can direct stage action, sanctioning improvised continuation of dialogue. No mere 'crutch' for the 'lame' writer, *etcetera* has possibilities undreamt of in Brenan's philosophy.

The list of early modern uses of *etcetera* in the previous paragraph is not as eclectic as it may seem. All four categories are linked in that *etcetera* directs the

---

[2] The reader has signed his name—John Pulley—with the date '1541' on sig. E1r. For Pulley's 'mode of engagement that we might begin to think of as performative reading', see Tamara Atkin, *Reading Drama in Tudor England* (London: Routledge, 2018), pp. 177–8.

[3] Brenan, *Composition and Punctuation Familiarly Explained for Those Who Have Neglected the Study of Grammar*, 14th edn (London: Virtue Brothers & Co., 1865), p. 16.

[4] Brenan, *Composition and Punctuation*, p. 16.

eye to a vacancy. We can see why it might be associated with aposiopesis, a rhetorical figure that is paradoxically about silence. Conceptually, *etcetera* is related to the list and to asyndeton; its typographical cousins are ellipsis and the dash, features that call attention to what is not there. *Etcetera* plays with possibility, exploits its status as a margin or boundary, tantalizes with surplus and remainder, offers and denies completion simultaneously. Even when it functions as an abbreviation, *etcetera* plays a conceptually sophisticated game with boundaries and cusps, with abruption and continuation, with suspension and extension of meaning. It can indicate both continuation and failure to continue: *etcetera* both appeals to what is known and therefore has no need to continue articulating and it stops because it cannot go on, can only gesture beyond itself.[5]

Umberto Eco identifies in Homer's *Iliad* a swing between what he calls a 'poetics of "everything included"' (represented by Achilles' shield) and a 'poetics of the "etcetera"' (represented by the catalogue of ships: lists can go on indefinitely).[6] It is clear that the list is an *etcetera* in that it gestures beyond itself. Eco notes that research on the list typically confines itself to verbal lists 'because it is very hard to say in what way a picture can present things and yet suggest an "et cetera"',[7] and he is quoted as saying that the world of sculpture does not have lists or *etceteras*: 'it is hard to imagine a statue that conveys an "et cetera", i.e. one that suggests it may continue beyond its own physical limits'.[8] I disagree. Sculpture has *etceteras*: missing limbs. So does painting: the *Mona Lisa*'s smile is an *etcetera* (the background is not). *Etcetera* also extends to narrative and structure. *Hamlet* is a five-act exploration of *etcetera*—of what it means to be an extension, an aftermath. Trevor Ross suggests that we

> consider literary canons as lists as much as standards of excellence. Among the earliest forms of writing, lists are the simplest of texts, held together by the most arbitrary of syntaxes, the page they are written on.... Canons are similarly the

[5] For excellent theoretical accounts of the list, relevant to *&c/etcetera*, see Umberto Eco, *The Infinity of Lists* (London: MacLehose Press, 2009); Tony Thwaites, 'Currency Exchanges: The Postmodern, Vattimo, Et Cetera, among Other Things (Et Cetera)', *Postmodern Culture: An Electronic Journal of Interdisciplinary Criticism* 7:2 (1977), DOI:101.1353/pmc.1997.0015; and Robert Belknap, *The List* (New Haven, CT: Yale University Press, 2004).

[6] Eco, *The Infinity of Lists*, p. 8.   [7] Eco, *The Infinity of Lists*, p. 9.

[8] Quoted by Mary Beard in 'The Infinity of Lists by Umberto Eco', *Guardian*, 12 December. Available at: <https://www.theguardian.com/books/2009/dec/12/umberto-eco-lists-book-review>. However, in his introduction, Eco simply says that one needs to work a little harder to find visual *etceteras*.

products and signs of literate cultures, texts of texts in effect...[and] are wholly arbitrary as syntactical units.[9]

Ross' view of canon is kin to Eco's view of the *Iliad*, with its swing between completion and definiteness. It is this balancing act that characterizes the *etcetera*. Like the blank of Chapter 1, *etcetera* both pauses and moves forward, it links and it separates; it takes the reader, in Geoffrey Hartman's paradox, 'beyond, though not away from'.[10]

I have been spelling out *etcetera* in full, although to do so is to obliterate a crucial part of its visual identity. Like the blank, early modern *etcetera*s come in many forms—*et cetera, etcetera, Etcetera, et-cetera, et caetera, etcaetera, & cetera, &c*—and can be pronounced with a hard or a soft 'c'. The word(s) have a long history, as the Latin form suggests; it was frequently used by Romans in lists.[11] The abbreviated form with the ampersand has a two-stage development. The first comes via Cicero's secretary, Tiro. In the first century BCE Tiro was instructed by Cicero, who had been impressed by Greek shorthand, to devise a system of Latin abbreviations.[12] Tironian shorthand comprised a vast number of glyphs but only its abbreviation for *et* remains in use today; depending on the font or hand, it varies in shape from a right angle through a hoop to a curl. The second stage, which was the innovation of the first century, was to speed up cursive with a ligature: the *et* symbol and the *c* were joined. (We have since lost all other Roman cursive ligatures.) Some italic fonts show clearly the visual etymology in the union of *et* and *c*: *&c* and *&c*. The *&c* varies strikingly in appearance between roman, black letter, and italics.[13]

Because in this book I am interested in the visual page, we need to ponder the effect of the abbreviated form: *&c*. The abbreviation is artistic in ways the two separate words are not: it provides 'a canvas for calligraphers and

---

[9] Trevor Ross, *The Making of the English Literary Canon from the Middle Ages to the Late 18th Century* (Montreal and Kingston: McGill-Queen's University Press, 1998), p. 23.

[10] Geoffrey Hartman, quoted in Christopher Ricks, 'William Wordsworth 1', in Christopher Ricks, *The Force of Poetry* (Oxford: Oxford University Press, 1997), pp. 89–116 (p. 91).

[11] Thus Cicero: 'slave, animal, furniture, food etc.'. See Cicero, *Topica*, in *Cicero: De Inventione, De Optimo Genere Oratorum, Topica*, trans. H. M. Hubbell (Cambridge, MA: Harvard University Press, 1993), p. 399.

[12] Keith Houston, *Shady Characters* (London: Penguin, 2013). Given that Latin did not separate words with spaces, abbreviations of words and phrases would significantly enhance the clarity of the reading experience. Ancient Greek also shortens *kai ta loipá* to *ktl*.

[13] The word *ampersand* is of nineteenth-century origin. Houston gives entertaining folk etymologies before describing the abbreviation's stand-alone place at the end of alphabet: 'and *per se* and' (*Shady Characters*, p. 76).

typographers to indulge their artistic proclivities'.[14] This is particularly clear in its italic form (in early modern texts its Latin status is regularly indicated with italics), which Houston views as 'much more playful'.[15] Like the blank space, the '&c' is much more eye-catching than the two words it represents. The ampersand is curvaceous and cursive, standing tall over its companion *c*. When italicized, it inclines tipsily forward or leans rakishly backwards. It kicks its legs in the air, a laughing, open, carnivalesque figure. Furthermore, '&c' is much more frequent in early modern printing than *etcetera* and its titillating typography calls our attention, inviting us to dwell on it in the way the blank beckons. As such, the visual aspect is part of its 'meaning'.[16]

Throughout the rest of this chapter, I use the hyphenated compound *&c-etcetera* in italics when I am talking generally about this rhetorical and typographical feature in early modern texts. When I discuss specific examples, my quotations will use the form in which it appears in the source text. Let us now consider *&c-etcetera*'s contributions to a textual history of the blank.

Part I: Interpretations

Bawdy and the Body

Substitutes

I begin with Chaucer's *Manciple's Tale*. Here is the crow telling the husband that he has been cuckolded:

> ...blered is thyn ye
> With oon of litel reputacioun,
> Noght worth to thee, as in comparisoun,
> The montance of a gnat, so moote I thryve!
> For on thy bed thy wyf I saugh hym swyve.[17]

In the earliest surviving copy, the early fifteenth-century Hengwrt manuscript, the scribe (Adam Pinkhurst) replaces the word *swyve* with '&c': 'For on

---

[14] Houston, *Shady Characters*, p. 75.   [15] Houston, *Shady Characters*, p. 69.

[16] Lighting departments sell lamps in the shape of an ampersand. Brand names such as Moët & Chandon and the V&A depend on it. The logo of the poetry website <divedapper.com> (the name comes from the waterfowl in *Venus and Adonis*) places the ampersand at the centre of its graphic design. It is an artistic letter.

[17] *The Manciple's Tale*, ll. 252–5, in *The Riverside Chaucer*, ed. Larry Benson (Boston, MA: Houghton Mifflin Co., 1987).

thy bed thy wyf I saugh hym &c.'[18] Whether '&c' is actually voiced or is just the mark(er) of what is omitted is not clear; what is clear is that by Shakespeare's day *&c-etcetera* has become not just a substitute for a bawdy verb or noun but a bawdy term itself. It now means the thing it previously only stood in for.

Mercutio in Q1 *Romeo and Juliet* (1597) describes Romeo's lovesick behaviour:

> Now will he sit under a Medler tree,
> And wish his Mistris were that kinde of fruite,
> As maides call Medlers when they laugh alone.
> Ah *Romeo* that she were, ah that she were
> An open *Et caetera*, thou a poprin Peare.   (D1r)

This is part of the play's unPetrarchan imagery in which Romeo imagines having sex (and paying for sex) with Rosaline (1.1.214). Here Mercutio envisages Romeo's imaginings. Not sighing under a sycamore (the pun on 'sick amour' was common in courtly love) as Benvolio first encountered him (1.1.121), Mercutio imagines Romeo under a medlar tree. The ripe medlar fruit looked provocatively like the female vagina, although its slang name 'open arse' indicated the other opening with which it was associated.[19]

In Q1, the relation between Romeo's phallic fruit and Rosaline's open '*Et-caetera*' is clear: the shape of the poperin pear (from Poperinghe in Flanders) resembled a penis and scrotum; '*Et caetera*' denotes the vagina. Q2 (1599) reads 'O *Romeo* that she were, ô that she were / An open, or thou a Poprin Peare' (D1v), a reading followed by the Folio of 1623. Arden 2 reads 'O Romeo, that she were, O that she were / An open-arse and thou a poperin pear!' (2.1.37–8); Arden 3 is the same without the conjunction: 'O Romeo, that she were, O that she were / An open-arse, thou a poperin pear!' (2.1.37–8).[20] Both the Ardens' 'open-arse' is an emendation based on the likelihood that Q2's 'open, or' is a compositorial misreading, a misunderstanding, or a legitimate alternative spelling. The question is whether the Q1 reading saw itself as a blank ('*Et caetera*' as a deletion of open-arse) or as a substitute term ('*Et caetera*' as an acceptable bawdy epithet). Both Gibbons and Weis explain Q1's reading as a euphemistic replacement (2.1.38n).

---

[18] Hengwrt 154 (Peniarth 392D), National Library of Wales, Aberystwyth.

[19] For the vaginal reading, see Peter J. Smith, 'Medlers and Meddlers: John Davies' *The Scourge of Folly* and Another Look at Rosaline's Open *Et Cetera*', *Cahiers Elisabéthains* 46 (1994), 71–3; for the anal interpretation, see Jonathan Goldberg, '*Romeo and Juliet*'s Open R's', in *Romeo and Juliet: William Shakespeare*, ed. R. S. White (Basingstoke: Palgrave, 2001), pp. 194–212.

[20] *Romeo and Juliet*, ed. Brian Gibbons (Arden 2; London: A. & C. Black, 1990) and *Romeo and Juliet*, ed. René Weis (Arden 3; London: Bloomsbury, 2012).

Similar bawdy meanings are activated in *2 Henry IV* (Q1600) when Pistol uses '& caetera' as a noun: 'come we to ful points here? and are & caeteraes, no things?' (D4v). The punning here is complex: not only are '& caetera' and 'no thing' both sexual slang for the same body part, the vagina, but 'no things' also activates the literal meaning of nothing.[21] A rough paraphrase might read: 'Am I aroused and vaginas not available?'

Robert Greene's *Farewell to Folly* (1591) offers an illuminating angle on the question of whether *&c-etcetera* is an acceptable euphemism. A group of Florentine courtiers, debating in a Lyly-influenced style, embark on an anatomy of folly. Lady Katherine is critical of male folly. Pressed by her brother, she explains:

> [Y]ou can not heare the name of folly but you must frowne, not that you mislike of it in thought, but that deckt in your *pontificalibus* [in the full flow of your finery] a man may shape *& cetera* by your shadow: *Benedetto* let not this bitter blow fall to the ground, but told hir hir Latine was verie bad and worst placst: for *& cetera* was no word of art for a foole, but in deede he did remember Parrats spake not what they thinke, but what they are taught [.]   (B4r)

It is hard to decode Lady Katherine's phrase 'a man may shape *& cetera* by your shadow' word by word but it is clear from her brother's reprimand that she has committed a linguistic faux pas. Although she has realized correctly that '& cetera' is a substitute term, she thinks it is an innocent synonym, a 'word of art' (presumably something like '*pontificalibus*') for a fool. Benedetto points out that '& cetera' does not mean what she thinks it means and accuses her of repeating what she has heard without any understanding. What was a stand-in for a bad word has now become a bad word itself.

This is not uncommon in the history of rude words, but the process by which the acceptable substitute (the euphemism) comes to mean the same as the thing for which it substitutes is complex. An Elizabethan would say 'sir-reverence' (meaning 'saving your reverence', 'pardon me') apologetically before mentioning something that might offend—for example, something scatological; 'sirreverence' then came to mean excrement. In Robert Greene's coney-catching pamphlet, *The Black Book's Messenger* (1592), a man rises in the middle of the night to make 'a double use of his Chamber pot' (D2v). There is an intruder at the window (a 'curber'—the hook of the coney-catch) and the contents of the chamber pot are emptied over the curber's head with the

---

[21] Gordon Williams, *A Dictionary of Sexual Language and Imagery in Shakespearean and Stuart Literature*, 3 vols (London: Athlone Press, 1994).

result that 'his face, his head, and his necke, were all besmeared with the soft sirreverence, so as hee stunke worse than a Jakes Farmer [someone who tends privies]' (D3r).[22] The passage twice holds the body at linguistic arm's length, first with the euphemistic description of the man's dual excretory needs and then with the substitute noun for the substance with which the curber is smeared.

Euphemism offers an acceptable substitute for an unacceptable term, as its etymology indicates: < Greek εὐφημισμός, < εὐφημίζειν 'to speak fair' (*OED* 1). Euphemism minimizes offensive impact; 'sirreverence' can be said whereas 'shit' cannot. Is this also true of *&c-etcetera*? Benedetto's correction of Katherine initially implies that she has said a bad word although what is at fault is simply her understanding. But although *&c-etcetera* is sayable, it is clearly not sayable by ladies like Katherine. As a noun in its own right, *&c-etcetera*—like sexual slang generally, and like euphemism—both conceals and draws attention to the thing it conceals. Therefore, to know what it conceals is, for a lady, a breach of decorum (in the way that Henrietta Bowdler could not be credited with expurgating Shakespeare: making Shakespeare's vocabulary acceptable means that she understands the unacceptable terminology).[23] Greene's joke is that Lady Katherine is so far from any acquaintance with sexual and scatological vocabulary that she does not know what *&c-etcetera* means. She violates decorum because of innocence rather than knowledge.

In William Haughton's city comedy *Englishmen for my Money* (*c*.1598, Q1616), one of the heroines fears that 'if I fall sicke, / Theyle say, the *French (et-cetera)* infected mee' (D2r). The line is interesting typographically. If *&c-etcetera* is an indication of omission, a textual substitute for a more explicit term, so too are round brackets.[24] In Florio's translation of *The Essays of Montaigne* (1603), Florio uses round brackets to indicate omission of a scatological term in Montaigne: 'A (   ) in the fooles teeth'.[25] In Chapter 1 we saw that John

---

[22] See Melissa Mohr, *Holy Shit: A Brief History of Swearing* (Oxford: Oxford University Press, 2013), p. 159.

[23] For other Victorian examples of this female dilemma, see Mohr, *Holy Shit*, pp. 173–226.

[24] See John Lennard, *'But I Digress': The Exploitation of Parentheses in English Printed Verse* (Oxford: Oxford University Press, 1991).

[25] Book I, p. 117, L5r. The original (Bordeaux, 1580) uses the French word/phrase for 'turd' ('bren du fat'). The phrase occurs in the essay 'Comme nous pleurons & rions d'une mesme chose', in a passage that Montaigne revised (adding the passage 'bren du fat'); he also expanded the essay considerably. The revised version is in the Rouen edition (no date), whose title page advertises it as an annotated, corrected, and expanded version (British Library copy, shelfmark 840s.ccc.2). William H. Hamlin explores Florio's sanitisations of Montaigne's vocabulary in *Montaigne's English Journey: Reading the Essays in Shakespeare's Day* (Oxford: Oxford University Press, 2014), p. 262, n.30 (cf. p. 262, n.29).

Marston's *The Malcontent* (1604) uses round brackets for a sexual insult (the missing word must rhyme with 'locks' in the second line):

Mal. The Dutchman for a drunkard.
Maq. The Dane for golden lockes:
Mal. The Irishman for Usquebath [Usquebaugh].
Maq. The Frenchman for the (   ) [H1r][26]

But unlike the Florio and Marston examples, Haughton's text gives us two marks of omission: the '*et-cetera*' and the brackets. It is typographically tautologous.[27]

As a slang term, *&c-etcetera* is not confined to sex. John Eliot uses it for another bodily function, defecation. His *Ortho-Epia Gallica* (1593) is a French-language phrase book, offering dialogues for travellers. It works like modern phrase books, with its dialogues arranged in parallel columns of French, phonetic pronunciation, and English translation, depicting situations for which a visitor might need vocabulary.[28] One such dialogue takes place in the apothecary's shop, where a customer asks about a medicine, 'Fait il restraindre ou laischer?' ('Does it constipate or loosen?'). Enthusiastically affirming the latter verb, the apothecary replies: 'Oy, oy & tres bien chier' ('Yes, yes, it makes you shit really well') (L3v). Eliot's English translation is coyer than mine: '*Yea, yea, and make a man go to the &c. lustily*' (L4v). Florio also uses '&c' for defecation:

---

[26] I quote from the version expanded by Webster in 1604 (STC 17481), although the passage (but not the pagination) is the same in the first edition of the same year, STC 17479.

[27] Lloyd Kermode suggests that the parentheses in *Englishmen for my Money* indicate typographically the bandy-legged gesture the actor made at this stage to indicate the effects of syphilis (*Englishmen for my Money*, in *Three Renaissance Usury Plays*, ed. Lloyd Kermode (Revels; Manchester: Manchester University Press, 2009), 2.1.98–9n). This is also John Lennard's explanation for the brackets in *The Malcontent*—— 'a graphic joke, not censorship' ('*But I Digress*', p. 40). In these cases, then, the typography embodies stage action for the reader's benefit. It is not unknown for typography to embody stage business as we saw in the Introduction (e.g. in *The Miseries of Enforced Marriage* (1607) where the dash provides for stage action). Parentheses are used to indicate stage business in the 1600 quarto of Ben Jonson's *Every Man Out* (1600) when Fastidious Brisk puffs tobacco, indicated repeatedly as '(*Tab.*)'. The stage business is explicitly spelled out in the subsequent dialogue: 'Troth sweet Ladie I shall (*Tab.*) be prepar'd to giue you thankes for those thanks, and (*Tab.*) studie more officious and obsequious regards (*Tab.*) to your faire beauties: (*Tab.*) mend the pipe boy'; Maciente comments (presumably aside), 'I ne're knew Tabacco taken as a *parenthesis* before' (K4v; see Lennard, '*But I Digress*', p. 49).

[28] The volume is genuinely useful but it is also partly parodic of Florio's exhaustive dialogues, *First Fruits* (1578). The copy of *Ortho-Epia* in the Huntington Library has been treated seriously and marked up by Gabriel Harvey (with one cross-reference to Florio). Harvey's annotations stop once the book reaches the illustrative situations; he is clearly more interested in the translation theory of the introductory section.

'*Aesope* that famous man, saw his Maister pisse as he was walking: What (saide he) must wee not &c. when wee are running?'[29]

Florio again makes a joke whose punchline is less obvious to modern than to early modern ears when, in *First Fruits* (1578), he poses this question: 'tel me also one thing that I wil aske you, if you can, What is the heavyest thing?' The reply is: 'the heaviest thing that is, as I beleeve, is one Etcetera, for if it take you by the way [unexpectedly], you cannot cary it farre [further], one foot more' (Kii'). The answer to the riddle is likely scatological. If something catches the traveller short ('take you by the way'), you cannot go on ('not cary it farre, one foot more').

Let us return to the sexual meanings of *&c-etcetera*. In Randall Cotgrave's *Dictionarie* (1611), Cotgrave translates 'vit' (penis) as '*A mans yard; a beasts pizle*' (Mmmmii'). He uses a different euphemism for the female noun, 'vitte': '*A womans &c.*' (Mmmmii'). He defines '*con*' (cunt) as '*A woman's &c*' (T3v). Glossing 'Bergamasque', he translates his illustrative phrase 'Il boucle sa feme à la Bergamasque' with '*As the* (Italian) *Bergamasks, who buckle up their wives &c. with a device like a trusse for a burst man*' (Kir). 'Wives' here is not an object but the possessive (singular or plural) of the object *&c-etcetera*; a 'burst man' is a man with a hernia. In other words: an Italian buckles up his wife's *&c-etcetera* with a gadget like a hernia support.[30]

This might make us revisit the Florio riddle and suspect a sexual answer: if the traveller is overcome by lust, he can't carry on. In view of the implied disbursement by evacuation ('you cannot carry it farre'), this seems less likely a meaning than the scatological. Although ejaculation is technically evacuation, it is less associated with weight ('carry it') than is excrement. Nonetheless, it is worth pausing over the sexual possibility, given that one *&c-etcetera* in Florio's *Dictionary* occurs in a sexual context.[31]

Apron-Strings

In the *Dictionary* Florio extends his definition of 'Fica' (fig): '*Also used for a womans quaint,* [cunt] *and women in Italie use it as an othe to sweare by as our*

---

[29] Montaigne, *The Essays*, trans. Florio, Kkk4v. Both Montaigne's original and Florio's translation lack the syntactical balance on which the punchline depends: if we piss when we walk, must we therefore shit when we run? 'Esope ce grand homme vid son maistre qui pissoit en se promenant, Quoy donq, fit-il, nous faudra-il chier en courant'; Montaigne, *Essais* (1580), Book IV, p. 281.

[30] Usually this slang term is given its full form when it refers to the female pudenda. I assume that the two-column dictionary format here occasions the reduction to '&c', even though space is not an issue.

[31] There may be more, but since one cannot do a digital search for '&c', this chapter is limited to examples I have observed in reading.

Englishwomen say by my apron-strings, &c.'.[32] 'By my apron-strings' does not occur as an oath in any extant early modern text but it is clear that the reference is sexual, with 'apron-strings' being a euphemism for the female pudenda. Thus the English oath is the exact equivalent of the Italian.

We can trace the way 'apron-strings' developed its sexual meaning—not because apron-strings are a piece of female attire (although that may be part of it) but because they function as a pair and so are seen as analogous to legs. In his *Owl's Almanac* (1618) Dekker describes how Libra followed Virgo 'as fast as her apron-strings would give her leave' and 'being almost breathlesse with taking such wide strides, in short language laide open her case, and courted *Jove* for revenge' (D1r). The reference to 'wide strides' explains the metaphor of 'fast' apron-strings, resulting in breathlessness. It is then a short step (literally) from female legs to what Mercutio describes as 'the demesnes that there adjacent lie' (*Romeo and Juliet* 2.1.20).

Many early modern references to apron-strings occur in narratives of cuckoldry or in images of sexual intimacy. In the anonymous *Penniless Parliament of Threadbare Poets* (1608) we read of a man who played 'fast and loose with womens Apron-stringes' (C1r). Marston's *Histriomastix* (1610) lists fictitious play titles and their genres, identifying *The Widow's Apron Strings* as a 'nocturnall' (this follows on from the genres of '*Tragedy*', '*Comedie*', '*Infernall*', and '*[P]astorall*'). The sexual joke in the fictitious title is tripled: widows were conventionally seen as lusty, 'nocturnall' indicates a night-time entertainment, and apron-strings complete the sexual allusion. Similarly, in Dekker's *Owl's Almanac*, the apron-string bawdy is extended by the pun on 'case' (*OED* case *n.* 2, 8. *slang* The vagina), where Dekker not only explains the licentious meaning in the text ('in short language laide open her case') but emphasizes it in the marginal note: '*A good Lawyer, she opens her owne case*' (D1r). In Middleton's *The Changeling* (*c.*1622, Q1653) Lollio is as close to his mistress as 'her Apron strings' (G4r) while the boy in Tomkis' *Lingua* (1607) boasts that he can go anywhere: 'in the Court your Gentlewomen hang me at their Apron strings' (C4v). The intimacy becomes part of misogynist aphorism: 'excuses are never further off women then their apron strings' where the ostensible textile meaning is overlaid with the sexual in this cuckold tale.[33]

---

[32] John Florio, *Queen Anna's New World of Words, or Dictionarie of the Italian and English Tongues* (1611), Q3v, p. 186.

[33] Anon, *Westward for Smelts* (1620), B3r. Williams' *Dictionary of Sexual Language and Imagery* has no entry for apron-strings but notes that the apron 'often carries sexual significance' (vol. I, p. 32).

To return to Florio's *Dictionary* entry for *fica*, then: it is impossible to dismiss the '&c' at the end of 'by my apron-strings, &c' as a benign example of continuation. In fact, in this context, it is hard to know what continuation would mean grammatically. While it might indicate that 'by my apron-strings' is only one illustrative example of a female oath and that there are other similar ones ('&c'), given that 'apron-strings' is an exact equivalent of 'by my fig', it would be an unnecessary extension.

Even so, the abbreviation requires comment, given that Florio's sentence does not require it: he has already completed his example ('*as our Englishwomen say by my apron-strings*') and '&c' has no additional 'meaning'. It often occurs in this way, underlining a bawdy allusion, like a textual wink. One can see it as a forerunner of the 'Nudge, nudge, wink, wink' sketch from *Monty Python* where double-entendres are followed by the catch phrase 'grin grin, wink, wink, nudge nudge, say no more'; '&c' and 'say no more' are direct equivalents.[34] When *&c-etcetera* functions as a noun, it tends to be spelled out in full, as in John Ford's *The Lady's Trial* (1639): 'Money is trash, and Ladies are *et caetera*'s' (D2r). Thus *&c-etcetera* nuances its meaning according to context or grammar (scatological or sexual, noun or verb) but is regularly used to cover up body parts and activities.

Women's &-caeteras

The female pudendum is the most frequent noun-use, as we saw in *1 Henry IV* and *The Lady's Trial*. By the eighteenth century, poetry is full of men touching women's *&c-etceteras*. In an anonymous poem ascribed (unsurprisingly) to Rochester we read:

> In a dark silent shady grove
> Fit for the delights of love
> As on *Corinna's* Breast I panting lay
> My right hand playing with *& caetera*.
>
> A thousand Words and amorous Kisses
> Prepar'd us both for more substantial Blisses;
> And thus the hasty moments slipt away
> Lost in the Transport of *& caetera*.[35]

The poem has four verses, each of which concludes with a sexual pun on '*& caetera*'. The titillating anonymous *Fable of the Cat Turned into a Woman* does the

---

[34] *Monty Python's Flying Circus*, series 1, episode 3, and repeated in different contexts in subsequent films.

[35] *Poems on Affairs of State from the Reign of K. James the First to this Present Year 1703*, vol. II (London, 1703), p. 271. Vieth does not include the poem in his edition of Rochester. See *The Complete Poems of John Wilmot, Earl of Rochester*, ed. David M. Vieth (New Haven, CT: Yale University Press, 2002).

same. The *Fable* is an eighteenth-century variant of the Pygmalion myth in which a beau falls in love with his cat ('Puss'). He woos her, composes sonnets to her, and 'Oft they'd little Scuffles / She'd scratch his Eyes and tear his Ruffles'. The poem concludes with Puss's metamorphosis into a woman. Her transformation is described (paws become hands and fur becomes skin) but some anatomical features 'in proper places stay / As Eye-brows, Head, *Et caetera*'.[36]

The sexual slang continues into the twentieth century. e. e. cummings' anti-war poem, 'my sweet old etcetera' (1926), rings the changes on *etcetera/et cetera* throughout, before concluding with an unmistakably sexual reference to 'Etcetera'. The poem contrasts the narrow domesticity of the soldier's sister, knitting, and the naivety of his parents' patriotic belief in the glories of war, with his own experiential reality:

> Isabel created hundreds
> (and
> hundreds) of socks not to
> mention fleaproof earwarmers
> etcetera wristers etcetera my
> mother hoped that
>
> I would die etcetera
> bravely of course my father used
> to become hoarse talking about how it was
> a privilege

The speaker's experience is different. The *etcetera*s quoted in the next part of the poem denote not useless overproduction or conventional pieties but the traumatic closing down of emotions and realities until the opening up of the optative and life-sustaining specificity of Etcetera:

> meanwhile my
> self etcetera lay quietly
> in the deep mud et
> cetera
> (dreaming
> et
>   cetera, of
> Your smile
> eyes knees and of your Etcetera)[37]

---

[36] *Miscellaneous Poems*, ed. Matthew Concaner (London, 1724), p. 368.
[37] *e. e. cummings: Complete Poems, 1904–1962*, ed. George J. Firmage (New York: W. W. Norton & Co., 1994).

The opening up is literal: 'etcetera' becomes 'et cetera'; then 'et cetera' is split across stanzas before the words are unified in a single capitalized form. cummings graphically represents emotional separation and union by manipulating the movement of 'et cetera' on the printed page. The vaginal *etcetera* has the opposite effect on a character in Edward Albee's radio play, *Listening* (1976), who expresses disgust at the female sexual body: 'I rose from the hot moist suffocating center of your etcetera'.[38]

Rape

Sexual slang has a darker side when *&c-etcetera* refers not just to a female body part but to rape of the female body. In James Calfhill's *An Answer to the Treatise of the Cross* (1565), a Catholic priest hides in a hollow image in his church to scrutinize female parishioners; when he sees one he likes, he instructs her to return to the church and spend the night in solitary penance. He himself returns by a secret tunnel and, from inside the hollow image, scares the woman into believing that she is being addressed by God: 'sodainly by a vice [device], all the candels goe out, he playeth the priest. &c. Thus in conclusion, many honest mens wives, many worshipful & honorable, under colour of holynesse, & by mere hipocrisie, were instrumentes many yeares, to satisfy the pleasure of the filthy priest' (LLii^v–LLiii^r). Calfhill uses sexual abuse by a priest as part of an anti-Catholic narrative. In the prose novella by George Gascoigne, *The Adventures of Master F. J.* mentioned in Chapter 1 (published in 1573 in *A Hundreth Sundrie Flowres*), we encounter rape in a wooing situation. F. J. forces his sexual attentions on Elinor 'and bare hir up with such a violence against the bolster, that before shee could prepare the warde [assume a defensive position], he thrust hir through both hands, and &c. wher by the Dame swoning for feare, was constreyned (for a time) to abandon hir body to the enemies curtesie' (Iivr). The conjunction that prefaces the '&c' makes clear that this is more than a trailing off. The conjunction propels us forward and the '&c' stops us short. The two work in conjunction, as it were, emphasizing the force of '&c' as indicating a narrative over which the writer is drawing a veil. I will return to Gascoigne's many uses of '*&c*' in this novella at the end of this chapter but here I want simply to draw attention to the way *&c-etcetera* stands in not just for a sexual word but for a larger sexual narrative. It no longer embodies a

---

[38] *Counting the Ways and Listening: Two Plays by Edward Albee* (New York: Athenaum, 1977). Cited in Philip C. Kolin, 'Bawdy Uses of Et Cetera', *American Speech* 58:1 (1983), 75–8.

single body part or a sexual act or an omission but all three: a sexual action inflicted on a body, too terrible to be articulated.

Interruption and Breaking Off

The Dash

Early modern *&c-etcetera* is also used typographically to signal an interruption in the text: it is pressed into service as a prototype of the dash. The em-dash is not yet a fully-fledged punctuation mark but it starts to become so in the early seventeenth century. (As we saw in the Introduction, Henry Woudhuysen traces this new fashion in punctuation to Ben Jonson.)[39] Before then, there had been two ways of indicating interruption via punctuation. One was to omit any kind of terminal punctuation. In *A Knack to Know a Knave* (anonymous, 1594) Philarchus is criticized and condemned by his father:

> Here I doe banish thee from *Englands* bounds,
> And never to
> King: There stay, now let me speake the rest: (C1v)

In the anonymous *Wit of a Woman* (1604) Gianetta interrupts Erinta:

> Erinta: Maister Doctor would faine bee a patient in steede of a Phisitian, and
>   I must bee his cure: but
> Gianetta: And what say you *Lodovica*?   (F1r)

An alternative way of indicating interruption was with a period. In Heywood's *How to Choose a Good Wife from a Bad* (1602), Aminadab asks the young school-boy Pipkin 'how many parsons are there?' and Pipkin starts to enumerate them ('*I*le tell you as many as *I* know, if youle give me leave to reckon them'). He begins: 'The Parson of *Fanchurch*, the Parson of *Pancridge*, and the Parson of.' (G2r). Pipkin's reckoning is clearly interrupted as Young Arthur says: 'Well sir about your businesse'. Although Pipkin's incomplete 'Parson of.' may look like an invitation for a specific name, the joke throughout the scene is that Pipkin is being questioned about his school grammar lessons (like William Page in the near-contemporary *Merry Wives of Windsor*, Folio-text version) and answers with non-grammatical examples. Asked about cases, he answers with lute cases and cap cases, and asked about grammatical persons, he

[39] See Henry R. Woudhuysen, 'The Dash—A Short but Quite Dramatic Account', paper delivered at 'The Jacobean Printed Book', Queen Mary College, University of London, September 2004.

answers with homonymic parsons. Justifiably impatient, Young Arthur interrupts and puts a stop to the sequence (literally).

Hotspur dies in the quarto of *1 Henry IV* (1598) as follows:

> no Percy thou art dust
> And food for.
> Prince: For wormes, brave Percy.   (K3r)

By 1623, in the Folio, we have the following:

> No *Percy,* thou art dust
> And food for ------------
> Prince: For Wormes, brave *Percy.*   (TLN 3050–2)

This is still not the em-dash: as Woudhuysen explains (and facsimiles show) a cut-down brass rule for framing the Folio columns has been recycled, here as elsewhere in the Folio, as a long dash. Obviously, there was a perceived need for a punctuation mark that was not yet in existence.

Some of the more baffling uses of *&c-etcetera* make sense if we think of them as a forerunner of the dash. This is clearest when we have two versions of a text for comparison. The first quarto of John Day's *Isle of Gulls* (1606, STC 6413) offers the following dialogue (I have not modernized speech prefixes here):

> *man,* yes Mopsa.
> *mop.* plain *Mop[sa].* I might be madam *Mopsa* in your mouth, goodman *&c.*
> whers Dorus.   (H1v)

'*&c*' here might invite improvised expansion of titles for 'goodman'. But it does not appear in the next quarto (1633, STC 6414), where '*&c*' is replaced by a punctuation mark—the dash: 'Plaine *Mopsa,* I might bee Madam *Mopsa* in your mouth, goodman — where's *Dorus?*' (H1v).

Two stage directions in George Gascoigne's *Glass of Government* (1575) make this meaning of *&c-etcetera* clear. A speech by the courtesan, Lamia, is printed between two stage directions whose phrasing makes clear what the '&c' at the end of her speech means.

> *She beginneth to tell a tale.*
> Lamia: Syr I have not power to rejecte your curtesie,
> You shall understand then, that being &c.
> *Pandarina interrupteth her.*   (E4v)

The verbs in the two stage directions are unusually specific and this makes them supremely helpful. Gascoigne's '*beginneth*' in the first direction indicates that the ensuing sentence is incomplete and the '*interrupteth*' in the second explains why. We could not hope for a clearer gloss on '&c'.

Interruption is also clearly indicated by the dialogue in Marston's *Dutch Courtesan* (1605). Beatrice is reading a poem to her sister:

> Purest lips soft banks of blisses
> Selfe alone, deserving kisses
> O give me leave to, &c.
> Crispinella: Pish sister *Beatrice*, pree thee readde no more, my stomacke alate stands against kissing extreamly.   (D3r)

At first sight, the '&c' looks like an invitation to continue reading a familiar poem (we shall see several examples of this use later in the chapter) but Crispinella's line shows that this is not the correct interpretation. She halts the reading and gives a reason for why she wishes to hear no more. Here '&c' is the mark of interruption, as it is in Q2 *Hamlet* (1604/5) when Polonius starts to read out a love letter from Hamlet to Ophelia that his daughter has given him:

> now gather and surmise,
>
> *To the Celestiall and my soules Idoll, the most beautified* Ophelia, *that's an ill phrase, a vile phrase, beautified is a vile phrase, but you shall heare: thus in her excellent white bos-ome, these &c.*
>
> Queen: Came this from *Hamlet* to her?
>
> Polonius: Good Maddam stay awhile, I will be faithfull,   (E4r)

Polonius is obviously interrupted by Gertrude ('Came this from *Hamlet* to her?') because he responds by requesting her patience while he completes the letter: 'Good Maddam stay awhile, I will be faithfull'.[40]

How editors treat Gertrude's interruption of Polonius varies. Those who use Q2 as their copytext retain its '&c.' (sometimes expanding to 'etc.').[41] Their retention of the '&c' is usually linked to their interpretation of it: Harold Jenkins explains the '&c' as 'a substitute for some formal phrase ... common in letter-headings' (2.2.112n); Ann Thompson and Neil Taylor view it as Polonius' abbreviation of Hamlet's commendation in the superscription (2.2.110–11n).

---

[40] The Folio version offers a full stop rather than '&c' after 'these' (TLN 1141); Q1 condenses the sequence so that Corambis (the Polonius figure) reads without interruption.

[41] *Hamlet* in Shakespeare, *The Riverside Shakespeare*, gen. ed. G. Blakemore Evans (1974; Boston, MA: Houghton Mifflin, rev. 1997), 2.2.113; *Hamlet*, ed. Edward Hubler (Signet Classic; New York: New American Library, 1963), 2.2.113; *Hamlet*, ed. Harold Jenkins (Arden 2; London: Methuen, 1982), 2.2.112; *Hamlet (Q2)*, ed. Ann Thompson and Neil Taylor (Arden 3; London: Thomson Learning, 2006), 2.2.111.

The Royal Shakespeare Company (RSC) edition (edited by Jonathan Bate and Eric Rasmussen), which uses F as its copytext, and the Arden 3 edition of F (edited by Thompson and Taylor), both realize that the Folio punctuation is not fit for purpose, and replace its terminal stop with a dash.[42] Those such as the Norton–Oxford that retain F's full stop make no sense: a punctuation mark indicating interruption is required.[43] One typographical way of embodying that interruption was '&c', developed later into the dash.

Aposiopesis

Why '&c' should function as a punctuation mark that indicates separation, interruption, or incompletion is explained by an otherwise odd line in Dekker's *Shoemaker's Holiday* (1600). Roland Lacy, in disguise as Hans, has premarital nerves as he anticipates the possible emotional alternatives of wedlock:

> This is the morning that must make us two happy, or miserable, therefore if
> you   (H3v)

The line lacks terminal punctuation and is clearly interrupted by Simon Eyre, who dismisses the bridegroom's nerves: 'Away with these iffes and ands Hauns, and these *et caeteraes*' (H3v). *Et caetera* here is a noun—which is presumably why it is spelt out in full. (In the examples quoted there is a tendency to distinguish between '&c' and 'etcetera', with 'etcetera' being a noun for Mercutio, Pistol, and Greene's Lady Katherine.) But a noun meaning what? There is evidence to suggest that Simon Eyre is using '*et caetera*' as a rhetorical term; '*et caetera*' is a synonym for the figure known as aposiopesis (a breaking off).

The clearest example comes from the eighteenth century when Joseph Addison writes 'I have by me an elaborate Treatise on the *Aposiopesis* call'd an "Et caetera".'[44] He explains that it is 'a Figure much used by some learned Authors'. Addison understands *&c-etcetera* as a 'Figure'—a figure of speech, a part of rhetoric. Early modern writers are not so explicit. Addison cites Coke's *Institutes* where Coke praises Littleton's oratory: 'Certaine it is that there is never a period nor (for the most part) a word, nor an (&c.) but affordeth excellent

---

[42] *Hamlet*, in Shakespeare, *The Complete Works*, ed. Jonathan Bate and Eric Rasmussen (New York: Random House, 2007), 2.2.116; *Hamlet (F)*, ed. Ann Thompson and Neil Taylor (Arden 3; London: Thomson Learning, 2006), 2.2.111.

[43] *The Norton Shakespeare based on the Oxford Edition*, ed. Stephen Greenblatt, Walter Cohen, Suzanne Gossett, Jean E. Howard, Katherine Eisaman Maus, and Gordon McMullan (New York: W. W. Norton, 1997).

[44] 'Dum Tacent, Clamant', *Tatler* 133, 11–14 February 1710, pp. 92–6 (p. 95).

matter of learning'.[45] Thus '&c' could indicate aposiopesis here but this is not entirely clear. What is clear is that Renaissance discussions of aposiopesis give examples which invariably conclude with '&c'. William Est in 1613 writes:

> O that thou haddest even knowne at the least in this thy day, those things which belong unto thy peace! &c

> ...These words expresse a passion proceeding of sorrow, which if it be vehement, is wont to interrupt and cut off some words which should make up and finish the speech:

> This figure is usuall among the *Rhetoritians* and is called in Greeke *Aposiopesis*, where something is left out, which must be understood for the perfecting of the speech.[46]

It is logical to assume that '&c' here means that the quotation continues (Est repeats the quotation in a shorter form a few lines on, stopping at 'even knowne', where the '&c' must indicate the continuation of the quotation). There are many examples where '&c' (always in this typographical form) does mean 'carry on this quotation', usually in quotations from foreign languages or school books, as in this double example from Thomas Tomkis' *Lingua* (1607):

> Phantastes: Pish, pish this is a speech with no action, lets here TERENCE, *quid igitur faciam. &c.* [So what am I to do?]

> Communis Sensis: *Quid igitur faciam? non eam ne nunc quidem cum accusor ultro?* [So what am I to do? Am I not to go, not even now, when she summons me of her own accord?]

> Phantastes: Phy, phy, phy, no more action, lend me your baies, doe it thus. *Quid igitur. &c.*   (H3r)

The lines from Terence are familiar enough to be continued after the opening '*quid igitur faciam. &c*' and Communis Sensis picks up the prompt; the '&c' in Phantastes' response refers us to the expansion as given in the previous line. But when Est uses '&c' to introduce an example of aposiopesis, the conventional use of '&c' to indicate that a quotation continues may not apply.

So we have '&c' as a punctuation mark for separation and as a rhetorical term for interruption; aposiopesis then becomes a metaphor for these items in action as we see in the anonymous play, *Every Woman in her Humour* (1609). Flavia reminds the audience it is unusual to have a female prologue, explaining

---

[45] Edward Coke, *The First Part of the Institutes of the Laws of England* (1628), ¶¶2r. The Early English Books Online (EEBO) copy is defective here (cf. footnote 102).

[46] William Est, *The Trial of True Tears* (1613), C5r.

that she has been sent on stage because 'men are apt to take kindelye any kinde thing at a womans hand' (A2r). Pursuing the associations of 'kindelye', she continues: 'wee poore soules are but too kinde, if we be kindely intreated, [if the audience is nice to the actors] marry otherwise, there I make my *Aposiopesis* [I will exit]'. 'Aposiopesis' is used to indicate breaking off—here, breaking off by leaving the stage.

As befits a book on *The Rhetoric of the Page*, Chapter 1 looked at the blank as a textual form of the rhetorical term *apophasis*, something that calls attention to what it professes to conceal. In this chapter, I suggest that '&c' is associated with the rhetorical term *aposiopesis*. It separates, it breaks off, it interrupts. In fact, in one of its functions, as a noun, it is not just associated with aposiopesis but is a synonym for aposiopesis, as we saw in *The Shoemaker's Holiday*.

If *etcetera* indicates aposiopesis, we need to question the assumption that Brutus reads out 'Shall Rome &c' when he receives the conspirators' letter in Shakespeare's *Julius Caesar*. Let us consider letters and formulae before returning to aposiopesis.

Letters and Formulae

The full passage in the Folio text of *Julius Caesar* reads:

> *Opens the Letter, and reades.*
> *Brutus thou sleep'st; awake, and see thy selfe:*
> *Shall Rome, &c. speake, strike, redresse.*
> *Brutus, thou sleep'st: awake.*
> Such instigations have beene often dropt,
> Where I have tooke them vp:
> *Shall Rome, &c.* Thus must I piece it out:
> Shall Rome stand under one mans awe?   (TLN 664–71)

It is not unusual to find '&c' in letters but it is always used for formulae. This is true of letters in plays as well as real epistles. It occurs at the beginning of letters for formulaic compliments to the addressee, as in Marlowe's *Edward II* (1594):

> To you my lord of Gloster from *Lewne.*
> *Edward.* Reade.
>   *Spencer reades the letter.*
> My dutie to your honor promised, &c. *I* haue according to instructions [...]
>   (H2r)

It also occurs at the beginning of letters (private and public) with regard to the addressee's titles. The epistolary dedication to Richard Barnfield's *Cynthia* (1595) begins with the heading 'To the Right Honorable, and most noble-minded Lorde, William Stanley, Earle of Darby, &c.' (A2r), after which the body of the epistle begins. The formula extends even to play titles: 'The two tragicall Dis*courses of mighty* Tamburlaine, the Scythian Shepheard. &c.'.[47] It occurs regularly at the end of letters for valedictory formulae. In the 1598 version of Jonson's *Every Man in his Humour* (Q1601), Bobadilla tells how he put off some gentlemen importuning him to attend their fencing match; his rejection is couched in the elaborately polite style of a letter, complete with the valedictory '&c': 'well, I tolde them that to come to a publique schoole they should pardon me, it was opposite to my humor but if so they would attend me at my lodging, I protested to do them what right or favour I could, as I was a gentleman. &c.' (I1v).

We also find copious examples of '*&c*' in legal documents from the medieval period onwards, again as a substitute for formulaic phrases.[48] But Brutus' abbreviation is not an obvious substitute for something formulaic. He seems puzzled by the phrase; he goes back to it and says he must 'piece it out'. The metaphor comes from clothing: to 'piece' is to add fabric to a garment. In *Merry Wives of Windsor*, the jealous husband Ford fulminates about his friend's trust in his wife: 'he pieces out his wive's [*sic*] inclination [he adds to his wife's adulterous desire], he gives her folly motion and advantage [encouragement and opportunity]' (3.2.34–5).[49]

---

[47] Christopher Marlowe, *Tamburlaine the Great* (1590), A3r.

[48] This is why Smallwood and Wells' explanation of '*et caeteras*' in *The Shoemaker's Holiday* must be wrong. Their footnote at scene xvii, line 5 glosses Simon Eyre's '*et caeteras*' as 'uncertainties (probably by parody of legal phraseology)'. While '*&c-etcetera*' is indeed used in legal documents—it persisted until the advent of the photocopier, in fact—it usually appears as a substitute for formulae (in other words, the opposite of 'uncertainties'). See Thomas Dekker, *The Shoemaker's Holiday*, ed. Robert Smallwood and Stanley Wells (Revels; Manchester: Manchester University Press, 1999). We also find formulaic uses of '&c' in medieval letters and legal documents, and in liturgical contexts ('To which glorious Son of God, *&c.*'; 'To whom, etc'; '*Blessed be God, even the Father, &c.*'). See *The Sermons of John Donne*, ed. George R. Potter and Evelyn M. Simpson (Los Angeles: University of California Press, 1957), pp. 224, 225, 273 (sermons 9, 11, 12). The Oration which concludes Pageant 5 of *The Magnificent Entertainment* (1604) ends with 'The Almighty etc.' (see Malcolm Smuts' footnote at line 2044 of the text in *Thomas Middleton: The Collected Works*, ed. Gary Taylor and John Lavagnino with Macd. P. Jackson, John Jowett, Valerie Wayne, and Adrian Weiss (Oxford: Clarendon Press, 2007)). Ramie Targoff pointed out to me that in his *Survey of London* (1598) John Stow uses '*&c*' to indicate formulae in Catholic prayers on tombs—phrases that can no longer be said, such as 'Orate pro nobis'. Middleton does the same thing critically with 'and so forth' in *Papistomastix* (1606): 'this is my bodie and so forth' (O3v, O4v). Here in Stow and Middleton the *&c-etcetera* formula works as religious censorship/self-censorship. Of all the Elizabethan writers, Stow appears to use '&c' most frequently and in the most varied ways, with Robert Burton in *Anatomy of Melancholy* a close second.

[49] Ford sees marriage in terms of textile ownership. Convinced of his wife's infidelity, he laments: 'There's a hole made in your best coat, Master Ford. This 'tis to be married! This 'tis to have linen and buck-baskets!' (3.4.141–3).

Shakespeare's later use of '&c' in the letter from Bertram to Helena in *All's Well that Ends Well* does not assist in interpreting the example from *Julius Caesar*. In Act 3, Helena receives a letter from her husband, detailing the apparently impossible conditions she must fulfil before she can claim him as her husband. Helena read this rejection letter aloud to her mother-in-law:

> Looke on his Letter Madam, here's my Pasport.
> *When thou canst get the Ring upon my finger, which never shall come off, and shew mee a childe begotten of thy bodie, that I am father too, then call me husband: but in such a (then) I write a Never.*
> This is a dreadfull sentence.   (TLN 1459–64)

She manages to fulfil these conditions and retains the letter to confront Bertram with it in quasi-legal fashion in Act 5:

> And looke you, heeres your letter: this it says,
>   When from my finger you can get this Ring,
>   And is by me with childe, &c. This is done,
>   Will you be mine now you are doubly wonne?   (TLN 3049–52)

In 1987 the Oxford editors suggested that '&c' is Shakespeare's reminder to himself to check the wording he had used previously in Act 3.[50] More plausible is Tiffany Stern's reminder that letters are props; as such, they are not written into the actor's Part ('anything . . . that could reduce the learning load was very useful'). Detached from the text, they live in the props store.[51] In this context, '&c' in an actor's Part may be an instruction to the actor meaning 'read out the property letter you read out previously'.

An '&c' analogous to Brutus' occurs in Samuel Harsnett's *A Declaration of Egregious Popish Impostures* (1603). This book, commissioned by the Anglican Church, was the result of an enquiry into the public exorcisms performed by Catholic priests in the 1580s.[52] Harsnett includes witness statements by the possessed. At first glance, the quotation that follows seems to be another example of the bawdy '*&c*' as Sara Williams describes how the devil worked his way up her body: '*Sometime* (she saith) *they lodged the devill in her toe, sometime in her legge, sometime in her knee. Sometime, &c.*' (I4r). But when Harsnett continues

[50] Stanley Wells and Gary Taylor, with John Jowett and William Montgomery, *William Shakespeare: A Textual Companion* (Oxford: Clarendon Press, 1987), p. 499 (5.3.315/2833n).

[51] Tiffany Stern, *Making Shakespeare: From Stage to Page* (London: Routledge, 2004), pp. 113–18 (p. 117).

[52] Shakespeare consulted it for Mad Tom's lists of devil's names in *King Lear*. The British Library website has an excellent account of the book, with illustrative digitalized pages. See <https://www.bl.uk/collection-items/a-declaration-of-egregious-popish-impostures-by-samuel-harsnett-1603>.

'Let the devil, and his holy charmers make up the rest', the implication is that he has broken off. (We saw a parallel example at the start of this chapter in a similarly anti-Catholic sexual context with James Calfhill's *Answer to the Treatise of the Cross*.) In fact, '*&c*' can have it both ways here: it fills in euphemistically and breaks off aposiopetically, like the duality of the example from Haughton's *Englishmen for my Money* where the round brackets indicate something missing and the '*et-cetera*' does too, even as '*et-cetera*', the mark of omission, fills up the gap in the brackets, the mark of omission.

This varied evidence suggests that, on balance of probability, '&c' in Brutus' letter indicates incompletion or self-interruption. This need not mean that he does not say it aloud—Elizabethans may have understood '&c' as a way of underlining that the speaker was breaking off. The challenge for modern actors who voice '&c' is to avoid the cavalier tone that we associate with '&c' as a mark of laziness. At Shakespeare's Globe in 2014 (*Julius Caesar*, dir. Dominic Dromgoole) Tom McKay's Brutus was briskly decisive in 'piecing it out'. In Gregory Doran's RSC production in 2012 Joseph Paterson gave a wry smile at the obviousness of how to complete the sentence. Richard Pasco's Brutus for the BBC in 1979 (dir. Herbert Wise) swallowed hard on '&c'. In the 1953 MFM film (dir. Joseph Mankiewicz), James Mason's voice had a nervous question mark over '&c': the stakes of (mis)interpretation are high.

Aposiopesis (Continued)

Non-epistolary examples in which *&c-etcetera* seems to mean a dash or its rhetorical equivalent, aposiopesis, appear in many plays. It is instructive to compare two moments of self-interruption in Marlowe's *Dr Faustus*. In both A- and B-texts Faustus responds sceptically to Mephistopheles' statement that they are in hell by citing as contrary evidence their familiar academic activities; however, the exact phrasing in A and B differs. In the A-text (1604) Faustus says, 'How? now in hell? nay. and this be hell, Ile willingly be damnd here: what walking, disputing, &c. But leaving off this, let me have a wife' (C2r). In the B-text (1616) he says, 'Nay, and this be hell, I'le willingly be damn'd. / What sleeping, eating, walking and disputing? / But leaving this, let me have a wife' (C1r). Michael Keefer says that the A-text replaces 'two of the four participles that appear in B by "*et cetera*"'.[53] Keefer thinks the compositor in

[53] Michael Keefer, 'The A and B Texts of Marlowe's *Doctor Faustus*', *Papers of the Bibliographical Society of America* 100:2 (2006), 227–57 (255). In Christopher Marlowe, *Doctor Faustus: A 1604-Version*, ed. Michael Keefer (Peterborough, ON.: Broadview Press, 1991) Keefer considers 'the vagueness of "&c."' as evidence of imperfect memory on the part of a reporter (p. lxix).

the A-text saw sexual implications in the line (Faustus immediately justifies his request for a wife on the grounds that he is 'wanton and lascivious') and so '&c' functions as a censorious substitute for bawdy. But in both texts it is clear that Faustus breaks off his list of participles ('but leaving this') and each text has a different way of signalling that self-interruption.

Only two modern editions indicate the interruption, and both use ellipses to do so (one deletes the '&c'). In David Ormerod and Christopher Wortham's edition of the A-text we read: 'What? walking, disputing . . . But leaving off this, let me have a wife' (ll. 586–7).[54] Roma Gill's revised New Mermaids edition of 1989, based on the A-text, retains the '&c' (as 'etc') and then adds ellipses: 'What, walking, disputing, etc . . . But leaving off this' (scene 5, ll. 139–40).[55] In Ben Jonson's *Poetaster* (1602), Act 5, scene 2 ends with Virgil's recitation, describing the monster Rumour: '*As covetous she is of Tales, and Lies, / As prodigall of Truth: This Monster, &c.*' (K4r). Realizing that this is an interruption, Alexander Leggatt comments, 'On the words "this monster", the monster actually appears'.[56] M. J. Kidnie's edition represents the moment as follows:

> As covetous she is of tales and lies,
> As prodigal of truth. This monster ---
> [*He is interrupted by shouting off-stage*].   (5.2.96–7)

Editorially acknowledging that the speech is interrupted, she silently replaces the '*&c.*' with a dash and adds a stage direction indicating why.[57]

A comic example of '&c.' as interruption comes in the third of the *Parnassus* plays, *2 Return from Parnassus* (*c.*1601, Q1606).[58] These three plays were written by Cambridge undergraduates at St John's College at the end of the sixteenth century; they are structured as a series of episodic skits, a forerunner of the Cambridge Footlights, showcasing aspects of the characters' lives as students

---

[54] Christopher Marlowe, *Dr Faustus: The A-Text*, ed. David Ormerod and Christopher Wortham (Nedlands: University of Western Australia Press, 1985), ll. 586–7. However, the editors' justification is that 'part of the line may be missing' although they are correct that '&c' is 'best rendered in modern typography by three dots' (587n).

[55] Christopher Marlowe, *Dr Faustus: Based on the A-Text*, ed. Roma Gill (London: A. & C. Black, 1989). Mark Thornton Burnett presents both A- and B-texts in his Everyman edition, as do Bevington and Rasmussen in their Revels edition, following the respective copy texts closely. See Christopher Marlowe, *The Complete Plays*, ed. Mark Thornton Burnett (London: J. M. Dent, 1999).

[56] Alexander Leggatt, *Ben Jonson: His Vision and Art* (London: Methuen, 1981), p. 99.

[57] Ben Jonson, *Poetaster*, in *The Devil is an Ass and Other Plays*, ed. M. J. Kidnie (Oxford: Oxford University Press, 2000).

[58] The manuscript is dated 1601; the play reached print in 1606. I quote from the printed quarto version. For the MS see Anon, *2 Return from Parnassus; or the Scourge of Simony*, Folger Shakespeare Library MS V.a. 355.

and beyond. Act 4, scene 3 of the last play shows the two unemployed graduates, Studioso and Philomusus, auditioning as actors with William Kemp and Richard Burbage. Burbage first expresses interest in Studioso as a potential Hieronimo:

> I thinke your voice would serve for *Hieronimo*, observe how I act it and then imitate mee.

The quarto here misses out a line, present in the manuscript version, in which Burbage demonstrates: 'Who calls Jeronimo from his naked bedd.' The omission is clearly accidental since Burbage has said he would demonstrate. The quarto then continues as follows:

> Studioso: Who call[s] *Hieronimo* from his naked bed?
> And &c.[59]
> Burbage: You will do well after a while. (G3v)

Kemp now turns his attention to Philomusus:

> Now for you, methinkes you should belong to my tuition, and your face me thinkes would be good for a foolish Mayre or a foolish justice of the peace: marke me -------

Instead of Burbage's short sample from a familiar play, Kemp launches into a long and syntactically balanced piece of rhetoric:

> Forasmuch as there be two states of a common wealth, the one of peace, the other of tranquility: two states of warre, the one of discord, the other of dissention: two states of an incorporation, the one of the Aldermen, the other of the Brethren: two states of magistrates, the one of governing, the other of bearing rule [...]

It continues like this for over a dozen lines. It is an impossibly long speech for Philomusus to attempt, but he is not given much of an opportunity:

> Philomusus: Forasmuch as there be. &c.
> Kemp: [T]hou wilt do well in time.   G3v–G4r)

On both occasions, the '&c' may indicate the students' continuation of the demonstrated speech. As we have seen, there is plenty of precedent for this, the standard, meaning of '&c', and given that the MS duplicates the '&c' ('Forasmuch as there bee 2 states &c. &c.'), it could simply mean 'continue'. But the comedy of the scene may derive from the fact that both amateurs are

---

[59] The MS reads 'Who calls &c'.

interrupted after the briefest of moments, the professionals' interruptions functioning as the Elizabethan equivalent of today's directors' brutal stereotype call, 'Next'.

A related example occurs in the MS version of this play when Academico says: 'I pray you S^r &c.' (Act 2, scene 5). In this episode he repeatedly asks a stranger for money but the unphilanthropic stranger pretends to misunderstand what Academico wants, offering him hunting advice in response; Academico keeps trying to get back on topic but is repeatedly interrupted by the unwanted advice. When the play reaches print in 1606, the quarto removes the '&c' and represents the line as: 'I pray you sir ——' (D2r). At least, this is how J. B. Leishman's collation represents the quarto, and his note reads:

> *I pray you sir* ——] So 1606; MS 'I pray you S^r &c.'[60]

In fact, Q reads: 'I pray you sir.' (D2r). Leishman has, I think rightly, but without comment, interpreted the line as being interrupted. The compositor, like the compositors of Q *1 Henry IV* and *How to Choose a Good Wife from a Bad* that we looked at earlier in this chapter, used a full stop to represent interruption.

A revised passage in Act 5 of Chapman's *The Widow's Tears* (1612) has a stray '*&c.*' in the dialogue. Lysander hesitates to disinter the corpse with the crowbar that he has brought into the tomb for the purpose, whereupon Cynthia snatches it and offers to act: 'No, Ile not lose the glorie ant [on't]. This hand, *&c.*' (K3v). Editors have long noticed the textual disruption (Cynthia three lines later refers to her hand) and the assumption is that the first reference is an imperfectly deleted cut. If it is, the ensuing dialogue is inadequately rewritten. Possibly the '*&c.*' indicates an interruption: Cynthia vows to 'assay [her] strength', boasting 'Ile doot my selfe'. Lysander says he cannot simply be a spectator and requests the crowbar. Cynthia protests ('No, Ile not lose the glorie ant. This hand, *&c.*') but Lysander insists, interrupting her at 'hand' with 'Pray thee sweet, let it not bee said the savage act was thine; deliver me the engine'. Cynthia continues to resist, maintaining that the crowbar is 'in a fitter hand', hence the later reference.

The association of '&c' with interruption may explain appearances of '&c' in the margins of MSS when lines have been inserted: it indicates an interruption, or resumption after an interruption, the marginal equivalent of a caret mark. In Middleton's *The Second Maiden's Tragedy* the mark '*&cS*' appears at the end of speeches which are to be inserted; the '*&cS*' indicates the lines which

---

[60] Anon, *The Three Parnassus Plays*, ed. J. B. Leishman (London: Nicholson & Watson, 1949), p. 276.

overlap (see lines 239ff, 249, 642).[61] We find similar in the manuscript of *Sir Thomas More*: see, for example, lines 9 and 26 in Addition V in W. W. Greg's transcript for the Malone Society.[62] Daniel Wakelin notes the use of *&c-etcetera* in medieval manuscripts to indicate abridgement and excerption: the scribe of Ezekiel and the Minor Prophets 'marks the places where he skips by trailing off with *et cetera*'.[63] So '&c' can be helpful in understanding authorial revision—which is itself a process of interruption and resumption.

Continuation

If *&c-etcetera* means 'break off', 'don't complete', it also means its opposite: 'fill in', 'continue'. This is the use of *&c-etcetera* with which we are most familiar, and it is the primary definition offered by the *OED*: '*1.* As phrase... indicating that the statement refers not only to the things enumerated but to others which may be inferred from analogy'. Thus, John Eliot's list of comestibles in *Ortho-Epia Gallica* (1593) fulfils the *OED* criterion: '*plentie of bread, of flesh, cheese, butter, salt fish, wilde fowle, &c.*' (Kiir). So too does Phallax's announcement in Whetstone's *Promos and Cassandra* (1578) that he has 'an office got, / By force wherof every lycence, warrant, pattent, pasport, / Leace, fyne, fee, *et cetera*, pas and repas, through *Phallax* hands' (Civ).[64] In Greene's *James IV* (1598) Slipper posts an advertisement, boasting that as a serving man he can '*sleep with the soundest, eate with the hungriest, work with the sickest, lye with the lowedest, face with the proudest, &c. that can wait in a Gentlemans chamber*' (C2r). John Manningham's description of the counterfeit letter in *Twelfth Night* as 'prescribing his [Malvolio's] gesture in smilinge, his apparaile, /&c/' may also come into this category although, since Manningham collapses two aspects of the prescribed apparel (the colour yellow and the cross garters) into one general noun ('apparaile'), there is, arguably, nothing more to come in this list.[65]

---

[61] Thomas Middleton, *The Second Maiden's Tragedy*, ed. W. W. Greg (Malone Society Reprints; Oxford: Oxford University Press, 1909).

[62] Anthony Munday and Henry Chettle, revised by Henry Chettle, Thomas Dekker, Thomas Heywood, and William Shakespeare, *Sir Thomas More*, ed. W. W. Greg (Malone Society Reprints; Oxford: Oxford University Press, 1911).

[63] Daniel Wakelin, 'When Scribes Won't Write: Gaps in Middle English Books', *Studies in the Age of Chaucer* 36 (2014), 249–78 (257).

[64] Note that the examples from *Ortho-Epia* and *Promos and Cassandra* are both in lists but vary in morphology.

[65] See 2 February 1602, British Library Harley MS 5353, fol. 12v.

Lists are a characteristic of stage directions where early modern playtexts offer abundant examples of the things that *&c-etcetera* invites us to supply. I attempt to subdivide them in the section 'Stage Directions'.

Stage Directions

Characters

We can supply characters. '*Enter John of Gaunt sicke, with the duke of Yorke, &c.*' (Shakespeare, *Richard II*, 1597, C3r); 'Ent. Lord Maior &c' (Munday et al., *Thomas More*, l. 252); '*Enter the King, Lancaster, Mortimer senior, Mortimer junior, Edmund Earle of Kent, Guie Earle of Warwicke, &c*' (Marlowe, *Edward II*, 1594, A3r); '*Exit Cardinal, &c*' (Middleton, *Women Beware Women*, 1657, M8r); '*Enter . . . After her the duke whispering with Medice, Lasso with Bassiolo, &c*' (Chapman, *The Gentleman Usher*, 1606, C3r); '*Enter the Duches with her daughters, Demetrius, Lisander. &c.*' (Day, *The Isle of Gulls*, 1606, C3v); '*Enter the Lord de Averne / and his Lady etc*' (Heywood, *The Captives*, ll. 869–71).[66] An untypical variant appears in Q1 *Othello* (1622): '*Enter* Desdemona, Iago, *and the rest.*' (C3v).

Props

We can supply props. '*Enter Ariell, loaden with glistering apparell, &c.*' (*The Tempest*, TLN 1868); '*Enter* Merry *and* Rachel *to execution with Officers with Halberdes, the Hangman with a lather [ladder]. &c.*' (Robert Yarington, *Two Lamentable Tragedies*, 1601, K1v); '*Enter six Saxon Kings ghosts crown'd, with Scepters in their hands, &c.*' (Richard Brome, *The Queen's Exchange*, 1657, D4v). Oddly, the editor of *The Queen's Exchange* for the online Brome edition, Marion O'Connor, changes '*&c.*' to '*and so forth*'.[67]

Sound

We can supply sound. In John Day's *The Isle of Gulls* (1606) a marginal direction instructs: '*Musicke of Bels &c.*' (E2r); Dekker's *Shoemaker's Holiday* (1600) invites the extension of human sound: '*They passe over the stage, Rafe falles in amongest them, Firke and the rest cry farewel, &c. and so Exeunt.*' (C1r).

---

[66] Thomas Heywood, *The Captives*, ed. Arthur Brown (Malone Society Reprints; Oxford: Oxford University Press, 1953). In this last example, note that the imprecision of 'etc' has been clarified but not eliminated by a second ink (possibly a second hand) which adds 'Dennis and others', thereby solving one ambiguity while creating another.

[67] See: <http://www.hrionline.ac.uk/brome>.

Action

We can supply action. Ben Jonson's *The Devil is an Ass* (1631) instructs: '*He growes more familiar in his Court-ship. playes with her paps, kisseth her hands, &c.*' (R1r).[68] George Peele's *The Love of King David and Fair Bethsabe* (1599) gives direction for a scene of mourning: '*They use all solemnities together, and sing, &c.*' (D3v). Note that '*&c*' has become almost a technical term in stage directions. An earlier, variant form of saying 'carry on with these actions' is seen in Skelton's *Magnyfycence* (*c.*1520) where the stage direction instructs: 'Hic ingrediatur Foly quesiendo crema et faciendo multum feriendo tabulas et similia' ('Here let Folly enter, shaking a bauble and making a commotion, beating on tables *and suchlike*' (no date, C4v, my emphasis)).

Costume

We can supply costume. Thomas Tomkis' *Lingua* (1607) explains how both Tragedy and Comedy are to be dressed: '*next him Tragedus appareled in black velvet, faire buskins, a fauchion &c. then Comedus in a light colloured greene taffata robe, silke stockings, pumps, gloves. &c.*' (H2v). Sometimes directions to supply costume are combined with directions to supply action: '*Enter Lysander like a Souldier disguisde at all parts, a halfe Pike, gorget, &c. he discovers the Tombe, lookes in and wonders, &c.*' (George Chapman, *The Widow's Tears*, 1612, H1v). A later occurrence of '*&c*' in this play is not quite so clear. Like Lysander before him, Ero is instructed to open the tomb and respond to what he sees inside: '*Ero opens, and hee sees her head layd on the coffin, &c.*' (K1v). What part of the sentence does '&c.' extend? Does it extend the verb 'sees', requiring additional actions and responses from Ero? Or does it govern the coffin, implying that there is more than just Cynthia's head lying on the coffin?

Song

We can supply the continuation of dialogue or the repetition of song. The jailer's daughter, singing one of her mad songs, exits as follows in the 1634 Q of *Two Noble Kinsmen*: '*Sings. I will be true, my stars, my fate, &c. Exit. Daugh.*' (K2v).[69] She is almost certainly to continue singing a known song rather than

---

[68] The gradation here is intriguing: familiarity increases from breasts to hands rather than vice versa.

[69] Lois Potter suggests that the songs the Daughter sings in her mad scenes may be too bawdy to have their lines printed in full; see *Two Noble Kinsmen*, ed. Potter, 4.1.104n.

improvise some musical continuation; we see this indication of familiarity repeatedly in snatches of songs.[70]

In Jonson's *Poetaster* (1602) Gallus asks Crispinus 'What is't you sing Sir?' to which Crispinus responds '*If I freely may discover, &c.* Sir, I'le sing that' (D1r). The italics suggest that he illustrates his proposed song by singing it, and the '*&c*' (also in italics) invites him to continue the known material. The return to roman indicates the return to speech.[71] A similar sequence of song-followed-by-speech occurs in the anonymous *Every Woman in her Humour* (1609) where Philautus, prevailed upon to sing, protests 'My love can sing no other song but still complaines I did her. &c. I beseech your Majestie to let me goe' (H2r). In *Patient Grissil* (1603) Babulo enters 'singing with a boy after him' and the line following the stage direction combines speech and song, with '&c' indicating musical continuation:

> *Bab.* Boy how sits my rapier: *la fol la fol. &c.*   (D4v)

The second drinking song in Dekker's *Shoemaker's Holiday* has an '&c' in each of its refrains; it concludes with an additional instruction. I begin the song at the refrain after the first verse:

> Trowle the boll, the jolly Nut-browne boll,
> And here kind mate to thee:
> Let's sing a dirge for Saint Hughes soule,
> And downe it merrily.
>
> Downe a downe, hey downe a downe,
> Hey derie derie down a down, *Close with the tenor boy*:
> Ho well done, to me let come,
> Ring compasse gentle ioy.
> Trowle the boll, the Nut-browne boll,
> And here, kind &c. *as often as there be men to drinke.*

The '&c' in the refrain indicates the repetition of the words while the italicized direction instructs that the repetition of the line be matched to the number of singers available. When the number of men have sung the equivalent number of lines, we are given this conclusion:

> At last when all haue drunke, this verse.
> Cold's the wind, and wet's the raine,

[70] See, for instance, Whetstone, *Promos and Cassandra* (1578), Ciiiv and Civr, where the first occurrence is given in full, the second with '&c'.

[71] This song is loosely based on one of Martial's *Epigrams* and the words are printed just a few lines later (when Crispinus sings them), without any '&c'.

> Saint Hugh be our good speede:
> Ill is the weather that bringeth no gaine,
> Nor helpes good hearts in neede.   (A4r)[72]

The Folio text of *Twelfth Night* indicates repeated lines in Feste's final song:

> *Clowne sings.*
> *When that I was and a little tine* [tiny] *boy,*
> *with hey, ho, the winde and the raine:*
> *A foolish thing was but a toy,*
> *for the raine it raineth every day.*
>
> *But when I came to mans estate,*
> *with hey ho, &c.*
> *Gainst Knaves and Theeves men shut their gate*
> *for the raine, &c.*
>
> *But when I came alas to wive*
> *with hey ho, &c.*
> *By swaggering could I never thrive,*
> *for the raine, &c.*   (TLN 2559–71)

The abbreviations continue for all five verses: this is obviously typographic-ally efficient, saving the compositor repetitive typesetting labour. The same happens with Desdemona's willow song in F *Othello*, where the line '*Sing Willough, Willough, Willough*' is subsequently given, three times, as '*Sing Willough, &c.*' (TLN 3014–25). Editors today tend to copy this shorthand. But in an era of electronic typesetting there seems no practical reason to continue the abbreviation and one important aesthetic reason not to: it denies the reader the acoustic experience and pleasure afforded an audience—the pleasure of repetition. Poems and songs with repeated refrains are aurally hypnotic. The eye deserves to experience this as well as the ear. The RSC Shakespeare edi-tion, edited by Bate and Rasmussen, is inconsistent in its treatment of '&c.': Desdemona's '*Sing Willough, &c.*' is expanded to 'Sing willow, willow, willow' (4.3) whereas Feste's '*with hey ho, &c.*' and '*for the raine, &c.*' is left abbreviated. The Riverside edition is inconsistent in an identical way. Bevington's edition, however, expands both abbreviations, as does the New Oxford Shakespeare.[73]

---

[72] A similar direction for an appropriate but undetermined amount of repetition, but without the '&c', occurs in the interlude by Ulpian Fulwell, *Like Will to Like* (after 1568?): 'Hee may sing this as oft as hee thinketh good' (D4r).

[73] Shakespeare, *The Complete Works of Shakespeare*, ed. David Bevington, 4th edn (New York: Longman, 1997); Shakespeare, *The Complete Works: Modern Critical Edition*, ed. Gary Taylor, John Jowett, Terri Bourus, and Gabriel Egan (Oxford: Oxford University Press, 2016).

Improvisation

In stage directions, '&c' indicates structured or sanctioned improvisation. In *Patient Grissil* (1603) repeated dialogue occurs in the same sequence as repeated song where an exhortation to the singing workmen, 'Worke apace, apace, apace, apace' is, on its second appearance, presented as 'Worke apace, apace, &c.' (B1r). Invited repetition or continuation need not be of material from within the text—'&c' can be an indication to continue known material such as proverbs. In *Wily Beguiled* (1606) we are told that Gripe 'gapes after golde, / And still relies upon the olde sayd Saw; / *Si nihil attuleris &c*' (C3r). In Jonson's *The Devil is an Ass* (1631) Fitdottrel has (or rather, pretends to have) a mad fit: 'Yellow, yellow, yellow, yellow, &c.' (Y3v). Extending his ravings is logical as, confined to bed, he clutches the bedcovers, shakes and quivers, resists interference, and accompanies his actions with mad repetition. More surprising is Jonson's acoustic choreography in the same scene: '*Ha, ha, ha, ha, ha, ha, ha, ha, &c.*' (Y3r). The incongruous authorial permission here simply signals that the actor may laugh for as long as he feels appropriate: something one feels falls within an actor's decision-making powers. Coordinating the length of dialogue with stage business is indicated in the combination of '&c' and stage direction in Robert Wilson's *The Cobbler's Prophecy* (1594) where the speech and action are those of a madwoman:

> Ile looke in thy purse by and by:
> And if thou have any money in it,
> wele drinke the Divell dry, Divell dry, &c.
> *Here she runnes about the stage snatching at everie thing shee sees.*   (A4v)

These examples blur the borderline between simple repetition and improvisation. Several stage directions use '&c.' to invite the actor to supply his own dialogue or noise—that is, to improvise. In *Guy, Earl of Warwick* (1661) the Clown discovers the sleeping Rainborn and decides to wake him:

> [T]herefore I'le wake him sure, Whoop whow, *&c.*
>   *He Hollowes in his Ear.*   (E2v)[74]

In *The Honest Lawyer* by S. S. (1616), Bromley calls for sack and ekes out his line with some mutterings: 'Giue's some Sacke, I say: mun tut, &c.' (I2r). Neither

---

[74] B. J., *The Tragical History, Admirable Atchievments and Various Events of Guy Earl of Warwick*. The play was first published in 1661 but is of earlier composition. Estimates range from early 1590s to the 1620s; see Helen Moore, introduction to Malone Society Reprint, vol. 170 (Manchester: Manchester University Press, 2006), pp. xiii–xxv.

he nor anyone else has used this phrase before so it is not a catchphrase. It is the sole occurrence of the phrase between 1550 and 1650 on Early English Books Online (EEBO).

In Dekker's *Patient Grissil*, Babulo enters carrying a baby whom he proceeds to soothe. The '&c' indicates that he repeats the phrase 'dance mine own child' (dance = dandle; *OED* v. 6b):

> Hush, hush, hush, hush, and I daunce mine own childe and I dance mine owne childe, &c: ha ha, whoop olde Master, so ho ho, looke heere, and I dance mine own childe, &c: heere's sixteene pence a weeke, and sixteene pence a weeke, eight groates, sope and candle, I met her in Osier grove, crying hush, hush, hush, hush: I thought it had been some begger woman, because of her pitcher, for you know they beare such houshold stuffe, to put drinke and porrage together, and I dance mine, &c.   (G4r)[75]

In Greene's *James IV* (1598), Act 1 ends with Sir Bartram and Sir Eustace exiting together while in conversation about the beautiful and virtuous Lady Ida (the 'she' of the last line of the extract). Sir Bartram says:

> Guid bony *Dick*, my wife will tel thee more,
> Was never no man in her booke before:
> Be Gad shees blyth, faire lewely, bony, &c.
> *Exeunt.*   (C4r)

The rhyming couplet indicates the end of the scene, and the following line, with its '&c', invites the actors to continue talking to cover their exit.[76]

As well as using '&c' for the jailer's daughter's songs, *Two Noble Kinsmen* (1634) has one '&c' in dialogue, when Arcite pledges Palamon. Arcite has brought food and drink (the stage direction specifies '*Meate, Wine*'; F4v) and invites the weakened Palamon to picnic with him:

> Sit downe, and good now
> No more of these vaine parlies; let us not
> Having our ancient reputation with us
> Make talke for Fooles, and Cowards, To your health, &c.
> *Pal.* Doe.   (F4v)

---

[75] This text has also used '&c' for the refrains of songs on A4v and D4v. All three occurrences are in the part of Babulo, the comic servant (in the first song, others join him); comic roles often capitalize on an actor's improvisatory ability so finding '&c' here should not surprise us.

[76] In Heywood's *2 Edward IV* (1600) we have '*Jockie is led to whipping over the stage, speaking some words, but of no importance*' (L5r). In Greene's *Orlando Furioso* (1594) we have (of song) 'he playes and sings any odde toy' (F4v).

The '&c' here could cover action or it could cover language.

In support of language, we might adduce the moment above from Greene's *James IV*, in which case the '&c' in *Two Noble Kinsmen* could indicate a continuation of the verbal etiquette of pledging. On the other hand, it is hard to know what Palamon means by 'Doe'. He has clearly not responded to Arcite's instruction to 'sit downe' as Arcite has to repeat it after Palamon's 'Doe' ('Pray sit downe then'), nor has he agreed to pledge Arcite: he only agrees to do this four lines later ('Well Sir, Ile pledge you'). One can imagine that the action performed by Arcite on '&c' is a tentative or encouraging raising a goblet to Palamon, awaiting Palamon's approval to pledge him. Lois Potter suggests that the '&c' indicates 'ceremonial pouring and saluting' (3.3.12n). The New Oxford Shakespeare imagines that the stage business is Palamon's, not Arcite's: 'Palamon might uncork the bottle of wine or hand it to Arcite at this moment' (3.3.12n).[77]

Since Palamon was hesitant about drinking (he suspects Arcite of having poisoned the wine), Arcite must first drink to convince his cousin. Palamon clearly drinks seven lines later, after his belated agreement to do so, as Arcite says: 'Drinke a good hearty draught [has Palamon taken a still-suspicious sip?], it breeds good blood man'. Palamon must then drink a second time, presumably a greater quantity, as Arcite asks, 'Doe not you feele it thaw you?'; Palamon, beginning to relax, responds with 'Stay, Ile tell you after a draught or two more' (presumably now drinking more eagerly). The momentum of the scene is obvious and can even be comic as the reluctant but hungry and thirsty Palamon now enthusiastically quaffs. One production described by Lois Potter attached the comedy to the '&c': 'Arcite filled out the *&c.* by a comically melodramatic performance of death by poison, thus rebuking what he saw as unworthy suspicion' (3.3.12n).

The play that shows the greatest scope for improvisation is the university drama *2 Return from Parnassus* where the layout of the manuscript enables us to work out whether expansion or cutting is the cause of the difference in length between the MS version of Act 2, scene 2 (ten lines) and its printed counterpart (thirty-eight lines). The author originally intended the MS scene to conclude after ten lines, writing a right-justified '*Exit*' on the same line as the final line of dialogue. He subsequently deleted the *Exit*, and in the blank horizontal space between the last line of dialogue and the margin, wrote '*&c &c &c &c.*' (see Figure 2.1). Is this an instruction to the actors to continue in the same

---

[77] I am grateful to Rory Loughnane, the New Oxford Shakespeare editor, for helpful correspondence about the theatrical options here.

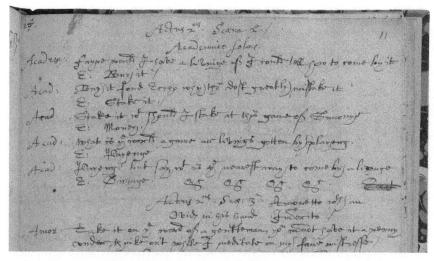

FIGURE 2.1   Anon, *2 Return from Parnassus*, *c.*1606, fol. 11r. Shelfmark Folger
MS V.a.355. Used by permission of the Folger Shakespeare Library.

echoing vein, improvising? Or did the actors improvise of their own accord,
their continuation of the scene then being indicated in the manuscript text
with the four '&c's? What is clear is that the extended scene is brilliant, a rhyming equivalent of a contest in holding your breath (how long can he keep
going?); the concluding echo also dexterously gets the plot back on track,
motivating Academico's exit and commenting on the scene:

> [Academico]:   Wel, if he give me good words, it's more then I have from an *Eccho*.
> Eccho: goe. (C3r)

Part II: Complexities

Complications

So far I have attempted to categorize *&c-etcetera*, offering tidy taxonomies:
censorship/euphemism/bawdy slang; interruptions in the form of a punctuation
mark (the dash) and a rhetorical figure (aposiopesis); invitations to supply
or complete. Such taxonomies are, however, foreign to the early modern
spirit of *&c-etcetera*, where, as we shall see, the Gascoignes of the world can
offer creatively multiple uses of '&c' in a single text. In this section I want to

introduce some early modern instances in which we cannot be sure what
&c-etcetera embodies.

The title page of the collaborative *The Witch of Edmonton* (Q1658) advertises
the play as 'A known true STORY. / Composed into / A TRAGI-COMEDY /
By divers well-esteemed Poets; / *William Rowley, Thomas Dekker, John Ford*,
&c.'. As Brian Vickers remarks wryly, 'Scholars could have done without
the &c.'.[78] In *Palladis Tamia* (1598), Francis Meres praises Shakespeare: 'As the
soule of *Euphorbus* was thought to live in *Pythagoras*: so the sweete wittie
soule of *Ovid* lives in mellifluous & hony-tongued *Shakespeare*, witnes his
Venus and *Adonis*, his *Lucrece*, his sugred Sonnets among his private friends,
&c.' (O01v–2r). Katherine Duncan-Jones suggests that '&c' has allusively
bawdy overtones but it seems too far from its referent ('Sonnets') to function
this way (unless the bawdy is simply a general 'nudge nudge, wink wink').[79]
An '&c' crops up in Jonson's *The Devil is an Ass* as part of a list: 'Such *oyles*; such
tinctures; such *pomatumn's*; / Such *perfumes*; *med'cines*; *quintessences*, &c.' (1616,
Q1631, R2v). It is in the middle of a speech, and the middle of a list; neither
the metre nor the grammar makes obvious how to interpret this occurrence.[80]
Is it an invitation to extemporize? It occurs at the foot of a crammed page: six
speech prefixes and their lines are added to the end of another character's line.
Some material may have been sacrificed and Mark Bland suggests that '&c.'
may be Jonson's way of indicating an omission.[81] (The 1641 reprint retains the
'&c' (E2v) but not its position at the foot of the page.) In Holinshed's account
of the murder of Arden of Faversham, a marginal summary note tells us that
'*Arden's wife visiteth, succoureth, emboldeneth and directeth Black Will, &c. how to
accomplish his bloody purpose*'.[82] Logically the '&c' should refer to Black Will's
accomplice, Shakebag, but grammatically the singular 'his' in the following
phrase works against that. One wonders if 'his' is a misprint for 'hir'? Or
whether the narrow format of the margin necessitated an omission?

---

[78] Brian Vickers, *Shakespeare, Co-Author* (Oxford: Oxford University Press, 2004), p. 15.

[79] Katherine Duncan-Jones (ed.), *Shakespeare's Sonnets* (London: Thomas Nelson, 1997), p. 2.

[80] However, the next line changes the content and structure of the list: 'And such a Mistresse of behaviour' (R3r).

[81] Mark Bland, personal communication. Bland also notes that Jonson complained about the printer of *The Devil is an Ass*. In a letter to his patron, the Earl of Newcastle, Jonson wrote 'My printer and I, shall afford subject enough for a Tragi-Comoedy. For wth his delayes and vexation, I am almost become blind'. In *The Cambridge Works of Ben Jonson*, ed. David Bevington, Martin Butler, and Ian Donaldson (Cambridge: Cambridge University Press, 2012), vol. VI, p. 343.

[82] Raphael Holinshed, *Chronicles of England, Scotland and Ireland* (1587), vol. VI, Kkkkk2r, p. 1063. See: <http://english.nsms.ox.ac.uk/holinshed/texts.php?text1=1587_8333>.

To unpick some of these complications, let us look at a variant of *&c-etcetera*: the phrase 'and so forth'.

'And so forth'

In 1623 Johannes Posselius published his *Dialogues Containing All the Most Useful Words of the Latin Tongue*. The format was unusual and ingenious: the Latin dialogues were provided with a running translation in English after each word or phrase. Thus, in the first dialogue we read as follows (the participant in the dialogue is a boy, whose noun functions as a speech prefix):

> *Puer* the boy [:] *Oculi* the eyes *omnium* of all things *spectant* doe looke in towards *te* thee *Domine* O Lord *&c.* and the rest (or so forth.)   (A3r)

Posselius translates the Latin abbreviation for 'et cetera' literally ('and the rest') and then, in parenthesis, offers a synonym: 'and so forth'.

For early moderns, 'and so forth' seems to have the limited meaning that 'etc.' does for us today: it invites continuation and it concludes lists. We find it in sequences itemized by numbers (*'fower, five, sixe and so forth'*) and by nouns ('plats, spoons, glasses and so forth').[83] In *Twelfth Night* (F 1623) Olivia itemizes her beauty: 'Item two grey eyes, with lids to them: Item, one necke, one chin, & so forth' (TLN 538–9) and the forged letter instructs Malvolio to adopt a 'tricke of singularity', itemized as 'a sad face, a reverend carriage, a slow tongue, in the habite of some Sir of note, and so foorth' (TLN 1594–6). Justice Shallow in *2 Henry IV* (1600) invites Falstaff to his orchard where 'in an arbour we will eate a last yeeres pippen of mine owne graffing, with a dish of car-rawaies and so forth' (K1v–K2r). In *Love's Labour's Lost* (1598), Sir Nathaniel reels off Latin: *'Facile precor gellida, quando pecas omnia sub umbra ruminat*, and so foorth' (E1v). In *Hamlet* (1604) Polonius lists the fictitious pastimes with which Reynaldo is permitted to slander Laertes: 'gaming...or took in's rowse, / There falling out at Tennis, or perchance / I saw him enter such a house of sale, / *Videlizet*, a brothell, or so foorth' (1604, E1v). All of these examples are at the ends of lines or lists. Unlike *&c-etcetera*, which is flexible, multifunctional, and imaginative, *and so forth* is circumscribed and fixed. Among such consistent end-of-list patterning, then, the use of 'and so forth' in Q1 *Hamlet* (1603) stands out as unusual, untypical, unShakespearean: 'Lady will you giue me leaue, and

---

[83] William Ames, *A Fresh Suit against Human Ceremonies in God's Worship* (1633), Ss4v; George Chapman, *May Day* (1611), I2r.

so forth: / To lay my head in your lappe?' (F3r). Given that the copy for Q1 is not generally believed to have come from Shakespeare's pen, this exception merits investigation in terms of Q1's textual transmission.

But my point here is not textual but sexual. We saw earlier how *&c-etcetera* is used as a noun to tarnish women. Women are *etceteras* (whores) as we saw in Ford's *The Lady's Trial* (1639): 'Money is trash, and Ladies are et caetera's' (D2r). In *The Winter's Tale* Shakespeare, uniquely, invents a male sexual noun, turning 'and so forth' into a noun for cuckold. Imagining the gossip about him, the sexually suspicious Leontes soliloquizes:

> Didst perceive it?
> They're here with me already; whisp'ring, rounding:
> Sicilia is a so-forth: 'tis farre gone   (TLN 301–3)

Glossing 'so-forth', Frank Kermode says 'he [Leontes] can't quite bring himself to say cuckold' (1.2.215).[84] John Pitcher's gloss reads 'the king is such and such a thing... because the whisperers daren't say "cuckold" or because he can't bear to say it' (1.2.216n).[85] This substitute for vocalization chimes with all the uses of *&c-etcetera* I have chronicled in this chapter. But 'and so forth' is never used, like 'etcetera', as a noun. In fact, according to EEBO, this is the only use of 'so forth' as a noun between 1580 and 1623, and it is *OED*'s only citation. Shakespeare, it seems, is trying to fashion a masculine equivalent for the female *etcetera*. *Etcetera* has such a specific meaning that Shakespeare can avoid it and adapt it.[86]

Earlier, in *Merchant of Venice* (1600), he had varied it morphologically as a feature of Shylock's linguistic Otherness. Shylock already commits the grammatical solecism of forming plurals of collective nouns with a terminal 's'— 'my moneys and my usances' (1.3.108), 'we would have moneys' (1.3.116), 'moneys is your suit' (1.3.119). But so too does the Athenian usurer in *Timon of Athens* ('Importune him for my moneys', 2.1.16), so this may just be usurer-speak. In *Merry Wives of Windsor* the Welsh Parson Evans talks of 'seven hundred pounds of moneys' (1.1.50–1) so it may, in fact, just be outsider-speak. But to Shylock's unorthodox plural is added an unorthodox variant of 'and so forth'. When he declines Bassanio's invitation to dinner on religious dietary

---

[84] William Shakespeare, *The Winter's Tale*, ed. Frank Kermode (New York: New American Library, 1963).

[85] William Shakespeare, *The Winter's Tale*, ed. John Pitcher (Arden 3; London: Methuen/A. & C. Black, 2010).

[86] This is an appropriate play in which to experiment: the 'so forth', the bit of narrative that doesn't need to be filled in, is a version of the 'wide gap' of time to which the Chorus draws our attention in 4.1.7.

grounds, Shylock first itemizes the things he is prepared to do with Christians: '*I wil buy with you, sell with you, talke with you, walke with you, and so following*' (1600, B2v, my emphasis). Shylock is marked as a non-Venetian outsider, both by religion and by (tiny details of) language.[87]

Thomas Heywood harnesses 'and so forth' for linguistic comedy in *1 Edward IV* (1600) where the citizen, Ralph Josselyn, rarely finishes his sentences, breaking off with 'and so forth':

> Simple though I am, yet I must confesse,
> A mischiefe further off, would, and so forth,
> You know my meaning, things not seene before,
> Are, and so forth, yet in good sadnes,
> I would that all were well, and perchance,
> It may be so, what, were it not for hope,
> The heart, and so forth.   (A6r–v)

He uses 'and so forth' fifteen times in his three scenes. Ned Spicing is the character with whom Josselyn is most frequently in dialogue (the two are political opponents). Spicing is impatient with Josselyn's linguistic tic and he ridicules it by inventing appropriate nicknames for Josselyn. His first is 'good master "and so forth"' (scene 5, line 103, B1v).[88] His second comes in response to unexpectedly hearing Josselyn speak when the Mayor and his men arrive at Mile End. He identifies Josselyn by his speech habit:

Josselyn. I [Ay] but you know what followed, and so forth.

Spicing. Et cetera? are you there? mee thinks the sight of the dun Bull, the *Nevels* honored crest, should make you leave your broken sentences, and quite forget ever to speake at all.   (B5v, scene 9, lines 104-07)

A modern edition should put 'Et cetera' in inverted commas to indicate its status as a tag phrase.[89] (Spicing's sequence, 'Et cetera? Are you there?' could be paraphrased in *Much Ado* fashion as 'Good Master "*et cetera*"! are you yet living?' as Spicing catches sight of his adversary.) The encounter concludes with the rebel leader Falconbridge saying 'Away with this parentheses of words'

---

[87] I am grateful to Lois Potter for discussing this example with me.

[88] I quote from Richard Rowland's edition where the modernized punctuation makes Spicing's tone clear. See Thomas Heywood, *1 Edward IV*, ed. Richard Rowland (Revels; Manchester: Manchester University Press, 2005). The original reads 'good M. and so forth'.

[89] Richard Rowland does this for Spicing's earlier mockery of 'and so forth', as we saw in footnote 88: 'We'll talk more anon, good master "and so forth"' (5.103).

(parenthesis is an interruption or digression).[90] Here Heywood is using 'Et cetera' to characterize Josselyn's self-interruptions ('leave your broken sentences'), but, like Posselius, he uses it interchangeably with 'and so forth'.

One final question is whether 'and so forth' is used like &c-etcetera as a euphemism for bawdiness or whether it is consistently neutral? The answer, it seems, is: generally the latter but with some experimental attempts at the former. In *The Wit of a Woman* (1604), Isabella imagines what people will say if she marries the old man who is wooing her: 'she surely married his purse and not himselfe, and she wil have a gallant in a corner, that shall and so foorth: why he must bee but a countenance [cover]' (E4v). Earlier, Ventero has introduced himself as a schoolmaster, advertising his skills in 'the Arte of Charactering, writing and reading and so forthe' (E1v). Given that Germaine Greer characterizes the wives in *Westward Ho!* (a play of the same decade) as erotically transgressive for learning to write, one wonders if similar associations apply here under cover of the 'and so forth'.[91] *Northward Ho!* (1607) presents a conversation in which sexual familiarity is being reported:

Greenshield: [F]amiliar with her.
Mayberry: Kissing and so forth.
Green: I [aye] Sir.   (A3r)

Nicholas Breton's *Old Man's Lesson and a Young Man's Love* (1605) inveighs against adulterous women:

it is a fine jest, to see how the devil teacheth them, to excuse their owne sin, as thus: flesh is fraile, these wicked men are ful of temptation, and my husband is such a, and so foorth: but this will not serve, when time shall serve, that they shall answere for their service to God, and their husbands.   (F1r)

In all of these instances 'and so forth' seems to be a genuine breaking off, with the preceding sexual term perhaps underlining the necessity of breaking off for decorum's sake.[92] From these examples, it seems that 'and so forth' flirts with but does not develop the identifiable meanings that &c-etcetera does.[93]

---

[90] B6r. See Jonathan P. Lamb, *Shakespeare in the Marketplace of Words* (Cambridge: Cambridge University Press, 2017), pp. 140–75.

[91] Dekker and Webster, *Westward Ho!* (1604); Germaine Greer, *Shakespeare's Wife* (London: Bloomsbury, 2007), pp. 56–7.

[92] Despite the indefinite article in the last example from Breton, 'and so foorth' is unlikely to be a noun because the article is followed by a comma. And if it is a noun, it cannot mean 'cuckold', à la Leontes, because the husband is already a 'something' that justifies the wife now making him a cuckold.

[93] Of potential relevance is the cluster of dates in these examples: they are all early seventeenth century. The breaking off in association with sexual vocabulary and allusions may be an attempt to foster an identity for 'and so forth' analogous to &c-etcetera.

George Gascoigne

In the A-text of *Dr Faustus* (1604), one of the clowns, accused of stealing a goblet from the vintner, appeals incredulously to his companion, Rafe, for support before turning to insult his accuser: 'I a goblet *Rafe*, I a goblet? I scorne you: and you are but a &c.' (D3v). In Gascoigne's *Supposes* (1566, in *A Hundreth Sundrie Flowres* (1573)) the comic Cleon indulges in insults like the clown in A-text *Faustus*, and they are indicated in the same way: 'I had thought to have given him these hose when I had worne them a litle nearer, but he shall have a. &c.' (Ciiv).[94] Lois Potter writes that Gascoigne is here indebted to the Italian tradition of improvisation.[95] This he may be but Ariosto, Gascoigne's source, does not indicate improvisation at this point or at anywhere else in *I Suppositi*. However, the home-grown English comic tradition does provide a model for Gascoigne to follow. In Henry Medwall's *Fulgens and Lucres* (written late 1400s, published 1512–16) the servants play 'Farte Pryke in Cul' (a jousting match played in a squatting position, using wooden staffs).[96] The game concludes with one of the clowns being thrown to the ground, apparently letting out a prodigious fart. Exaggerating his fall as fatal, he requests a priest for confession, to which his fellow responds, 'it is nede, / For he is not in clene lyfe indede, / I fele it at my nose .for fo. &c'.[97] Editors emend the line to 'I feel it at my nose [*faugh faugh* &c]', the bracketed material providing the direction for the *whaaaw* sound that indicates the clown's reaction to an offensive smell.[98]

When Gascoigne indicates improvisation in *Supposes* ('he shall have a. &c.') it is one of the few places outside *Master F. J.* that he uses '&c'. In *F. J.* he uses it six times, always in a different way. At the start of this chapter we saw his use of '&c' as a substitute for a rape narrative. For his other examples we may turn to the summary of one of Gascoigne's editors: 'etc: used by "G. T." a number of times *rhetorically*, with either, as here, a weary shrug, or a lascivious leer, as

---

[94] In this example, as in the example from A-text *Faustus*, the form of the indefinite article preceding &c ('a' not 'an') shows that the '&c' is not to be pronounced: 'you are but a &c'; 'he shall have a. &c'. It is a material stand-in for the improvised insults that the actor must say.

[95] Lois Potter, 'Plays and Playwrights', in *The Revels History of Drama in English*, vol. II: *1500–1576*, ed. T. W. Craik, Clifford Leech, and Lois Potter (London: Methuen, 1980), pp. 288–9.

[96] See Meg Twycross with Malcolm Jones and Alan Fetcher, 'Fart Pryke in Cul: The Pictures', *Medieval Theatre* 23 (2001), 11–121.

[97] Henry Medwall, *Fulgens and Lucres*, ed. F. S. Boas and A. W. Reed (Oxford: Clarendon Press, 1926), ll. 1210–12.

[98] The emendation of 'for fo' to 'faugh' receives support from Jonson's *Poetaster* where Tucca's response to the apothecary is 'fough: out of my Nostrils, thou stinkst of *Lotium*, & the *Syrringe*' (E3v).

on page 61'.[99] These are only two of six ways. The variety of uses within a single text means that when we read '&c' in *F. J.* we have to treat it as a stylistic phenomenon, like Emily Dickinson's dashes, and pay serious attention to it as a mark of Gascoigne's (or G.T.'s?) style, every bit as important as his other imaginative innovations in this text.

Edward Coke, *Institutes*

If we return to Coke's *Institutes* (1628), we see something similar. Littleton's text, which Coke is translating and annotating, is densely populated with *&c-etceteras*. In his preface, Coke praises the stylistic variety of these *&c-etceteras*,[100] and throughout the work he regularly explains them, treating them as a textual feature with linguistic meaning:

> &c. And here (&c.) implieth, Distresse, Escheat, and the like (Bb1r, p. 97)[101]
>
> *Que il doit faire, &c.* Here by (&c.) is understood Temporall or Spirituall Service (Bb1r, p. 97)
>
> &c. This &c. in the end of this Section, implieth any other heire lineall or collateral (Bbb3v, p. 192v)
>
> &c. There is nothing in our Author but is worthy of observation. Here is the first (&c.) and there is no (&c.) in all his three Bookes (there being as you shall perceive very many) but it is for two purposes. (E1r–v, pp. 17r–v)[102]

---

[99] Paul Salzman (ed.), *An Anthology of Elizabethan Prose Fiction* (Oxford: Oxford University Press, 1987), p. 393, my emphasis. Gascoigne uses '&c' formulaically ('she gave him thanks as etc.'; p. 7); dismissively ('This sonnet is short and sweet, reasonably well, according to the occasion etc.'; p. 37); as continuation of excuses ('he was tied to the invention, troubled in mind etc.'; p. 52); as narrative continuation ('although I could wade much further, as to declare his departure, what thanks he gave to his *Hope* and etc., yet I will cease'; p. 80); to continue a quotation ('[*r*]*ugier qual semper fui, etc.*'; p. 28); to continue a list (as 'the Dame', 'the Lady', 'Mistress', and etc.'; p. 80); as a possible interruption ('Bess and etc'; p. 68). None of these examples precludes irony. All references are to Salzman's edition although he expands the 1573 text's consistent use of '&c' to 'etc'. He prints 'Bess and etc.' where the 1573 edition prints 'Besse &c' (K4r), which changes the meaning.

[100] Addison wrote in 1710: 'the great *Littleton*, who, as my Lord Chief Justice *Coke* observes, had a most admirable Talent at an &c' (*Tatler* 133, 11–14 February 1710, p. 95). Like his reference to Littleton's use of this 'Figure'—a rhetorical technique—Addison sees this as something for which one has a 'Talent'.

[101] The printer uses parentheses as a form of inverted commas, indicating the citational nature of '&c'. This is not unusual (for more on experimental typography in quotations, see the Epilogue to this book).

[102] Coke, in *First Part of the Institutes*, then explains the two purposes, subdividing the second into three categories. The *&c-etcetera* implies 'other necessary matter' and sends the student away to follow it up. His subsequent reasons are familiar from classical rhetoric: they help the reader uncover (classical *inventio*), understand, and remember. The EEBO copy of this edition is defective here, omitting 17v and 18r.

What Brenan would edit out in the nineteenth century as the hallmark of a lazy author, Coke praises and glosses in Littleton as the mark of a skilful stylist.

Coke himself knew the value of *&c-etcetera* in his own writing. Coke had investigated the scandal of Sir Thomas Overbury's murder; he had also investigated associated rumours that Overbury's murderers had poisoned Prince Henry. Queen Anne rewarded him with a large diamond ring 'for the discovering of the poysoning of Sr Thomas Overbury, etc'.[103] Allen Boyer comments:

> that *et cetera* deserves italics—even underlining. Coke knew and used this abbreviation as a coded reference, a signal that 'doth imply some other necessary matter'. That something lay behind every *et cetera* was a topic on which Coke was insistent, perhaps obsessive; in his own masterpiece, the commentary upon Littleton, he devoted a paragraph to indexing the 119 occasions upon which *&c* appeared in Littleton's *Tenures*. Coke had discovered the truth about the poisoning of Sir Thomas Overbury; that was universally known; it could be mentioned in describing a jewel he prized. Coke's reference to *&c* is something different—almost a personal memorandum. It offers a subtly coded statement that Anna had rewarded him for investigating the poisoning of someone beyond Overbury.[104]

This reference appears in an inventory of Coke's plate, pictures, 'rarities', and 'household stuff' taken in 1631. His jewels appear under 'rarities' and the full item reads: 'A ringe sett with a great diamond cutt with fawcetts. Given to Sr. Edw. Coke by Q. Anne for the discovering of the poisoning of Sr. Thomas Overbury, etc.'.[105] One wonders what the chances are that the inventory's phrasing originates with Coke himself rather than with an assistant. On the one hand, taking an inventory is a clerical job; but on the other, given the nature of the precious jewels and plate, one does not want to run the risk of an assistant carelessly or deliberately omitting an item. Since the phrase about the diamond ring from Queen Anna describes a jewel that has a backstory, this amount of inventory detail is more likely from the owner of the jewel than a secretary. Another jewel is described with an art-historical knowledge that seems unusual for a secretary: 'A ringe sett with a great Turkys which K. Henry 8 used to wear and was pictured with it on his forefinger'. Another reference

---

[103] C. W. James, *Chief Justice Coke, his Family and Descendants at Holkham* (London: Country Life Ltd; New York: Charles Scribner's Sons, 1929), p. 318.

[104] Allen D. Boyer, 'Sir Edward Coke: Royal Servant, Royal Favourite', Harvard Law School website, pp. 1–24 (p. 11). Available at: <http://www.law.harvard.edu/programs/ames_foundation/BLHC07/Boyer%20Sir%20Edward%20Coke%20-%20Royal%20Servant%20and%20Royal%20Favorite.pdf>.

[105] James, *Chief Justice Coke*, p. 318.

to Henry VIII shows political-diplomatic knowledge: 'A great picture in Gould of Kinge Henrye the 8th with inscription of Hebrew and Greek characters on the reverse, concerning his supremacie which he sent abroad to this friends and allies'. Later in the inventory it becomes clear that Coke must at least have supervised the itemization as he distinguishes between items that already belonged to him and those that came via his second wife. Furthermore, although he uses the third person in the itemized lists, he also uses the first person, describing Henry Beck as a gentleman who looks after the house and plate at Godwick for which 'he hath a yearly fee and reward allowed unto him by me Sir Edward Coke'.[106] We can have some confidence that the 'etc.' originates with Coke.

On the two occasions in which *&c-etcetera* appears elsewhere in the inventory (at least, in the excerpts published by Charles James), they are used in a conventional way: 'Faire coynes of Ferdinand and Elizabeth King and Queene of Spain, of Philipp King of Portugal, of Charles Duke of Savoye, the Duke of Mantou, etc.'.[107] The second 'etc.' comes in a paragraph describing the duties of the Godwick custodian (he looks after 'plate etc'.) and so is not in an itemized list.[108] Boyer probably overstates the case when, in explaining this inventory, he describes Coke's comments in *Institutes* E1r–v (pp. 17r–v) as an 'index' of Littleton's *&c-etceteras* in one paragraph, but it is true that, as we have seen, Coke is alert throughout the *Institutes* to the varying meanings of *&c-etcetera*. In this inventory's reference to Overbury it is hard to see what the concluding 'etc.' could gesture to in inventory terms so Boyer's reading of it as an allusion is tempting.

John Ford, *Love's Sacrifice*

We can see how an apparently straightforward occurrence acquires complexity in Ford's *Love's Sacrifice* (1633). In this Caroline tragedy (written between 1621 and 1633 but probably post-1626), the comic character Mauriccio ('an old antique') closes a scene with a promise of poetry and a reflection on food:

> I am big with conceit and must be delivered of poetry, in the eternall commendation of this gracious *Tooth-picker*: but first, I hold it a most healthy policy to make a slight supper.

---

[106] All quotes in this paragraph: James, *Chief Justice Coke*, p. 320.
[107] James, *Chief Justice Coke*, p. 320.   [108] James, *Chief Justice Coke*, p. 321.

> For meat's the food that must preserve our lives,
> And now's the time, when mortals whet their knives
> on thresholds, shoo-soles, Cart-wheeles, &c. Away *Giacopo*.
>
> *Exeunt.* (E3v)

The comic structure of the speech is clear: an overblown promise of grandiloquent poetry directed to a minor object, the toothpick, is followed by a deferral of the poetry for practical reasons—an exit to supper. The exit is then motivated by a rhyming couplet although the couplet's rhyme is followed by an incomplete sentence in which the phrase 'mortals whet their knives' is extended to provide three objects of the whetting: thresholds, shoe soles, and cart wheels (and presumably more, if the '&c' invites the actor to improvise further objects). The exit that was motivated at the start of the speech, 'Come behind me, *Giacopo*', is finally achieved with the variant command at the end: 'Away *Giacopo*.'

I have described the two lines of rhyme as a couplet, and the compositor clearly saw them that way as he indented the two lines, emphasizing their pairing (see Figure 2.2). Later editors have followed suit. Gifford's edition of 1827 italicizes the couplet and makes clear the additional nature of the final line by adding a dash after the couplet.[109] Henry Weber's 1811 edition italicizes all three lines but adds an ellipsis before the last line, which he indents.[110] The couplet has a terminative emphasis (which is the effect of couplets when they

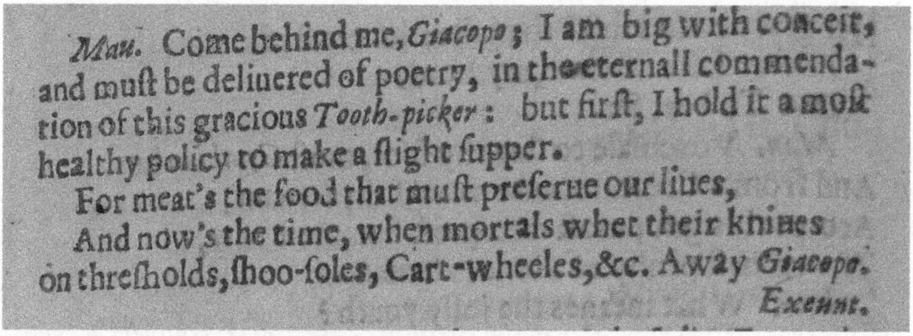

FIGURE 2.2 John Ford, *Love's Sacrifice* (1633, STC 11164), E3v. Courtesy of the President and Fellows of Magdalen College, Oxford.

[109] John Ford, *The Dramatic Works of John Ford*, 2 vols, ed. William Gifford (London: John Murray, 1827), p. 421.

[110] John Ford, *The Dramatic Works of John Ford*, 2 vols, ed. Henry Weber (Edinburgh: A. Constable, 1811), p. 386.

close scenes) and so the final non-rhymed line understandably looks like an addition or improvisation. This deduction is supported by the '&c', which typically invites further extension.

But the rhyming couplet did not start life as a couplet, nor is the apparently extraneous final line an addition. The second line of the couplet and the last line of the scene belong together as a quotation from Francis Beaumont's popular comedy, *The Woman Hater* (1607). In this play, the comic gourmand, Lazarillo, a 'humours' character defined by his love of food, seeks a rare fish head at the Duke's court. He has been given advice about verbal etiquette at court and told to respond to the Duke in circumlocutions. Asked what time it is, Lazarillo replies:

> About the time that mortals whet their knives
> On thresholds, on their shoe soles, and on stayres:
> Now bread is grating, and the testy cooke
> Hath much to doe now, now the Tables all.   (D1r)

Impatient for a plain answer, the Duke interrupts Lazarillo's last sentence and punctures his metaphors bathetically with the clarifying question: ''Tis almost dinner time?'

The Ford lines are clearly a quotation from Beaumont, cued by the appropriate context: a speech about food. This tells us a lot about the importance of Beaumont's play in its own time, and for years after. (It also tells us a lot about what impressed Ford.) The appropriateness is not just limited to food. Mauriccio, like Lazarillo, is attempting a poetical conceit: 'I am big with conceit and must be delivered of poetry' (E3v).[111]

I was therefore wrong in suggesting that the rhyme in Ford (lives/knives) is a couplet to conclude the scene (although the compositor has, understandably, set it as an indented couplet) and that the final line ('on thresholds...') is an addition. But it is hard to know exactly what is going on here. Is the '&c' in *Love's Sacrifice* an indication to continue with the Beaumont quotation? Is 'Cart-wheeles' a deliberate or accidental substitution for 'stayres'? What is clear is that textual appearance, the rhetoric of the page—couplets as well as *&c-etceteras*—can be misleading.

---

[111] The only Ford scholar to have noticed the source in Beaumont is Curtis Perry in *Eros and Power in English Renaissance Drama: Five Plays by Marlowe, Davenant, Massinger, Ford and Shakespeare* (Jefferson, NC: McFarlane & Co., 2008).

Cue Words

Ben Jonson, *Every Man in his Humour*

Further complications come when '&c' is a cue word. Let us look at a revision
Ben Jonson made in the text of *Every Man in his Humour*. The play was written
in 1598 with an Italian setting and a cast of Italian characters. Jonson later converted it to an English setting; this was the version published in the 1616 Folio.
In the 1598 version (Q1601) Bobadilla tells how he put off some gentlemen
importuning him to attend their fencing match; his rejection is couched in the
elaborately polite style of a letter, complete with the valedictory '&c': 'well, I
tolde them that to come to a publique schoole they should pardon me, it was
opposite to my humor but if so they would attend me at my lodging, I protested to do them what right or favour I could, as I was a gentleman. &c.'
(I1v).[112] In the 1616 Folio version this speech remains relatively untouched
('attend me at my lodging' becomes 'give their attendance at my lodging', for
instance) but in the sign-off '&c' has been replaced by 'and so forth' (E3r). A
practical explanation perhaps underlies Jonson's revision. Bobadilla's witty
spoken parody of epistolary written style leaves '&c' as the end of his speech.
This is perfectly acceptable in a letter or a legal document but potentially dis-
astrous in an actor's cue word. Given the multiple functions of *&c-etcetera* that
I have outlined, the actor who sees '&c' as his cue (or '[was] [a] [gentleman]
&c') does not know what he is listening out for. Is his interlocutor to improvise here? Does his interlocutor say the words '*et cetera*'? Is it an aposiopetic
dash and is the listening actor meant to interrupt? Such uncertainty would be
problematic in a cue; accordingly it has to be revised to 'and so forth'.

Or does it? Heywood's *A Woman Killed with Kindness* (1607) uses '&c' three
times. They are used in different ways but all are cue words. Let us scrutinize
them.

Thomas Heywood, *A Woman Killed with Kindness*

The first occurrence of '&c' is in a bawdy context when Nick, the servant,
offers a rhyming couplet to conclude the scene:

> If they proceed as they haue done before,
> *Wendols* a knave, my Mistris is a &c. (D1r)

---

[112] This is 4.2.25–9 in the Revels edition, ed. Robert S. Miola (Manchester: Manchester University
Press, 2000). It is Act 4, scene 6 in the Folio.

The form of the indefinite article makes it clear that '&c.' is not spoken. So too does its abbreviated form: as we saw at the start of this chapter, when it is a bawdy noun to be spoken, *etcetera* tends to be written out in full. (Q3 of *Woman Killed* (1617) replaces the ampersand with a dash.) We know that '&c.' here in *Woman Killed* stands in for 'whore' but is it 'a piece of overnice reticence' on the part of the character,[113] an indication to the actor to complete the rhyme,[114] or a textual mark of editorial/compositorial censorship? The last is a tempting explanation. One wonders how often printing-house compositors are involved in choosing '&c.' when it functions as a somatic substitution. The examples from Florio at the start of this chapter are unexpected, given that Florio is not elsewhere coy or euphemistic in his translation of Montaigne, and the examples throughout this chapter tend to come from a few printing houses (albeit not so few as to enable us to draw a correlation). However, the missing word in Wendoll's speech, 'whore', is not always offensive. In Robert Tailor's *The Hog hath Lost his Pearl* (1614) Haddit has the couplet:

> *Undone by folly, fortune lend me more,*
> *Canst thou, and wilt not, pox on such a whore.*   (B4r)

Why, we might ask, does he not say, 'pox on such an &c'?

The next two '&c's in Heywood's *Woman Killed* are interruptions. When Malby delivers the impoverished Susan a bag of gold from the man who wants to seduce her, Sir Francis Acton, Susan recoils at Acton's name, preventing Malby from completing his announcement:

> Malby: This Gold *Sir Francis Acton* sends by me,
> And prays you &c.
> Susan: *Acton*: oh God that name I am borne to cursse.   (E2v)

Several editors interpret the '&c' as an indication for the actors to whisper (both Van Fossen's and Fraser and Rabkin's gloss at this point is 'indicating whispering').[115] Kidnie's edition replaces the '&c' with a dash to indicate that the speech is interrupted. She does the same for the final occurrence of &c in

---

[113] Thomas Heywood, *A Woman Killed with Kindness*, ed. R. W. van Fossen (Revels; London: Methuen, 1961), vi.183n.

[114] Margaret Jane Kidnie notes that when Broadsides Theatre Company completed the rhyme, they 'introduc[ed] a term of abuse that the play otherwise entirely avoids'. Thomas Heywood, *A Woman Killed with Kindness*, ed. Margaret Jane Kidnie (Arden; London: Bloomsbury, 2017), 6.184n.

[115] Van Fossen, ix.51n; *A Woman Killed with Kindness*, in *Drama of the English Renaissance I: The Tudor Period*, ed. Russell A. Fraser and Norman Rabkin (New York: Macmillan, 1976), ix.51n.

the play on G2r (scene xiv) when Susan bemoans her lack of fortune and value: 'I owe even for the clothes upon my backe, / I am not worth, &c.' Her brother contradicts her, apparently interrupting her to do so: 'Oh sister say not so'. Brian Scobie comments, 'The ampersand in Q1 seems here to indicate interruption'.[116]

Although the meaning of each of these Heywood *&c-etcetera*s is clear or can be reasonably supposed, their position compromises my interpretation of them: all are cue words. If Jonson saw the need to revise the cue word, why didn't Heywood?[117] Here then is a dilemma: many of the *&c-etcetera*s I have cited conclude a speech. This is inevitable when it signals a breaking off or an interruption. But the improvisations and the insults also occur at ends of speeches—surely a problematic location in a Part-based system. One systematic difference between the interruptions and the insults is that the insults are prefaced by an indefinite article: 'a. &c' in *Supposes*, 'a &c' in A-*Dr Faustus*. An actor seeing this as his cue would know that a noun is to follow. A variant grammatical help is the use of an adjective which may indicate to the listening actor the status of '&c' as a noun to be provided by the preceding actor ('Out you Rogue, you arrant &c.' in *Wily Beguiled*, C4r). This quasi-system may distinguish the first occurrence in *Woman Killed* (a noun) from the last two (interruptions).

In *The Contention between Liberality and Prodigality* (1602), the formulaic lines of an indictment, read out by the Clerk and repeated by the Cryer, are indicated in the printed text of the Cryer's Part by repeating the Clerk's first words followed by '&c' (F3r). These are ends of lines and hence cue words but this is obviously a compositorial labour-saver, and is unlikely to reflect the underlying manuscript copy. In a case like this, *&c-etcetera* in drama gives us a small window onto the different worlds of manuscript and print.

---

[116] *A Woman Killed with Kindness*, ed. Brian Scobie (New Mermaids; 1985; London: A. & C. Black, 1991), xiv.20n.

[117] When Middleton uses *etcetera* in a speech, it is not the last word and he makes its vocalization as a noun quite clear by varying its Latin form. In *The Phoenix* (1607), Tangle lists and explains his twenty-nine current lawsuits; when he gets to the ninth, the dialogue reads 'Nine, *& sic de coeteris.* I haue so vext and beggerd the whole parish' (C1v). Similarly, in Webster's *Duchess of Malfi* (1623) Bosola reads the paper that Antonio has dropped with its horoscope for his newborn child. It forecasts a short life and violent death, and then: 'Caete[r]a non scrutantur' (E2r, 2.3.63). This may be part of the paper, meaning that the astrologer did not investigate further. But since it is in roman type and the horoscope is in italic, it could be a PS by the astrologer or a comment by Bosola. I am grateful to Lois Potter for this reference and for correspondence about the performance options. Both these examples, occurring in a Latin phrase, suggest that '*coeteris* / Caete[r]a' are pronounced with a hard 'c'.

Part III: Extensions

Extending Meaning

Exaggeration and Ambiguity

Although by the nineteenth century Brenan has a reductive view of '&c' as an imprecision, it is this very ability of '&c' to extend what is said that enables it to be used for exaggeration (and its opposite, understatement) and ambiguity. McEnery finds an example of the first category with three '*etc*.'s in a document which 'exaggerat[es] the range of sins to be combated, and hence amplif [ies] the moral panic discourse'.[118] Ambiguity was at the heart of political manoeuvrings in the infamous Etcetera Oath of 1640.[119] A response to the Bishops' War of 1638–40 in which Charles tried to impose English Laudian ceremonies on Scotland, the Etcetera Oath was '*injoyn'd for the preventing of all Innovations in Doctrine and Government*' (E1v). Every graduate had to swear not to give consent 'to alter the Government of this Church by Arch-bishops, Bishops, Deanes, and Arch-deacons, &c., as it stands now established, and as by right it ought to stand' (E2r). The title page of Thomas Bray's 1641 pamphlet against the oath (see Figure 2.3) indicates the ways in which the '&c' was 'contrived': it 'cunningly oblig[ed] the Consciences of his Majesties Subjects to observe and obey whatsoever errours they would impose'.[120] As Touchstone might have said, 'Much virtue in &c.'.

Swift uses *etcetera* with parodic effect when he describes the genealogy of critics in *The Tale of a Tub*:

> Every *True Critick* is a Hero born, descending in a direct Line from a Celestial Stem, by *Momus* and *Hybris*, who begat *Zoilus*, who begat *Tigellius*, who begat *Etcætera the Elder*, who begat *B[en]tly*, and *Rym[e]r*, and *W[o]tton*, and *Perrault*, and *Dennis*, who begat *Etcætera the Younger*.[121]

---

[118] Tony McEnery, *Swearing in English: Bad Language, Purity and Power from 1586 to the Present* (Abingdon: Routledge, 2006), p. 170. He prints the document on page 171 but does not give its source, although it is *circa* or post-1700. His information comes from the SRMC (Society for the Reformation of Manners Corpus) which he compiled—a total of 120,709 words—from 1699 to 1745 (see his p. 14).

[119] Church of England, *Constitutions and Canons Ecclesiastical* (1640).

[120] See 'Samoth Yarb' [Thomas Bray], *The Anatomy of Etcetera* (1641); John Spurr, '"The Strongest Bond of Conscience": Oaths and the Limits of Tolerance in Early Modern England', in *Contexts of Conscience in Early Modern Europe 1500–1700*, ed. Harold E. Braun and Edward Vallance (Basingstoke: Palgrave Macmillan, 2004), pp. 151–65 (esp. pp. 158–9).

[121] Jonathan Swift, *A Tale of a Tub and Other Satires*, ed. Kathleen Williams (London: J. M. Dent & Sons, 1975), section III, p. 57. I am grateful to Thomas Roebuck for drawing my attention to this passage.

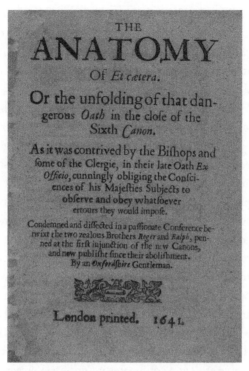

FIGURE 2.3 'Samoth Yarb' [Thomas Bray], *The Anatomy of Etcetera* (1641, Wing B4284), title page. Shelfmark B4284. Used by permission of the Folger Shakespeare Library.

The appropriation of *Etcætera* as a proper name here indicates the line of carpers stretching out till doomsday. By the nineteenth century, *&c-etcetera* had come a long way from its early modern somatic and sexual meanings. Kate Nickleby's boarding school in Devonshire costs 'fifty guineas a-year without the etceteras'.[122] Although the *OED*'s last citation for 'usual additions, extras, sundries' is 1884 (its first is 1817), in the 2000s a gentleman's tailor in England adopted the noun for luxury accessories: 'Clements & Church. Fine Tailoring and Etceteras'.[123] Now 'Et Cetera' is the name of their online newsletter.

Sound: Bathos, Rhyme, Music

Byron's *Don Juan* offers the comic bathos of 'Hail muse! etcetera' where the *etcetera* has to be written out in full to scan.[124] The parodic effect is not simply

[122] Charles Dickens, *Nicholas Nickleby*, ed. Michael Slater (Harmondsworth: Penguin, 1978), p. 416.
[123] See <www.clementsandchurch.co.uk>.
[124] Lord George Gordon Byron, *Byron*, ed. Jerome J. McGann (Oxford: Oxford University Press, 1986), Canto III, I.1.

because of the reduction of an epic convention. It is compounded by the belatedness of the invocation (appearing at the beginning of the third canto), by being despatched quickly in order to move to Juan sleeping on 'a fair and happy breast', and by the rhythm in which the spondee followed by the multi-syllabic 'etcetera' trails off acoustically.

Carol Anne Duffy created a similarly bathetic effect when she adapted *Everyman* for the National Theatre in 2015 (dir. Rufus Norris). *Etcetera* first completes a list of nouns, depicting Everyman squandering his 'God-given time on pleasure, treasure, leisure, etcetera' where the reversal from trochaic to iambic is as unexpected as the offhand tapering-off. At the end of the play, when a desperate Everyman panic-prays, Death ridicules him: 'What's this? "Forgive me, I could have been betterer"? / Et-fucking-cetera'. The ungrammatical double comparative and the comic tmesis of 'et-fucking-cetera' combine to create a reductive rhyme. The medieval *Everyman* had already played with 'et cetera' in a number of ways. Mischief concludes a speech by combining 'and so forth' tautologically with 'et cetera'. His ten-line speech is linguistically parodic, containing mock-Latin ('*firibusque*') and mock-biblical exegesis; part of the acoustic joke is that he needs a rhyme for ' "*Chaff horsibus et reliqua*" ', provided two lines later by 'And so forth, *et cetera*'.[125] James Joyce both puns on *etcetera* ('etsitaraw etcicero') and conjugates it ('etcaetera etcaeterorum').[126]

Because today (perhaps influenced by Brenan) *&c-etcetera* is seen as insouciant sloppiness, actors need do little to bring out the term's propensity for comic anti-climax. When Dickon Tyrell played Adam Overdo in Ben Jonson's *Bartholomew Fair* (Sam Wanamaker Playhouse 2019, dir. Blanche McIntyre), his formal and precise articulation of Ovid's Latin was followed by an offhand, litotical 'etcetera': 'I will sit down at night and say with my friend Ovid, *Iamque opus exegi, quod nec Jovis ira, nec ignis, &c.*'.[127] The unexpected ending triggered audience laughter.

The obvious next step for acoustic play with *etcetera*'s polysyllables is music. Zadie Smith's *On Beauty* provides a bridge when Howard Belsey focuses on the

---

[125] Anon, *Mankind*, ed. Douglas Bruster and Eric Rasmussen (Arden; London: Methuen/A. & C. Black, 2009), ll. 60–4. Latin forms lend themselves to parody in early modern texts. In *The Unfortunate Traveller* (1594) Nashe satirizes an orator whose mouth was full of '*quemadmodums* [quaemodums] and *quapropters*' (F1r).

[126] James Joyce, *Finnegans Wake*, ed. Robert-Jan Henkes, Erik Bindervoet, Finn Fordham, and Jeri Johnson (Oxford: Oxford University Press, 2012), pp. 152, 154.

[127] Ben Jonson, *Bartholomew Fair*, ed. Suzanne Gossett (Revels Student Editions; Manchester: Manchester University Press, 2000), 2.4.70.

rhythm of the four syllables as uttered by a colleague: 'Howard enjoyed the tuneful Nigerian musicality of "etcetera".'[128] This musicality is literalized in Jackie Wilson's classic jive song, 'Etcetera', with its refrain 'et-cet-er-a, and so forth, you know', and in The Smiths' 'Sweet and Tender Hooligan' with its sequence of ten emphatic ETCs:

> And...
> 'In the midst of life we are in death ETC.'
> Don't forget the hooligan, hooligan
> Because he'll never, never do it again
> And...
> 'In the midst of life we are in death ETC.'
>
> ETC! ETC! ETC! ETC!
> IN THE MIDST OF LIFE WE ARE IN DEATH ETC
> ETC! ETC! ETC! ETC!
> IN THE MIDST OF LIFE WE ARE IN DEBT ETC[129]

Here the capitalized abbreviation has only a visual emphasis since the word is sung in full, with the emphasis coming from the repetition coupled with the prayer-book pun on death/debt which brings out the Elizabethan homophone. In the twentieth century, we find Rodgers and Hammerstein's King of Siam doubling and even tripling the phrase, creating a catchphrase.[130] There is something about 'etcetera' that invites repetition, perhaps because its scansion is fluid: it can be four syllables in two iambs (ĕt cét ĕr á) or given an exaggerated emphasis as two spondees (ét cét ér á) or it can be a dactyl (ét cĕt'ră). Because the feminine endings of dactyls are invariably comic in English poetry (their 'dying fall' is anti-climactic) *&c-etcetera* often has a double trailing-off, in sound as well as in meaning.

Location, Location, Location

Borges breaks the unwritten rule of *etcetera*—that it should conclude a list:

> In its remote pages it is written that the animals are divided into: (a) belonging to the emperor, (b) embalmed, (c) tame, (d) sucking pigs, (e) sirens, (f) fabulous,

---

[128] Zadie Smith, *On Beauty* (London: Penguin, 2005), p. 20.

[129] For Jackie Wilson's 'Etcetera' see <http://www.youtube.com/watch?v=Z8SNHNphi2o>; for The Smiths' 'Sweet and Tender Hooligan', see: <http://www.azlyrics.com/lyrics/smiths/sweetandtenderhooligan.html.> I am grateful to Sam Plumb and Philip Schwyzer respectively for directing me to these songs.

[130] Margaret Landon, *Anna and the King of Siam* (London: Longman's, Green & Co., 1944); Rodgers and Hammerstein, *The King and I* (1951). Cf. our tautological pairing: 'and so on and so forth'. Modern German does the same with 'und so fort und so weiter'.

(g) stray dogs, (h) included in the present classification, (i) frenzied, (j) innumerable, (k) drawn with a very fine camelhair brush, (l) et cetera, (m) having just broken the water pitcher, (n) that from a long way off look like flies.[131]

He grabs the reader's attention simply by relocating the expected position of 'etcetera'.

In the Introduction we looked at Georges Perec's imaginative and quirky essay 'On the Page' in which he plays with blank spaces. As the essay continues, he enlists the *&c-etcetera* as part of his playfulness with blanks. His section on writing things down has only four sentences and is a combination of parentheses and *&c-etceteras*. The *&c-etceteras* usually conclude lists and are always in the abbreviated form 'etc.'. The last lines of the section, however, offer a juxtaposition:

> ticking, in a journal containing a summary of almost all the others in the field of the life sciences, the titles that may be of interest to the research-workers whose bibliographical documentation I am supposed to provide, filling in index-cards, assembling references, correcting proofs, etc.
>
>   Et cetera.[132]

The first 'etc.', like the others in this section of his book, is used as the conventional indication of continuation; it is not entirely neutral, however, overlaid as it is with implied boredom at the necessity of providing these forms of documentation. The next sentence, with the full form 'Et cetera' seems to be an abbreviation for a longer, more impatient, sentence: 'I could go on writing paragraphs like these (but I won't)'.[133]

Form

Susan Wheeler's poem 'The Split' (2012) chronicles the deterioration of a relationship. An itemized list of thirty domestic grievances from both partners' viewpoints ('24. She hated the Dave Clark Five') includes the haunting (and hinting) '26. He went out for gum etcetera'.[134] Here 'etcetera' means 'you

---

[131] Jorge Luis Borges, 'John Wilkins' Analytical Language', quoted in Michel Foucault, *The Order of Things* (1966; London: Routledge, 1989), p. xvi. Some translations offer 'miscellaneous' for 'et cetera' but Borges' original reads 'etcétera'. See *Otras Inquisiciones* (Buenos Aires: Emécé Editores, 1960), p. 142.

[132] Georges Perec, *Species of Spaces and Other Places*, trans. and ed. John Sturrock (Harmondsworth: Penguin, 1999), pp. 12–13.

[133] I am grateful to David Hillman for bringing Perec's essay to my attention and for helpful correspondence on interpreting it.

[134] Susan Wheeler, *Meme* (Iowa City: University of Iowa Press, 2012), p. 43.

know the rest of this story', avoiding all the conventional, tired narratives of separation and infidelity: he needed space and gum was just an excuse; he was seeing someone else and gum was a thin cover-up. The poetic doyenne of 'etcetera', however, is Alice Oswald. Reviewing Oswald's collection *Woods etc.*, Kate Kellaway observed, 'She has succeeded in finding a freshness of her own—and a playfulness. Take the serious tease of the title's "etc". She says: "I love etc and dot dot dot. I feel the universe is constructed with an etc. I am really happy starting a sentence, it is finding an end that is difficult." She is a sparing user of full stops'.[135] In this respect, Oswald maps herself on to the Dawn in her long poem 'Tithonus: 46 Minutes in the Life of the Dawn' (2014), where we read 'she never quite completes her sentence but is always almost'. The last page of the poem uses visual typography to convey the fading away elsewhere favoured by Oswald with ellipses or 'etc.': the black ink becomes progressively lighter until it is only just legible.[136] The sun has risen; darkness has become light.

The poem was first published as a pamphlet in 2014. After explaining the myth of Tithonus and the dawn, Oswald offers a crisp summary of the poem in performance: 'what you are about to hear is the sound of Tithonus meeting the dawn at midsummer. His voice starts at 4.17, when the sun is six degrees below the horizon, and stops 46 minutes later, at sunrise'. Each page of the pamphlet has parallel columns: the right-hand column prints the poem, the left depicts diagrammatically the changing number of degrees below the horizon as the sun moves towards dawn. When the poem was republished two years later in the collection *Falling Awake* (2016), the prefatory explanation included the additional line 'The performance will begin in darkness' and removed the diagrams in the left-hand column although the page was still divided in two by a vertical dotted line, 'pacing' the poem towards dawn.[137] Neither edition has page numbers: this is a poem that is measured in time, not in pages.

In addition to the two printed versions, there is an abridged BBC radio recording.[138] There are variants between all versions (the variants affect the

<hr>

[135] *The Observer*, Sunday 19 June 2005.

[136] The effect is even more marked in the pamphlet version where the last stanzas are printed on the back inside cover, which is coloured red.

[137] Katie Mennis, 'Alice Oswald and Homer', unpublished dissertation (Oxford University, March 2018), p. 1.

[138] Alice Oswald, *Tithonus* (abridged) on *The Echo Chamber*, BBC Radio 4, 27 December 2014, noted and collated by Mennis. Available at: <https://learningonscreen.ac.uk/ondemand/index.php/prog/084752EB>.

poem's references to minutes and seconds, which are adjusted accordingly).[139] Nearly halfway through the version published in *Falling Awake* is a double-page spread that contains only the vertical dotted line on each page (Mennis describes this as an 'endless vertical ellipsis'[140]) and the one-word 'Etc.' at the bottom of the right-hand page. There is nothing corresponding to this in the pamphlet version, and the *Falling Awake* version resumes with text that is completely different to that in the pamphlet. At this point in performance, the audience hears 'rapid repetitions of formulae not found in either textual version';[141] for Mennis the 'etc.' represents 'a poem in ring composition'.[142]

Like Alice Oswald, Julian Barnes elevates '*etc.*' to a book title: *Love, etc.* In this novel he also devotes an entire chapter to '*etc.*' (chapter 14) where it becomes a theory of love. The plot revolves round a love triangle, and the novel explores *&c-etcetera*'s conceptual siblings—lists, endings, unintended effects, alternatives—while a running trope offers *&c-etcetera* in other forms (*und so weiter*, and so on, blah blah). The German poet Christian Morgenstern (1871–1914) manipulates the abbreviation of '*und so weiter*' ('usw') visually and acoustically in his nonsense poem 'Die Trichter' ('The funnels'). In this poem, two funnels take a walk in the wood, and the poem is funnel-shaped:

> Zwei Trichter wandeln durch die Nacht.
> Durch ihres Rumpfs verengten Schacht
> fließt weißes Mondlicht
> still und heiter
> auf ihren
> Waldweg
> u.s.
> w.

First published in a collection of poems in 1905 (the influence of Lewis Carroll is obvious), 'Die Trichter' was not translated in English until 1962 when the American Jerome Lettvin rendered it as follows:

> Through darkest night two funnels go;
> and in their narrow necks below
> moonbeams gather to cast

---

[139] The complex nature of the variants has been studied by Mennis in 'Alice Oswald'; I am grateful to her for sharing her unpublished work and allowing me to quote from it.

[140] Mennis, 'Alice Oswald', p. 2.   [141] Mennis, 'Alice Oswald', p. 6.

[142] Mennis, 'Alice Oswald', p. 7. She links this 'etc.' to the title poem in *Woods etc.* where the speaker walks into 'increasing / woods' where 'etc.' stands for continuation of/into the woods.

the better a
light upon
their
path
et
c.

In Morgenstern, the abbreviation 'u.s.w.' is visually essential to the poem's tapered shape of the funnel but aurally the rhyme is dependent on the speaker saying the full form of the 'w'—'weiter'. (This contrasts with the Byron example from *Don Juan* where sound and appearance go together.) Lettvin has managed to reproduce both visual and aural effects with 'c.'/'cetera'.[143]

It is rare to find 'and so forth' being used as creatively as *&c-etcetera*. 'Ballad for Americans' (1939) is an exception. It is a patriotic puzzle to identify the first-person narrator (America in all her infinite variety).[144] The narrator insists 'you know who I am' and explains, opaquely, 'I'm an engineer, musician, street cleaner, carpenter, teacher...'; 'I was baptized Baptist, Methodist, Congregationalist...'; 'I'm just an Irish, Negro, Jewish, Italian...' The lists lead to the summary line, 'I am the "etceteras" and the "and so forths" that do the work'. Here *etcetera* and *and so forth* stand in for the nameless citizens who make the country.

And one must not ignore *etcetera*'s—or is it *and so forth*'s?—modern equivalent—yada, yada—as initiated by Seinfeld.[145] It is clear that, from the early modern period to the twenty-first century, *etcetera* is so much more than Brenan's 'lame' typographical abbreviation.

Continental *&c-etceteras*

The question of how early modern *&c-etceteras* work in other languages is beyond the scope of this chapter but examples from Spain and France suggest it might also indicate the female pudenda. Alexandra Wingate cites two

---

[143] Lettvin's translation appeared in his essay on Morgenstern, 'Morgenstern and Mythopoetry', *The Fat Abbot: A Literary Review* 4 (1962), 12–20. The essay is a coda to Lettvin's translation of twelve of Morgenstern's poems from *Galgenlieder* ('Gallows-songs')—the volume in which 'Die Trichter' appears. The essay occupies pages 1–11 of the journal; it describes Morgenstern's method of composition and his linguistic theory, and illustrates it with further translations.

[144] Music by Earl Robinson; words by John La Touche. I am grateful to Peter Holland for bringing this ballad to my attention.

[145] The phrase is the title of episode 19 of season 8 (24 April 1997).

examples from the Spanish *Diccionario de Autoridades*. The first is from the poet
Luis de Góngora (1561–1627) in *Fábula de Píramo y Tisbe*(1618):

> El etcétera es de marmol, [The etcetera is of marble,]
> cuyos relieves ocultos, [whose hidden reliefs,]
> ultrage mórbido eran [the sickly/white insult were]
> a los divinos desnúdos. [naked to the gods.]

Since this follows a discussion of breasts, Wingate feels it is not too much of a
stretch of the imagination to deduce that 'etcétera' here means 'vagina'.

The second example is from a poem by Francisco de Quevedo (1580–1645)
about Orlando el Enamorado:

> Y otros muchos Gentiles y Christianos, [And many other gentlemen and Christians,]
> Que son en los etcéteras Fulanos. [Who are in the etceteras, simply men.]

Wingate explains: 'The modern definition of "fulano" is "some guy", "what-
sisname" or "so-and-so", so in the context of this early modern work, "fulano"
probably refers to a lower-class male, the antithesis of the "gentiles y cristianos"'.
'Etcétera' could then refer to the penis, Wingate suggests, but given the tendency to use it for 'vagina' in early modern English, it more probably means
that the gentlemen and Christians behave like less-educated men when it
comes to sexual matters.[146]

French also seems to use *&c-etcetera* titillatingly for the female pudenda, at
least on the evidence of an eighteenth-century translation of Laurence Sterne's
A Sentimental Journey. In English the novel ends with a blank. Yorick 'is sus-
pended in a never-to-be-completed gesture':[147]

> I stretch'd out my hand, I caught hold of the Fille de Chambre's
> END OF VOL. II

Joseph Frénais' 1769 translation extends and adapts Sterne's ending:

> & en etendant le bras, je saisis la femme de chambre, &…&c. &c. &c.…. Mais *honi
> soit qui mal y pense*. Le jour parut, & nous n'eûmes point a rougir de nous voir.[148]

---

[146] Rabelais uses thirty-eight synonyms for penis in *Gargantua and Pantagruel* (1653) but '&c' is not
one of them. I am grateful to Alexandra Wingate, who searched for Spanish examples after the
Panizzi lectures, emailed me these citations, provided the translations, and engaged in helpful correspondence on the subject. Juan-Carlos Condé also searched but found no further references beyond
these two; I am grateful to him, too, for his labours.

[147] M.-C. Newbould, *Adaptations of Laurence Sterne's Fiction: Sterneana, 1760–1840* (London:
Routledge, 2013), p. 20.

[148] *Voyage Sentimental par M. Stern, sous le nom d'Yorick; traduit de l'Anglois par M. Frénais*, 2 vols in 1
(Amsterdam and Paris, 1769), pp. 231–2, quoted in Newbould, *Adaptations*, p. 21.

Although the three '&c's would seem to indicate which part of the *chambre de fille*'s anatomy Yorick caught, Frénais assures the reader that there was no embarrassment when the two met the next day. Newbould weighs up interpretations of the three '&c's. She finds some support for a suggestive '&c' in the *honi soit* ('what, exactly, is the *mal* that the reader might *pense*?') but concludes in favour of an innocent '&c' based on the subsequent reassurance about lack of embarrassment.[149] I think, however, that Frénais treads an ironic line between the two positions: the lack of embarrassment is due to the *chambre de fille*'s lack of displeasure at Yorick's action. It looks, tentatively, as though both Spanish and French see the bawdy potential in *&c-etcetera*.

Conclusion

Although I said that in Shakespeare 'and so forth' concludes a list, that is true only in terms of its location in the list, not in terms of the function it serves conceptually. Like *etcetera*, 'and so forth' never ends anything: it concludes (or seems to conclude) only by inviting continuation. Thus *&c-etcetera* is not just what is absent from the text but also what refuses to go away: it is the ghost character of early modern writing, the site of perpetual exchange between the potential and the actual in knowledge. It is a textual moment which gestures beyond the text—whether in prose or in performance. It is a textual embodiment of absence. And if one accept its invitation to complete, one negates its status as *&c-etcetera*, as something which exists only in incompletion and interruption and breaking off.

Sir John Davies' poem on dancing, *Orchestra* (1622), has a hiatus at stanza 126 as we saw in Chapter 1: '*Here are wanting some Stanzaes describing Queene Elizabeth. / Then follow these.*'[150] It resumes for five stanzas (the 'these'), before concluding with stanza 132 as follows (L3r):

132

So &c. &c. *   *   *

The combination of '&c' with asterisks invites attention: the asterisk is the focus of Chapter 3.

---

[149] Newbould, *Adaptations*, p. 21.   [150] Davies, *Orchestra* in *Nosce Teipsum* (1622), L2r.

The Asterisk; or, the Gnomic Page

We do not know the full meaning of these signs, and our ignorance should be part of our sense of them. (George K. Hunter) [1]

Introduction

Like the blank and the *&c-etcetera* in previous chapters, the asterisk is a typographical sign that draws attention to what it professes to conceal. So we are in familiar territory and I want to begin by looking at what the asterisk stands in for, what kind of absence it represents. But we saw in previous chapters that the blank and the *&c-etcetera* had multiple meanings and the asterisk is no different. Although it represents absence it also does the opposite: it *is* the thing it represents—a star—so I want to look at this paradox in representation. However, where early modern readers most often encountered the asterisk was in the margin and so in Part II of this chapter I look at early modern systems of navigating books, the material around the text (notes and indexes and stage directions), in all of which the asterisk has a role to play.

Both parts of this chapter are about the *mise-en-page* and therefore fit the theme of this book, *The Rhetoric of the Page*, where I have been using 'rhetoric' in the sense of graphic meaning as part of a text's rhetorical strategy—negotiating the layout of the printed page. However, in previous chapters I have also been considering rhetoric literally, thinking about the typography of the page as a visual extension of rhetorical terms. The asterisk takes us into the territory of the *gnome*: the rhetorical term for something that points beyond itself, what

---

[1] George K. Hunter in John Marston, *The Malcontent*, ed. George K. Hunter (1975; Revels; Manchester: Manchester University Press, 1999), p. xxxix.

The Rhetoric of the Page. Laurie Maguire, Oxford University Press (2020). © Laurie Maguire.
DOI: 10.1093/oso/9780198862109.001.0001

Puttenham in *The Arte of English Poesie* (1589) calls the 'Directour' (Dd1r).[2] Puttenham explains it as 'a maner of speach to alleage textes or authorities of wittie sentence'; the gnome directs you to wisdom beyond the immediate (con)text, citing other 'textes or authorities' (Dd1r).

In 1624, John Gee makes the same point about the asterisk's role as a director when he uses 'Index' as an equivalent term for 'asterisk': 'It is here expressed *Notanter et innuendo*, by <u>pointing</u> to it, *quod habes*, *That which thou hast*. And so these words are a kind of <u>*Index or Asterisk*</u> to direct us by a signe or marke to a thing thereby signified' (C2r, my underlining).[3] Instructing the would-be orator in 1633, Charles Butler devoted a section to *sententiae*, similarly advocating the use of asterisks or manicules in the margin to indicate gnomic pointing.[4]

Gee was using 'index' in its etymological sense of pointing, indicating; we are most familiar with this as the manicule, the pointing index finger in the margin.[5] Consequently, this chapter looks at the place the asterisk has in a suite of symbols in the margins of texts (numerals, letters, the obelus, and idiosyncratic purpose-made symbols) directing the reader: symbols that mark items of note—moral note, literary note—in the text for extraction into commonplace books. The gnomic, pointing asterisk is associated with wisdom, with knowledge (Puttenham offers the Latin *sententia* and the English *sage sayer* as synonyms for *gnome*) and the question this chapter ultimately poses is: what kind of knowledge does the asterisk broker in the margins of early modern texts?

Part I: Representation

Representation I: Absence

Ben Jonson

In 1598/9 Ben Jonson wrote an occasional tribute to Sir Thomas Palmer (1540–1626). It is a straightforward poem (Colin Burrow describes it as an

---

[2] See George Puttenham, *The Arte of English Poesie*, ed. Gladys Willcock and Alice Walker (Cambridge: Cambridge University Press, 1936), pp. 235–6. In Greek, *gnome* means thought, judgement, opinion; in English it becomes 'A short pithy statement of a general truth; a proverb, maxim, aphorism, or apophthegm' (*OED n.1*).

[3] John Gee, *Hold Fast* (1624).   [4] Charles Butler, *Oratoriae Libri Duo* (1633), A4v.

[5] William H. Sherman, *Used Books: Marking Readers in Renaissance England* (Philadelphia: University of Pennsylvania Press, 2008).

'early unfinished rhapsody rather in the manner of George Chapman'[6]). Palmer had compiled a manuscript book of botanical emblems, *The Sprite of Herbs and Trees*, for presentation to Elizabeth's Lord Treasurer, William Burghley. (Burghley died while the book was in preparation so it was presented to his son, Robert Cecil, as a New Year's Gift on 1 January 1599.) Jonson first met Palmer in 1589, and his dedicatory poem to Palmer appears at the head of the manuscript along with tributes by six other poets.[7] Jonson's poem was never printed in any of his subsequent collections, for reasons which are unclear: 'Jonson may have lost the poem or have come to outgrow it quite rapidly, or may have become uneasy about the poem as a result of its apparent references to the persecution of Palmer as a result of his Catholicism'. The enigmatic reference to unspecified 'travails' in the poem's conclusion is an oblique reference to religious suffering, and the reference to plants that survive storms and thunder in the poem's opening is allegorical; the Christian etymology of the dedicatee's surname provides an easy springboard to these more specific, Catholic references.[8]

The poem is only thirty lines long and at line 25 it breaks off—or breaks down—to indicate the way in which the author has broken down: he has fainted, lost consciousness.

> Till giddy with amazement I fell down
> In a deep trance *   *   *   *   *
> *   *   *   *   *   When lo, to crown thy worth
> I struggled with this passion that did drown
> My abler faculties, and thus brake forth

This is what we might call the aphasic asterisk: the asterisks coincide with the trance. What is missing here is textual—hence the asterisks; but consciousness is missing and the asterisks are the textual representation of the trance (see Figure 3.1).

---

[6] Colin Burrow, 'The Poems: Textual Essay', in *The Cambridge Edition of the Works of Ben Jonson Online*, vol. VII, ed. David Bevington, Martin Butler, and Ian Donaldson (Cambridge: Cambridge University Press, 2012). Available at: <https://universitypublishingonline.org/cambridge/benjonson/k/essays/The_Poems_textual_essay/>.

[7] For the relation between Jonson and Palmer, see Ian Donaldson, *Ben Jonson: A Life* (Oxford: Oxford University Press, 2011), pp. 146–7. For the placing of Jonson's poem, see Colin Burrow (ed.), 'From Thomas Palmer, *The Sprite of Trees and Herbs*', in *The Cambridge Edition*, vol. I, ed. Bevington, Butler, and Donaldson, p. 229.

[8] Burrow, 'The Poems'; Donaldson, *A Life*, p. 147, and Robert S. Miola, 'Ben Jonson, Catholic Poet', *Renaissance and Reformation/Renaissance et Réforme* 25:4 (2001), 101–15 (104).

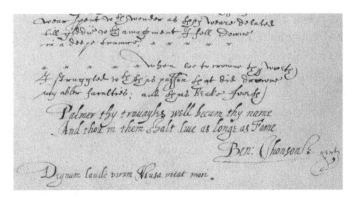

FIGURE 3.1 Ben Jonson, 'To Thomas Palmer', fol. 10. British Library Add MS 18,040. © The British Library Board.

Stars are often used to represent a dazed state or unconsciousness: all cartoon characters see stars when they get beaten up. But it is not necessary to have a blow to the head to see stars. The experience is triggered by pressure, so sneezing or rubbing one's eyes or suffering a drop in blood pressure is sufficient. The pressure stimulates the cells of the retina, and the optic nerve translates this pressure into star-shaped images called phosphenes. These pressure phosphenes remain for a few seconds after the pressure of sneezing or rubbing stops so when the eyes are opened, the stars are still visible. Neurologists describe this as a visual experience in which one sees light without light actually entering the eye. So although I am using the Jonson example to illustrate absence (the absence of consciousness), it also depicts presence, in a nice visual pun: Jonson falls down in a trance and he sees stars.

Jonson was a master of obliquity, often for good political or religious reasons.[9] This means that his readers have to make an interpretive effort but even Ian Donaldson, the great Jonson biographer and editor, admits defeat here: 'For reasons never explained—the inadequacy of the poet? the nature of the emblems? the private allegiances of their maker?—the central subject of this poem remains finally unutterable, issuing merely in a set of typographical markers'.[10] In fact, I will offer a reason when I return to the poem at the end of this chapter, but for now I simply want to note it as an example of affective typography: the asterisk is a marker of emotional overload.

---

[9] See Donaldson, *A Life*, p. 147, and Miola, 'Ben Jonson'.   [10] Donaldson, *A Life*, p. 147.

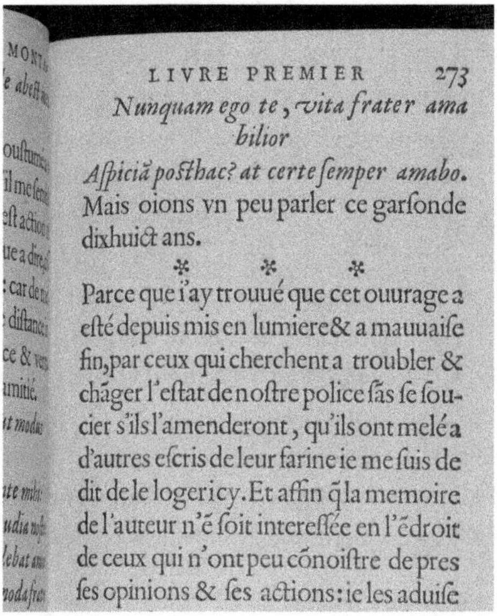
LIVRE PREMIER 273

Nunquam ego te, vita frater ama bilior

Aſpiciã poſthac? at certe ſemper amabo.

Mais oions vn peu parler ce garſonde dixhuict ans.

* * *

Parce que i'ay trouué que cet ouurage a eſté depuis mis en lumiere & a mauuaiſe fin, par ceux qui cherchent a troubler & chãger l'eſtat de noſtre police ſãs ſe ſoucier s'ils l'amenderont, qu'ils ont melé a d'autres eſcris de leur farine ie me ſuis de dit de le logericy. Et affin q̃ la memoire de l'auteur n'ẽ ſoit intereſſée en l'ẽdroit de ceux qui n'ont peu cõnoiſtre de pres ſes opinions & ſes actions: ie les aduiſe

FIGURE 3.2 Montaigne, *Essais* (1580), S1r, p. 273. Shelfmark Arch. B. f. 59. By permission of the Bodleian Libraries, University of Oxford.

Montaigne

Twenty years before Jonson's poem, in 1580, Montaigne's essay 'On Friendship' offered a line of three asterisks (see Figure 3.2). Montaigne intended to include in this essay a work written by his close friend, Étienne de La Boétie (1530–1563). Etienne was a judge in the Bordeaux parliament (where he and Montaigne met), a philosopher, and the author of sonnets, translations, and a political essay on tyranny ('De la Servitude Volontaire ('Discourse on voluntary servitude')). It was this essay that Montaigne planned to reprint but just as the *Essais* was going to press, the material became too politically sensitive. Montaigne explains:

> [h]aving discovered that this work of his has since been published to an evil end by those who seek to disturb and change the state of our national polity without worrying whether they will make it better, and that they have set it among works of their own kidney, I have gone back on my decision to place it here.[11]

In other words, La Boétie's essay was being seditiously appropriated by Protestant republicans in the French religious wars and to print it would

[11] Michel de Montaigne, *The Complete Essays*, ed. M. A. Screech (Harmondsworth: Penguin, 1991), p. 218.

inevitably associate Montaigne with this faction. Montaigne therefore cut the material and replaced it with a separate chapter containing twenty-nine of La Boétie's sonnets. But the first edition (1580) contains both the substitute—the sonnets—and a line of asterisks indicating the omitted material.[12]

Saul Frampton gives a wonderful, anthropomorphized description of this line: 'the three cold and distant five-fingered stars—in the place where La Boétie's words should have run on from his own—mark the cold and irredeemable distance of his loss, like hands reaching out but never touching'.[13] This is not poetic exaggeration. Montaigne did not alter his original text around the omission which still cues La Boétie's words, even though the words are no longer there: 'Mais oions [voyons] un peu parler ce garcon de dixhuict [huit] ans [Let us hear this eighteen-year-old boy speak]'.

The closeness of La Boétie and Montaigne was immortalized by Montaigne in this essay on friendship, most memorably in his expression of intersubjectivity:

> In the friendship which I am talking about, souls are mingled and confounded in so universal a blending that they efface the seam which joins them together so that it cannot be found. If you press me to say why I loved him, I feel that it cannot be expressed except by replying: 'Because it was him: because it was me'.[14]

La Boétie's words were here designed to mix with Montaigne's, textually blending and effacing the seam which joins them together. The absence of La Boétie's words is therefore more than just a textual excision: it is a profound ontological hole in Montaigne's very being for which the only expression is the asterisk.[15]

George Saunders, *Lincoln in the Bardo*

We see the asterisk standing in for the emotionally unspeakable in *Lincoln in the Bardo*, George Saunders' Booker Prize-winning novel of 2017.[16] On the

---

[12] The sonnets occupy sigs S3v–T2v. For an account of the political circumstances that led to the excision of the sonnets, and Montaigne's decision to indicate their absence, see Saul Frampton, *When I am Playing with My Cat, How Do I Know that She is Not Playing with Me: Montaigne and Being in Touch with Life* (New York: Vintage Books/Random House, 2011), p. 39 and Donald M. Frame, *Montaigne: A Biography* (New York: Harcourt, Brace & World Inc., 1965), pp. 72–3.

[13] Frampton, *When I am Playing*, p. 39.   [14] Montaigne, *Essays*, pp. 211–12.

[15] When the second edition was published, eight years later, it just included the twenty-nine sonnets: there is no line of asterisks. But in the 1580 Bordeaux copy even the sonnets are absent. M. A. Screech's headnote explains: 'Montaigne simply struck them all out. . . . No attempt is made to conceal the omission: the gaps are like blank columns in a censored newspaper' (*Essays*, p. 220).

[16] George Saunders, *Lincoln in the Bardo* (London: Bloomsbury, 2017).

page this novel looks like a play. Generically liminal, it appropriately explores boundaries and juxtapositions—between this world and the next, between the slave and the free, between historical voices and fictional voices. The novel's narrators are speaking spectres who are not aware that they are dead and use an idiosyncratic vocabulary to describe things and relationships (a coffin is a 'sick box' from which they expect to recover). The novel is, among other things, a linguistic experiment in the emotional states that can and cannot be articulated—grief, for example. Even minor characters contribute to this. Litzie Wright is so brutalized by her soldier-rapists that she is rendered utterly silent about the experience, her speech reduced to a series of asterisks. The asterisks vary in number. On page 221 we find this dialogue:

Go ahead, Litzie. It's now or f——— never.

betsy baron

****

litzie wright

Silent.

eddie baron

As always.

betsy baron

What the f——— must've been done to her? To shut her up so tight?

eddie baron

Stepping up beside the mulatto came a stout negro woman of some years, by all appearances a large, outwardly jolly presence in that previous place, who was not jolly at all now, but livid, and scowling; and her feet, worn to nubs, left two trails of blood behind her, and as she placed her hands (also worked to nubs) on the mulatto's hips, in support, she left bloody prints in two places there on the pale smock, as the mulatto continued to thrum and shake.

the reverend everly thomas

****

litzie wright

In this sequence, the asterisks don't represent anything textual (a narrative or sequence of words) that we could source elsewhere or supply by imagination. The asterisks stand in for an emotional horror, untranslatable into words, so deep is its trauma. They are followed by a near-full-page paragraph of paradoxically horrendous lyricism in which Mrs Francis Hodge imagines Litzie's story.

The Eighteenth Century: Swift, Pope, Sterne

Eighteenth-century texts experimented with punctuation: dashes, asterisks, manicules, sequences of 'XXX', and blank spaces.[17] The century began with fairly orthodox uses. In 1704 Jonathan Swift comically exploited the asterisk's traditional representation of absence, using it to present a faux-hiatus in the *Battle of the Books* (see Figure 3.3). But he also harnessed its genuine power to represent omission. 'The Author Upon Himself' (1713) begins with the explanation '*A few of the first Lines were wanting in the Copy sent by a Friend of the Author's from* London', followed by four lines of asterisks (see Figure 3.4). (This poem actually begins with a double blank, as the opening line reads, 'By an ——— ——— ——— pursu'd'.[18]) In 'An Epistle to Mr Gay' (1731) the word 'STATESMAN' is artistically self-censored with a zigzag arrangement of asterisks (see Figure 3.5).[19]

A sequence of four asterisked lines in Pope's *Dunciad* (1728–43) cancels an attack on Thomas Hanmer's Shakespeare edition (the edition did not appear until 1743–4; it was an eclectic, undocumented mixture of emendations by Pope, Theobald, and Hanmer himself and was self-published). Hanmer-as-editor was lampooned by Pope in Book IV of the *Dunciad* as the knight Montalto, where Pope glosses the 'Knight' in a footnote as 'An eminent person, who was about to publish a very pompous Edition of a great Author, *at his own expense*' (emphasis original) (see Figure 3.6).[20]

These are broad-brush summaries of complex personal and textual relations; the point here is simply to note the asterisk's traditional role in representing omission (although not always concealment). For experiments with the asterisk

[17] For 'XXX' see Leonard MacNally, *Sentimental Excursions to Windsor and Other Places* (London, 1781), p. 171, cited in M.-C. Newbould, *Adaptations of Laurence Sterne's Fiction: Sterneana, 1760–1840* (London: Routledge, 2013); Newbould says that 'the "X" is a diminished version of the "★"' (p. 165).

[18] Jonathan Swift, *Poems on Severall Occasions* (Dublin: George Faulkner, 1735), p. 343. At least, it begins this way in the cancelled state; the uncancelled reads 'By an †old red-Pate murd'ring Hag pursued', with the obelisk directing us to a footnote, '*The late D* --------*s of S*--------*t*' (*Poems*, p. 343). A copy of volume II of the Faulkner edition, now in the Bodleian English Faculty Library, contains leaves that were subsequently cancelled still in place, and all the cancels (except ★Z) bound in at the end of the book. See Margaret Weedon, 'An Uncancelled Copy of the First Collected Edition of Swift's Poems', *Library* 5th series 22 (1967), 44–56. This copy was unique until recently: see Andrew Carpenter and James Woolley, 'Faulkner's *Volume II. Containing the Author's Poetical Works*: A New Uncancelled Copy', in *Münster 2019: Reading Swift: Papers from the Seventh Münster Symposium 2017*, ed. Hermann J. Real (Munich: Verlag Wilhem Fink, 2019), pp. 47–58. I am grateful to James McLaverty for bringing the variant states to my attention and for communicating the discovery of a second extant copy with the cancelled and uncancelled leaves.

[19] Swift, *Poems*, p. 419. The uncancelled state has the word in full.

[20] Alexander Pope, *The Dunciad in Four Books Printed According to the Complete Copy Found in the Year 1742 with the Prolegomena of Scriblerus and Notes Variorum* (London: M. Cooper, 1743), IV, ll. 113–20, p. 165.

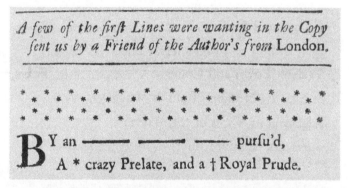

Goddefs *Diffidence*, came unteen, and caft
a Mift before his Eyes) tho'
Vid. Homer. his was of Gold, and coft a
hundred Beeves, the others but of rufty
Iron. However, this glittering Armor
became the *Modern* yet worfe than his
Own. Then, they agreed to exchange
Horfes, but when it came to the Tryal,
Dryden was afraid, and utterly unable to
mount. * * * * * *
Alter hiatus * * * * * * * *
in MS. * * * * * * *
* * * * * * *Lucan* appeared upon
a fiery Horfe, of admirable Shape, but
head-ftrong, bearing the Rider where he
lift, over the Field ; he made a mighty
Slaughter among the Enemy's Horfe ;

FIGURE 3.3 Jonathan Swift, *The Battle of the Books*, in *A Tale of a Tub* (1704), p. 264.
Shelfmark 147959. Courtesy of the Huntington Library, San Marino.

*A few of the firft Lines were wanting in the Copy
fent us by a Friend of the Author's from* London.

B Y an ———— ———— ——— purfu'd,
A * crazy Prelate, and a † Royal Prude.

FIGURE 3.4 Jonathan Swift, *Works* (Dublin: George Faulkner, 1735), p. 343.
Shelfmark XL 77 1735 29164. By permission of the Bodleian Libraries, University of
Oxford (English Faculty Library).

AND firft : To make my Obfervation right,
I place a S T *₊*₊* A N full before my Sight.

FIGURE 3.5 Jonathan Swift, *Works* (Dublin: George Faulkner, 1735), p. 419. Shelfmark
XL 77 1735 29164. By permission of the Bodleian Libraries, University of Oxford
(English Faculty Library).

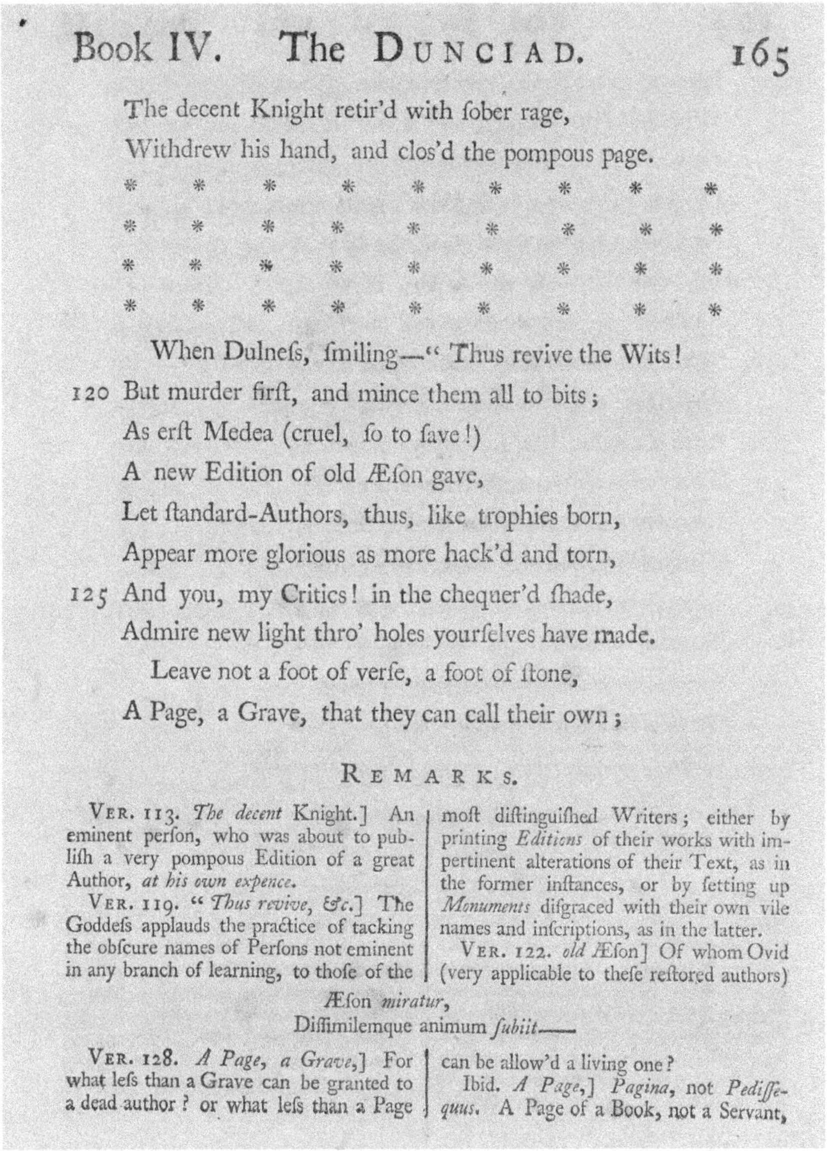

Book IV.   The DUNCIAD.   165

The decent Knight retir'd with fober rage,

Withdrew his hand, and clos'd the pompous page.

* * * * * * * * *

* * * * * * * * *

* * * * * * * * *

* * * * * * * * *

When Dulnefs, fmiling—" Thus revive the Wits!

120 But murder firft, and mince them all to bits;

As erft Medea (cruel, fo to fave!)

A new Edition of old Æfon gave,

Let ftandard-Authors, thus, like trophies born,

Appear more glorious as more hack'd and torn,

125 And you, my Critics! in the chequer'd fhade,

Admire new light thro' holes yourfelves have made.

Leave not a foot of verfe, a foot of ftone,

A Page, a Grave, that they can call their own;

REMARKS.

VER. 113. *The decent* Knight.] An eminent perfon, who was about to pub-lifh a very pompous Edition of a great Author, *at his own expence.*

VER. 119. " *Thus revive, &c.*] The Goddefs applauds the practice of tacking the obfcure names of Perfons not eminent in any branch of learning, to thofe of the

moft diftinguifhed Writers; either by printing *Editions* of their works with im-pertinent alterations of their Text, as in the former inftances, or by fetting up *Monuments* difgraced with their own vile names and infcriptions, as in the latter.

VER. 122. *old* Æfon] Of whom Ovid (very applicable to thefe reftored authors)

Æfon *miratur,*
Diffimilemque animum *fubiit——*

VER. 128. *A Page, a Grave,*] For what lefs than a Grave can be granted to a dead author? or what lefs than a Page

can be allow'd a living one?
Ibid. *A Page,*] *Pagina,* not *Pediffe-quus.* A Page of a Book, not a Servant,

FIGURE 3.6 Alexander Pope, *The Dunciad in Four Books* (London: M. Cooper, 1743), IV, ll. 113–20, p. 165. Shelfmark YL 64.1 [DUN] 1743; 26932. By permission of the Bodleian Libraries, University of Oxford (English Faculty Library).

we must turn to Laurence Sterne's *The Life and Opinions of Tristram Shandy* (1759–67)[21] which uses the asterisk in a typographically titillating way.

This shaggy-dog fictional autobiography chronicles the life of Tristram Shandy from conception. It is volume II before we get even close to him being born. What will become a turning point in his biography (the moment of delivery) hinges on who will attend his mother in pregnancy and labour. Mrs Shandy prefers the attendance of a female midwife to Dr Slop because, Uncle Toby explains, she 'does not care to let a man come so near her ****'.[22] Uncle Toby may break off here out of modesty (Tristram, the narrator, won't say whether the sentence was completed or not) and Sterne/Tristram draws our attention to this verbal moment, or non-verbal moment, as a challenge in writerly representation. He repeats it, first identifying it as a rhetorical moment (an example of aposiopesis) and then considers alternative ways (non-asterisked ways) of representing Uncle Toby's missing word in print: ' "My sister, mayhap", quoth my Uncle *Toby*, "does not care to let a man come so near her ****". Make this dash, --- 'tis an Aposiopesis. – Take the dash away, and write *Backside*, --'tis Bawdy. Scratch Backside out, and put *Covered way* in, 'tis a Metaphor'.[23]

Most readers, if they think about these notational systems at all, would probably be content to leave the four asterisks as a vague indication of Mrs Shandy's nether regions rather than a coded representation of specific sexual slang. 'Four-letter word' was a phrase not yet in existence. *Tristram Shandy* is full of asterisks, replacements for vocabulary from single words to whole sentences, and they seem playful teases rather than cryptographic codes. The novel prompted a commentary, published within a year of the first two volumes: *Explanatory Remarks upon the Life and Opinions of Tristram Shandy; wherein the Morals and Politics of this Piece are Clearly Laid Open*, by Jeremiah Kunastrokius MD (1760). The name is obviously a pseudonym, an obscene Latin pun, so there is a witty appropriateness in this scurrilous pseudonym for a writer who claims to investigate modesty in *Tristram Shandy*. From its very first pages, the exaggerations of the *Explanatory Remarks* prepare us for parody:

> the beauties and excellencies of his [Tristram Shandy's] work, may not only be passed over by many of the inhabitants of *Asia-minor*, *Monomotapa*, some of the

---

[21] Volumes I and II were published in 1759, volumes III and IV in 1761, volumes V and VI in 1762, volumes VII and VIII in 1765, and volume IX in 1767. As Newbould notes, the novel's publication 'was not a static event, but a constant process of evolution' (*Adaptations*, p. 18).

[22] Laurence Sterne, *The Life and Opinions of Tristram Shandy*, vol. II (York: Ann Ward, 1759), p. 91.

[23] Sterne, *Tristram Shandy*, vol. II, p. 92.

Mickmacs, Cherokees, and Catawbas, but, at least, by seven hundred and fifty of the inhabitants of *London*, and *Westminster*, the *Borough of Southwark*, and parts adjacent.... I now set down to write for the seven hundred and fifty *incomprehensible readers* of *Tristram Shandy*, in and about the purlieus of this metropolis, — and *no other*. To them be it known, then, that Mr. *Tristram Shandy* is one of the greatest moralists, and most refined politicians this, or any other age whatever has produced.[24]

The obscene etymology of 'Kunastrokius' receives extended attention in the author's own Shandy-esque biography published later in 1760.[25] In it he claims that the success of his *Explanatory Remarks* had not only sold out the entire print run and occasioned a second larger impression but had prompted speculation about his true identity. Some denied his existence, some alleged he was not a true doctor, and some believed he was none other than Tristram Shandy himself. Accordingly, he has felt obliged to publish his own *Life and Opinions*. Like Tristram, he begins before his birth, with a genealogical table tracing his ancestry back to Adam via Alexander the Great, Cyrus, and Nimrod. He then explains the origin of his surname in a discussion which constantly raises and dismisses the sexual. Considering the variant Latin morphology *cunnus* taxes the 'Chastity of [his] Pen';[26] he denies that there is any *double entendre* in 'To stroke';[27] and he concludes the introduction by printing a fan letter from a reader, 'Diana Morelove' (the name paradoxically couples the Goddess of Chastity with a demand for more love), who thanks him for explaining Tristram Shandy's 'four stars' and says 'you have so pleased and tickled *me ****, that I am resolv'd to have a further Acquaintance with you'.[28] In a footnote Kunastrokius says he has emended the lady's 'my ****' to 'me'; but this emended possessive pronoun makes her request for further activity with the sexual body part denoted by the asterisks all too clear.

This fescennine autobiography follows naturally from Kunastrokius' *Explanatory Remarks*, which were devoted to decoding Sterne's asterisks. Kunastrokius assumes an equivalence between the number of asterisks—there are four of them—and the number of letters in the missing word in Uncle Toby's statement. He concludes that they represent 'the *third*, the *twentieth*, the

---

[24] Jeremiah Kunastrokius, *Explanatory Remarks upon the Life and Opinions of Tristram Shandy; wherein the Morals and Politics of this Piece are Clearly Laid Open* (London: E. Cabe, 1760), pp. 6–7, emphasis original.

[25] Jeremiah Kunastrokius, *The Life and Opinions of Jeremiah Kunastrokius* (London: E. Cabe, 1760).

[26] Kunastrokius, *Life and Opinions*, p. viii.   [27] Kunastrokius, *Life and Opinions*, p. ix.

[28] Kunastrokius, *Life and Opinions*, p. xii. The single asterisk denotes a footnote; the sequence of four represents an omission.

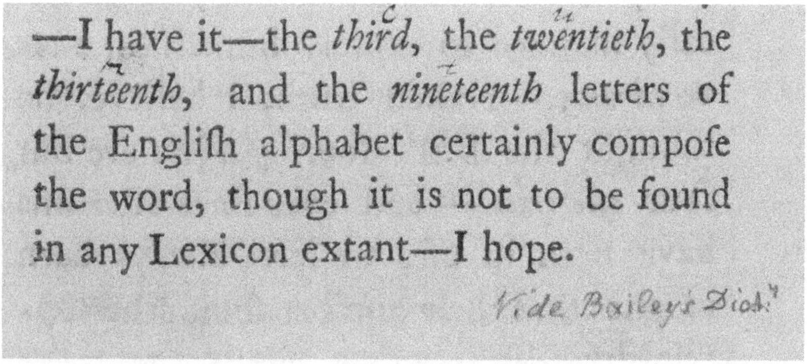

> —I have it—the *third*, the *twentieth*, the *thirteenth*, and the *nineteenth* letters of the Englifh alphabet certainly compofe the word, though it is not to be found in any Lexicon extant—I hope.
>
> *Vide Bailey's Dict.*

FIGURE 3.7 Jeremiah Kunastrokius, *Explanatory Remarks upon the Life and Opinions of Tristram Shandy* (London: E. Cabe, 1760), p. 28. Shelfmark Godw. subt. 111–112 (v.3–4). By permission of the Bodleian Libraries, University of Oxford.

thirteenth and the *nineteenth* letters of the English alphabet'.[29] (If one checks his arithmetic and finds oneself a letter out, it is because i/j still counted as one letter.) The ostensible raison d'être of Kunastrokius' work is to argue for morality and modesty in *Tristram Shandy*; in practice he provides a treatise on the asterisk. He works his way through Sterne's novel, asterisk by asterisk.

The reader of the copy now in the Bodleian Library spelled out Kunastrokius' circumlocutions—literally (see Figure 3.7). He inked in the four letters of the alphabet above Kunastrokius' numerals. He also responded to Kunastrokius' vain hope that the offensive word did not feature in any lexicon by actually checking a dictionary: 'Vide Bailey's Dict', a reference to Nathan Bailey's hugely popular *Dictionarium Britannicum* (1730 onwards), a forerunner of the *Oxford English Dictionary*.[30]

It is not often that we can follow a reader so closely in the act of reading. He first dwells on the sentence on the page and then consults another book.

Swearing

A brief digression on the history of obscenity is necessary because what counts as a bad word varies through history and so, too, does the typography

---

[29] Kunastrokius, *Explanatory Remarks*, p. 28.
[30] *Bailey's Dictionary* does indeed contain the noun, defined decorously in its usual ameliorative Latin form (*pudendum muliebre*). The British Library website entry on dictionaries highlights Bailey's, with an explanation of its importance (such as its inclusion of rude words). See: <https://www.bl.uk/learning/langlit/dic/bailey/1730bailey.html>.

used to sanitize it.[31] The avoidance of sexual body parts via euphemism has a complicated development, related to the history of swearing. 'Swearing' itself is a difficult term to unpack because it encompasses oaths (swearing *by* or *to* or *that*), which are not necessarily offensive, and swearing *at*, which is.[32] Tony McEnery explains that 'while profligate swearing in the seventeenth century may have been a cause of offence, it was distinct from obscene language, which was much closer to what one may term modern swearing'. He discusses oaths, obscenity, blasphemy, and morally offensive terms under the general heading 'bad language'.[33] Melissa Mohr notes that 'it was only at the end of the nineteenth century that "swearing" began to indicate both oaths and obscene words'.[34] Chaucer's Pardoner denounces swearing (ironically, given his own hypocrisies), describing the roisterers' breaking of verbal taboos:

> And many a grisly ooth thane han they sworn
> And Cristes blessed body they al torente.[35]

Ophelia swears 'by Gis [Jesus], and by Saint Charity' (*Hamlet*, 4.5.58). The offensive religious swearing—in public—is evidence of her madness.[36]

In early modernity the really unmentionable words were religious not sexual. Swearing by God or by parts of God's body was taboo: God's wounds (zounds), God's eyelid (slid), God's nails (snails), God's foot (sfoot), God's blood (sblood), God's bones (sbones), God's body (sbody). Thus, 'a turd in your teeth'

---

[31] For excellent accounts of this subject, see Geoffrey Hughes, *Swearing: A Social History of Foul Language, Oaths and Profanity in English* (Oxford: Blackwell, 1991); Tony McEnery, *Swearing in English: Bad Language, Purity and Power from 1586 to the Present* (Abingdon: Routledge, 2006); and Melissa Mohr, *Holy Shit: A Brief History of Swearing* (Oxford: Oxford University Press, 2013). For more general obscenity in relation to objects and viewing, see Deana Heath, 'Obscenity, Censorship, and Modernity', in *A Companion to the History of the Book*, ed. Simon Eliot and Jonathan Rose (Oxford: Blackwell, 2008), pp. 508–19.

[32] See Hughes, *Swearing*, p. 4.   [33] McEnery, *Swearing in English*, p. 61.

[34] Mohr, *Holy Shit*, p. 12.

[35] *The Pardoner's Tale*, ll. 708–9, in *The Riverside Chaucer*, ed. Larry Benson (Boston, MA: Houghton Mifflin Co., 1987).

[36] It is hard for modern productions to convey the transgressive vulnerability of Ophelia in this scene: a teenager swearing and singing bawdy songs does not have the shock value of 1601. The production of *Hamlet* at the Royal Shakespeare Company in 2008 (directed by Gregory Doran) used modern dress to stage an equivalent. Ophelia entered in a cotton floral bra and underpants and was compassionately covered up by Gertrude with her pashmina. We might be inured to a teenager's bad language and sexual knowledge but we understand that something is wrong when she appears in public in her underwear.

was ok; 'by God's bones' was not.[37] There was a superstition that oaths had illocutionary force, in the J. L. Austin sense: by dismembering God's body verbally you were actually doing physical violence to it.[38] Censored oaths (or self-censored oaths) were represented by dashes, empty brackets, or dashes within brackets, as we saw in Chapter 2. In Marston's *Dutch Courtesan* (1605), we find 'Will I: I [Aye] by the (   )' and 'By (   ) but I do now' (F4r, F2r.) In Jonson's *Cynthia's Revels* (1601), we read: 'by (—) *'tis good*' (*Works*, Z3r).[39] This was especially the case after the 1606 'Act to Restrain Abuses', which prohibited religious oaths on stage. When the contract replaced the oath, 'the great age of oath swearing was over, and the rise of obscenity was beginning'.[40] Christopher Hill locates this transition in the age of Hobbes although we can see signs of it earlier: the 1590s play *Arden of Faversham* contrasts a world based on contracts with one based on honour.[41]

Despite its varied forms, all swearing tends to mix the sacred and the profane and to serve the same functions: emphasis, cathartic release, desire to shock. The Restoration perfected this mix as in the opening of Rochester's 'Satire on Charles II':

> I' th'isle of Britain long since famous growne
> For breeding the best cunts in Christendome   (ll. 1–2)

It is the alliterative juxtaposition in the second line that attracts attention, rather than the licentiousness per se.[42]

Modern swearwords are coupled with body parts and functions. The development of privacy, architecturally and conceptually, means that physical

---

[37] Mohr, *Holy Shit*, p. 93. In Jonson's *Bartholomew Fair*, 'a turd in your teeth' is Humphrey Wasp's repeated overexcited refrain. For Prospero's effect on Caliban, see 'You taught me language, and my profit on't / Is, I know how to curse' (*Tempest*, 1.2.363–4). Margaret Atwood develops this theme in *Hag Seed* (London: Hogarth Press, 2016) where the prison inhabitants rehearsing *The Tempest* are only permitted to curse using phrases from the play.

[38] This is part of a debate about whether linguistic terms are *ad placitum* (arbitrary and conventional) or *ex congruo* (motivated and mimetic). The terms are Francis Bacon's but the question and categories go back as far as Plato's *Cratylus*. For Bacon's position on words versus things see Brian Vickers, 'Bacon and Rhetoric', in *The Cambridge Companion to Bacon*, ed. Markku Peltonen (Cambridge: Cambridge University Press, 1996), pp. 200–31.

[39] At least, this is how it appears in the 1616 *Works* (STC 14752). The quarto of 1601 reads '*By God*' (M2v).

[40] Mohr, *Holy Shit*, p. 143.

[41] For Hobbes, see Mohr, *Holy Shit*, p. 142; for *Arden*, see Alexander Leggatt, '*Arden of Faversham*', *Shakespeare Survey* 36 (1983), 121–36.

[42] Hughes, *Swearing*, p. 140.

activities that were once performed in public places (urinating, defecating, having sex) become hidden in the Renaissance, and the vocabulary for them became concealed too. 'Sixteenth-century people were ashamed of more things than their medieval forebears, and ashamed in front of more people. It became more and more important to conceal these various shameful body parts and actions, in public life and in polite language'.[43] We saw evidence of this development in Chapter 2 in the use of &c-etcetera. The eighteenth century saw the rise of ameliorative Latin terms and orthophemisms—defecate, osculate, perspire—and the Victorian period was the heyday of euphemism (the 'etcetera' of Chapter 2 is a Victorian synonym for underwear). Table legs and chicken legs became, along with human legs, 'unmentionables', and the textiles that clothed legs—trousers—were similarly verbally off limits. In *Oliver Twist*, Giles the butler explains that he got out of bed in the night and '"drew on a pair of ----"' but is interrupted with the cautionary reminder, '"Ladies present"', before continuing '"--- Of *shoes*, sir"...laying great emphasis on the word'.[44]

Sterne (Continued)

Melissa Mohr does not deal specifically with the asterisk in her history of swearing but it is present on her book's dustjacket where it conceals the scatological: *Holy Sh*t*. Jeremiah Kunastrokius was possibly right to detect a system in *Tristram Shandy*, although perhaps not one that is as literal as he argued (where four asterisks equals a four-letter word). Sterne used various typographical forms to represent omissions. For instance, chapter 27 of volume IV begins as seen in Figure 3.8. But the asterisks come into their own when sexual explicitness is being avoided (see Figures 3.9 to 3.11).[45]

---

[43] Mohr, *Holy Shit*, p. 156.

[44] Charles Dickens, *Oliver Twist*, ed. Peter Fairclough (Harmondsworth: Penguin, 1986), p. 260. For the age of euphemism see Hughes, *Swearing*, pp. 139–63 (who cites several examples from Dickens, pp. 152–3), and Mohr, *Holy Shit*, pp. 173–226. For orthophemisms, see Mohr, *Holy Shit*, pp. 197–8. For the relation of obscenity and censorship see McEnery, *Swearing in English*, pp. 61–82.

[45] Layout differs slightly between London and Dublin editions in the 1760s and 1770s. In the opening of chapter 20 in volume IX (Dublin: Henry Saunders, 1779) for instance, the lines of asterisks form a single paragraph (B2r, p. 27). Whether dividing them into two 'paragraphs' or uniting them in one, the compositor is interpreting the asterisks and giving them a logical structure. On the way editors treat nonsense as if it has meaning, see Randall McLeod's analysis of chough's language in *All's Well that Ends Well*: Random Cloud [= Randall McLeod], 'Shakespear Babel', in *Reading Readings: Essays on Shakespeare Editing in the Eighteenth Century*, ed. Joanna Gondris (Newark, DE: Associated University Presses, 1997), pp. 1–70.

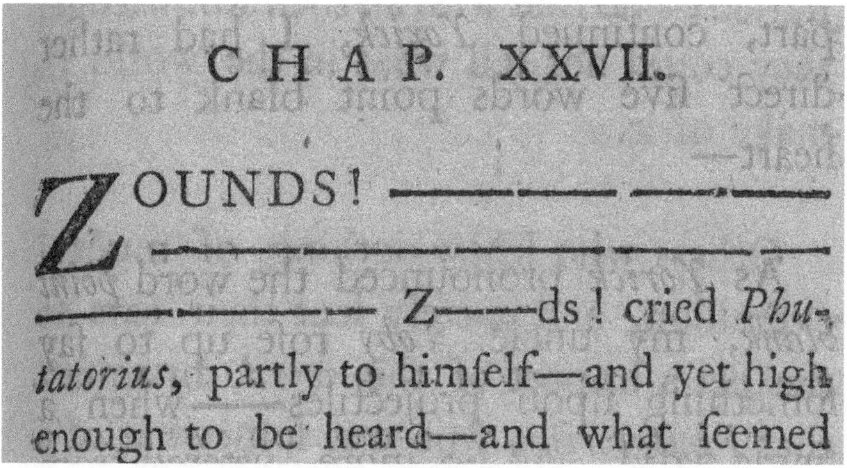

CHAP. XXVII.

ZOUNDS! ——— ———
——— ——— ——— ———
——— ——— Z——ds! cried *Phu-*
tatorius, partly to himſelf—and yet high
enough to be heard—and what ſeemed

FIGURE 3.8 Laurence Sterne, *The Life and Opinions of Tristram Shandy*, vol. IV (London: R. & J. Dodsley, 1761), p. 168. Shelfmark 77051. Courtesy of the Huntington Library, San Marino.

These examples all relate to Tristram's conception ('the other causes for which matrimony was ordained'; Figure 3.10) or delivery and circumcision ('there is a possibility . . . that the forceps'; Figure 3.11), or the widow Wadham's alarmed excitement at being shown the 'very place' where Uncle Toby was wounded (she anticipates being shown his groin rather than a map of the battlefield; Figure 3.9).

Sterne's novel was published serially in nine volumes over eight years; when the first two volumes were published in 1759, they were an immediate literary sensation. Kunastrokius' is only one of many parodic responses that included imitations of Sterne's digressions, his addresses to the reader, his typography, and the memoir genre. (There were also appalled complaints about the volumes' scurrility, given that Sterne was a clergyman.)[46] In the immediate aftermath of publication of the first two volumes, it was the punctuation that got most of the attention, with salacious jokes based on Sterne's asterisks becoming in-jokes. In one literary response analysed by Newbould, Leonard MacNally's *Sentimental Excursions to Windsor and Other Places* (1781), the heroine falls over backwards while exiting a coach (the hoop of her dress is caught in the doorway). Seeing her on her back with her legs in the air, the hero modestly averts his gaze. He forces himself to concentrate on a nearby inn sign, which

[46] See Newbould, *Adaptations*, pp. 16–20. Newbould documents eighty years of responses to Sterne's work in paintings as well as printed texts.

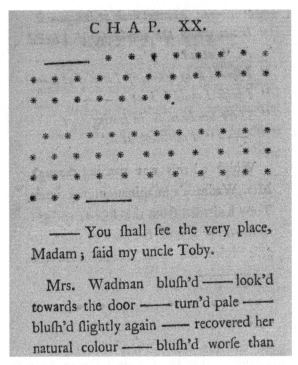

FIGURE 3.9 Laurence Sterne, *The Life and Opinions of Tristram Shandy*, vol. IX (London: T. Becket & P. A. Dehondt, 1767), F4r, p. 71. Shelfmark 86885. Courtesy of the Huntington Library, San Marino.

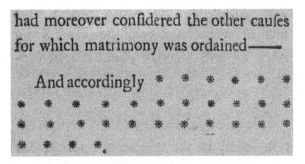

FIGURE 3.10 Laurence Sterne, *The Life and Opinions of Tristram Shandy*, vol. IX (London: T. Becket & P. A. Dehondt, 1767), F8v, p. 80. Shelfmark 86885. Courtesy of the Huntington Library, San Marino.

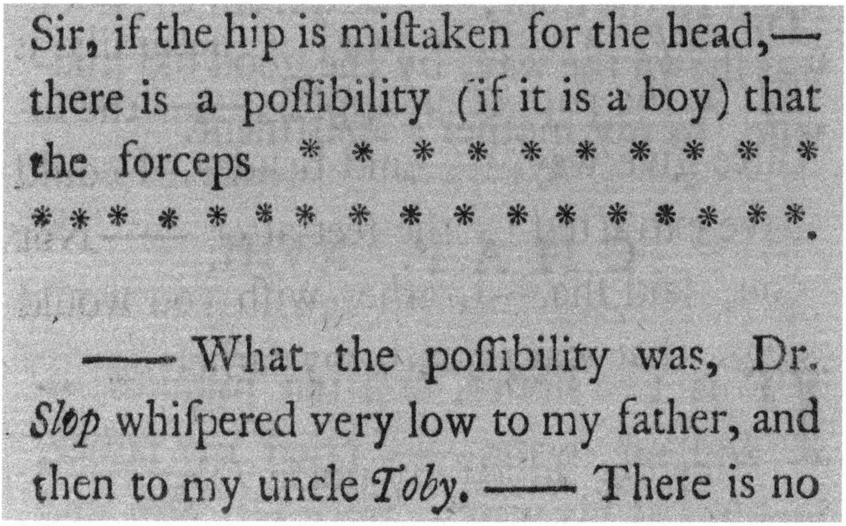

Sir, if the hip is miſtaken for the head,——
there is a poſſibility (if it is a boy) that
the forceps * * * * * * * * * *

* * * * * * * * * * * * * * *.

—— What the poſſibility was, Dr.
Slop whiſpered very low to my father, and
then to my uncle *Toby.* —— There is no

FIGURE 3.11 Laurence Sterne, *The Life and Opinions of Tristram Shandy*, vol. III (London: R. & J. Dodsley, 1761), E5r, p. 73. Shelfmark 77051. Courtesy of the Huntington Library, San Marino.

unfortunately happens to be the Star and the Garter—the two sexual provocations he is trying not to think about. This joke is a measure of the distance from the Renaissance to the eighteenth century. The Elizabethan printer, Richard Tottel, who had a print shop at Temple Bar on Fleet Street, had as his shop sign the 'Hand and Star'. His sign is an altogether innocent pun: it 'alludes to "his dependence on imported paper" since the hand and star was "a common watermark in early English imprints, signalling paper imported from France or Italy" '.[47]

Tristram Shandy invites readerly interventions, from its appeals to imagine scenes and paintings to its invitation to fill in blank space.[48] It is a supersized example of the phenomenon outlined in the Introduction to this book, where

[47] Tamara Atkin, *Reading Drama in Tudor England* (London: Routledge, 2018), p. 129, citing John Bidwell, 'French Paper in English Books', in *The Cambridge History of the Book in Britain*, vol. IV: *1557–1695*, ed. John Barnard and D. F. McKenzie with Maureen Bell (Cambridge: Cambridge University Press, 2002), pp. 583–601 (p. 585).

[48] The serial publication means that it was able to react to these responses, becoming a *chassé-croisé* (Anne Bandry's term, cited by Newbould, *Adaptations*, p. 18). For more on the response enabled by serial publication see Newbould, *Adaptations*, pp. 18–20 and Thomas Keymer, 'Dying by Numbers: *Tristram Shandy* and Serial Fiction', *The Shandean* 8 (1996), 41–67, and 9 (1997), 34–69 and Sterne, *The Moderns and the Novel* (Oxford: Oxford University Press, 2002).

the blank invites the reader to speculate or supply. This is particularly true when Sterne's asterisks replace something sexual. Christopher Wagstaff makes this the topic of an entire book. Wagstaff's parodic memoir *The Life, Travels and Adventures of Christopher Wagstaff, Gentlemen, Grandfather to Tristram Shandy* (1762) addresses the sexual nature of Sterne's asterisks. The book professes to be an edited version of an older text (by 'Wagstaff') 'originally published in the latter end of the last century. Interspersed with a suitable variety of matter by the editor. The whole being intended as a full and final answer to everything that has been, or shall be, written in the out-of-the-way way' (title page). It is intended 'as a proof that *Shandeism* (or something very like it) had an existence in this kingdom long before a late well-known publication' (A4r). The first chapter, by the anonymous 'editor', contains definitions and rules of punctuation, typography, and style *'which all editors and authors ought to learn by heart'* (B1r). Among them, it explains how to interpret asterisks:

> A short train, or half a dozen lines of asterisks, as * * *, or * * * * * * *
> * * * * * * * * * * * * * * * *
>
> signifies, that an author's meaning is not to be understood, when he speaks *plain*, but does not *speak out*; or denotes something of body or blasphemy (if need be) *innocently* left out to be *wickedly* and *absurdly* supplied by the reader's imagination. Thus— (B2r)

The example provided is none other than Uncle Toby's explanation of his sister's reluctance to use a male midwife.

For Montaigne and George Saunders, the asterisk stands in for the emotionally unspeakable; for Sterne and his adapters the asterisk represents the physically unspeakable. Sterne's unspeakable is comic (perhaps because it is knowable: it is a lexical void not an emotional one) but it has a serious literary side. Sterne's punctuation (and parodies of his punctuation) marks the beginning of a serious enquiry about how graphic appearance—type—contributes to portraying sensibility on the printed page. The eighteenth-century sentimental novel would go on to develop the dash as the typography of Modesty and Affect (especially with swooning heroines, a development itself parodied in Jane Austen's juvenilia). The dash becomes, like the *&c-etcetera* and the asterisk before, a narrative technique. And the development began, as Mary Newbould shows, with parodies of Sterne's asterisks and dashes. Barbara Benedict calls this typographic legibility the 'face of the page'—what in this book I call the 'rhetoric of the page'. Benedict's term is appealing because of its allusion to physiognomy, which is itself a late eighteenth-century fashion, like the novel.[49] In her analysis, the two forms of learning to read go together. We decode the mind's construction in the face; we decode the page.

The modern equivalent of the asterisk as typographical veil is to be found on the Internet where the asterisk indicates not a rude word but a distasteful concept from which one wishes to dissociate oneself emotionally or politically. A common current example of this, according to a recent *Guardian* article about Twitter, is a proper name—D*n*ld Tr*mp.[50] Individuals and concepts are now treated as if they are bad words and the asterisk holds things at a distance.[51]

What can't be represented, what is present only through a typographical indication of absence, paradoxically has its opposite in the asterisk's visual power to represent.

Representation II: Presence

Printers of early modern texts regularly use the asterisk non-representationally: that is, ornamentally. They use it singly, in chapter subheadings or on title pages; they print three in a horizontal line (known as a 'dinkus'); they group three or five asterisks into triangles or inverted triangles (known as 'asterisms'). They repeat asterisks in a single line to form a decorative border.[52] In the twenty-first century, *BBC Good Food* magazine depicted a circular arrangement of pear slices in a pie recipe, commenting that the cook should 'arrang[e] the pears in a neat asterisk'.[53] By 'neat', I assume they mean symmetrical: 'neat' is not an adjective usually associated with the asterisk.

Flowers

At the same time as the asterisk's decorative nature made it suitable for non-representation, its floral shape made it aesthetically appropriate for representing

---

[49] Barbara M. Benedict, 'Reading Faces: Physiognomy and Epistemology in Late-Eighteenth-Century Sentimental Novels', *Studies in Philology* 92:3 (1995), 311–28 (326).

[50] See <https://www.theguardian.com/books/booksblog/2018/nov/02/thank-s-for-asterisks-the-maligned-punctuation-enjoying-twitter-revival>.

[51] It tends to be vowels that are replaced by asterisks, but not always, as in this creative placard from the anti-Brexit protest in London in March 2019: 'FOR *U*K's SAKE, STOP BREXIT'. The asterisk has an acoustic equivalent in the bleep, which targets the entire word.

[52] Cf. Juliet Fleming, 'How to Look at a Printed Flower', *Word & Image* 22:2 (2006), 165–87 and 'Changed Opinion as to Flowers', in *Renaissance Paratexts*, ed. Helen Smith and Louise Wilson (Cambridge: Cambridge University Press, 2011), pp. 48–64. See also A. E. B. Coldiron, *Printers without Borders* (Cambridge: Cambridge University Press, 2015), pp. 228–40 (esp. p. 239).

[53] *BBC Good Food*, October 2017, front cover and pp. 60–1.

flowers. We see this most imaginatively in Stephen Hawes' *Conversion of Swearers* (1509). Hawes (fl. 1502–21) was a Tudor poet and courtier who served as Groom of the Chamber to Henry VII, as Hawes, or his printer, explains at the end of *Conversion* (A7v). He is the author of a long allegorical poem, *The Pastime of Pleasure* (1506, printed in 1509).[54] Four little-read shorter works— *The Example of Virtue* (1509), *The Conversion of Swearers* (1509), *A Joyful Meditation* (1509), and *The Comfort of Lovers* (1515)—were edited for the Early English Text Society in 1974.[55]

These poems have never recovered from C. S. Lewis' damning summary that Hawes 'seems ever on the point of becoming much better than he actually is'. Gordon Kipling holds Lewis responsible for the view that 'critical opinions of Stephen Hawes have traditionally distinguished between the dreadful poems he actually wrote and the brilliant ones he might have written'.[56] The denigration of Hawes tends to focus on his metrical technique (he suffers in this respect by comparison with Lydgate, whom, according to Anthony à Wood, he revered[57]). Hawes himself may inadvertently have contributed to this critical response through litotic modesty-*topoi*: the autobiographical first-person preface to the *Conversion of Swearers* confesses that he is 'lytell or nought expert in poetrye' (A2r) and it ends with the familiar *envoi* to the personified book, here coupled with an appositive description of the work which is modest to the point of disparagement: 'Go lyttel treatyse *devoyde of eloquence*' (A8r, my emphasis).

The Conversion of Swearers is a first-person address by the crucified Christ; its repetitive structure is an appeal to kings and their subjects to cease swearing. This summary makes the work sound homiletic (which, of course, it is). But it is also a moving account of the physical pain caused to Christ by human swearing for, as we have seen, oaths were deemed to have illocutionary force: the swearer 'tears' and 'rends' and 'razes' Christ's body anew (these verbs appear over twenty times in the eleven pages of the poem).

[54] The full title is *The History of Graunde Amour and la Bel Pucel, conteining the Knowledge of the Seven Sciences and the Course of Man's Life in this Worlde*. The poem details the education of a knight, and although it is traditional to say that it influenced *The Faerie Queene*, the *Spenser Encyclopedia* finds no evidence to support this assertion and much to refute it. See A. C. Hamilton (gen. ed.), *The Spenser Encyclopedia* (Toronto: University of Toronto Press, 1990), p. 348.

[55] Stephen Hawes, *The Minor Poems*, ed. Florence W. Gluck and Alice B. Morgan (Oxford: Oxford University Press, 1974).

[56] Gordon Kipling, review of Stephen Hawes, *The Minor Poems* ed. Gluck and Morgan, *Review of English Studies* 27 (1976), 457–8. This quotation, and that from C. S. Lewis, appear on p. 45.

[57] Anthony à Wood, *Athenae Oxonienses*, ed. P. Bliss (London: F. C. & J. Rivington et al., 1813), I, columns 9–11.

The poem uses seven-line stanzas in rhyme royal (*ababbcc*); it begins with the poet addressing us in this form before Christ starts to speak in the same rhyme scheme.[58] The metre is predominantly, sometimes clumsily, iambic, but the poem's form shows Hawes' interest in technical experimentation.

After the poet's address to us, the poem proper begins with eight stanzas of Christ's incredulity that swearers would rather go to the devil than inhabit the 'moost gloryous mansyon' (A3r). It then changes completely in both metrical format and in visual layout as Christ speaks in three-line stanzas. The printer uses pilcrows to indicate not just each new unit of stanzaic speech but changes of metre: the stanzas progress from monometer through dimeter, trimeter, tetrameter, pentameter to a pivotal hexameter stanza before descending through pentameter again down to monometer, like a virtuoso piano scale. The poem here has a visual, verbal symmetry. Furthermore, each three-line stanza is completed with a word or phrase in the right of the line, to which it is linked by a bracket (see Figure 3.12).

This horizontal linking in metre is interwoven with a vertical linking in rhyme: the completing rhymes in the right-hand side of the page increase their syllables (obviously) in tandem with the increase in metrical feet ('kynde' in lines 2/3, 'in mynde' in lines 5/6, for the monometer and dimeter sequence and so on). The eye (and ear) read and hear both horizontally and vertically. We thus see two kinds of *disjecta membra*: scattered limbs and scattered words; indeed, the scattered words *represent* the scattered limbs. The page extends this graphicological representation: its white space is strewn with ten floral asterisks which represent flowers strewn over Christ's limbs or aestheticized drops of Christ's blood.[59]

The final two lines of Christ's inset poem, which are printed on the following recto page, scatter geometric printers' ornaments instead of asterisks in the white space. Two horizontal lines of ornaments then stretch across the page as a section break before the poem resumes its regular seven-line stanzas.[60] The

---

[58] He later offers a sequence of anaphoric litanies ('Wo worthe' for four stanzas, followed by 'Blessyd be' for four stanzas on Aviv–Aviir) but the stanzaic rhyme scheme is unchanged. Gluck and Morgan note that these lines 'serve as a rhetorical flourish rather than as part of the poem's statement' (Hawes, *The Minor Poems*, ed. Gluck and Morgan, p. xxxviii). They were attractive enough for their eight stanzas to be copied out by a sixteenth-century reader in BL Harley 4294 (Hawes, *The Minor Poems*, ed. Gluck and Morgan, p. xx).

[59] Mohr reads the asterisks as flowers (*Holy Shit*, p. 121), Jonathan Sawday as blood (*Print, Space, and Void*, in progress).

[60] The Early English Books Online (EEBO) image of the Huntington copy misrepresents the visuals: a reader has copied the type ornaments in ink so the EEBO image looks busier and less symmetrical than the printed page actually is.

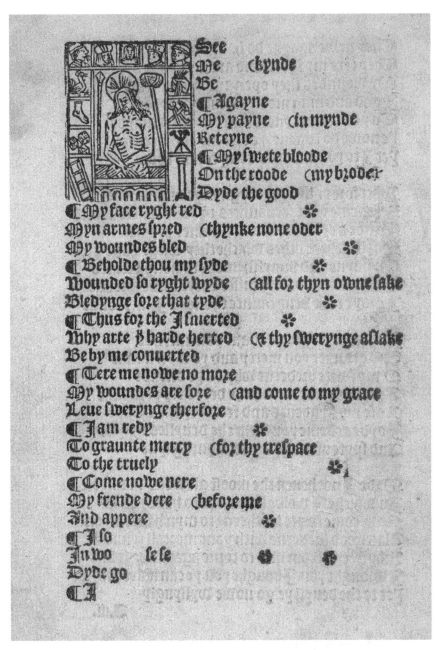

FIGURE 3.12 Stephen Hawes, *The Conversion of Swearers* (1509) STC 12943.5, A3v. Shelfmark 61309. Courtesy of the Huntington Library, San Marino.

inset poem is emotionally painful to read, so the two lines of type ornaments function as does the Chorus in Greek tragedy, giving the reader—and perhaps the poet—an emotional break before the poem resumes its interrupted stanzaic form. But at the same time the grammar shows that there is no severance, for, despite this double interruption of visual break (with ornaments) and stanzaic break (with change of form), the inset poem continues grammatically in the resumed sequence of seven-line stanzas. What initially seems like an incomplete conclusion to the inset poem (Christ says: 'I / Crye / Hy the[e]') resumes grammatically after the lines of ornaments with '[u]nto me dere broder'. As we saw with Herbert's 'Church Monuments' in the Introduction, typographical division can make a theological point. Here nothing, not even printers' ornaments, can come between God and mankind.

My description of this sequence is unavoidably convoluted as I want to emphasize how much is going on. Gluck and Morgan are more succinct. They describe the stanzas as four-line units, with a 'tail-rhyme' scheme where 'the final line of each stanza appear[s] in a parenthesis after the second line' (p. 147, ll. 113–58n). This is technically correct but I do not think it is an accurate description of the visual effect (which is why I have chosen to describe the stanzas as three-line units plus an extra line). In fact, Gluck and Morgan edit out the rhetoric of the page, presenting this section of the poem entirely as a conventional vertical reading experience:

See
Me
Be
(kynde
¶Agayne
My payne
Retyne
(in mynde
¶My swete bloode
On the roode
Dyde the good
(my broder   (ll. 113–24)

They compensate by providing a photographic plate on the opposite page, although they print only the verso, missing out the inset poem's completion on the adjacent recto and that page's variant typography.

The Conversion of Swearers is clearly not a shape poem, as it has sometimes been described, since the poem straddles two pages (it even orphans the last two lines of the final stanza which no shape poem would do); in addition, the tiny woodcut of Christ which begins the inset sequence I have been discussing forces the first two stanzas to wrap (and hence detracts from the vertical visual symmetry of the stanzas with their increasing metre).[61] Nonetheless, the entire poem is typographically self-aware. We see this in the conclusion when Christ reminds the kings and lords that they have torn the charter He sealed with His blood: 'Beholde this lettre with the prynte also / Of myn owne seale by perfyte portrature / Prynte it in mynde and ye shall helthe recure' (A7v). The printed seal, with 'perfyte portrature' is the tiny woodcut in the inset poem; the 'lettre' is the poetic device of the frame poem with its address to Christian princes:

> Ryght myghty prynces of every crysten regyon
> I sende you gretynge moche hertly & grace...
> And all your lordes I greete in lyke cace
> By this my lettre your hertes to enbrace
> Besechynge you to prynte it in your mynde
> How for your sake I toke on me mankynde   (A2v)

From the printed and metaphoric document they (and by extension, we) are holding, we are then urged to undertake emotional printing, stamping Christ's sacrifice on our mind.[62]

The floral asterisks at the start of this poem form part of its metatextual movement towards a conclusion whose language harks back to the typography of its beginning. Hawes presumably discussed the asterisks with the printer, Wynkyn de Worde (whose printer's device with its burst of asterisks, discussed in the section 'Stars', features as the colophon to Hawes' work). The poem unites thematic content and typesetting, the language of the text and the body of the text, in a countermove to the swearers whose language tears the body apart.

Although the *croix pattée* or Maltese cross is technically a variant of the obelisk (the dagger or cross symbol: see the section 'Readers' Stars'), it overlaps with the representational function of the asterisk so I want to make brief mention

---

[61] When the poem was reprinted in 1531 by Johan Butler, the typography was different. The inset woodcut is much larger (5.5cm x 4cm to the 1509's 4cm x 3.4cm) and depicts a different scene: Christ sits on the Father's lap on His throne, and the woodcut lacks the border of thirteen images that featured in 1509. The poem itself has no asterisks; instead it has seventeen right-justified rectangular type ornaments. There is no horizontal two-line rule of ornaments to separate the inset poem from its continuation.

[62] Harry Newman's wide-ranging discussion of images of printing (from seals, coins, and the printing press) in early modern drama seems relevant to this poem. See Harry Newman, *Impressive Shakespeare: Identity, Authority and the Imprint in Shakespearean Drama* (London: Routledge, 2019).

of it here. We find it in Roman Catholic services 'to indicate points at which the priest must make the sign of the cross'[63] and it occurs in a surprisingly analogous way in the Tudor interlude of *Johan the Evangelist* (printed *c*.1550 although probably written *c*.1520). In this play, centred speech prefixes are generally prefaced by fleurons, with the exception of three long moral speeches of the Evangelist; the exceptions have different typographical symbols, including a *croix pattée*. The result, as Claire Bourne observes, is that the Evangelist is taken 'out of the fictional world of the play and into the here and now of the reader's engagement with the spiritual argument'.[64]

Moving from the sublime to the ridiculous: Kurt Vonnegut's *Breakfast of Champions* (1973) uses the asterisk to illustrate the sphincter. The narrator is honest about the juvenile nature of his humour (see Figure 3.13). This page of

I am programmed at fifty to perform childishly—to insult "The Star-Spangled Banner," to scrawl pictures of a Nazi flag and an asshole and a lot of other things with a felt-tipped pen. To give an idea of the maturity of my illustrations for this book, here is my picture of an asshole:

▶ I think I am trying to clear my head of all the junk in there—the assholes, the flags, the underpants. Yes—there is a picture in this book of underpants. I'm throwing out characters from my other books, too. I'm not going to put on any more puppet shows.

FIGURE 3.13 Kurt Vonnegut, *Breakfast of Champions* (London: Jonathan Cape, 1973), p. 5. Courtesy of Penguin Random House.

[63] Keith Houston, *Shady Characters* (London: Penguin, 2013), p. 106.

[64] Claire Bourne, 'Dramatic Pilcrows', *Papers of the Bibliographical Society of America* 108:4 (2014), 413–52 (437).

the novel is very popular printed on T-shirts (perhaps because of the shock value of the headline 'Kurt Vonnegut's asshole'). However, several of the online T-shirts are misleading: a comparison of the T-shirt with the text reveals that the T-shirt asterisk lacks Vonnegut's central circle and twelve points. The Internet is full of fakes, even fake asterisks.[65]

Stars

Given the asterisk's etymology as 'little star', there should be no surprise at its ability to represent the heavens. In fact, one reviewer of *Tristram Shandy* wrote that four stars have now become 'a new method of talking bawdy *astronomically*'.[66] A counter-response to this 'new method' came in 1672 in a book that depicts the night sky dotted with stars on a black page, only to follow it with a white page depicting the rising sun. Rather than representing nocturnal sexual activity, the asterisk joke is that sometimes a star is just a star.[67]

We see this most obviously in early modern astronomical texts and in those whose background illustrations depict the heavens. The printer's device of Wynkyn de Worde (1455–1534) uses a sliding scale of asterisk shapes and sizes to depict the stars, two planets, and the sun (see Figure 3.14). Johann Comenius' language manual, *Orbis Pictus* (1672), is a series of double-page spreads, with an illustration on the verso page and Latin/English vocabulary on the recto. The illustration for Philosophy shows the philosopher looking at the heavens (see Figure 3.15).[68] Stars circle round the astronomical chart in John Blagrave's *The Mathematical Jewel* (1585) (see Figure 3.16).[69] Some of the most beautiful astronomical depictions occur in astrological commentaries by Galileo in 1610 and Johannes Kepler in 1611. Galileo's 1610 text is punctuated by various sizes and shapes of asterisks in single, mostly horizontal, lines (see Figure 3.17). Kepler's commentary on Galileo, in the *Dissertatio* of 1611, has several pull-out charts (see Figure 3.18).[70]

---

[65] For an authentic Vonnegut asterisk T-shirt see: <https://www.redmolotov.com/vonnegut-ahole-tshirt>.

[66] 'An Account of the Rev. Mr. ST ✱✱✱✱, and his Writings', *Grand Magazine* 3 (June 1760), 308–11, reprinted in *Sterne: The Critical Heritage*, ed. Alan B. Howes (London: Routledge/Kegan Paul, 1974), pp. 95–9 (p. 96) and cited by Newbould, *Adaptations*, p. 156.

[67] George Stayley, *Life and Opinions of an Actor* (Dublin: George Faulkner, 1762). The pages are reproduced in Newbould, *Adaptations*, pp. 158–9.

[68] Johann Comenius, *Orbis Pictus* (1672), O7v.

[69] John Blagrave, *The Mathematical Jewel* (1585), Aiiiv.

[70] Not all the editions of 1611 contain the illustrations or pull-out charts. I am grateful to Daryl Green for alerting me to this edition.

FIGURE 3.14 Stephen Hawes, *The Conversion of Swearers* (1509, STC 12943.5), colophon. Shelfmark 61309. Courtesy of the Huntington Library, San Marino.

In all these astronomical representations, the asterisk functions like Antony's crocodile: 'it is shap'd, sir, like itself' (*Antony and Cleopatra*, 2.7.42).

Readers' Stars

If the asterisk's visual relationship to star is exploited, its etymon is also often noted. Elyot defines 'asteriscus' as 'a lytle marke in wrytynge like a sterre'. In his depiction of the activities that take place in the study, Comenius shows the scholar copying *mots justes* into his commonplace book, or, explains Comenius, he 'marks them in them [his textbook, his source book] with a dash, or a little star in the Margent'.[71] Indeed, readers often show considerable artistic individuality through their marks. A reader of Euripides adorns his/her marginal asterisk with serifs (see Figure 3.19). A differently formed asterisk occurs elsewhere in the same text, alongside a manicule (C5v) (see Figure 3.20).

---

[71] Thomas Elyot and Thomas Cooper, *Bibliotheca Eliotae* (1559, STC 7663), Hiiir; Comenius, *Orbis Pictus*, O4v–O5r.

FIGURE 3.15 Johann Comenius, *Orbis Pictus* (1672, Wing C5524), O7v. Shelfmark
Douce CC 216. By permission of the Bodleian Libraries, University of Oxford.

The printer has already marked up this text with the standard sixteenth-
century method: quotation marks. In this period, quotation marks did not
mean that these lines in the text were quoted from elsewhere; they meant that
they were quot*able* by the reader, a ready-reckoner for easy extraction to a
commonplace book. As such, they appeared only at the start of lines; they
were in the form of modern closing quotation marks; and they often sat on the
line rather than being superscripted.[72] In the first illustration from Euripides,
the editor and printer have used two means to draw the reader's attention to
the beauty of the lines: a footnote (indented and centred beneath the speech)
and commonplace markers. Thus, by adding an asterisk, the reader is gilding

---

[72] The classic article on the subject is G. K. Hunter, 'The Marking of *Sententiae* in Elizabethan
Printed Plays, Poems, and Romances', *The Library* 5–6: 3–4 (1951), 171–88. It has since been updated
and qualified by many scholars (see, for instance, Laura Estill, 'Commonplace Markers and Quotation
Marks', in *ArchBook* (Architecture of the Book), 7 March 2014, updated 25 February 2019. Available at:
<http://drc.usask.ca/projects/archbook/commonplace.php>), but Hunter's taxonomy of marks
remains stable.

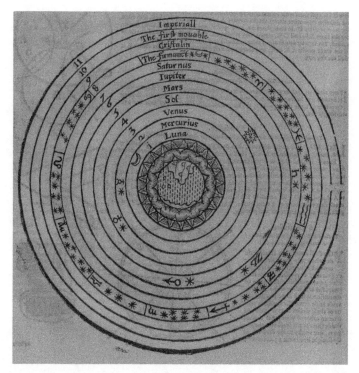

FIGURE 3.16 John Blagrave, *The Mathematical Jewel* (1585, STC 3119), Aiiir. Shelfmark
STC 3119. Used by permission of the Folger Shakespeare Library.

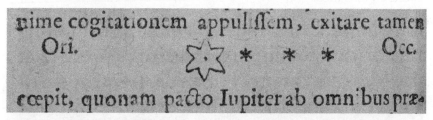

FIGURE 3.17 Galileo Galilei, *Sidereus Nuncius Magna, longeque admirabilia spectacula
pandens* (1610), CIv (p. 18). Shelfmark Savile CC 8. By permission of the Bodleian
Libraries, University of Oxford.

the lily; but he is also personalizing the text, adding his agreement to that of
the publisher.[73]

In the British Library copy of *A Continued Inquisition against Paper Persecutors*
(1625), the four spaces between an asterisk's crossbars are dotted, giving it a

[73] Cf. forms of digital reading where one can see previous readers' highlighted passages.

FIGURE 3.18 Johannes Kepler, *Dissertatio cum Nuncio Sidereo Nuper ad Mortales Misso a Galilaeo Galilaeo Mathematico Patavino* (Frankfurt, 1611), between A5v and A6r (pp. 10–11). Shelfmark Savile CC 8. By permission of the Bodleian Libraries, University of Oxford.

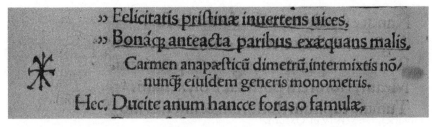

FIGURE 3.19 Euripides, *Hecuba and Iphigenia in Aulis*, trans. Erasmus (Basil, 1518), A8v. Shelfmark 216–1999q. Used by permission of the Folger Shakespeare Library.

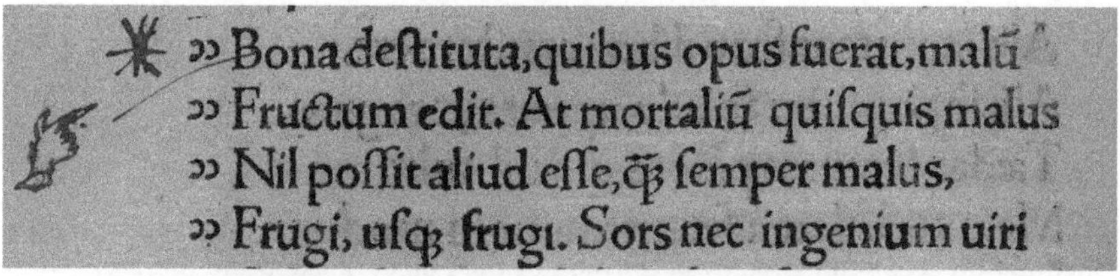

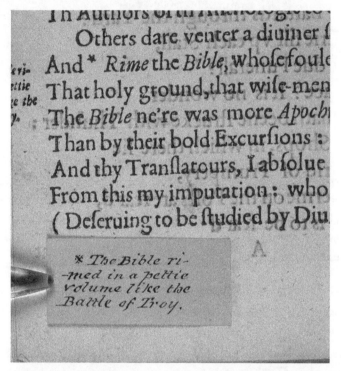

※ ›› Bona deſtituta,quibus opus fuerat,malū
›› Fructum edit. At mortaliū quiſquis malus
›› Nil poſſit aliud eſſe,q̃ ſemper malus,
›› Frugi, uſq̃ frugi. Sors nec ingenium uiri

FIGURE 3.20 Euripides, *Hecuba and Iphigenia in Aulis*, trans. Erasmus (Basil, 1518), C5v. Shelfmark 216-1999q. Used by permission of the Folger Shakespeare Library.

FIGURE 3.21 John Davies of Hereford, *A Continued Inquisition against Paper-Persecutors* appended to *A Scourge for Paper-Persecutors* (1625, STC 6341), A1v. Shelfmark C.39.e.55. © The British Library Board.

classical look (see the end of this section for the classical derivation of the asterisk) (see Figure 3.21).[74] A reader of Sidney's *Countess of Pembroke's Arcadia* (1593) in the Folger Library (copy 1) has used a fine nib to draw tiny stars between the printed lines (see Figure 3.22).[75] A reader of the Huntington

[74] The manuscript note supplies a marginal note that was printed in the original but has been cropped.

[75] Philip Sidney, *The Countess of Pembroke's Arcadia* (1593, STC 22540), Folger Library copy 1, N1r.

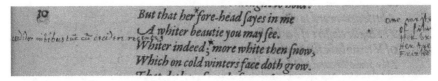

FIGURE 3.22 Philip Sidney, *The Countess of Pembroke's Arcadia* (1593, STC 22540), N1r. Shelfmark STC 22540. Used by permission of the Folger Shakespeare Library.

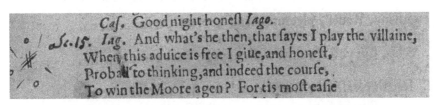

FIGURE 3.23 Shakespeare, *Othello* (1622, STC 22305), F3v. Shelfmark 69337. Courtesy of the Huntington Library, San Marino.

Library copy of *Othello* (1622) marked the margins with an exploding firework. He adorns a hashtag to turn it into a giant asterisk (F3v) (see Figure 3.23).[76]

Asterisks made by readers' pens are everywhere in the margins of early modern books. The asterisk is part of a system of gnomic pointing, of marking *sententiae*, of commonplacing. In 1670 Owen Price provided a list of marks that one might find in the margin:

1 *Asterisk*, is a note of Illustration, so called from its Star-like form, thus, *.

2 " Is a Note of Citation, when a thing is quoted from another Authour, thus".

3 *Index* is a Note like a fore-finger, pointing at what is remarkable in the Page, thus, ☞

4 *Obelisk* is a Note of referring to the Margin, thus, †.

5 *Section* is the beginning of a new head, marked thus, §.

6 *Paragraph* is a mark put before an Authors name quoted, thus ¶.[77]

---

[76] Shakespeare, *Othello* (1622, STC 22305), Huntington Library copy, F3v. This copy was owned by George Steevens (1736–1800) and it is he who has supplied the scene number. For more on the marginal additions, see 'Reading *Othello*'.

[77] Owen Price, *English Orthographie* (1670), D2r.

Price makes a neat division between the function of the asterisk (first in his list) and that of the obelisk (fourth in his list.)[78] This distinction might have been the case in 1670 but it was not a hundred years previously (just as Price's explanation of quotation marks might hold true for 1670 but not in the previous century, as we have seen).

We need to dwell briefly on the evolution of the obelisk because the asterisk's history is linked to that of the obelisk. (They go together even in comic books: Astérix and Obélix are boon companions.) The two kinds of type are discussed together in Keith Houston's book on typography, *Shady Characters*. Houston explains that both are ancient marks (they originate in the fourth century BCE in the great library of Alexandria in Egypt) and both were editorial marks. The obelisk came first. It was a marginal mark for identifying spurious lines of Homeric text, introduced by Zenodotus of Ephesus, the first librarian, as part of an editorial project. One of his successors, Aristarchus, introduced the dotted asterisk for genuine Homeric material that had been accidentally duplicated. By the Middle Ages the asterisk and the obelisk were used simply as marginal markers to call attention to points on a page, and by the sixteenth century they had developed alongside the marginal note or gloss. I want to look at experiments with citational systems in the margins of early modern books: this is now a story about margins, and the asterisk is a key player.

Part II: The Margin

Occupying the Margin; or, a Star is Born

The margin is a complex space in early modern printed books.[79] As William Slights points out, the belittling concept of the marginal as something subordinate was not yet in existence. The endnotes in John Hagthorpe's *Divine Meditations and Elegies* (1622) are actually in larger font than the text, destabilizing

---

[78] The name 'obelisk' comes from the Greek for skewer.

[79] For excellent discussions of the early modern margin see Evelyn Tribble, *Margins and Marginality: The Printed Page in Early Modern England* (Charlottesville: University of Virginia Press, 1993); William W. E. Slights, 'The Edifying Margins of Renaissance English Books', *Renaissance Quarterly* 42:4 (1989), 682–716 and *Managing Readers: Printed Marginalia in English Renaissance Books* (Ann Arbor: University of Michigan Press, 2001); Sherman, *Used Books*; and Jane Griffiths, *Diverting Authorities: Experimental Glossing Practices in Manuscript and Print* (Oxford: Oxford University Press, 2015). Griffiths' work is particularly valuable as it situates the printed marginal gloss in the history of pre-print texts and thus illuminates the experimental nature of the early modern margin.

the idea of a conceptual centre and subsidiary text.[80] Samuel Daniel self-consciously worries about burdening his margin with too many scholarly notes.[81] In *The Shepherd's Garland* (1593), Drayton talks about the 'learned margent' where 'learning's lines are ever enterlined' and in *Poly-Olbion* (1622) he instructs his readers, 'If the Page satisfie not, inquire in the Margine'.[82] When Horatio tells Hamlet 'you must be edified by the margent' (5.2.155), he reveals he comes from a reading culture in which margins were visually prominent and intellectually important.[83]

The various kinds of material contained in marginal notes can be seen in a single text, Drayton's *The Barons' Wars* (1603), reprinted in his *Poems* (1619).[84] We find summaries ('*The Queene is greatly perplexed, whilst things sort not out to her desire*', B4r), commentary ('*Good consideration of the King*', C2r), a pointer to recipe ingredients for a '*sleepie Potion*' mentioned in the text (E4v), cross-references ('*Looke to the 23. Stanza of the first Canto*', F4r), literary criticism ('*The Socke, or soft Shoo, used in Comicke and light Poesies, from which hee ascendeth to this Tragique poeme*', D1v), linguistic glossing ('*A Metaphor taken from Card-play*', F3v), and historical, genealogical explanation (G4v).

Textual commentary and glosses were experimental in the sixteenth and seventeenth centuries, with no standardized convention about layout (sidenotes, footnotes, or notes between stanzas of poems?), notation (should keying devices—numerals, letters, symbols—be in both text and margin?) or, as we shall see, content. Visually, it was not always easy to negotiate the relationship of margin to text. The folio pages of Hugh Broughton's *A Concent of Scripture* (1590) have two columns of text but seven columns of marginal notes.[85] The notes of explanation in John Davies' *A Select Second Husband for Sir Thomas Overbury's Wife* (1616), occupy a centred line between the poem's stanzas. The narrow margins of the quarto format explain this interlined location; but the side effect of having horizontal, interlined notes is that they look misleadingly like part of the poem.

If sidenotes are used in a variety of ways, so too are the symbols which link to them: most often, a mixed economy of asterisks, obelisks, numerals, lowercase

---

[80] John Hagthorpe, *Divine Meditations and Elegies* (1622), C7v–C8v.

[81] Samuel Daniel, *Collection of the History of England* (1634), A2v.

[82] Michael Drayton, *The Shepherd's Garland* (1593, F1v); *Poly-Olbion* (1622, ❧1r). *Poly-Olbion*'s explanation to the notes, and the notes themselves, appear to be by John Selden; see the section 'Dialogue'.

[83] Slights, *Managing Readers*, p. 20.   [84] The marginal notes were added in the 1619 edition.

[85] A page from Broughton's book is reproduced in Slights, *Managing Readers*, p. 271.

letters, and no typographical sign at all. In John Dee's *General and Rare Memorials . . . to the Art of Navigation* (1577), we see different systems and different functions on a single page (D4r). One marginal note, without a symbol, simply advises 'Note this Poynt'. Another, also without a symbol, is a gloss on the text's 'Twenty sundry Places' (the margin explains: 'The Twenty Ports for the Pety-Navy-Royall'). Three marginal asterisks attached to numerals 1 to 3 help the reader extract the principal categories in a lengthy paragraph. Thus we encounter injunction, explanation, and enumeration within a few inches.

When texts use a (predominantly) single system such as the asterisk, the patterns still vary. Sometimes an asterisk in the text is matched by an accompanying asterisk in the margin, as in the following examples. George Chapman explains a mythological reference to Diana and Acteon in his epyllion, *Ovid's Banquet of Sense* (1595), C2v. George Gascoigne's sidenotes explain simple vocabulary and provide basic information, glossing '*Yewle*' as 'Christmas' and '*Delfe*' as 'A towne in Holland'.[86] The 'path to that rare Vesterie' in Ariosto's *Seven Planets* (1611) receives a lengthy historical explanatory sidenote: '*In former times* there was a Church or Temple without a Vestery . . .' (Q2v, my emphasis). Sometimes a single asterisk in the margin has no corresponding asterisk in the text, functioning as a general nota bene, an alternative to the manicule. Anthony of Guevara's *The Dial of Princes* (1577) sprinkles its densely printed pages with floral asterisks in the margins (h2r) without any in the body of the text.

The key for indicating the note's relation to the text is typographically flexible but its location—in the margin rather than at the foot of the page—is the most typical. It was the eighteenth century before the sidenote became the footnote.[87] This changed the rhetoric of the page from a horizontal and fluid reading experience to one that was vertical and interrupted. Slights finds footnotes less interruptive but I disagree.[88] Footnotes are certainly less intrusive than endnotes (which involve the hand as well as the eye) but the sidenote foregrounds its dialogic role with the text more visibly than does its foot-of-the-page equivalent. I want to pursue the concept of dialogue because it is foregrounded not just in the visual relationship (note side-by-side with text) but in content (note in debate with text).

---

[86] Gascoigne, 'Dulce Bellum Inexpertis', in *Poesies* (1575), i5v.
[87] Lawrence Lipking, 'The Marginal Gloss', *Critical Inquiry* 3:4 (1977), 609–55, cited in Tribble, *Margins and Marginality*, p. 131; Slights, *Managing Readers*, p. 16.
[88] Slights, *Managing Readers*, p. 16.

Dialogue

In *A Scourge for Paper-Persecutors* (1625), John Davies of Hereford asterisks a line that contains the words '*Embellish*', '*Blandishment*', and '*Equipage*'. His marginal note observes, '*These words are good: but ill-used: in over-much use savouring of witlesse affectation*' (B1v). In 'Dulce Bellum Inexpertis', Gascoigne, who (as we saw) glossed Delft neutrally as '[a] towne in Holland', has more to say about the Hague: 'The pleasauntest village (*as I thinke*) that is in Europe' (i6v, my emphasis). Notes often criticize the Pope. When George Goodwin's *Of the Pope's Supremacy* says 'the Pope is not a *Sheepe*', the marginal comment adds, '*No, for he is a Wolfe in a Sheepes coat*' (C4v). Lawyers too receive criticism. The margin of Thomas Wilson's *Art of Rhetoric* (1563) notes that '[l]awiers, ne[ve]r dye beg[ga]rs' (Ciii^v). Gascoigne makes a similarly non-neutral observation in the margins of *Supposes*: 'Lawyers are never weary to get money'.[89] This is in the margin of a play in which all Gascoigne's other marginalia offer literary criticism relevant to the plot of the play (primarily pointing out the kinds of 'supposes' in the plot as it develops: 'A shrewde suppose'; 'A knavish suppose'). The comment about lawyers takes us outside the world of the fiction—which is exactly what the margin does. Of course, literary criticism does this too: when Gascoigne directs us to the play's multiple 'supposes', his notes prompt a cognitive, analytical response that is distinct from our immersive experience of reading the fictional world. The two types of marginal comment are not separated because they are not separate: the only distinction to be made is spatial (between text and margin), not conceptual (between different kinds of marginal content).[90]

The margin points to features in the text but is itself on the edge of the text, negotiating the boundary between author and reader, between text and response. This is something that the horizontal footnote at the bottom of the page cannot do, and the endnote is even worse: both are easy to ignore. Many contemporary online texts compound the problem: their endnotes are impossible to check while reading the main body of a chapter and often they are excluded from the PDF download facility. (However, there are signs that this is changing: footnote numbers are increasingly coded as links so one can toggle easily.) The vertical margin is an aside—spatially, literally—and we know how powerful asides are in the theatre. In fact, just as we can view the marginal

---

[89] Gascoigne, *Supposes*, in *Poesies* (1575), Eviii^v.
[90] On margins conducting dialogue with the text they gloss, see Griffiths, *Diverting Authorities*, especially ch. 7.

note as the *platea* of the page, we can view the theatrical aside as a dramatized marginal note: the asterisk is given embodiment, translated into time and space.[91]

The character of the Bastard in Shakespeare's *King John* provides an extended example of this. He is developed from a 'single sentence' in Holinshed's *Chronicles*: 'Philip, bastard son to King Richard . . . killed the viscount of Limoges, in revenge of his father's death'.[92] In *King John*, as critics point out, Philip is given a surname, a brother, a mother, a servant (who is also given a name), and a personality. In short he is given an identity. He is also given a dramatic function: chorus or commentator on history.

I say 'dramatic' function because the Bastard has no plot function. Despite his physical and rhetorical prominence in the play, one could remove him from the play with no detriment to the action.[93] The Bastard is there solely to write his name in the history books, as we see in his asides in the parley before Angiers:

> King John: Doth not the crown of England prove the King?
> And if not that, I bring you witnesses,
> Twice fifteen thousand, hearts of England's breed –
> Bastard: Bastards, and else.
> King John: To verify our title with their lives.
> King Philip: As many and as well-born bloods as those –
> Bastard: Some bastards too.   (2.1.273–9)

The Bastard's asides insert him, and those like him, in the historical text.

In a play which contests two patrilineal inheritances—Robert Faulconbridge's of his father's estate, and King John's of the throne of England—history's marginal characters (illegitimate children and their mothers) become crucial. The first scene reverberates with family terms—'brother', 'mother', 'father'[94]—and the family here is literally the blood unit rather than a metaphor for the state. History has a political, public side and a personal side; but the personal

---

[91] For the distinction between *locus* (representational place—the fictional place of the play world) and *platea* (presentational place—the front of the stage where the performer addresses the audience), see Robert Weimann, *Author's Pen and Actor's Voice: Playing and Writing in Shakespeare's Theatre* (Cambridge: Cambridge University Press, 2000).

[92] Jean E. Howard and Phyllis Rackin, *Engendering a Nation: A Feminist Account of Shakespeare's English History Plays* (London: Routledge, 1997), p. 128: Geoffrey Bullough, *Narrative and Dramatic Sources of Shakespeare*, vol. IV (London: Routledge/Kegan Paul, 1962), p. 28.

[93] Julia C. van de Water, 'The Bastard in *King John*', *Shakespeare Quarterly* 11 (1960), 137–46.

[94] Nicholas Woodeson, 'King John', in *Players of Shakespeare 3*, ed. Russell Jackson and Robert Smallwood (Cambridge: Cambridge University Press, 1993), pp. 87–98 (p. 94).

becomes political when it involves Richard I siring an illegitimate son. Women receive scant attention in the official history books but their sexual activities and their position as mothers are of great significance in determining feudal or allodial allocation, as the Faulconbridge episode attests. Richard I is renowned for his military exploits (hence his cognomen, 'the Lionheart') but scene 1 of *King John* reminds us of Richard's nocturnal sexual activities and promotes the Bastard from the margins of history to centre stage.

How to Read an Elizabethan Book

The Elizabethan printed page is a work in progress and readers benefit from help in navigating its innovative features. Drayton's *Poems* (1619) instruct readers how to use the notes to *England's Heroical Epistles* (first published in 1597). The 1619 title page to the *Epistles* advertises the poem as having 'Some short Annotations... *To which, the* Reader is directed, by this Marke * in the beginning of every Line, to which the Annotations are pertinent' (O2r). Readers are being taught how to use their books and how to read the rhetoric of the page.

This may, in part, be a response to anxiety about reception. George Gascoigne describes how readers 'doutfully construed' the first edition of *The Adventures of Master F.J.* as 'scandalous'.[95] He inveighs against readers 'who (having no skill at all) will yet be verie busie in reading all that may be read, and thinke it sufficient if (Parrot like) they can reherse things without booke: when within booke they understand neither the meaning of the author, nor the sense of the figurative speeches' (¶¶ii^r). Thomas Nashe taxes readers with the opposite habit: over-interpretation. In *Pierce Pennilesse* (1592), he laments this 'moralizing age' in which 'every one seeks to shew himselfe a Polititian by mis-interpreting' (STC 18372, ¶2v.) Michael Drayton complains about the negative responses to the first edition of his epic chorographical poem, *Poly-Olbion* (1622): in contrast to his friends' encouraging reactions, those of the public were characterized by 'barbarous Ignorance..., below all Ballatry' (*The Second Part*, STC 7229, A2r). John Taylor the Water Poet addresses those of his readers who 'know how to reade, and *not merre [mar] the sense with hacking or mis-construction*'.[96] George Chapman is worried that the reader's intention trumps that of the author: in his *Free and Offenceless Justification of... Andromeda*

---

[95] Gascoigne, *Pleasantest Works* (1587), ¶ii^r.
[96] John Taylor the water poet, *Works* (1630), Bbb5r.

Liberata (1614) he writes that an author can 'meane what he list' but 'his writing notwithstanding must be construed *in mentem Legentis*...to the intendment of the Reader' (**Ir). The development of sidenotes and footnotes in part responds to these anxieties, directing the reader to rhetorical beauties or moral interpretations.

The index comes into this category of development (a gnomic pointer, as we saw at the beginning of this chapter, in John Gee's definition). Leonard Mascall gives an explanation of how the reader should use the index to his book on trees, *The Art and Manner How to Plant and Graft All Sorts of Trees* (1572). We are to look at the page number attached to each term in the index and then locate that number in the book: '*Here foloweth a necessary table (by Alphabete) to finde out quickly all several particulars in thys booke afore mentioned, by the numbers in this table, seeking the lyke number on the pagine or leafe*' (Piir).

Mascall's index is where today's indices are: at the end of the book. The index ('A Table to the Chiefest Passages') to Drayton's *Poly-Olbion* (*A Chorographicall Description*, STC 7228) is at the beginning; it is an index only to the notes and it does not have our modern expectation that an index should be neutral.[97] It is in dialogue—corrective, argumentative dialogue—with the book's material. The entry on the Hawthorn reads:

> *Hawthorn blossoming on Christmas day, as report wonders; but the truth is, that it blossometh indeed in Winter, not observing any particular Day, no more then the Walnut tree in the Abbey observes S.* Barnabies *(although that go's for truth in report also).* (❧2v)

This index entry directs us to page 54 for the discussion of the Hawthorn. The discussion takes place in one of the notes to Drayton's poem, where the writer offers a personal, potentially sceptical, comment but is not blatantly contradictory. 'It goes for currant truth that a Hawthorne thereby on Christmas day alwayes blossometh: which the Author tels you in that, *Trees yet in winter &c.* You may cast this into the account of your greatest wonders' (F3v). The distancing tactics—'it *goes for* currant truth', 'the *Author* tells you', the reference to 'wonders'—slant the discussion, separating the opinions of the note-writer from the author. But he does not contradict the author as he does in the index.[98] Indexing *Poly-Olbion*'s references to the history of the Dukedom of Clarence, he notes their source in 'Francis Matenesi *a Divine, and professor of*

---

[97] *Poly-Olbion* was first published in 1612; the index was added to the edition of 1613.

[98] Elsewhere in the notes he distances himself from the author even as he praises his learning or chides previous scholars for their errors. See Angus Vine, *In Defiance of Time: Antiquarian Writing in Early Modern England* (Oxford: Oxford University Press, 2010), p. 191.

Story and Greeke in Cologne'. He then supplements the information he is indexing ('*which indeed is also slanderously reported among* Rablais *his tales*') and in a further supplement offers moral commentary: '*But it worst of all becomes a profest Historian as* Matenesi *is*'(❧2r.) The index does not simply enable the retrieval of information: it offers additional opinion.

This kind of dialogic commentary is characteristic of marginal notes as we saw. The index is thus linked to the sidenote. And notes enter into dialogue with the text for the simple reason that the writer of the notes is not always the author.

In the preface to *Poly-Olbion* Drayton explains that he has provided three 'especiall helps' to the reader 'for the further understanding of my Poeme' (A1v). The first reading aid is the 'Argument', the second is the maps, and the third are the notes (for which the technical term is 'illustrations'): 'Then hast thou the Illustration of this learned Gentleman, my friend, to explaine every hard matter of history, that, lying farre from the way of common reading, may (without question) seem difficult unto thee' (A1v). The learned gentleman appears to be no less a figure than John Selden.[99]

Selden's erudition is everywhere evident in the 'often digressive, frequently allusive, and always fiendishly learned illustrations'.[100] Their dialogic quality was noted by readers at the time: Selden was asked 'whether he wrote the commentary to his "Polyolbion" and "Epistles" or Mr. Drayton made those verses to his notes'.[101] Certainly, as Vine notes, Selden's 'antiquarian urge to compile and complete threatens to overrun Drayton's original text' and it is 'not always clear who is annotating whom'.[102]

This Author of Illustrations and Table (index) then addresses the reader. He explains his glossarial principles. He has glossed allusions that might only be understood by 'a full knowing Reader' and he explains how to use his notes: 'By *Paragraph's* [pilcrow signs] in the Verses [lines of the poem] you know what I meddle with [interpose; the verb does not yet have the sense of negative interference] in the *Illustrations*' (A4r). Like Mascall explaining how to match the number in the index to the page number, Selden explains how to

---

[99] I am grateful to Thomas Roebuck and Philip Schwyzer for helpful correspondence about the notes and about Selden. For the Arts and Humanities Research Council (AHRC) Drayton Poly-Olbion project, directed by Andrew McRae and Philip Schwyzer, see <http://poly-olbion.exeter.ac.uk>.

[100] Vine, *In Defiance*, p. 186.

[101] Sir Edward Bysshe in *Aubrey's Brief Lives*, quoted in Vine in *In Defiance*, p. 190. As Vine points out, Bysshe did not realize that Drayton wrote his own notes for the *Epistles*.

[102] Vine, *In Defiance*, p. 190.

match the symbol in a line of the poem to the margin. Sjoerd Levelt further unpacks Selden's marginal note, 'If the Page satisfie not, inquire in the Margine'.[103] This is not just a plug for the supplementary margin but an explanation of how to use the margin as index: 'if you look for a subject indicated in the table and you notice you can't find it in the main text column, look at the notes in the margin to see if the subject is mentioned there'.[104]

The gnomic asterisk in the margin, pointing to sidenotes, has taken us into the larger territory of annotation. (Erasmus referred to his annotations on the New Testament as 'pointers'.[105]) Let me conclude this exploration of the margins by gathering together some of the big literary questions that the asterisk in the margin cues us to ask.

The first concerns early modern authorship. What does it mean to be the author of a note? What does it mean to be the author of an index? When Selden refrains from 'vaine loading my Margine'—the margins of Drayton's *Poly-Olbion*—one cannot help but notice the possessive pronoun. In Holinshed's *Chronicles* some of the notes have initials, some are anonymous. This segregation of textual parts unsettles current critical notions of authorship. Is this collaboration? Is it editing? Is editing authorship? Is indexing editing? Despite Selden's distancing himself from material in Drayton's poem, he is sufficiently involved to care about its printing. He provided an errata list; and, as we saw in Chapter 1, when the printer miscalculated space in a way that would have left blank pages, Selden provided a genealogical table of Welsh kings.[106] The 'Table' was added in 1613 so, as Philip Schwyzer points out (personal communication), Selden 'clearly maintained his interest in *Poly-Olbion* even after the initial printing'.

When Selden's 'Hawthorn' entry distances itself from material in the text, how different is this from the gloss of a modern editor indicating her or his historical distance from a Renaissance text's cultural, superstitious, or misogynist beliefs?

---

[103] See footnote 82.

[104] Sjoerd Levelt, blogpost at: <https://levelt.wordpress.com/tag/john-selden/>. In an interesting sidelight on Elizabethan printing, Selden apologizes that he has not had enough time to compose the notes as Drayton only asked him to provide notes once the poem was in press. It may be this haste that accounts for the lengthy errata list: Selden was 'unable to revise or correct his text' (Vine, *In Defiance*, p. 186).

[105] He was aware of the difficulty of naming this innovation: 'I have added these pointers (*so to call them*)'. See Erasmus, *The Correspondence of Erasmus: Letters 298–445*, trans. and ed. R. A. B. Mynors and D. F. S. Thomson, annotated by James K. McConica (Toronto: University of Toronto Press, 1976), p. 199, ll. 48–54, my emphasis.

[106] Vine, *In Defiance*, p. 186.

Liver] The *supposed* seat of the passions
(AYLI, 3.2.422)

The mandrake...*was said* to shriek when pulled from the ground
(Duchess of Malfi 2.5.1–2)

Giovanni refers to a *stereotype* of women as inconstant
('Tis Pity She's a Whore 3.2.11)[107]

The second question is familiar to us from Chapters 1 and 2: the question of editorial attitudes to, and treatment of, asterisks by modern editors. Ben Jonson's poem to Sir Thomas Palmer provides a succinct example. In the Penguin edition of *The Complete Poems*, the asterisks become ellipses; the rhetoric of the Elizabethan page gets changed.[108]

Thomas Nashe provides a more extended test case. In *Pierce Pennilesse* (1592) Nashe conducts a relationship with the reader through his marginalia as well as through the body of the text.[109] As we have seen, Nashe was derided by Gabriel Harvey for these notes; whether for this reason, or some other, he deleted many of them in the second 1592 edition. The marginal notes vary from the summary ('The pride of the Italian'; D2r) through the sententious ('Little men for the most part are most angry'; E3r) to the satiric (fleshly minded '*Belials*' are punningly explained: 'Or rather belly-alls, because all theyr minde is on theyr belly'; G1r). The notes often directly address the reader: 'Marke these two letter-leaping Metaphors good people' (D4r); a complaint against the 'tyred Jade belonging to the Presse' who upbraided Nashe in print is extended into the margin with the mocking addendum, 'I would tell you in what booke it is, but I am afrayde it would make hys booke sell in hys latter dayes, which hetherto hath lien dead & bin a great losse to the Printer' (F2v). The margins, in short, are as full of personality as the main body of the pamphlet.

Some of the notes are keyed to the narrative, with asterisks in both margin and central text, but many have no notational key to cue them. This is not as haphazard as it sounds for there is a quasi-system. The general comments— summaries, sententiae—are unasterisked (logically so: they relate to a section

[107] John Webster, *The Duchess of Malfi*, ed. E. M. Brennan, 3rd rev. edn (New Mermaids; London: A. & C. Black, 1993); John Ford, *'Tis Pity She's a Whore*, ed. Simon Barker (London: Routledge, 1997).

[108] Ben Jonson, *The Complete Poems*, ed. George Parfitt (London: Penguin, 1975). Ellipses also feature in most internet editions although one does not expect editorial rigour from general poetry websites.

[109] There were two editions this year by different printers and publishers: John Charlwood for Richard Jones (STC 18371) and Abel Jeffes for John Busby (STC 18372). The first edition was unauthorized, and Nashe did not see proofs for either edition (he was in the countryside avoiding the London plague). I quote here from STC 18371.

rather than to a specific line). The asterisked comments tend to be keyed to a specific reference. This is not consistent (it is a trace rather than a structure) but it is clear that the asterisks are part of the reading experience. Do they originate with the author or the compositor? In other words, are they substantives or accidentals? The former is more likely. As Cathy Shrank points out, the asterisk within the text, linking reference to margin, is the sort of thing that the author would know and which a compositor is unlikely to spend time working out. However, any 'system' holds only for the first edition: the second edition erratically copies over asterisks from the first edition, retaining some in the text without repeating them in the margin.[110]

Grosart retains the asterisks in his edition, as does McKerrow.[111] John Payne Collier's so-called facsimile of 1886 does not.[112] In J. B. Steane's Penguin edition of 1972, the sidenotes become footnotes and the asterisks are removed: the rhetoric of the page is flattened.[113] Stanley Wells' edition of 1964 has no sidenotes although he occasionally adopts them as section headings. When we reach the textual appendix, we find this explanation:

> A includes a number of marginal notes, one of which was omitted from B, considerably more from C. Some are merely brief statements of content; these are omitted from the present edition except for those that mark major sub-divisions of the text, here incorporated as headings. Other notes provide comment or additional material. Notes of this kind left standing in C are here printed as footnotes.[114]

In *Diverting Authorities* Jane Griffiths provides a superb analysis of the way the notes are not ancillary to the text but part of it. They play with voice: is this Ovid's voice in the note or Nashe's?[115] They play with authority: the reader who expects explanatory glosses encounters only further self-reflexive interpolations.[116] They play with the very form of the gloss: the juxtaposition

[110] I am grateful to Cathy Shrank for the information in this paragraph and for helpful correspondence on Nashe's margins. For an enlightening discussion of Nashe's marginalia in this text, see Griffiths, *Diverting Authorities*, ch. 7.

[111] Thomas Nashe, *The Complete Works of Thomas Nashe*, vol. II, ed. A. B. Grosart (London: privately printed, 1883); Grosart wraps the text round the marginalia so that they are, in fact, left- and right-justified and so not marginalia at all. Thomas Nashe, *The Works of Thomas Nashe*, vol. I, ed. R. B. McKerrow (London: Sidgwick & Jackson, 1910).

[112] Thomas Nashe, 'Pierce Penilesse', in *Illustrations of Early English Literature*, vol. II, ed. John Payne Collier (London: privately printed, 1867–70).

[113] Thomas Nashe, *The Unfortunate Traveller and Other Works*, ed. J. B. Steane (Harmondsworth: Penguin, 1972).

[114] Thomas Nashe, *Pierce Penilesse et al.*, ed. Stanley Wells (London: Edward Arnold, 1964), p. 329.

[115] Griffiths, *Diverting Authorities*, p. 181.   [116] Griffiths, *Diverting Authorities*, pp. 176, 182.

of note forms (place-marker, source, first-person response) 'implies what is physically impossible: that the margins of the page record temporally distinct layers of annotation'.[117] And above all, they play with the boundary between orality and print: the glosses 'return the text to the condition of speech'.[118] Nashe's canon is interested in orality throughout,[119] and here, 'in minimizing the distance between reader and writer', Nashe stages 'the equation of writing with speech which recurs throughout his work'.[120] Physically adjacent to the text, these notes are nonetheless thematically, crucially, playfully, part of the text.

Thirdly: what happens when asterisks move from being used by the reader as a marginal mark to being used by the writer or the printer? The causal evolution in my question is misleading. It might be better posed as: are asterisks used differently by readers, by authors, and by printers? Can we assign asterisks in printed texts to a source? Do asterisks dissolve the boundary between writers and printers? At what stage does the compositor become a co-creator? What happens if this co-creation does not fulfil the author's vision of the *mise-en-page*? Drayton complains that the printer of *The Legend of Great Cromwell* (1607) did not consult him about the font size and therefore there was no room in the margins for the notes. Unhappily, therefore, he has to include in the preface the material that should have been in the notes; he likens it to a cook having to put in one dish what should have been distributed across several plates (A2v). Chapman complains that the notes to his *Memorable Masque* (1613) are not in their proper places (they were supposed to follow the relevant speeches) because of the 'unexpected haste' of the printer 'who never let me know, and never sending me a proofe, till he had past those speeches; I had no reason to imagine hee could have been so forward' (a1v). Readers' attention is drawn to the ideal layout and the imperfect substitute in their hands.

My fourth point is about the boundary between books and plays. When playtexts attach asterisks to stage directions in the margin do they see themselves as a book or a play? It is helpful to think of the stage direction as a marginal gloss—which it is: a gloss on the action. There are very few asterisks in early modern stage directions. One is in the *Two Noble Kinsmen*; others are in

---

[117] Griffiths, *Diverting Authorities*, p. 178.   [118] Griffiths, *Diverting Authorities*, p. 185.

[119] See, for example, Neil Rhodes, 'Nashe, Rhetoric and Satire', in *Jacobean Poetry and Prose: Rhetoric, Representation and the Popular Imagination*, ed. Clive Bloom (Basingstoke: Macmillan, 1988), pp. 25–43.

[120] Griffiths, *Diverting Authorities*, p. 183.

plays by John Marston. (I will explore these in the next section, 'The Synaptic Asterisk'.)[121]

My fifth point concerns the note as 'gnome'. The gnome is etymologically linked to knowledge. Its Sanskrit root, *gnâ* leads to two separate Latin forms, the adjective *gnarus* (knowing) and the verb *gnarro* (I tell), a form of *gnaro* (elided from *gnarum facio*: I make known). What kind of knowledge does the asterisk mediate, what kind of story does it tell?

These last two questions are too large to leave as rhetorical and so I will deal with both in the next section, 'The Synaptic Asterisk'. This requires me to revisit two items I looked at briefly earlier (Ben Jonson's poem to Thomas Palmer and the early modern reader's annotation of the 1622 *Othello*) to explore what I call the 'synaptic' asterisk.

The Synaptic Asterisk

Ben Jonson, 'To Thomas Palmer'

Thomas Palmer's manuscript quarto book of emblems, *The Sprite of Trees and Herbs*, comprises 223 beautifully illustrated poems (each illustration is in colour and measures roughly 7cm by 6.5cm).[122] The poems unite the moral and the botanical as Palmer reads the plant world allegorically. The palm represents 'the conquest of malice' as it stands tall (cap. 18); the 'pitch', whose stem does not produce any sprigs, is a warning to man not to die childless (cap. 24); the mustard seed (cap. 25), 'symbolises Christian faith, since it grows to a large size from tiny beginnings'.[123] The book made a huge impression on the young Jonson, whose literary career was just beginning in the late 1590s. It is this impression that he struggles to articulate in the poem.

Jonson's first response to the book is 'admiration' (4), 'wonder' (5, 23), 'amazement' (6). These nouns carry a stronger, more superlative quality than today's diluted meanings, stressing excitement, surprise, astonishment, the marvellous, the remarkable and extraordinary. Marlowe's Helen of Troy is the 'admirablest Lady that ever lived' (*Dr Faustus*, 1604, E3v). 'Amazement' foregrounds the paralysis occasioned by '*overwhelming* wonder' (*OED* amazement *n.*, 1 and 4, my emphasis). As here in Jonson, 'amazement' and 'admiration' are often paired terms: Hamlet's behaviour strikes Gertrude 'into amazement and

---

[121] Others appear in the MS of Heywood's *The Captives*, added by a playhouse annotator, and in the 1631 edition of Ben Jonson's *Staple of News*. See note 141.

[122] Damage to the pages means that some of the boxes for illustrations are now blank.

[123] Burrow in *The Cambridge Edition*, vol. I, p. 229. I quote the poem from this edition.

admiration' (*Hamlet*, 3.2.327). 'Wonder' has a magical quality (*OED n.1a* and 1*b*): Macbeth's encounter with the witches leaves him 'rapt in the wonder of it' (*Macbeth*, 1.5.6). Jonson is describing no ordinary emotional experience.

But the poem develops the interplay between the emotional and the cognitive. A second strand of vocabulary characterizes a more familiar, rational Jonson: the book impresses his 'brain' (21), it creates 'worlds of thoughts' (22; 'thoughts' is repeated at line 23), and taxes his 'abler faculties' (29). This strand of imagery works both with and against the affective. Jonson is 'rapt' (13), he 'struggle[s] with this passion' (29), his thoughts are 'circumvolved in gyre-like motion' (23), they spiral and expand ('dilate', 24), making him 'giddy with amazement'—which is when and why he 'fell down / In a deep trance' (25–6). This is the point at which the reader encounters the lines of asterisks.

Jonson critics interpret these asterisks differently. Colin Burrow describes the poem as an 'inspired rhapsody which lapses into asterisks'.[124] Ian Donaldson describes it as 'climaxing curiously in a rapturous run of asterisks'.[125] Is it a climax or an anti-climax? An ascent or a falling-off?

'Trance' comes from Old French *transir* (to depart) and the Latin *transire* (to go across). Movement is at the heart of the metaphor we use today for reading when we talk about being 'lost in a book'.[126] Cognitive psychologists study the phenomenon called 'immersion' or 'transportation' as a response to a literary or playworld—what Jonson calls a 'trance'.[127] Colin Burrow says that in the

---

[124] Colin Burrow, 'Ben Jonson', in *The Cambridge Companion to English Poets*, ed. Claude Rawson (Cambridge: Cambridge University Press, 2011), pp. 122–38 (p. 125).

[125] Donaldson, *A Life*, p. 147.

[126] See Victor Nell, *Lost in a Book: The Psychology of Reading for Pleasure* (Ann Arbor: Michigan State University, 2005).

[127] Also called 'narrative engagement' and 'literary allusion', the phenomenon is the subject of a growing literature. For representative examples, see: M. Bortolussi and P. Dixon, 'Transport: Challenges to the Metaphor', in *The Oxford Handbook of Cognitive Literary Studies*, ed. Lisa Zunshine (Oxford: Oxford University Press, 2015), pp. 525–40; Thalia R. Goldstein and E. Winner, 'Enhancing Empathy and Theory of Mind', *Journal of Cognition and Development* 13 (2012), 19–37; Thalia R. Goldstein and P. Bloom, 'Characterizing Characters: How Children Make Sense of Realistic Acting', *Cognitive Development, Special Issue: Cognizing the Unreal* 34 (2015), 39–50; Timothy Chesters, 'Social Cognition: A Literary Perspective', *Paragraph* 37 (2014), 62–78; R. J. Gerrig, *Experiencing Narrative Worlds: On the Psychological Activities of Reading* (Boston, MA: Yale University Press, 1993); Melanie C. Green, T. C. Brock, and G. F. Kaufman, 'Understanding Media Enjoyment: The Role of Transportation into Narrative Worlds', *Communication Theory* 14 (2004), 311–27; Melanie C. Green, 'Transportation into Narrative Worlds: Implications for the Self', in *On Building, Defending and Regulating the Self: A Psychological Perspective*, ed. Abraham. Tesser, J. V. Wood, and D. A. Stapel (New York: Psychology Press, 2005), pp. 53–76; Marie-Laure Ryan, *Narrative as Virtual Reality: Immersion and Interactivity in Literature and Electronic Media* (Baltimore, MD: Johns Hopkins University Press, 2001); Blakey Vermeule, *Why Do We Care about Literary Characters?* (Baltimore, MD: Johns Hopkins University Press, 2010); Lisa Zunshine, *Why We Read Fiction: Theory of Mind and the Novel* (Columbus: Ohio State University Press, 2006).

1590s Jonson was 'experimenting with how to represent poetic inspiration'.[128] I think that he was also experimenting with how to represent readerly excitement. This is how we can reconcile Donaldson's Jonson, who climaxes into asterisks, and Burrow's, who lapses into them. Alison Scott sees the poem as concerned with giddiness, 'as a simultaneously and interactively cognitive and emotional process'. I would add that this interactive simultaneity of emotion and cognition is how Jonson comes to understand reading.[129]

Reading—the excitement of reading—takes Jonson outside himself; entranced, he falls in a trance. The asterisks represent loss of consciousness, or perhaps loss of self-consciousness: this is what happens when you get lost in a book. But they also represent connection: the synaptic explosion as the book acts on the mind and emotions. The asterisk is a proto-emoji, suggesting both excitement and an event (in the etymological sense, *ex-venire*: that which happens as a result of something).[130] Reading explodes our brains, and the asterisk represents this excitatory synaptic charge.

We see this in the early modern reader who marked up Q1 *Othello*. We met this reader in the section 'Readers' Stars'; let us look at his marginal asterisks more closely.

Reading *Othello*

The 1622 quarto of *Othello*, now in the Huntington Library, was owned by George Steevens (1736–1800), who marked it up with an editorial eye (his edition of twenty Shakespeare quartos was published in 1766 and his ten-volume edition of *The Works of Shakespeare* in 1773). Steevens divided the undifferentiated acts of *Othello* into scenes and he collated the 1622 quarto with one of 1630, then collated both with an edition of 1655 (which, he observes, simply reprints the 1630 quarto). He noted Q/F variants in the margins throughout, sometimes (when the margin provided insufficient space) at the foot of the page. These collation notes are in a characteristic red ink.

The Q also contains annotations in two or possibly three other inks, as well as in pencil: underlinings, asterisks, other marginal hieroglyphics, additional stage directions, and corrections. Some seem to be by Steevens but some are

---

[128] Burrow, 'Ben Jonson', p. 125.

[129] Alison V. Scott, 'Making a Virtue of Giddiness: Rethinking Troilus' (E)Motion', in *Shakespeare and Emotions: Inheritances, Enactments, Legacies*, ed. R. S. White, Mark Houlahan, and Katrina O'Loughlin (Basingstoke: Palgrave Macmillan, 2015), pp. 124–36 (p. 133).

[130] For concepts of arrival, irruption and the 'evental subject' in Shakespeare, see Nicholas Luke, *Shakespeare Arrivals* (Cambridge: Cambridge University Press, 2017). Luke proposes that Shakespeare characters irrupt into the play via an event, where 'event', following Alain Badiou, is defined as an ethically charged moment that arises actively and unpredictably from within a situation.

certainly by an early modern reader (they are written in Elizabethan secretary hand). This early modern reader looked up vocabulary on twelve occasions, using the blank signature N2v at the end of the book to compile a neat glossary of terms such as *Epilepsia, Anthropophagi, Equivoce, Exufflatio, Defunctus.*[131] These are indeed exotic, unfamiliar, and difficult words in Q *Othello* (F *Othello* tones down some of Q's vocabulary). The reader has a good sense of staging and adds key stage directions to his text. He notes the crucial moment when Desdemona drops her handkerchief (H1v) and when Othello strikes her (K2v) and when Iago strikes Emilia with a sword (M4r). In the reciprocal pledge scene of 3.3, he balances the quarto stage direction for Iago's genuflection with the addition of a parallel one for Othello (H3v). He notes an aside for Iago (E1r) and he adds a stage direction for Roderigo's death, accompanying the text's 'o, o, o' (L4r). He corrects or completes erroneous, damaged, or badly inked readings. On D2v 'm[ealt]' is noted as 'melt' beneath the blotted word (2.1). The illegible verb in Act 3—'That Cuckold lives in blisse, / Who certaine of his fate, l[es] not his wronger' (G3v)—is guessed at (incorrectly), with 'hates' in the left margin. Steevens later correctly supplies 'loves' in the right margin. The early modern reader inserts 'without remorce' on H3v where Q reads 'shall be remorce'.

Thus, we have two attentive readers, one an eighteenth-century reader interested in textual variants, and one an Elizabethan reader interested in understanding vocabulary and in stage action. Faced with Othello's 'provulgate' in Act 1 (B4r), the editor underlines it in red and uses the margin to note the Folio reading 'promulgate'; the early modern reader adds the Q reading to his glossary: '*provulgo, as* • to show a broad, to professe opneley [sic]'. The two readers are easy to distinguish because of their handwriting as well as their interests. But the quarto is marked up extensively with a variety of notational symbols so, when we encounter marks that are not words or phrases, it is less easy to know who made them. There are eighty octothorpes (what we now call the hash tag), fifteen curly brackets (once in triplicate), twelve dotted diple, two crosses, a number of idiosyncratic marks such as lines with arrows and dots, and a capital omega (three times). Speeches are underlined on no fewer than 117 occasions. Othello's rhetoric and Iago's brazen audacity are the prime

---

[131] This process began from the moment he began to read: the first two items in his glossary, *evade* and *epithet*, occur on the first page of the play (where he has underlined them in black). Steevens may, of course, be responsible for these underlinings, but elsewhere on this page he has underlined in red, and since the words underlined in black feature in the early modern glossary, it is reasonable to assume that the underlining and glossarial actions were coordinated.

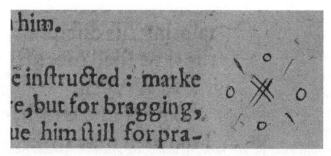

FIGURE 3.24 Shakespeare, *Othello* (1622, STC 22305), E2r. Shelfmark 69337. Courtesy of the Huntington Library, San Marino.

draws in this respect, often receiving a combination of underlinings and marginal marks. On a dozen occasions these underlinings are accompanied by what I have called an exploding asterisk: a hashtag surrounded by four dashes and four tiny circles that give it the appearance of a firework or exploding asterisk (see Figure 3.24).

Steevens is certainly the author of the precisely penned small asterisks (of which there are five) since they are in red and sometimes accompany his collation notes. But many of the black-pen underlinings of speeches seem to predate Steevens' red underlinings (he often underlines a word or phrase in red below a speech which is already underlined in black). This may be Steevens on two occasions rather than two readers: the two rust-coloured marginal hieroglyphs on D2r are written over one of Steevens' distinctive red-ink marginal collation notes, as are the curly bracket on E2r and the octothorpe on E2v. But elsewhere, such as on G4v, black ink in the margin identifies an unattributed speech as belonging to 'Iago', where the 'g' matches the formation of 'g' in the glossary; and the 'Iago' is followed by Steevens' red-ink note making the same point (and citing the Folio). The red ink is an emendation based on collation not on logical guesswork (the probable source of the black ink's emendation) and it is an unusual addendum had Steevens also been the author of the black-ink point.

I am tempted to view the bulk of the black-ink underlinings and marginalia as the product of the early modern reader rather than the eighteenth-century editor. But whichever reader was responsible for these annotations, it was one who felt readerly excitement at the rhetoric of Othello and conveyed his excitement with underlinings and exploding asterisks. This takes us back to Jonson's poem to Thomas Palmer. Jonson read Sir Thomas Palmer's book and it exploded his mind; he represented it in the only way he could, with a series of asterisks. The experience of reading *Othello*—the rhetoric of Othello and the gall of Iago—exploded this reader's mind. The asterisk shows us that explosion: it is the mark in the margin when a brain connects with a text. In this respect, then, it matters little whether it is a reader's or an editor's brain (and editors are readers as A. E. Housman reminds us: 'before I edit a work, I read it').[132] Like Ben Jonson in 1599, the reader of the 1622 *Othello* represents his electrified response with asterisks. It is perhaps no coincidence that neuroscience would later do the same in depicting synaptic flashes. Reading is an electrifying experience and, in an era before brain scans, the margins of *Othello* show us nothing less than the experience of reading.

Part III: Mediation

Mediating Knowledge and Ignorance

I said in the Introduction that this book is about the history of reading, about the ways in which readers interact with their books. Chapters 1 and 2 explored what is not there: blank space or the inferred continuation that *&c-etcetera* prompts. The asterisk is slightly different. The asterisk is there but it's in the margin, on the edge, a boundary marker. It mediates between the text and the reader: it points out what to admire or it identifies a source or explains vocabulary to us. But it also gives us personal responses—John Davies' 'good words if not ill-used', Gascoigne's Hague as the 'pleasauntest village'. It represents the dialogue between a personal response and an intellectual (as we saw in Jonson's attempts to reconcile the two). It represents the interplay of emotional reaction and literary criticism—which is the activity of reading. The asterisk, then, is a metaphor for everything in the previous chapters: it represents the interactive cusp between writer and reader, between stimulus and response, between what is in the text and what is outside, between what the author writes and what the reader brings to that writing, between what we know and don't know, between what we are told and not told, between centre and margin. It is the child of the technical and the theoretical—the printed page and the stakes of writing—signalling and embellishing something epistemologically important about the adjacent text. And it sits gnomically in the margin, indicating its helpful mediating position.

---

[132] A. E. Housman, 'Transpositions in the Ibis of Ovid', in *The Classical Papers of A. E. Housman*, vol. III, ed. J. Diggle and F. R. D. Goodyear (London: Cambridge University Press, 1971), p. 976.

I'd like to dwell on the concept of mediation via George Hunter's statement about gnomic pointing in Marston's *The Malcontent*. With a combination of resignation and theoretical insight, Hunter concluded, 'We do not know the full meaning of these signs, and our ignorance should be part of our sense of them'.[133] This was written in 1975, when Hunter edited *The Malcontent* for the Revels series, but his interest in Marston's gnomic pointing began decades earlier. In 1951 Hunter surveyed gnomic pointing in early modern texts, dramatic and non-dramatic.[134] He identified five ways in which print calls attention to *sententiae*: different font; double commas (the forerunner of what we now call quotation marks) at the beginning of the gnomic passage and subsequent lines but not at the end; commas at the beginning of the gnomic passage and subsequent lines but not at the end; asterisks; manicules. He identified patterns and trends: gnomic pointing is a phenomenon of print not manuscript; it appears frequently in the work of some authors and compositors but not others; the single comma became old-fashioned by the 1630s. Several of his observations about the development of gnomic markers relate to material we encountered in the development of the sidenote in Part II: The Margin. He notes for example that many Drayton poems (*England's Heroical Epistles*, *The Barons' Wars*, *Robert of Normandy*, *Matilda*, and *Cromwell*) have no gnomic pointing before the 1619 *Poems*.[135] As we have seen, two of these poems acquired notes and an index after their first publication. There is a developing sense of a bookish identity.

Hunter dwells on the prominence of gnomic marking in Marston's plays, particularly in the editions of *The Malcontent* in 1604. He concludes that Marston exercised an editorial function in the reprints, adding more gnomic pointing, although he (Marston) was inconsistent about the methods adopted. Hunter extended this consideration when he came to edit the play in 1975. There he provided an editorial rationale:

> I have resisted temptation to modernise the 'gnomic pointing' which is a significant feature of the original text, and one whose detailed alteration between quartos implies finicky care by author or compositors.... *We do not know the full meaning of these signs, and our ignorance should be part of our sense of them.*[136]

Our ignorance is a lot less than it was, thanks to the work of scholars such as Laura Estill, Margreta de Grazia, Zachary Lesser, Beatrice Montedoro, and

---

[133] Hunter in Marston, *The Malcontent*, pp. xxxviii–xxxix.   [134] Hunter, '*Sententiae*'.
[135] Hunter, '*Sententiae*', 177.
[136] Hunter in Marston, *The Malcontent*, pp. xxxviii–xxxix, my emphasis.

Peter Stallybrass.[137] But I want to emphasize Hunter's phrasing because it is precisely this boundary between ignorance and knowledge that, I have been arguing, the asterisk gnomically negotiates. How does a text ask itself questions about what it is doing? For the printed text, the answer is: via the asterisk. The asterisk is the double of literary history, sitting between *hors-texte* and *mise-en-page*, on the boundary of epistemology and physical page, constructing that boundary and simultaneously dissolving it.

That is a huge symbolic weight for a piece of type to carry. And we have downgraded its significance. We have reduced it to a location marker not just as a footnote but in the literal, geographical sense, on information boards where asterisks inform us, 'you are here'. Outside academic writing, the locational, asterisked footnote is mainly negative. It directs us to the small print, introducing exclusions and qualifications which are never to our benefit. We cannot use frequent flyer points over Christmas; we cannot combine special offers in restaurants; sales last only as long as the stock does. So standard is this exclusionary association that it can be transferred parodically to social situations (see Figure 3.25). As I hope has become clear, in no previous century would people have thought of the asterisk in this limited and negative way.

Mediating Play and Book

In the previous section I looked at the asterisk's role in the boundary between knowledge and ignorance. In this section I want to look at its role in the boundary between play and book. Asterisks occur in the stage direction of two plays printed thirty years apart: Marston's *The Malcontent* (1604) and

[137] Margreta de Grazia, 'Shakespeare in Quotation Marks', in *The Appropriation of Shakespeare: Post-Renaissance Reconstructions of the Works and the Myth*, ed. Jean I. Marsden (New York: St Martin's, 1991), pp. 57–71; Ann Moss, *Printed Commonplace-Books and the Structuring of Renaissance Thought* (Oxford: Clarendon Press, 1996); Peter Stallybrass, 'The Library and Material Texts', *Publications of the Modern Language Association* 119:5 (2004), 1347–52; Zachary Lesser and Peter Stallybrass, 'The First Literary *Hamlet* and the Commonplacing of Professional Plays', *Shakespeare Quarterly* 59:4 (2008), 371–420; Laura Estill, *Dramatic Extracts in Seventeenth-Century English Manuscripts: Watching, Reading, Changing Plays* (Newark: University of Delaware Press, 2015); Fred Schurink, 'Manuscript Commonplace Books, Literature, and Reading in Early Modern England', *Huntington Library Quarterly* 73:3 (2010), 453–69; Laura Estill, 'Commonplacing Readers', in *Shakespeare and Textual Studies*, ed. M. J. Kidnie and Sonia Massai (Cambridge: Cambridge University Press, 2015), pp. 149–62; Estill, 'Commonplace Markers'. See also the database curated by Laura Estill and Beatrice Montedoro, DEx: A Database of Dramatic Extracts. Available at: <https://dex.itercommunity.org/>

* not included

FIGURE 3.25 Cartoon, *Man Excluded*. Cartoon reproduced courtesy of <https://www.cartoonstock.com>.

Fletcher and Shakespeare's *Two Noble Kinsmen* (1634). I approach them in reverse chronological order.

John Fletcher and William Shakespeare, Two Noble Kinsmen

Two Noble Kinsmen (1634) uses an asterisked stage direction on only one occasion.[138] It occurs in the scene (Act 3, scene 6) when Palamon and Arcite meet to contest their title to Emilia's love. This is their first, unofficial combat; Emilia knows nothing of their love, and both men are technically exiles from Athens. Although their combat is private, they observe formal ceremonies. Palamon appeals formally to abstractions for protection ('My Cause and honour guard me') and Arcite appeals to his love for Emilia ('And me[,] my love'). A stage direction in the left-hand margin indicates their observance of physical as well as linguistic formalities: 'They bow severall wayes: then

---

[138] I am grateful to Rory Loughnane, who edited the play for the New Oxford Shakespeare, for helpful correspondence on this asterisk and the dramatic moment it accompanies.

advance and stand' (H1v). There is no marginal asterisk with this stage direction although one is placed midline in the corresponding dialogue. There it occurs between two phrases, keying the end of the first phrase (Arcite's appeal to Love) to the stage business, after which the Arcite-actor resumes his line with the uncertain question, 'Is there ought else to say?'

Many of the stage directions in this quarto are in the left-hand margin, often in advance of their related moment in the dialogue, and it is clear from their location, as well as their locution, that the underlying manuscript copy was what we would now call a prompt book: 'Chaire and stooles out' (G2v); '3. Hearses ready' (C4v). Thomas Cotes the printer (d. 1641) had a long, successful career in the Jacobean and Caroline periods and was accustomed to setting marginal notes: they appear in almost all the books he printed between 1628 and 1634, keyed to the text by lowercase letters, by asterisks, or without a notational symbol. Prior to the *Two Noble Kinsmen*, however, the bulk of his work was non-dramatic. A reprint of Fletcher's *Faithful Shepherdess* in 1629 and Shakespeare's Folio in 1632 were his first forays into drama. With *Two Noble Kinsmen* Cotes simply followed his normal typesetting procedure and did not see much distinction between this book—a playtext—and the other non-dramatic texts he had printed previously. The typical location of manuscript prompt-book stage directions in the margin would have made the manuscript closely resemble others of his experience.[139]

John Marston, *The Malcontent*

A different explanation underlies the use of asterisks in the drama of John Marston. At the beginning of *The Malcontent* (1604), a speech by Malevole begins, '*Yaugh, godaman what dost thou there', with a marginal stage direction, '*Out of his chamber'.[140] Someone is thinking about staging—specifically, the relationship between the upper and lower stage.[141]

[139] The year before *Two Noble Kinsmen* was published, Marlowe's *Jew of Malta* was printed. Although it contains an asterisk, the situation is not analogous. The asterisked sidenote is part of three historical explanations in the margin of a prologue explaining allusions to Christopher Marlowe, Edward Alleyn, and Richard Perkins. (The notes are signalled respectively by an asterisk, an obelisk, and a double obelisk.) It is not part of the dramatic experience, in that the audience at the Cock-Pit would have heard the allusion ('best of poets') without its gloss. The audience for *Two Noble Kinsmen* would have *seen* the gloss in action: 'They bow several ways'.

[140] I quote from STC 17481, B1r.

[141] Analogous asterisks occur for similarly practical reasons in Heywood's *The Captives* (c.1632) where the playhouse annotator adds marginal asterisks to direct attention to major stage directions. British Library MS Egerton 1994, fols 52–73. See the Malone Society Reprint prepared by Arthur Brown (Oxford: Oxford University Press, 1953). Marginal asterisks also preface stage directions in the first and last acts of Jonson's *Staple of News* (1631).

This 'someone' in *The Malcontent* is theatrically alert throughout the printed text. The margins indicate to whom a speech is directed, sometimes with an asterisk in both margin and dialogue ('*To Prepasso*', B2r), sometimes without ('*To Bilioso*', B2r; 'Aurelia to Pietro', I3r). They indicate action that accompanies speech ('*Ferneze privately feedes Maquerelles hands with jewells during this speech*', C1v). They indicate blocking: the speech prefixes for Malevole and Pietro on I2v have prefatory asterisks, alerting us to the corresponding (but unasterisked) directions in the margin, 'Malevole takes his wife to daunce' and 'Pietro taks his wife Aurelia to dance.'

Who speaks to whom in the final scene is carefully choreographed. In the last nine lines of the play, we have one stage direction for action ('*kicks out Mend.*') and six directions indicating whom Malevole addresses as he metes out punishments and rewards. Four of these addressee-directions are without any marginal symbol, one has an asterisk in text and margin, and one has a § in the text although the corresponding (blurred) marginal mark looks more like an asterisk. This printed playtext functions as a director, trying to help readers dramatically by orienting them to a visual experience. This is a printed play that is very aware of its status as play.[142]

Simultaneously, however, the text is aware of itself as a book. It begins with a prefatory epistle to the reader. The epistle calls attention to the difference between a play as a performance artefact and as a printed object. (We see this distinction again on the last page which prints 'an imperfect Ode', explaining that it comprises only 'one staffe' because it was spoken as/by the prologue (I4r).) There is a *dramatis personae* list, providing detailed explanations of characters' relationships (e.g. Ferneze is 'A yong Courtier, and inamored on the Dutchesse'; A2v). And it prefaces several lines with double commas, helping readers extract choice *sententiae*.[143] In the prefatory epistle in which he argues for a play's rightful destination as performance, Marston concedes that *The Malcontent* would have made its way to the press somehow, so '*I have my selfe*

---

[142] The source of this helpfulness is more probably the author than the printer. The dramatic details are too precise throughout to be inserted without a careful reading or knowledge of the play. There were two editions of *The Malcontent* in 1604 but the first was corrected so heavily, with some formes reset, that 'the distinction between corrected states of one edition and a new "edition" embodying corrections' is 'blurr[ed]' (Hunter, in Marston, *The Malcontent*, p. xxxiii). Collating the two/three versions, Hunter concludes that there was someone with an editor's eye in the printing house—someone he identifies as Marston. For further discussion of this issue, see Holger Schott Syme, 'Unediting the Margin: Jonson, Marston, and the Theatrical Page', *English Literary Renaissance* 38:1 (2008), 142–71.

[143] See D2r, D4v, E1v, G1v. These also occur in other Marston plays: see, for example, *The Fawn* (1606), A4r, A4v.

therefore set forth this Comedie' (A2r). In *The Fawn* he offers the same distinction between drama and book, explaining again that he has been responsible for converting the former into the latter: '*If any shall wonder why I print a Comedie, whose life rests much in the Actors voice Let such know, that it cannot avoide publishing: let it therefore stand with good excuse, that I have been my owne setter out*' (A2r). Unlike *Two Noble Kinsmen*, then, which was printed posthumously, Marston seems to have been both concerned about, and involved with, his text's journey from stage play to book. The asterisks in *The Malcontent* are part of a system of annotating the action, translating a reading experience back into a viewing experience.[144]

Awareness of the relation between media (in this case, between play and book) can also be seen in the metatextual relations between fictional prose narratives and the printed book. Children's fiction is often wittily metatextual, as we saw in Chapter 1 with the case of the page snail. But so too is concrete poetry, as we saw when we looked at Jerome Rothenberg's edited collection of concrete poetry, *Technicians of the Sacred*, many of which exploit typographical symbols (the forward slash, ellipses, the plus-sign) to create visual meaning. In my final section I want to look at two works—a novel and a poem—that do playful things with asterisks for different reasons and with different effects.

Tradition and Innovation

Jerome Rothenberg, *Technicians of the Sacred*

In 1967 Jerome Rothenberg edited a collection of what he would later variously call an 'omnipoetics' and an 'ethnopoetics'. Interested in non-Western traditions of the poetic past, he collected poems and translations from mainly indigenous peoples;[145] these are the 'technicians' of the title whose poems, songs, picture-poems, oral poetics, repetitions, and gaps have been labelled primitive but are simply technically very different from Western/Anglophone

---

[144] Valentine Sims was an experienced printer of plays, and had also previously printed several books with marginal notes, but in neither case had he used asterisks. I quote *The Malcontent* from the 1604 version with the added induction (STC 17481). The first edition that year (STC 17479) also has the prefatory epistle and choreographic margins with asterisks. I enjoyed several discussions with Rory Loughnane about asterisks in *The Malcontent* when we were discussing *The Two Noble Kinsmen* and am grateful to him for his editorial expertise.

[145] Jerome Rothenberg (ed.), *Technicians of the Sacred*, 3rd edn (Los Angeles: University of California Press, 2017). The 1967 edition was expanded in 1984 and again in 2017; the third edition (from which I quote) runs to 643 pages. I am grateful to Gillian Woods for bringing this collection, and its dedication, to my attention. Page numbers in parentheses in this section refer to this work.

poetic frameworks. The book's manifesto (indeed, the first three words of the first edition) is that 'primitive means complex'. Rothenberg rethinks inherited definitions of poetry, and cautions readers against the binary division of tribal versus literate poetics and the assumption that orality totally defines 'them' or that writing totally defines 'us' (p. xxviii).

His caution is salutary given how many of the poems play with graphic form and printing conventions. Type size is manipulated: 'Coyote and Junco', by Native American Zuni poet Andrew Peynetsa, juxtaposes small and regular font sizes, superscript, capitals, and italics (pp. 190–2). In the Nyigina Australian poem, 'From "George Dyungayan's Bulu Line"', four different font sizes are used, along with ellipses and empty brackets. The Cherokee *The Killer* uses two lines of inverted commas (unattached to speech) in a poem that regularly begins each line with 'listen' (p. 63). In 'The Myth of the Dragon-Fly' the pages are sprinkled with single inverted commas, colons, and full stops (interspersed with scattered word and phrases), patterned like constellations in a night sky (pp. 397–401) and representing the dragonflies of the title and the mosquitoes of the introduction. 'Midé Picture-Songs' include 'An Imploration for Clear Weather', which is a series of pictographs (pp. 173–5); but equally pictorial are the repetition poems, whether the repetition is of a line, a phrase, or a single letter. In the African American 'Ol' Hannah' (pp. 67–70), we find repetition of one letter within a word ('Ohhhhhhhhhh') and 'partneeeeeer' rhymes with 'riveeeeeer'; the Ayahuasca sound-poem (from the Kaxinawás of Brazil and Peru) comprises a single letter: a rectangle composed of 'e (arranged in fifteen lines, with six 'es per line).[146] The Borneon 'A List of Bad Dreams Chanted as a Cause & Cure for Missing Souls' (pp. 60–2) begins each line anaphorically with 'To dream that one', 'To dream that she', 'To dream of resting'. The three pages of repeated lines form a pattern like a designer textile, but they also create a dizzying optical glare, like snow blindness or an optician's chart testing for astigmatism. Nestled in among the repetitions are tiny variations which stand out because of their visual clarity, separated from the identically repeated forms that surround them. These variations alter the pace of the reading experience and attract the reader's visual, lexical, and emotional attention. If visual form is manipulated, so is generic form: the South African Vendan 'Language Event' is structured as a Q and A (pp. 102–3), with its

---

[146] Rothenberg's introduction raises interesting questions about how we define a single line in poetry. Is it still single if it is repeated? How do repeated lines become unified? How do we identify a group? (*Technicians*, p. xxxii).

answers becoming increasingly sinister; the Aztec 'Coronation Event' is structured as a play, with five main characters, extras, dialogue, and stage directions
(pp. 118–23). Poetic form is constantly defamiliarized. These 'near-poems'
(p. xix) both question twentieth-century definitions of poetry and foreground
primitive poetry's link to contemporary concrete poetry and visual art.[147]

This is the context in which asterisks make their appearance in *Technicians of
the Sacred*. We first encounter them in the book's dedication which reads as in
figure 3.26. Visually arresting but cryptic to the point of impenetrability, these
asterisks require one to turn to page 396 for illumination. Here we find 'Old
Man Beaver's Blessing Song', a translation (by J. R. and Richard Johnny John)
of a traditional Senecan song-poem used ceremoniously to renew friendship
ties. One characteristic of Senecan song poetry is 'its minimal use of words

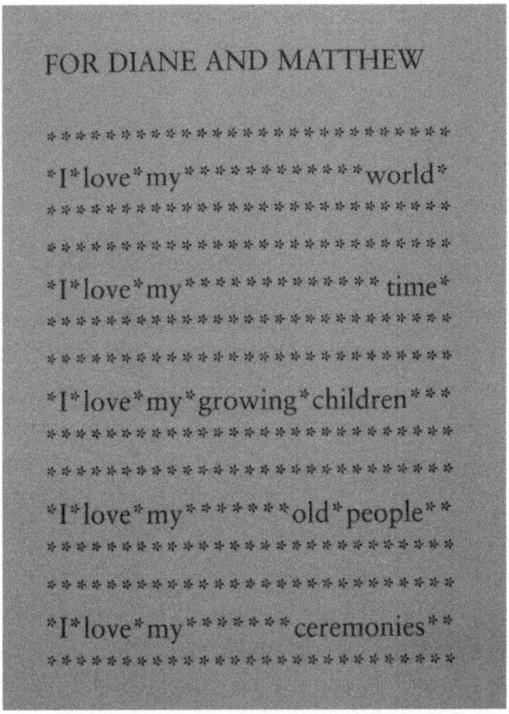

```
FOR DIANE AND MATTHEW

*********************************
*I*love*my*************world*
*********************************
*********************************
*I*love*my**************time*
*********************************
*********************************
*I*love*my*growing*children***
*********************************
*********************************
*I*love*my*******old*people**
*********************************
*********************************
*I*love*my*******ceremonies**
*********************************
```

FIGURE 3.26 Jerome Rothenberg, ed. *Technicians of the Sacred* (3rd edition.
Oakland, CA: University of California Press, 2017). Courtesy of University of
California Press.

---

[147] We recall from Chapter 1 that Simon Armitage felt as a poet that he has more kinship with
visual artists.

and vocables'. How, then, to present a 'centuries-old minimalism in a printed format'? (p. 624). The translators' solution is the asterisk. They couple this with repetition, the acoustic 'heheeHOHO' and a mixture of upper- and lowercase. The sixteen-line song begins as follows:

*OLD*MAN*BEAVER'S*BLESSING*SONG
*all*i*want*'s*a*good* *5¢*seegar*
heeheeHOHOheeheeHOHOheeheeHOHO

It repeats lines 2 and 3 six times (without the italics on *5¢*seegar*) before concluding with a repeat of the first line. In appropriating this form for his dedication, then, Rothenberg invokes an ancient friendship ritual to pay tribute to his family and to renew their bonds.

In his introduction, Rothenberg notes how central are a woman and a child to the 'oldest' cultures he studies (p. xxxviii); they are also the centre of his own dedicatory poem. His introduction also ponders the ways that new forms of writing are created and the way in which unity is achieved in any unfamiliar and disaggregated new form so that the poem becomes more than a collection of parts. Unity requires one constant item against which all disparate materials can be measured. But he also identifies readerly involvement as a key constituent. Gaps in poems, whether of physical space or understanding, leave 'room for fill-in and it is "the spectator" as (ritual) participant who pulls it all together' (p. xxxiv). The dedication thus does not stand outside the collection but becomes the first poem in it (as befits a volume whose editor is also a poet) and the reader becomes 'maximal[y] involve[d]' (p. xxxiv; this is a familiar refrain throughout *The Rhetoric of the Page*). The sequence of asterisks sets the scene for a collection of poems in which graphics are as important as words, in which typography is paradoxically centre stage in oral forms, and in which the reader is constantly drawn in through shape.

For a different kind of readerly involvement, and the role of the asterisk, I turn to Edith Nesbit's children's novel, *The Wouldbegoods* (1901).[148]

E. Nesbit, *The Wouldbegoods*

Edith Nesbit's children's novel *The Wouldbegoods* (1901) is a sequel to her best-seller, *The Story of the Treasure Seekers* (1899). Here the asterisk plays a more playful, metaphoric role.

---

[148] I am grateful to Alison Shell for bringing this novel to my attention.

Having tried their elders' patience, the Bastable children have been sent away from London for the summer. They formalize the experience of trying to be good by founding a society: the society of the Wouldbegoods. Each chapter of the novel describes a day's attempt at generous and helpful actions; inevitably the children's well-intentioned activities get out of hand and each episode ends with them being lectured or punished.

The young narrator introduces his family in the first chapter but declines to repeat explanations that we can find in the first novel. In the first of many direct addresses to the reader, he gives a cross-reference: 'We are the Bastables— Oswald, Dora, Dickie, Alice, Noel, and H. O. If you want to know why we call our youngest brother H. O. you jolly well read *The Treasure Seekers* and find out'.[149] We are not entering the world of the Bastable children so much as watching that world be constructed. References to the act of writing abound: 'I hope all this is plain. I have said it as short as I can' (p. 24). The author notes his experiments with vocabulary. A description of someone as 'dejected' prompts the parenthetical observation: '(That is a good word, and one I have never used before)' (p. 11). An entire paragraph in parenthesis worries: '(I hope you do not think that the words I use are getting too long. I know they are the right words. And Albert's uncle says your style is always altered a bit by what you read. And I have been reading the Vicomte of Bragelonne. Nearly all my new words come out of those.)' (p. 96). Sometimes he foregrounds his authorship by describing himself in the third person: his sisters 'are strangely fond of kissing [babies]. The author never could see anything in it himself' (p. 130). He tries out different narrative styles: 'But let me to my narrating. I hope you will like it. I am going to try to write it a different way, like the books they give you for a prize at a girls' school [...] Here goes:' (p. 112). After four paragraphs of sentimental maidens and elevated vocabulary ('umbragipaeous beech tree'), the project is abandoned: 'It's no use. I can't write like these books. I wonder how the books' authors can keep it up' (p. 113).[150]

The plot of the children's daily escapades is itself nested within a writing project. The children are staying with Albert's uncle who is writing a work of

---

[149] E. Nesbit, *The Wouldbegoods* (London: Ernest Benn, 1958), p. 10. Page numbers in parentheses in this section refer to this work.

[150] The *OED* has no citation for *umbragipaeous* although its meaning and etymology are clear. The narrator's subsequent 'plain English' summary as he rejects his own style helps any young reader who might not have worked it out: 'What really happened was that we were all eating black currants in the orchard' (p. 113).

fiction. And his frame story itself ends like a work of fiction when he finds a bride. This is not the kind of conclusion our young narrator likes: 'I am afraid it is rather dull but it was very important (to him), so I felt it ought to be narrated' (p. 254). With the action concluded, he tells us: 'So that is the end of the Wouldbegoods, and there are no more chapters after this. But Oswald hates books that finish up without telling you the things you might want to know about the people in the book. So here goes' (p. 255).

The novel's relationship with the fictional world underpins every chapter, where imaginative activities are described as if they are real. In the circus chapter, for instance, the farm animals are referenced as the exotic creatures they are deemed to represent. This is typical of children at play, as the many psychological and neuroscientific articles about children's play worlds attest. But the narrator's imaginative world encounters slippage (mainly when things go wrong and the real world intrudes): 'The old horse—I mean the trained elephant from Venezuela...' (p. 105). The author's lapses from consistent inhabitation of the fictional world only serve to underline the narrative control that goes into creating and maintaining a fictional world in the first place.

These are more than just self-reflexive comments on the process of writing. The constant foregrounding of genre, structure, vocabulary, and style (and, as we shall see, typography), means that we are never allowed to forget that we are reading a book. There are cross-references to the book we are reading. Oswald's suggestion that the children 'do something' is given a footnote directing us forward sixteen pages to a short story. When the narrator suspects we may not have noticed a detail of his plot, he admonishes, 'if so, don't look back for it' (p. 256). This is a novel of stories *qua* book-product as well as storytelling.

Chapter 6 details the children's attempts to cast the farmyard animals in a circus. None of the animals—the goats, the donkeys, the pigs, the old horse, the turkeys—behaves as expected; or rather, they behave entirely as one would expect untrained animals to behave. When Billy, the 'well-known acrobatic goat' independently does his 'Alpine feat of daring' in the kitchen by ascending a chair onto the dresser, causing crockery to crash, the housekeeper, Mrs Pettigrew, is enraged. She had already been brandishing a mop against the goat while screaming (outside, 'Noël...wondered whether Mrs Pettigrew was being robbed, or only murdered'). Now she and Albert's uncle direct their angry invective to the children, at which point the narrator says, 'I will draw a veil and asterisks over what Mrs Pettigrew said' (p. 105). This is the narrator's first use of zeugma but not his first metaphorical allusion to typographical representation. A few paragraphs before this, describing the circus turn in which the goat was to climb the Andes, he reflects, parenthetically: '(We thought we could make the Andes out of hurdles and things, and so we could have but for what always happens. (This is the unexpected. (This is a saying father told me—but I see I am three deep in brackets so I will close them before I get into any more).).).' (p. 103).[151]

When he writes 'draw a veil and asterisks', he shows us that he understands decorum in writing and (self-)censorship in print. He does this in two ways. The first is literary, with a metaphor for concealment: 'I will draw a veil'. The second is typographical: 'and asterisks'. His creative coup, however, is to unite the two methods, turning asterisks into a metaphor. The young narrator is telling a story, with due attention to the tools of narration (language, apostrophe, narrative content, and so on). But he is also aware that stories are written down and printed—indeed, that we can only access his story through print. With the allusion to asterisks, he reminds us that we are reading a book. This brings us back full circle to my Introduction where I noted that 'nothing is more calculated to remind a reader he is reading than the deliberate foregrounding of graphic form'.[152] The evolution of Allen Ginsberg's *Howl* shows something similar in the medium of poetry performance when the poet blurs the boundary of orality and print. The original typescript's 'mother finally fucked' (recorded at a poetry reading in 1956) was published the same year as 'mother finally ******' but then developed in later performance into 'mother finally asterisked'. Ginsberg turns the self-censorship of his six asterisks into a verb that is simultaneously a sexual euphemism and a typographical nod, treating 'the printed asterisks as the poem's literal words'.[153]

---

[151] In the same paragraphs, the children dress the pig in a Union Jack 'we made out of Daisy's flannel petticoat and cetera'. It is tempting to see this as another play with print forms. However, as we saw in Chapter 2, 'etcetera' was a Victorian euphemism for underwear so its appearance here could just be an appropriate coincidence. The unusual form 'and cetera' may suggest that the narrator is activating the literal Latin meaning rather than employing a euphemism: the Union Jack, in other words, was formed of Daisy's petticoats and the rest of her undergarments. So this may be part of the narrator's sensitivity to language rather than to print.

[152] Edward A. Levenston, *The Stuff of Literature: Physical Aspects of Texts and their Relation to Literary Meaning* (Albany: State University of New York Press, 1992), p. 119.

[153] Hannah Sullivan, *The Work of Revision* (Cambridge, MA: University of Harvard Press, 2013), p. 251. For 'mother finally fucked' see Allen Ginsberg, *Howl: Original Draft Facsimile, Transcript and Variant Versions, Fully Annotated by Author*, ed. Barry Miles (London: Harper Perennial 2006), p. 18; for 'mother finally ******' see Ginsberg, *Howl and Other Poems* (San Francisco, CA: City Light Books, 1956), p. 15. For 'asterisk' as a verb, see Epilogue footnote 13.

In the Epilogue I want to look at how graphic form—the punctuation and typographical signs I have been exploring in these three chapters—assumes a metaphoric life beyond the page. But I also want to look at a different kind of experiment: the ways in which printers, alert to the rhetoric of the page, experiment with other kinds of typographical effects in plays. Let us look now at these two types of innovation.

Epilogue

Print and Metaphor

Punctuation acquired personality in Elizabethan texts, not just typograph-ically on the page but metaphorically in speech. In Marston's *Antonio and Mellida* (1602), Mellida tells Antonio 'weele point [punctuate] our speech / With amorous kissing, kissing com[m]aes' (G4r). Heywood's Lord de Averne warns his scribe against inserting a 'suspitious dash / or doubt-full Coma' (*The Captives*, 1380–1).[1] Parenthesis receives the lion's share of metaphoric uses. John Donne several times uses 'parenthesis' to denote inset moments in life: 'I am in such a parenthesis now (in convalescence) when I thought myself very near to my period' he writes to a lord in 1624, while in his *Meditations* he com-pares time to punctuation: 'Tyme is a short *parenthesis* in a longe *period*'.[2] Like Donne, a character in the anonymous *The Wit of a Woman* (1604) links paren-thesis to the grammatical period. When Gerillo offers idealized praise of women, Veronte interjects sceptically. Commenting on the interjection, Filenio asks, 'What's that? a parentheisis?' [*sic*]; Veronte counters with 'Better so then a foole point'(G1r). The pun on 'foole / full point' extends the punctuation allusion and turns it into a misogynistic joke. Cuckolds' horns are often compared to parentheses because of the similarity of shape: 'doost see Vulcan with the horning parenthesis in his fore-head' asks Polymetes in John Day's *Law Tricks* (1608, E1r). Shape is also invoked when John Earle uses parenthesis to describe curled flecks of dust on a page. His antiquary loves

---

[1] Thomas Heywood, *The Captives*, ed. Arthur Brown (Malone Society Reprints; Oxford: Oxford University Press, 1953). The play was new in 1624 when Sir Henry Herbert entered it in his office book, and so the dating supports Henry Woudhuysen's argument about the development of the dash as a Jacobean punctuation mark. (See Introduction and Chapter 1.)

[2] 'Letter to a Lord upon Presenting Some of his Work to Him [1624]', in John Donne, *Complete Poetry and Selected Prose of John Donne*, ed. Charles M. Coffin (New York: Random House, 2001), pp. 395–6 (p. 395); *Devotions upon Emergent Occasions* (1634), P12r.

The Rhetoric of the Page. Laurie Maguire, Oxford University Press (2020). © Laurie Maguire.
DOI: 10.1093/oso/9780198862109.001.0001

manuscripts 'especially if the cover bee all moth-eaten and the dust make a *Parenthesis* betweene every Syllable'.[3]

But 'parenthesis' is expanded to indicate both the physical brackets which enclose an aside and the digression itself. Like the '&c' of Chapter 2, it develops from being an item of punctuation to denoting the rhetorical feature that the punctuation introduced.[4] The semantically clever characters in Lyly's *Sapho and Phao* (1584) manage to yoke/joke about both meanings several times in just a few lines. Callipho recounts his contribution to a debate where his 'sentence [opinion, but with grammatical pun]' was deemed 'so indifferent, that they all concluded it might aswel have beene lefte out, as put in, and so placed on each side of my head things lyke horns, and called me a *Parenthesis*' (D3r). This leads to jokes about Vulcan's parenthetical horns and the same 'full point' joke as in *The Wit of a Woman*, before the dialogue returns to rhetorical parenthesis with the characters commenting on their own structural digression within the scene. In *Pierce Pennilesse* (1592), Nashe moves from the physical to the rhetorical. Dame Niggardize's tiny kitchen has 'a little court chimney, about the compasse of a *Parenthesis* in proclamation print'; later, having digressed, Pierce bids 'farewell, good parenthesis'.[5]

The physical shape of parentheses finds an outlet in stage action. The clown in Lodge's *The Wounds of Civil War* (1594) says he must 'make a parenthesis of this pintpot, for words make men dry' (G3r); Joseph Houppert's gloss explains 'just as parentheses enclose a word, the clown's hands enclose his pint pot'.[6] Here the word 'parenthesis' cues stage action. As we saw in Chapter 2, Lloyd Kermode suggests that the printed parenthesis in *Englishmen for my Money* embodies the actor's performance of the bandy legs that are the side-effect of the pox: 'Theyle say, the *French (et-cetera)* infected mee' (D1r). This was also John Lennard's explanation for the empty brackets enclosing the missing word 'pox' in *The Malcontent*—'a graphic joke, not censorship'.[7] In these cases, typography represents metaphor in action.

---

[3] John Earle, *Mikrocosmografia*, 5th edn, enlarged (1629), C7r–v.

[4] On parenthesis as digression, see Jonathan P. Lamb, *Shakespeare in the Marketplace of Words* (Cambridge: Cambridge University Press, 2017), pp. 140–74.

[5] STC 18373, B1v, I3r. The digression itself is similarly aware of print conventions, characterizing itself as a belated Epistle to the Reader (I3r).

[6] Thomas Lodge, *The Wounds of Civil War*, ed. Joseph W. Houppert (Regent's Renaissance Drama Series; London: Edward Arnold, 1970), 4.2.8n.

[7] John Lennard, *'But I Digress': The Exploitation of Parentheses in English Printed Verse* (Oxford: Oxford University Press, 1991), p. 40.

The early modern stage was rhythmically aware (which is no more than to say that it was an extension of humanist schooling). Dramatic characters regularly comment self-reflexively on metre, rhyme, and on the difference between prose and blank verse. One of the clowns in *Dr Faustus* (1604) queries 'How, in verse?' (B3r) and Jaques' exit in Act 4 scene 1 of *As You Like It* is motivated by the scene's switch to blank verse: 'Nay, God buy you, and you talke in blanke verse' (TLN 1946–7). Inept rhymes are often meta-textually explained by the need to complete a couplet, as in Marston's *What You Will* (1607):

> Then for the Low-counties, hay for the *French*
> And so (to make up rime) god night sweete wench. (B2v)

In *The Wounds of Civil War* the Clown's rhyming trimeters first prove infectious (the third soldier adopts the form to ask his important political question about Antony's whereabouts) and then irritating when, denied a straight answer, another soldier is forced to rephrase the question in blunt prose: 'I pre thee, leave these rymes, and tell us where thy master is' (G3v). This aural awareness includes rhetorical pointing. Ambler's parenthetical qualifications and subclauses in *The Devil is an Ass* are obviously acoustically graspable, given Merecraft's response:

> Sir you'll laugh at me!
> But (so is *Truth*) a very friend of mine,
> Finding by conference with me, that I liv'd
> Too chast for my complexion, (and indeed
> Too honest for my place, Sir) did advise me,
> If I did love myself (as that I do,
> I must confesse) MER: Spare your *Parenthesis*.[8]

Of course, metaphors from punctuation and typography are simply a subdivision of larger book-related metaphors, and writers in the nascent world of professional publication were alert to printing-house imagery and the conversion of orality to print.[9] Halfpenny, a servant in Lyly's *Mother Bombie* (1594), is

---

[8] Ben Jonson, *The Devil is an Ass*, in *Bartholomew Fair, The Devil is an Ass, and The Staple of News* (1631), X2v. I present the speech prefix and its location as in this edition.

[9] Thomas Nashe is the most celebrated example. *The Unfortunate Traveller* is the history of a page (in both senses); *Pierce Pennilesse* is structured round printing metaphors, and its marginal notes blur the boundary between text and commentary. See Rachel Stenner, *The Typographic Imaginary* (London: Routledge, 2019); Jane Griffiths, *Diverting Authorities: Experimental Glossing Practices in Manuscript and Print* (Oxford: Oxford University Press, 2015); and Neil Rhodes, 'Nashe, Rhetoric and Satire', in *Jacobean Poetry and Prose: Rhetoric, Representation and the Popular Imagination*, ed. Clive Bloom (Basingstoke: Macmillan, 1988), pp. 25–43.

described as being 'bound up in *decimosexto* [physically small]' yet is 'a wit in *folio*' (C1v). The same bibliographical image is used in the induction to *The Malcontent* to compare the statures of boy actors with those in adult companies: 'why not Malevole [*The Malcontent*] in folio with us, as Jeronimo [*The Spanish Tragedy* or *The First Part of Don Horatio*] in Decimo sexto with them'.[10] Early in *The Wonderful Year* (1603), Dekker summarizes the effects of the plague in just four sentences. 'This is the Abstract', he says, yet, 'like *Stowes* Chronicle in *Decimo sexto* to huge *Hollinshead*', he will enlarge the narrative (C1r). In Henry Porter's *Two Angry Women of Abingdon* (1599), the proverb-quoting servant Nicholas is accused of being 'a whoreson proverb booke bound up in folio' (D1v) where the insult turns on the discrepancy between content (low) and form (high). The same joke about incongruity occurs in *Love's Labour's Lost* when the lovesick Don Armado declares that he will write volumes of sonnets 'in folio' (TLN 487): folio format, reserved for serious works, is an inappropriate publishing format for personal sonnets. In *A Farewell to Folly* (1591) Greene uses the metaphor of print to mean smartly dressed (H4r) and in Dekker's *2 Honest Whore* (c.1605, Q1630) Hippolito uses an analogy with bad printing to comment on Infelice's emotional illegibility: 'Your cheekes of late are (like bad printed Bookes) / So dimly charactred [printed], I scarce can spell [decipher] / One line of love in them' (E2r–v). In prose texts and play dialogue, 'new edition' or 'second edition' or 'edition with new revisions' are regular ways of saying 'up to date'.

Punctuation and typography have a rich metaphoric life in all eras. In the early modern period Johannes Eck responded to Martin Luther's *Ninety-Five Theses* with a refutation titled *Obelisci*. (We remember that the obelisk was invented to identify spurious passages in Homeric texts.) The critical metaphor was not lost on Luther who countered with *Asterisci* (as we saw in Chapter 3, the asterisk's function was to call attention to genuine Homeric material).[11] In the nineteenth century, Fred Vesey performs 'parenthetically' on the piano 'with one hand' in George Eliot's *Middlemarch*.[12] Modern speech, too, is full of metaphors from punctuation and writing. We 'put something in brackets' or 'bracket crucial issues'; we 'underline' a point; we 'join the dots' or 'draw a line between two items'; we offer 'a footnote' or 'a P.S.' or 'a sidebar'. We place something 'in inverted commas' and we pronounce the slash

---

[10] John Marston and John Webster, *The Malcontent* (1604, STC 17481), A4r.

[11] On Luther and Eck, see Keith Houston, *Shady Characters* (London: Penguin, 2013), pp. 105–6.

[12] George Eliot, *Middlemarch* (New York: Signet Classics/New American Library, 1964), Part 2, ch. 16, p. 158.

symbol to indicate borderlines and overlaps: 'that is optimistic-slash-unrealistic'. We put a 'question-mark' over something, we caution with 'small print', and we 'asterisk' things by qualifying a point with restrictions or conditions.[13] Computer and IT terminology have now joined textual terms. We talk about intellectual 'bandwidth'; we use 'control F' as a verb to mean 'search' or we say 'hashtag' as a compliment (#GreenFingers; #DivineCook). The textual and typographical material I look at in this book is not confined to the printed page.

Print and Punctuation

If early modern writers were experimenting with writing and printing as metaphors, early modern compositors were experimenting with type-as-punctuation. We saw in Chapter 2, for instance, how a compositor in Coke's *Institutes* (1628) used parenthesis where we would use inverted commas to indicate a citation:

> &c. And here (&c.) implieth Distresse, Escheat, and the like   (Bb1r, p. 97)
> *Que il doit faire*, &c. Here by (&c.) is understood Temporall or Spirituall Service   (Bb1r, p. 97)

The compositor in *Arden of Faversham* (1592) did the same over thirty-six years earlier. The conspirators discuss the need for a code word to cue the murder of Arden:

> Black will: What shall the watch word be?
> Mosby: (Now I take you) that shall be the word   (H3r)

Parentheses are used in this way in the anonymous *Wily Beguiled* (1606) when William describes 'an honest Dutch Cobbler, that wil sing *(*I wil noe meare to *Burgaine* goe*)* the best that ever you heard' (G2v). When the play was reprinted in 1623, the song title was emphasized by adding italics: 'an honest Dutch Cobler, that will sing (*I will no moare to Burgine goe*) the best that ever you did heare' (G2v). In *The Blind Beggar of Bednal Green* (written by John Day and Henry Chettle in 1600 although not published until 1659) Canbee protests when Hadland addresses him familiarly by his Christian name: 'How you base

---

[13] 'To asterisk' is a recent verb. Keith Houston traces it to a record-breaking baseball player who was subsequently found to have taken banned steroids and judged guilty in 2011. His record of achievement was asterisked with a footnote recording the circumstances under which the record was achieved. Houston, *Shady Characters*, pp. 114–19.

Rogue, nere an (*M.*) under your Gidle, have I preferr'd thee to my good Lord Cardinal here, and am I no better than your homesome *Franck*' (C2r). The word 'Master' ('*M*') that Hadland has omitted to say is quoted to him and is signalled to the reader by parenthesis. Greene's *Groatsworth of Wit* (1592) is a black-letter text but it prints its (adapted) quotation from Shakespeare ('Tygers hart wrapt in a Players hyde') in roman to indicate the phrase's status as a quotation (F1v). Compositors are looking at what is available in their type cases and considering how to use it to indicate quotations.

Throughout this book I have been thinking about readers' responses to typography; now, 'at the latest minute of the hour', I want to dwell briefly on the creators of that typography (and compositor creativity), in a period when systems and conventions were just coming into being and hence offered scope for flexibility and experimentation. The place where we see this most is in play layout. In Chapter 3 I looked at stage directions in *The Malcontent* as part of a carefully thought-through system about how to present plays to readers in a way that enables them to visualize the dramatic experience; but choreographing action via stage directions is only one such way. In conclusion, I want to consider some elements of dramatic experience that printers try to translate into print.

The Rhetoric of the Stage Page

The anonymous *Look About You* (1600) consistently represents Redcap's stammer:

> By my Ch Ch Christendome I ha have not b b been h heere this three nights, a p p p plage of him, that made me such a ch chaunting, and s sent me such a Ja Ja Jaunt, blud I was st stayd for Skinke, that il fa fa fac'd rogue.   (D2r)

This is authorial rather than compositorial (the compositor is presumably following what he found in his manuscript copy) but it is a logical next step to move from one kind of speech representation to another. In Middleton and Dekker's *The Roaring Girl* (1611), black-letter type is used in a roman text to indicate the Dutch accent and language of a character in disguise (see Figure E.1). (Although Tear Cat's lines are part of the dialogue, they are not presented as continuous with the rest of the dialogue but are framed by white space, a point to which I shall return later in this section when discussing changes in textual status.) This indication of sound is not an isolated occurrence of attention to the reader's auditory experience in this quarto. Enunciation (or rather, laboured pronunciation) is represented by separating syllables with hyphens—'Pan-da-rus' and 'Cres-sida' (F2v)—as Mistress Gallipot, reading a letter aloud, stumbles

> *Mol.* Me‡re rogues, put fpur‡s to 'em once more.
> *Iack Dap.* Thou look'ft like a ftrange creature, a fat butter-
> box, yet fpeak'ft Englifh,
> What art thou?
>
> *T.Cat.* Ick mine Here. Ick bin den ruffling Teare-Cat,
> Den braue Soldade, Ick bin dorick all Dutchlant.
> Guerefen: Der Shellum das meere Ine Beafa
> Ine woert gaeb.
> Ick flaag bm ftroakes ou tom Cop.
> Daffick Den hundzed tonzun Diuell balle,
> Frollick miue Here.
>
> *Sir Bewt.* Here, here, let's be rid of their iobbering,
> *Moll.* Not a croffd *Sir Bewtious*; you bafe rogues, I haue
> taken meafure of you, better then a taylor can; and I'le fit you,
> as you (monfter with one eie) haue fitted me‡,
> *Trap.* Your Worfhip will not abufe a foldier.

FIGURE E.1 Thomas Middleton and Thomas Dekker, *The Roaring Girl* (1611, STC 17908), K3r. Shelfmark STC 17908. Used by permission of the Folger Shakespeare Library.

over classical names (although she has no trouble with 'Demophon' in the previous line). Stage business or pausing is indicated by long dashes when, at the feather shop, Jack Dapper requests:

'Shew me —— a —— spangled fether.' (D1r)

Throughout the play, the directions are alert to stage movement, choreographing the timing of the traffic across the stage as the characters visit the various shops and stalls in scene 3, for instance. The acoustic attention is part of the quarto's concern to represent dramatic experience, visual and aural. Some of this concern is a feature of authorial imagination (the probable copy for Q is authorial papers) but the black-letter speech is a printing-house decision.

The Roaring Girl's representation of Tear Cat's localized language and accent is extended to an entire part throughout the anonymous *Alphonsus, Emperor of Germany* (published in 1654, although composed five or six decades earlier).[14]

---

[14] I am grateful to Elisabeth Dutton for bringing this text to my attention.

Here the Saxon Princess speaks no English and her foreign language and accent are signalled typographically by black letter (see Figure E.2). The black-letter treatment is also given to Hans and Jerick, the two German farmers.

Compositors often use parallel columns to signal simultaneity of speech and action or question-and-response. Ben Jonson's works (rightly) receive a lot of attention in this respect, although the focus tends to be on Jonson's authorial concern for control of presentation rather than his printers' creative innovation. Crispinus' formulaic repetition (in the role of Mercury) of Gallus' formal licensing (in the role of Phoebus) of their playing is printed in a narrow right-hand column with abbreviated repetitions: 'The great, &c. / Of his, &c. /

And now to thee lewd Whore, diſhonour'd ſtrumpet,
Thy turn is next, therefore prepare to dye.
  Edward. O mighty Duke of *Saxon*, ſpare thy Child.
  Sax. She is thy Wife *Edward*, and thou ſhouldſt ſpare her.
One Gracious word of thine will ſave her life.
  Edward. I do confeſs *Saxon* ſhe is mine own,
As I have marryed her, I will live with her,
Comfort thy ſelf ſweet *Hedewick* and ſweet Wiſe.
  Hede. **Ach, ach vnd wehe, warumb ſagt your Excellence nicht ſo before, now iſt to late, vnſer arme kindt iſt kilt.**
  Edward. Though thou be mine, and I do pittie thee,
I would not Nurſe a Baſtard for a Son.
  Hede. **O Edouard now ich mark your mening ich ſholdt be your whore, mein Watter ich begehr upon meine knee, laſt mich lieber ſterben, ade falce Edouart, falce Prince, ich begehrs nicht.**
  Saxon. Unprincely thoughts do hammer in thy head,
I'ſt not enough that thou haſt ſham'd her once,
And ſeen the Baſtard torn before thy face;
But thou wouldſt get more brats for Butcherie?
No *Hedewick* thou ſhalt not live the day.
  Hede. **O Herr Gott, nimb meine ſeele in deiner henden.**
  Saxon. It is thy hand that gives this deadly ſtroak.
  Hede. **O Herr Sabote, das mein vnſchuldt an tag kommen mocht.**

FIGURE E.2 Anon, *Alphonsus, Emperor of Germany* (1654, Wing C1952), G4v. Shelfmark C1952. Used by permission of the Folger Shakespeare Library.

Willing &c.'.[15] Comments from 'Within' in Q *The Alchemist* (1612) are presented within double-height curly brackets (C4v), and simultaneous speech is presented across eight lines in two columns with a centralized dividing line-cum-bracket (K2r). In the Folio version of the play the dividing line has developed into elaborate curly brackets in the centre of the columns.[16]

But before Jonson, Elizabethan compositors were also alert to such issues. The compositor has used layout to create the effect of Echo in Thomas Lodge's *The Wounds of Civil War* (1594), with italicized echoes in the right-hand margin (E3v) (see Figure E.3). In Henry Porter's *Two Angry Women of Abingdon* (1599), two portions of dialogue are laid out in parallel columns for a scene of confusion during darkness—an attempt to indicate simultaneous speech or parallel groups or physical distance (K1v) (see Figure E.4).[17] In *Jack Drum's Entertainment* (1601), the joyful reunion of Katherine and Pasquill is expressed in two rhyming couplets, the first spoken by Katherine, the second attached to Pasquill's speech prefix. '*Both speake*' is sandwiched between the two lines of Pasquill's

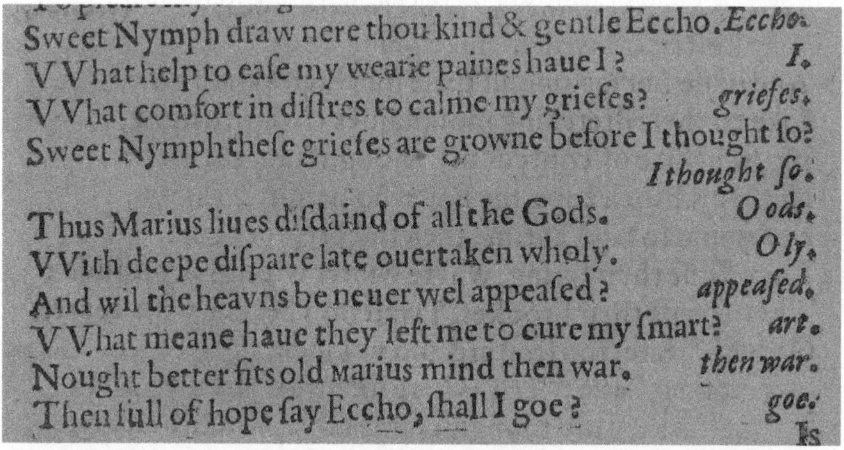
Sweet Nymph draw nere thou kind & gentle Eccho. *Eccho.*
VVhat help to eaſe my wearie paines haue I? *I.*
VVhat comfort in diſtres to calme my griefes? *griefes.*
Sweet Nymph theſe griefes are growne before I thought ſo?
I thought ſo.
Thus Marius liues diſdaind of all the Gods. *O ods.*
VVith deepe diſpaire late ouertaken wholy. *O ly.*
And wil the heavns be neuer wel appeaſed? *appeaſed.*
VVhat meane haue they left me to cure my ſmart? *art.*
Nought better fits old Marius mind then war. *then war.*
Then full of hope ſay Eccho, ſhall I goe? *goe.*
Is

FIGURE E.3 Thomas Lodge, *The Wounds of Civil War* (1594, STC 16678), E3v. Shelfmark STC 16678. Used by permission of the Folger Shakespeare Library.

15 *Poetaster*, in Jonson, *Works* (1616), Dd4r.

16 Jonson, *Works* (1616), Iii6r. For an excellent discussion of these effects, see Holger Schott Syme, 'Unediting the Margin: Jonson, Marston, and the Theatrical Page', *English Literary Renaissance* 38:1 (2008), 158–63.

17 There are two editions of 1599: one printed by Edward Allde for Joseph Hunt and William Ferbrand (STC 20121.5) and one printed by Allde for Ferbrand (STC 20122). They vary in use of italics and roman type, in spelling, and in layout of preliminaries, which affects pagination; the page layout of this nocturnal sequence is identical.

> *Raph.* So ho,   *M.Gour.* So ho.
> *Raph.* Whose there?   M.*Bar.*Heers on or two,
> *Raph.* Is Will there?   *M.Bar.* No, Phillip?
> M.*Gour.* Franke?   *Raph.* No, no.
> Was euer man deluded thus like me,
> I thinke some spirit leads me thus amisse:
> As I haue ofté heard, that some haue bin thus in the nights,
> But yet this mases me where ere I come,
> Some askes me still for Franke or Phillip,
> And none of them can tell me where Will is.
> *Wil.* So ho?   *Phil.* So ho.   *They hollo*
> *Hodg.* So ho?   *Boy.* So ho?   *within.*
> *Rap.* Sownes now I heere foure hollow at the least,

FIGURE E.4 Henry Porter, *The Two Angry Women of Abingdon* (1599, STC 20121.5), K1r. Shelfmark 62929. Courtesy of the Huntington Library, San Marino.

couplet (I1r): it looks as if Katherine speaks her two lines, Pasquill one, then both speak the final rhyme:

> *Kathe.* Once more let me be valued worth his love,
> In decking of whose soule, the graces strove.
> *Pas.* Spight hath outspent itselfe, and thus at last,
> *Both speake.*
> We clip with joyful arme each others wast.   (I1r)

Anthony Munday's *Fedele and Fortunio* (1585) indents rhyming couplets, even in the middle of speeches, when Victoria and Fedele speak in the verse form (*ababcc*) that structured the previous song (B3v–B4r). The reader's attention is being directed to an aural experience. In Marlowe's *The Jew of Malta* (*c.*1589–90, Q1633) Barabas' asides are given in italics (D1r, D4v, E4r).

Font type and font size are often changed by printers to indicate different textual status within a play—letters or proclamations, for instance. 'The Kings Pardon delivered by *Sir John Morton to the Rebels*' in the anonymous play, *Jack Straw* (1594) is printed under that heading, in black letter in a roman text, and is set off with white space and an indented woodcut (F1r). The play itself is very short and of poor stylistic quality; notwithstanding, the printer has taken care with it. The letter in Lodge's *The Wounds of Civil War* is similarly set off with white space, and printed in italics against the text's roman (D1r). These two examples may explain the white space round Tear Cat's speech in *The*

Roaring Girl: changes of textual status were signalled by a change of font accompanied by white space; the compositor saw a foreign-language speech as a change of textual status. When Lust enters 'like a gallaunt, singing this songe' in the anonymous *Trial of Treasure* (1567), his four lines of lyrics are given in larger font before he reverts to dialogue in regular type size, commenting on his musical entrance: 'What the Devill ailed me to singe thus, / I crie you mercy by my faith for entring, / Most like I have ridden on the fliyng Pegasus' (A3r). Whereas song extracts and titles were later italicized or enclosed within parentheses (as we saw in Chapter 2), the compositor here enlarges the type size. He is aware that these lines are part of the play but different in kind and he uses the rhetoric of the page to signal this (see Figure E.5). Just as writing and type make their way into orality as metaphor, orality makes its way into type: writers and compositors are thinking creatively about how to turn the visual and aural experience of drama into print.

Discussing plays published by Thomas Thorpe, Holger Schott Syme remarks that they 'look exactly as one would expect an early seventeenth-century play to look'.[18] This comes in the context of Thorpe's encouragement of innovation and eccentricity in his authors so it is a reasonable statement. But there was not really any expected 'look' for an Elizabethan or Jacobean play. Mid-century Tudor drama looks different from late-century translations of classical drama, and plays from the commercial stage look different again. As late as 1603 *Patient Grissil* was printed in black letter when the industry standard for plays had become roman. Stage directions were

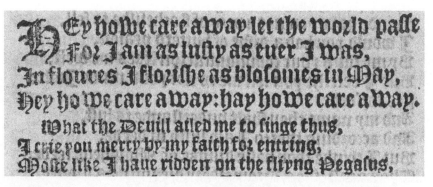

FIGURE E.5 Anon, *The Trial of Treasure* (1567, STC 24271), Aiiir. Shelfmark 69673. Courtesy of the Huntington Library, San Marino.

[18] Syme, 'Unediting', 157.

developing conventions; so too were speech prefixes and title pages.[19] There was some limited overlap between manuscript and print conventions but a complete lack of overlap between conventions for printing translations of classical drama and those for commercial drama. The rhetoric of the dramatic page was in development.

My topic in this book has been the experimental and creative uses of the page. I confined my enquiry to three specific areas (physical blanks, the &c-etcetera, and the asterisk) across a range of texts, genres, and periods. However, this enquiry is but a subset of a larger story about the journey from manuscript to print (as we saw briefly when we looked at physical blanks and at '&c') and it has its own subset story in the journey from stage to page. Levenston claims that 'only with the invention of printing did the actual appearance of the text on the written page begin to make any real contribution to the meaning of the work'.[20] This is perhaps an overstatement but it is true that we cannot ignore the relation between textual appearance and meaning—not just in the early modern world but in today's academic world where our representational (i.e. editorial) media are changing. Balachandra Rajan's investigation of the 'unfinished' aimed to 'eradicate ingrained reading habits' and Margaret Jane Kidnie makes a similar statement for the world of editing: 'as our assumptions about "completeness" change, so will the editions we prepare'.[21] Referentiality and fictionality are interrelated. Both Rajan and Kidnie aim to increase our understanding of the relation between the construction of meaning and the construction of the page. The blank, in its infinite variety, is a crucial part of this symbiosis.

[19] On stage directions see Linda McJannet, *The Voice of Elizabethan Stage Directions: The Evolution of a Theatrical Code* (Newark: University of Delaware Press, 1999) and Gillian M. Woods and Sarah Dustagheer (eds), *Stage Directions and Shakespearean Theatre* (London: Bloomsbury, 2018); on speech prefixes see Claire M. L. Bourne, 'Dramatic Pilcrows', *Papers of the Bibliographical Society of America* 108:4 (2014), 413–52; on title pages, see Tamara Atkin, *Reading Drama in Tudor England* (London: Routledge, 2018); on classical drama see Laurie Maguire, 'Classical and Commercial Drama in Print in Sixteenth-Century England', plenary conference talk at 'Academic Drama and the Popular Stage', University of St Andrews, June 2020.

[20] Edward A. Levenston, *The Stuff of Literature: Physical Aspects of Texts and their Relation to Literary Meaning* (Albany: State University of New York Press, 1992), p. 91.

[21] Balachandra Rajan, *The Form of the Unfinished: English Poetics from Spenser to Pound* (Princeton, NJ: Princeton University Press, 1985), p. 5; Margaret Jane Kidnie, 'The Staging of Shakespeare's Drama in Print Editions', in *Textual Performances*, ed. Lukas Erne and Margaret Jane Kidnie (Cambridge: Cambridge University Press, 2004), p. 161.

✣ finis.

Works Cited

Abbot, Robert, *True Ancient Roman Catholic* (1611, STC 54).

Addison, Joseph, 'Dum Tacent, Clamant', Tatler 133 (11–14 February 1710), 92–6.

Albee, Edward, Counting the Ways and Listening: Two Plays by Edward Albee (New York: Atheneum, 1977).

Ames, William, *A Fresh Suit against Human Ceremonies in God's Worship* (1633, STC 555).

André, Bernard, *The Life of Henry VII*, British Library MS Cotton Domitian A XVIII.

André, Bernard, The Life of Henry VII, trans. and intro. Daniel Hobbins (New York: Italica Press, 2011).

Anon, *2 Return from Parnassus; or the Scourge of Simony* (1606, STC 19309).

Anon, *2 Return from Parnassus; or the Scourge of Simony*, Folger Shakespeare Library MS V.a. 355.

Anon, 'An Account of the Rev. Mr. ST ****, and his Writings', *Grand Magazine* 3 (June 1760), 308–11.

Anon, *Alphonsus, Emperor of Germany* (1654, Wing C1952).

Anon, *Arden of Faversham* (1592, STC 733).

Anon, *A Brief Description of the Notorious Life of John Lamb* (1628, STC 15177).

Anon, *A Collection of the Contents of all the Chapters Contained in the Bible* (1605, STC 3020.5).

Anon, *The Contention between Liberality and Prodigality* (1602, STC 5593).

Anon, *A Continuation of More News from the Palatinate* (1622, STC 18507.51A).

Anon, *Every Woman in her Humour* (1609, STC 25948).

Anon, *Everyman and Mankind*, ed. Douglas Bruster and Eric Rasmussen (Arden; London: Methuen/A. & C. Black, 2009).

Anon, 'Fable of the Cat Turned into a Woman', in *Miscellaneous Poems*, ed. Matthew Concanen (London, 1724, ESTC T125249), pp. 366–8.

Anon, *A Funeral Elegy in Memory of Master William Peter* (1612, STC 21526).

Anon, *Interlude of Youth* (1557, STC 14111a).

Anon, *Jack Drum's Entertainment* (1601, STC 7243).

Anon, *Jack Straw* (1594, STC 23356).

Anon, *Johan the Evangelist* (c.1550, STC 14643).

Anon, *A Knack to Know a Knave* (1594, STC 15027).

Anon, *Locrine* (1595, STC 21528).

Anon, *Look About You* (1600, STC 16799).

Anon, *N-Town Plays*, British Library MS Cotton Vespasian D VIII.

Anon, *Nobody and Somebody* (1606, STC 18597).

Anon, *Pearl*, ed. E. V. Gordon (Oxford: Clarendon Press, 1974).

Anon, *Pearl*, ed. Sarah Stanbury (Kalamazoo, MI: Medieval Institute Publications, Western Michigan University, 2001).

Anon, *Pearl*, ed. William Vantuono (1995; Notre Dame, IN: University of Notre Dame Press, 2007).

Anon, *Pearl*, trans. Victor Watts (London: Enitharmon Press, 2005).

Anon, *Pearl: A New Verse Translation*, trans. Simon Armitage (London: Faber and Faber, 2016).

Anon, *Pearl: A New Verse Translation*, trans. Simon Armitage (New York: Liveright/W. W. Norton, 2016).

Anon, *Penniless Parliament of Threadbare Poets* (1608, STC 19307).

Anon, *Poems on Affairs of State: From the Reign of K. James the First, to this Present Year 1703*, vol. II (London, 1703, Wing T125689).

Anon, *The Puritan, or the Widow of Watling Street* (1607, STC 21531).

Anon, 'Review', *The Retrospective Review* 2 (1828), 1–22.

Anon, *Thomas, Lord Cromwell* (1602, STC 21532).

Anon, *The Three Parnassus Plays*, ed. J. B. Leishman (London: Nicholson & Watson, 1949).

Anon, *The Trial of Treasure* (1567, STC 24271).

Anon, *The Trial of Treasure, 1567*, ed. J. S. Farmer (Tudor Facsimile Texts; London: T. C. & E. C. Jack, 1908).

Anon, *Westward for Smelts* (1620, STC 25292).

Anon, *Wily Beguiled* (1606, STC 25818).

Anon, *Wily Beguiled* (1623, STC 25820).

Anon, *The Wit of a Woman* (1604, STC 25868).

Anon [England and Wales. Privy Council], *A Very Rich Lotterie Generall, without any Blanckes* (1567, STC 8000.3).

Anthony of Guevara, *The Dial of Princes*, trans. Sir Thomas North (1557, STC 12427).

Ariosto, Ludovico, *Seven Planets* (1611, STC 745).

Armitage, Simon, 'Mind the Gap: Omission, Negation and "a final revelation of horrible Nothingness—"', lecture delivered at Oxford University, 8 April 2016. Available at: <http://podcasts.ox.ac.uk/series/poetry-simon-armitage>.

Arnold, Matthew, *New Poems* (London: Macmillan, 1867).

Ashton, John, *The History of Gambling in England* (London: Duckworth, 1898).

Atkin, Tamara, *Reading Drama in Tudor England* (London: Routledge, 2018).

Atwood, Margaret, *Hag Seed* (London: Hogarth Press, 2016).

Bacon, Francis, *Essays* (1625, STC 1148).

Bacon, Francis, *New Atlantis* (1628, STC 1170).

Bacon, Francis, *Sylva Sylvarum* (1627, STC 1168).

Bailey, Nathan, *Dictionarium Britannicum* (London, 1730).

Bale, John, *The Pageant of Popes* (1574, STC 1304).

Barnfield, Richard, *Cynthia* (1595, STC 1484).

Barthes, Roland, 'From Work to Text', in *Textual Strategies: Perspectives in Post-Structuralist Criticism*, ed. Josué V. Harari (Ithaca, NY: Cornell University Press, 1979), pp. 73–91.

Beal, Peter, 'Anne, Lady Southwell', in *Catalogue of English Literary Manuscripts, 1450–1700*. Available at: <http://www.celm-ms.org.uk/introductions/SouthwellAnneLady.html>.

Beal, Peter, *Catalogue of English Literary Manuscripts, 1450–1700*, vol I, 1450–1625 (2 parts) (London: Mansell, 1980).

Beal, Peter, *Catalogue of English Literary Manuscripts, 1450–1700*. vol II, 1625–1700 (2 parts) (London: Mansell, 1980).

Beard, Mary, review of Umberto Eco, *The Infinity of Lists*, *The Guardian*, 12 December 2009. Available at: <https://www.theguardian.com/books/2009/dec/12/umberto-eco-lists-book-review>.

Beaumont, Francis, *The Woman Hater* (1607, STC 1693).

Belknap, Robert, *The List* (New Haven, CT: Yale University Press, 2004).

Bell, Terena, 'Th*nks for Asterisks', *The Guardian*, 2 November 2018. Available at: <https://www.theguardian.com/books/booksblog/2018/nov/02/thank-s-for-asterisks-the-maligned-punctuation-enjoying-twitter-revival>.

Benedict, Barbara M., 'Reading Faces: Physiognomy and Epistemology in Late-Eighteenth-Century Sentimental Novels', *Studies in Philology* 92:3 (1995), 311–28.

Bervin, Jen, *Nets* (Berkeley, CA: Ugly Duckling Presse, 2004).

Bidwell, John, 'French Paper in English Books', in *The Cambridge History of the Book in Britain*, vol. IV: *1557–1695*, ed. John Barnard and D. F. McKenzie with Maureen Bell (Cambridge: Cambridge University Press, 2002), pp. 583–601.

Bishop, William, *A Disproof of D. Abbots Counterproofe* (1614, STC 3094).

Blagrave, John, *The Mathematical Jewel* (1585, STC 3119).

Boogaart, Pieter, and Ritaa, *A272: An Ode to a Road*, rev. edn (2000; London: Pallas Athene, 2013).

Borges, Jorge Luis, 'El idioma analítico de John Wilkins' ['John Wilkins' analytical language'], in Jorge Luis Borges, *Otras Inquisiciones* (Buenos Aires: Eméce Editores, 1960), pp. 102–6.

Bortolussi, M., and P. Dixon, 'Transport: Challenges to the Metaphor', in *The Oxford Handbook of Cognitive Literary Studies*, ed. Lisa Zunshine (Oxford: Oxford University Press, 2015), pp. 525–40.

Bourne, Claire M. L., 'Dramatic Pilcrows', *Papers of the Bibliographical Society of America* 108:4 (2014), 413–52.

Boyer, Allen D., 'Sir Edward Coke: Royal Servant, Royal Favourite', Harvard Law School website, pp. 1–24. Available at: <http://www.law.harvard.edu/programs/ames_foundation/BLHC07/Boyer%20Sir%20Edward%20Coke%20-%20Royal%20Servant%20and%20Royal%20Favorite.pdf>.

Braden, Gordon, *The Classics and English Renaissance Poetry: Three Case Studies* (New Haven, CT: Yale University Press, 1978).

Braden, Gordon, *Hero and Leander: A Facsimile of the First Edition, London, 1598*, ed. Louis Martz (Washington, DC: Folger Shakespeare Library, 1972).

Braden, Gordon, 'Hero and Leander in Bed (and the Morning After)', *English Literary Renaissance* 45:2 (2015), 205–30.

Braunschweig, Hieronymus, *A Noble Experience of the Virtuous Handiwork of Surgery* (1525, STC 13434).

Brenan, Justin, *Composition and Punctuation Familiarly Explained for Those Who Have Neglected the Study of Grammar*, 14th edn (London: Virtue Brothers & Co., 1865).

Breton, Nicholas, *Old Man's Lesson and a Young Man's Love* (1605, STC 3674).

Brome, Richard, *The Queen's Exchange* (1657, Wing B4882).

Brotton, Jerry, *A History of the World in Twelve Maps* (London: Allen & Unwin, 2012).

Broughton, Hugh, *A Concent of Scripture* (1590, STC 3851).

Brown, Georgia E., 'Marlowe's Poems and Classicism', in *The Cambridge Companion to Christopher Marlowe*, ed. Patrick Cheney (Cambridge: Cambridge University Press, 2004), pp. 106–26.

Brown, Richard Danson ' "And dearest love": Virgilian Half-Lines in Spenser's *Faerie Queene*', *Proceedings of the Virgil Society* 29 (2018), 49–74.

Bullough, Geoffrey, *Narrative and Dramatic Sources of Shakespeare*, vol. IV (London: Routledge/Kegan Paul, 1962).

Bunting, Basil, *Collected Poems*, 2nd edn (Oxford: Oxford University Press, 1978).

Burrow, Colin, 'The Poems: Textual Essay', in *The Cambridge Edition of the Works of Ben Jonson Online*, ed. David Bevington, Martin Butler, and Ian Donaldson. Available at: <https://universitypublishingonline.org/cambridge/benjonson/k/essays/The_Poems_textual_essay/>.

Burrow, Colin (ed.), 'From Thomas Palmer, *The Sprite of Trees and Herbs*', in *The Cambridge Edition of the Works of Ben Jonson*, ed. David Bevington, Martin Butler, and Ian Donaldson, vol. I (Cambridge: Cambridge University Press, 2012).

Burton, Robert, *Anatomy of Melancholy*, 6th edn (rev. 1652, Wing B6182).

Butler, Charles, *Oratoriae Libri Duo* (1633, STC 4195).

Byron, Lord George Gordon, *Byron*, ed. Jerome J. McGann (Oxford: Oxford University Press, 1986).

Calfhill, James, *An Answer to the Treatise of the Cross* (1565, STC 4368).

Carlson, David R., 'André, Bernard (*c.*1450–1522)', in *Oxford Dictionary of National Biography*. Available at: <http://www.oxforddnb.com/view/article/513>.

Carlson, David R., 'King Arthur and Court Poems for the Birth of Arthur Tudor in 1486', *Humanistica Lovaniensia* 36 (1987), 147–83.

Carpenter, Andrew, and James Woolley, 'Faulkner's Volume II. Containing the Author's Poetical Works: A New Uncancelled Copy', in *Münster 2019: Reading Swift: Papers from the Seventh Münster Symposium 2017*, ed. Hermann J. Real (Munich: Verlag Wilhem Fink, 2019), pp. 47–58.

Carrión, Ulises, 'The New Art of Making Books', in *Artists' Books: A Critical Anthology and Sourcebook*, ed. Joan Lyons (Rochester, NY: Visual Studies Workshop Press/Peregrine Smith Books, 1985), pp. 16–27.

Chalmers Watts, Ann, 'Pearl, Inexpressibility, and Poems of Human Loss', *Publications of the Modern Language Association* 99:1 (1984), 26–40.

Chambers, E. K., *The Elizabethan Stage*, vol. II (Oxford: Clarendon Press, 1923).

Chambers, E. K., *William Shakespeare: A Study of Facts and Problems*, vol. I (Oxford: Clarendon Press, 1930).

Chapman, George, *All Fools* (1605, STC 4963).

Chapman, George, *A Free and Offenceless Justification of . . . Andromeda Liberata* (1614, STC 4977).

Chapman, George, *The Gentleman Usher* (1606, STC 4978).

Chapman, George, *May Day* (1611, STC 4980).

Chapman, George, *The Memorable Masque* (1613, STC 4981).

Chapman, George, *Ovid's Banquet of Sense* (1595, STC 4985).

Chapman, George, *The Widow's Tears* (1612, STC 4994).

Chaucer, Geoffrey, *The Canterbury Tales*, Hengwrt 154 (Peniarth 392D), National Library of Wales, Aberystwyth.

Chaucer, Geoffrey, *The Riverside Chaucer*, ed. Larry Benson (Boston, MA: Houghton Mifflin Co., 1987).

Chesters, Timothy, 'Social Cognition: A Literary Perspective', *Paragraph* 37 (2014), 62–78.

Chettle, Henry, *Hoffman* (1631, STC 5125).

Chettle, Henry, *The Tragedy of Hoffman*, in *Five Revenge Tragedies*, ed. Emma Smith (Harmondsworth: Penguin, 2012).

Church of England, *Constitutions and Canons Ecclesiastical* (1640, STC 10080).

Churchyard, Thomas, *Musical Consort of Heavenly Harmonie* (1595, STC 5245).

Cicero, *De Inventione, De Optimo Genere Oratorum, Topica*, trans. H. M. Hubbell (Cambridge, MA: Harvard University Press, 1993).

Clarke, Danielle, 'Marlowe's Poetic Form', in *Christopher Marlowe in Context*, ed. Emily C. Bartels and Emma Smith (Cambridge: Cambridge University Press, 2013), pp. 57–67.

Clegg, Cyndia Susan, *Shakespeare's Reading Audiences: Early Modern Books and Audience Interpretation* (Cambridge: Cambridge University Press, 2017).

Coate, Edmund, *The English Schoolmaster* (1630, STC 5714).

Cockerham, Henry, *The English Dictionary* (1623, STC 5461.2).

Coke, Edward, *The First Part of the Institutes of the Laws of England* (1628, STC 15784).

Coke, Edward, *The First Part of the Institutes of the Laws of England* (1629, STC 15785).

Coldiron, A. E. B., *Printers without Borders* (Cambridge: Cambridge University Press, 2015).

Colet, John, *The Ecclesiastical History of Dionysius*, ed. Daniel J. Nodes, *Studies in Medieval and Reformation Traditions*, 171 : 4: Texts and Sources (Leiden: Brill, 2013).

Collings, Matthew, 'Out on a Whim', *Evening Standard*, 29 November 2016, pp. 42–3.

Comenius, Johann, *Orbis Pictus* (London, 1672, Wing C5524).

Coogan, Robert, 'Petrarch's *Liber sine nomine* and a Vision of Rome in the Reformation', *Renaissance and Reformation* 19 : 1 (1983), 1–12.

Cooke, John, *Greene's Tu Quoque* (1614, STC 5673).

Cooper, Thomas, *Certain Sermons* (1580, STC 5685).

Cotgrave, John, *Treasury of Wit and Language* (1655, Wing C6368).

Cotgrave, Randall, *Dictionarie* (1611, STC 5830).

Cowley, Abraham, *A Poem on the Late Civil War* (1679, Wing C6679).

Creaser, John, 'The 1631 Folio (F2 (2)): Textual Essay', in *The Cambridge Edition of the Works of Ben Jonson Online*. Available at: <http://universitypublishingonline.org/cambridge/benjonson/k/essays/F2-2_textual_essay/2/>.

Crooke, Helkiah, *Mikrokosmographia* (1615, STC 6062).

Crooke, Helkiah, *Mikrokosmographia* (1631, STC 6063).

cummings, e. e., *Complete Poems, 1904–1962*, ed. George J. Firmage (New York: W. W Norton & Co., 1994).

Daniel, Samuel, *Collection of the History of England* (1618, STC 6248)

Daniel, Samuel, *Collection of the History of England* (1634, STC 6252).

Davies, John (of Hereford), *A Continued Inquisition against Paper-Persecutors* (1625, STC 6340).

Davies, John (of Hereford), *The Holy Rood* (1609, STC 6330).

Davies, John (of Hereford), *A Scourge for Paper-Persecutors* (1625, STC 6340).

Davies, John (of Hereford), *A Select Second Husband for Sir Thomas Overbury's Wife* (1616, STC 6342).

Davies, John, Sir, 'Orchestra', in *Nosce Teipsum* (1622, STC 6359).

Davison, Francis, *Poems, or A Poetical Rapsodie* (1621, STC 6376).

Day, John, *The Blind Beggar of Bednal Green* (1659, Wing D464).

Day, John, *The Isle of Gulls* (1606, STC 6412).

Day, John, *The Isle of Gulls* (1606, STC 6413).

Day, John, *The Isle of Gulls* (1633, STC 6414).

Day, John, *Law Tricks* (1608, STC 6416).

Day, John, and Henry Chettle, *The Blind Beggar of Bednal Green* (1659, Wing D464).

Dee, John, *General and Rare Memorials . . . to the Art of Navigation* (1577, STC 6459).

Dekker, Thomas, *2 The Honest Whore* (1630, STC 6506).

Dekker, Thomas, *The Owl's Almanac* (1618, STC 6515).

Dekker, Thomas, *Patient Grissill* (1603, STC 6518).

Dekker, Thomas, *Satiromastix* (1602, STC 6520.7).

Dekker, Thomas, *The Shoemaker's Holiday* (1600, STC 6523).

Dekker, Thomas, *The Shoemaker's Holiday*, ed. Robert Smallwood and Stanley Wells (Revels; Manchester: Manchester University Press, 1999).

Dekker, Thomas, *The Wonderful Year* (1603, STC 6535).

Dekker, Thomas, and John Webster, *Northward Ho!* (1607, STC 6539).

Dekker, Thomas, and John Webster, *Sir Thomas Wyatt* (1607, STC 6537).

Dekker, Thomas, and John Webster, *Westward Ho!* (1607, STC 6540).

Derrida, Jacques, *Of Grammatology* (Baltimore, MD: Johns Hopkins University Press, 2016).

Derrida, Jacques, *Spectres of Marx* (London: Routledge, 1993).

Derrida, Jacques, *Writing and Difference* (Chicago: University of Chicago Press, 1978).

Dickens, Charles, *Nicholas Nickleby*, ed. Michael Slater (Harmondsworth: Pryenguin, 1978).

Dickens, Charles, *Oliver Twist*, ed. Peter Fairclough (Harmondsworth: Penguin, 1986).

Dobranski, Stephen, *Readers and Authorship in Early Modern England* (Cambridge: Cambridge University Press, 2005).

Donaghy, Michael, *Errata* (Oxford: Oxford University Press, 1993).

Donaldson, Ian, *Ben Jonson: A Life* (Oxford: Oxford University Press, 2011).

Donne, John, *Complete Poetry and Selected Prose of John Donne*, ed. Charles M. Coffin (New York: Random House, 2001).

Donne, John, *Devotions upon Emergent Occasions* (1634, STC 7036).

Donne, John, *Poems* (1633, STC 7045).

Donne, John, *Poetical Works*, ed. Herbert Grierson (London: Oxford University Press, 1973).

Donne, John, *The Sermons of John Donne*, ed. George R. Potter and Evelyn M. Simpson (Los Angeles: University of California Press, 1957).

Drayton, Michael, *The Barons' Wars* (1603, STC 7189).

Drayton, Michael, *A Chorographicall Description [Poly-Olbion] and The Second Part . . . of Poly-Olbion* (1622, STC 7228 and 7229).

Drayton, Michael, *England's Heroical Epistles* (1602, STC 7197).

Drayton, Michael, *The Legend of Great Cromwell* (1607, STC 7204).

Drayton, Michael, *The Muse's Elizium* (1630, STC 7210).

Drayton, Michael, *Poems* (1619, STC 7223).

Drayton, Michael, *The Shepherd's Garland* (1593, STC 7202).

Drucker, Johannes, *Graphesis* (Cambridge, MA: Harvard University Press, 2014).

Drury, John, *Music at Midnight: The Life and Poetry of George Herbert* (London: Allen Lane, 2013).

Duncan, Dennis, and Adam Smyth (eds), *Book Parts* (Oxford: Oxford University Press, 2019).

Dunne, Derek, 'Rogues' Licence: Counterfeiting Authority in Early Modern England', *Shakespeare Studies* 45 (2017), 137–43.

Earle, John, *Mikrocosmografia*, enlarged 5th edn (1629, STC 7442).

Eco, Umberto, *The Infinity of Lists* (London: MacLehose Press, 2009).

Eco, Umberto, *The Open Work* (Cambridge: Cambridge University Press, 1981).

Edwards, Geraint, 'Erased Erased de Kooning Drawing'. Available at: <http://geraintedwards.com/?page_id=638>.

Eliot, George, *Middlemarch* (New York: Signet Classics/New American Library, 1964).

Eliot, John, *Ortho-Epia Gallica* (1593, STC 7574).

Elyot, Thomas/Thomas Cooper, *Bibliotheca Eliotae* (1559, STC 7663).

Erasmus, Desiderius, *The Correspondence of Erasmus: Letters 298–445*, trans. and ed. R. A. B. Mynors and D. F. S. Thomson, annotated by James K. McConica (Toronto: University of Toronto Press, 1976).

Est, William, *The Trial of True Tears* (1613, STC 10538).

Estill, Laura, 'Commonplace Markers and Quotation Marks', *ArchBook* (Architecture of the Book), 7 March 2014, updated 25 February 2019. Available at: <http://drc.usask.ca/projects/archbook/commonplace.php>.

Estill, Laura, 'Commonplacing Readers', in *Shakespeare and Textual Studies*, ed. M. J. Kidnie and Sonia Massai (Cambridge: Cambridge University Press, 2015), pp. 149–62.

Estill, Laura, *Dramatic Extracts in Seventeenth-Century English Manuscripts: Watching, Reading, Changing Plays* (Newark: University of Delaware Press, 2015).

Euripides, *Hecuba and Iphigenia in Aulis*, trans. Erasmus (Basil, 1518).

Fein, Susanna, '*Somer Soneday*: Kingship, Sainthood, and Fortune in Oxford, Bodleian Library, MS Laud Misc. 108', in *The Texts and Contexts of Oxford, Bodleian Library, MS Laud Misc. 108: The Shaping of Vernacular Narrative*, ed. K. K. Bell and J. N. Couch (Leiden: Brill, 2010), pp. 275–97.

Ferrante, Elena, 'Dialogue and Ellipsis', *Guardian*, 30 June 2018. Available at: <https://www.theguardian.com/lifeandstyle/2018/jun/30/elena-ferrante-dialogue-imposes-an-ellipsis>.

Fitzherbert, Anthony, *The Book of Justice of Peace* (1505, STC 14862).

Fleming, Juliet, 'Changed Opinion as to Flowers', in *Renaissance Paratexts*, ed. Helen Smith and Louise Wilson (Cambridge: Cambridge University Press, 2011), pp. 48–64.

Fleming, Juliet, *Cultural Graphology* (Chicago: University of Chicago Press, 2016).

Fleming, Juliet, 'How to Look at a Printed Flower', *Word & Image* 22:2 (2006), 165–87.

Fletcher, John, and William Shakespeare, *Two Noble Kinsmen* (1634, STC 11075).

Flood, Allison, 'First Novel Inspired by CIA's *Doctor Zhivago* Plan Nets $2m Book Deal', *Guardian*, 11 June 2018. Available at: <https://www.theguardian.com/books/2018/jun/11/first-novel-doctor-zhivago-2m-lara-prescott-we-were-never-here>.

Florio, John, *The Essays of Montaigne* (1603, STC 18041).

Florio, John, *The First Fruits* (1578, STC 11096).

Florio, John, *Queen Anna's New World of Words, or Dictionarie of the Italian and English Tongues* (1611, STC 11099).

Florio, John, *A World of Words* (1598, STC 11098).

Foakes, R. A., 'The "Part" of Orlando in Robert Greene's Play *Orlando Furioso*', Henslowe-Alleyn Digitalisation Project. Available at: <https://www.henslowe-alleyn.org.uk/essays/orlando.html>.

Foer, Jonathan Safran, *Tree of Codes* (London: Visual Editions, 2010).

Ford, John, *The Dramatic Works of John Ford*, ed. William Gifford (London: John Murray, 1827).

Ford, John, *The Dramatic Works of John Ford*, ed. Henry Weber (Edinburgh: A. Constable, 1811).

Ford, John, *The Lady's Trial* (1639, STC 11161).

Ford, John, *Love's Sacrifice* (1633, STC 11164).

Ford, John, *'Tis Pity She's a Whore*, ed. Simon Barker (London: Routledge, 1997).

Foxe, John, *Pandectae Locorum Communium Praecipua Rerum Capita et Titulos Ordine Alphabetico Complectentes* (1585, STC 11239.5).

Frame, Donald M., *Montaigne: A Biography* (New York: Harcourt, Brace & World Inc., 1965).

Frampton, Saul, *When I am Playing with my Cat, How Do I Know that She is Not Playing with Me: Montaigne and Being in Touch with Life* (New York: Vintage Books/Random House, 2011).

Fraunce, Abraham, *The Countess of Pembroke's Ivychurch* (1591, STC 11340).

Freedman, Barbara, 'Shakespearean Chronology, Ideological Complicity, and Floating Texts: Something is Rotten in Windsor', *Shakespeare Quarterly* 45:2 (1994), 190–210.

Frénais, Joseph, *Voyage Sentimental par M. Stern, sous le nom d'Yorick; traduit de l'Anglois par M. Frénais*, 2 vols in 1 (Amsterdam and Paris, 1769).

Fuller, Thomas, *The Worthies of England* (1662, Wing F2441).

Fulwell, Ulpian, *Like Will to Like* (after 1568? STC 11473).

Gaggero, Christopher, 'Pleasure Unreconciled to Virtue: George Gascoigne and Didactic Drama', in *Tudor Drama before Shakespeare, 1485–1590*, ed. Lloyd Kermode, Jason Scott-Warren, and Martine van Elk (Basingstoke: Palgrave Macmillan, 2004), pp. 167–94.

Gairdner, James (ed.), *The Chronicles and Memorials of Great Britain and Ireland during the Middle Ages* (London: Longman, Brown, Green, 1858).

Gardini, Nicola, *Lacuna: Saggio sul non detto* (Turin: Einaudi, 2014).

Gascoigne, George, *The Glass of Government* (1575, STC 11643a).

Gascoigne, George, *Grief of Joy: Certain Elegies*, in British Library Royal MS 18 A LXI.

Gascoigne, George, *A Hundreth Sundrie Flowres* (1573, STC 11635).

Gascoigne, George, *Pleasantest Works* (1587, STC 11639).

Gascoigne, George, *Poesies* (1575, STC 11636).

Gascoigne, George, *The Steel Glass* (1576, STC 11645).

Gee, John, *Hold Fast* (1624, STC 11705).

Gerard, W. B., *Laurence Sterne and the Visual Imagination* (Aldershot: Ashgate, 2006).

Gerrig, R. J., *Experiencing Narrative Worlds: On the Psychological Activities of Reading* (Boston, MA: Yale University Press, 1993).

Gibson, Jonathan, 'Significant Space in Manuscript Letters', *The Seventeenth Century* 12:1 (1997), 1–10.

Gilbert, W. S., *The Mikado*, in *The Savoy Operas*, vol. I (London: Macmillan, 1957).

Ginsberg, Allen, *Howl and Other Poems* (San Francisco, CA: City Light Books, 1956).

Ginsberg, Allen, *Howl: Original Draft Facsimile, Transcript and Variant Versions, Fully Annotated by Author*, ed. Barry Miles (London: Harper Perennial 2006).

Gitelman, Lisa, *Paper Knowledge: Towards a Media History of Documents* (Durham, NC: Duke University Press, 2014).

Godshalk, W. L., 'Hero and Leander: The Sense of an Ending', in *'A Poet and a filthy Play-Maker': New Essays on Christopher Marlowe*, ed. Kenneth Friedenreich, Constance B. Kuriyama, and Roma Gill (New York: AMS Press, 1988), pp. 293–314.

Goldberg, Jonathan, 'Romeo and Juliet's Open R's', in *Romeo and Juliet: William Shakespeare*, ed. R. S. White (Basingstoke: Palgrave, 2001), pp. 194–212.

Goldstein, Thalia R., and P. Bloom, 'Characterizing Characters: How Children Make Sense of Realistic Acting', *Cognitive Development, Special Issue: Cognizing the Unreal* 34 (2015), 39–50.

Goldstein, Thalia R., and E. Winner, 'Enhancing Empathy and Theory of Mind', *Journal of Cognition and Development* 13 (2012), 19–37.

Goodwin, George, *Of the Pope's Supremacy*, in *Babel's Balm* (1624, STC 12030).

Graves, Robert, *Poems Selected by Himself* (Harmondsworth: Penguin, 1957).

Grazia, Margreta de, 'Shakespeare in Quotation Marks', in *The Appropriation of Shakespeare: Post-Renaissance Reconstructions of the Works and the Myth*, ed. Jean I. Marsden (New York: St Martin's, 1991), pp. 57–71.

Green, Melanie C., 'Transportation into Narrative Worlds: Implications for the Self', in *On Building, Defending and Regulating the Self: A Psychological Perspective*, ed. Abraham. Tesser, J. V. Wood, and D. A. Stapel (New York: Psychology Press, 2005), pp. 53–76.

Green, Melanie C., T. C. Brock, and G. F. Kaufman, 'Understanding Media Enjoyment: The Role of Transportation into Narrative Worlds', *Communication Theory* 14 (2004), 311–27.

Greene, Robert, *The Black Book's Messenger* (1592, STC 12223).

Greene, Robert, *The Defense of Coney Catching* (1592, STC 5656).

Greene, Robert, *Farewell to Folly* (1591, STC 12241).

Greene, Robert, *Friar Bacon and Friar Bungay* (1594, STC 12267).

Greene, Robert, *A Groatsworth of Wit* (1592, STC 12245).

Greene, Robert, *James IV* (1598, STC 12308).

Greene, Robert, *John of Bordeaux*, unpublished manuscript, Alnwick Castle, MS 507.

Greene, Robert, *John of Bordeaux*, ed. W. L. Renwick (Oxford: Oxford University Press, 1936).

Greene, Robert, *A Maiden's Dream upon the Death of the Right Honorable Sir Christopher Hatton, Knight, Late Lord Chancellor of England* (1591, STC 12271).

Greene, Robert, *Orlando Furioso* (1594, STC 12265).

Greene, Robert, *The Spanish Masquerado* (1589, STC 12309).

Greer, Germaine, *Shakespeare's Wife* (London: Bloomsbury, 2007).

Greg, W. W. (ed.), *Two Elizabethan Stage Abridgements: The Battle of Alcazar and Orlando Furioso* (Oxford: Oxford University Press, 1922).

Griffiths, Andy, *Just Stupid!* (New York: Scholastic Printing, 1999).

Griffiths, Jane, *Diverting Authorities: Experimental Glossing Practices in Manuscript and Print* (Oxford: Oxford University Press, 2015).

Haddon, Mark, *The Porpoise* (London: Chatto & Windus, 2019)

Hagthorpe, John, *Divine Meditations and Elegies* (1622, STC 12602).

Hamilton, A. C. (gen. ed.), *The Spenser Encyclopedia* (Toronto: University of Toronto Press, 1990).

Hardman, Phillipa, 'Interpreting the Incomplete Scheme of Illustration in Cambridge Corpus Christi College MS 61', *English Manuscript Studies* 6 (1977), 52–69.

Hardman, Phillipa, 'Lydgate's "Life of our Lady": A Text in Transition', *Medium Ævum* 65:2 (1996), 248–68.

Hardman, Phillipa, 'Reading the Spaces: Pictorial Intentions in the Thornton MSS, Lincoln Cathedral MS 91, and BL MS Add. 31042', *Medium Aevum* 63:2 (1994), 250–74.

Hardman, Phillipa, 'Windows into the Text: Unfilled Spaces in some Fifteenth-Century English Manuscripts', in *Texts and their Contexts, Papers from the Early Book*

Society, ed. John Scattergood and Julia Boffey (Dublin: Four Courts Press, 1997), pp. 44–70.

Harris, Alexandra, *Virginia Woolf* (London: Thames & Hudson, 2016).

Harrison, Stephen, *The Arches of Triumph* (1604, STC 12863).

Harsnett, Samuel, *A Declaration of Egregious Popish Impostures* (1603, STC 12880).

Haughton, Hugh, 'Xanadu and Porlock: Thoughts on Composition and Interruption', in *The Book of Interruptions*, ed. David Hillman and Adam Phillips (Oxford and Bern: Peter Lang, 2007), pp. 27–43.

Haughton, William, *Englishmen for my Money* (1616, STC 12931).

Hawes, Stephen, *The Conversion of Swearers* (1509, STC 12943.5).

Hawes, Stephen, *The Minor Poems*, ed. Florence W. Gluck and Alice B. Morgan (Oxford: Oxford University Press, 1974).

Hawes, Stephen, [*The Pastime of Pleasure*]: *The History of Graunde Amour and la Bel Pucel* (1509, STC 12948).

Heath, Deana, 'Obscenity, Censorship, and Modernity', in *A Companion to the History of the Book*, ed. Simon Eliot and Jonathan Rose (Oxford: Blackwell, 2008), pp. 508–19.

Herrick, Robert, *The Hesperides* (1648, Wing H1595).

Heywood, Thomas, *The Captives*, British Library MS Egerton 1994, fols 52–73.

Heywood, Thomas, *The Captives*, ed. Arthur Brown (Malone Society Reprint; Oxford: Oxford University Press, 1953).

Heywood, Thomas, *1 Edward IV* (1600, STC 13342).

Heywood, Thomas, *1 Edward IV*, in *The First and Second Parts of King Edward IV*, ed. Richard Rowland (Revels; Manchester: Manchester University Press, 2005).

Heywood, Thomas, *2 Edward IV* (1600, STC 13342).

Heywood, Thomas, *The Fair Maid of the Exchange* (1607, STC 13317).

Heywood, Thomas, *How to Choose a Good Wife from a Bad* (1602, STC 5594).

Heywood, Thomas, *If You Know Not Me, You Know Nobody* (1605, STC 13328).

Heywood, Thomas, *The Rape of Lucrece* (1608, STC 13360).

Heywood, Thomas, *A Woman Killed with Kindness* (1607, STC 13371).

Heywood, Thomas, *A Woman Killed with Kindness*, in *Drama of the English Renaissance I: The Tudor Period*, ed. Russell A. Fraser and Norman Rabkin (New York: Macmillan, 1976).

Heywood, Thomas, *A Woman Killed with Kindness*, ed. R. W. van Fossen (Revels; London: Methuen, 1961).

Heywood, Thomas, *A Woman Killed with Kindness*, ed. Brian Scobie (1985; New Mermaids; London: A. & C. Black, 1991).

Heywood, Thomas, *A Woman Killed with Kindness*, ed. Margaret Jane Kidnie (Arden; London: Bloomsbury, 2017).

Hicks, Gary, *Fate's Bookie: How the Lottery Shaped the World* (Stroud: History, 2009).

Holinshed, Raphael, *Chronicles of England, Scotland and Ireland* (1587, STC 13569), vol. VI. Available at: <http://english.nsms.ox.ac.uk/holinshed/texts.php?text1= 1587_8333>.

Holland, Peter, 'Theseus' Shadows in *A Midsummer Night's Dream*', *Shakespeare Survey* 47 (1994), 139–51.

Homer, *The Odyssey*, trans. E. V. Rieu, rev. D. C. H. Rieu (Harmondsworth: Penguin Books, 1991).

Hood, Thomas, *The Use of Both the Globes* (1592, STC 13698).

Hooks, Adam, *Selling Shakespeare: Biography, Bibliography, and the Booktrade* (Cambridge: Cambridge University Press, 2016).

Hoppe, Harry R., '*John of Bordeaux*: A Bad Quarto that Never Reached Print', *Studies in Honor of A. H. R. Fairchild, University of Missouri Studies* 21 (1946), 119–32.

Housman, A. E., 'Transpositions in the *Ibis* of Ovid', in *The Classical Papers of A. E. Housman*, vol. III, ed. J. Diggle and F. R. D. Goodyear (London: Cambridge University Press, 1971), pp. 969–81.

Houston, Keith, *Shady Characters* (London: Penguin, 2013).

Howard, Jean E., and Phyllis Rackin, *Engendering a Nation: Shakespeare's Histories* (London: Routledge, 1997).

Howes, Alan B. (ed.), *Sterne: The Critical Heritage* (London: Routledge & Kegan Paul, 1974).

Hughes, Geoffrey, *Swearing: A Social History of Foul Language, Oaths and Profanity in English* (Oxford: Blackwell, 1991).

Hunter, G. K., 'The Marking of Sententiae in Elizabethan Printed Plays, Poems, and Romances', *The Library* 5–6: 3–4 (1951), 171–88.

Iser, Wolfgang, *How to Do Theory* (Oxford: Blackwell Publishing, 2006).

J. B. [i.e. 'B. J.'], *Guy, Earl of Warwick* (1661, Wing J5).

J. B. [i.e. 'B. J.'], *Guy Earl of Warwick*, ed. Helen Moore (Malone Society Reprint; Manchester: Manchester University Press, 2006).

James, C. W., *Chief Justice Coke, his Family and Descendants at Holkham* (London: Country Life Ltd; New York: Charles Scribner's Sons, 1929).

Johns, Adrian, *The Nature of the Book* (Chicago: University of Chicago Press, 1998).

Jonson, Ben, *The Alchemist* (1612, STC 14755).

Jonson, Ben, *Bartholomew Fair, The Devil is an Ass, and The Staple of News* (1631, STC 14753.5).

Jonson, Ben, *Bartholomew Fair*, ed. Suzanne Gossett (Revels Student Editions; Manchester: Manchester University Press, 2000).

Jonson, Ben, *The Complete Poems*, ed. George Parfitt (London: Penguin, 1975).

Jonson, Ben, *Cynthia's Revels, or The Fountain of Self-Love* (1601, STC 14773).

Jonson, Ben, *The Devil is an Ass* (1641, Wing J1011).

Jonson, Ben, *The Devil is an Ass*, in *Bartholomew Fair, The Devil is an Ass, and The Staple of News* (1631, STC 14753.5).

Jonson, Ben, *The Devil is an Ass and Other Plays*, ed. M. J. Kidnie (Oxford: Oxford University Press, 2000).

Jonson, Ben, *Epicoene*, ed. R. V. Holdsworth (New Mermaids; London: Ernest Benn Ltd, 1979).

Jonson, Ben, 'Epistle to Elizabeth, the Countess of Rutland', British Library Harley MS 4064 and Bodleian Rawlinson Poetry MS 31.

Jonson, Ben, *Every Man in his Humour* (1601, STC 14766).

Jonson, Ben, *Every Man in his Humour*, ed. Robert S. Miola (Revels Edition; Manchester: Manchester University Press, 2000).

Jonson, Ben, *Every Man out of his Humour* (1600, STC 14767).

Jonson, Ben, *Mortimer, his Fall*, ed. Karen Britland, in *The Cambridge Edition of the Works of Ben Jonson*, vol. VII, ed. David Bevington, Martin Butler, and Ian Donaldson (Cambridge: Cambridge University Press, 2012).

Jonson, Ben, *Poetaster* (1602, STC 14781).

Jonson, Ben, *The Staple of News* in *Bartholomew Fair, The Devil is an Ass, and The Staple of News* (1631, STC 14753.5).

Jonson, Ben, 'To Thomas Palmer', British Library MS Add. 18040, fol. 10.

Jonson, Ben, *Works* (1616, STC 14751).

Jonson, Ben, *Works* (1616, STC 14752).

Jonson, Ben, *Works* (1641, STC 14754).

Joyce, James, *Finnegans Wake*, ed. Robert-Jan Henkes, Erik Bindervoet, Finn Fordham, and Jeri Johnson (Oxford: Oxford University Press, 2012).

Keefer, Michael, 'The A and B Texts of Marlowe's *Doctor Faustus*', *Papers of the Bibliographical Society of America* 100:2 (2006), 227–57.

Kellaway, Kate, review of Alice Oswald, *Woods Etc.*, *The Observer*, 19 June 2005.

Kepler, Johannes, *Dissertatio cum nuncio sidereo nuper ad mortales misso a Galilaeo Galilaeo* (Frankfurt, 1611).

Kermode, Lloyd, ed. *Three Renaissance Usury Plays* (Revels; Manchester: Manchester University Press, 2009).

Keymer, Thomas, 'Dying by Numbers: *Tristram Shandy* and Serial Fiction', *The Shandean* 8 (1996), 41–67 and 9 (1997), 34–69.

Keymer, Thomas, *Sterne, the Moderns and the Novel* (Oxford: Oxford University Press, 2002).

Kidnie, Margaret Jane, 'The Staging of Shakespeare's Drama in Print Editions', in *Textual Performances*, ed. Lukas Erne and Margaret Jane Kidnie (Cambridge: Cambridge University Press, 2004), pp. 158–77.

King James VI, *Essays of a Prentice in the Divine Art of Poesie* (Edinburgh, 1584, STC 14373).

Kipling, Gordon, review of Stephen Hawes, *The Minor Poems* ed. Gluck and Morgan, *Review of English Studies* 27 (1976), 457–8.

Kirwan, Peter, *Shakespeare and the Idea of Apocrypha: Negotiating the Boundaries of the Dramatic Canon* (Cambridge: Cambridge University Press, 2015).

Kleon, Austin, *Newspaper Blackout* (New York: Harper Perennial, 2010).

Knight, Jeffrey Todd, *Bound to Read: Compilations, Collections, and the Making of Renaissance Literature* (Philadelphia: University of Pennsylvania Press, 2013).

Kolin, Philip C., 'Bawdy Uses of Et Cetera', *American Speech* 58:1 (1983), 75–8.

Krier, Theresa, 'Time Lords: Rhythm and Interval in Spenser's Stanzaic Narrative', *Spenser Studies* 21 (2007), 1–9.

Kunastrokius, Jeremiah, *Explanatory Remarks upon the Life and Opinions of Tristram Shandy* (London: E. Cabe, 1760).

Kunastrokius, Jeremiah, *The Life and Opinions of Jeremiah Kunastrokius, Doctor of Physick, &c. &c. &c.* (London: E. Cabe, 1760).

Lakoff, George, *Don't Think of an Elephant* (White River Junction, VT: Chelsea Green Publishing, 2004).

Lamb, Jonathan P., *Shakespeare in the Marketplace of Words* (Cambridge: Cambridge University Press, 2017).

Landon, Margaret, *Anna and the King of Siam* (London: Longman's, Green & Co., 1944).

Leggatt, Alexander, '*Arden of Faversham*', *Shakespeare Survey* 36 (1983), 121–36.

Leggatt, Alexander, 'Artistic Coherence in *The Unfortunate Traveller*', *Studies in English Literature, 1500–1900* 14:1 (1974), 31–46.

Leggatt, Alexander, *Ben Jonson: His Vision and Art* (London: Methuen, 1981).

Leland, John, *Principum, ac illustrium aliquot & eruditorum in Anglia virorum* (1589, STC 15447).

Lennard, John, '*But I Digress*': *The Exploitation of Parentheses in English Printed Verse* (Oxford: Oxford University Press, 1991).

Lesser, Zachary, and Peter Stallybrass, 'The First Literary *Hamlet* and the Commonplacing of Professional Plays', *Shakespeare Quarterly* 59:4 (2008), 371–420.

Lettvin, Jerome, 'Morgenstern and Mythopoetry', *The Fat Abbot: A Literary Review* 4 (1962), 12–20.

Levelt, Sjoerd, blogpost. Available at: <https://levelt.wordpress.com/tag/john-selden/>.

Levenston, E. A., *The Stuff of Literature: Physical Aspects of Texts and their Relation to Literary Meaning* (Albany: State University of New York Press, 1992).

Lodge, Thomas, *The Wounds of Civil War* (1594, STC 16678).

Lodge, Thomas, *The Wounds of Civil War*, ed. Joseph W. Houppert (Regent's Renaissance Drama Series; London: Edward Arnold, 1970).

Luke, Nicholas, *Shakespeare Arrivals* (Cambridge: Cambridge University Press, 2017).

Lyly, John, *Mother Bombie* (1594, STC 17084).

Lyly, John, *Sapho and Phao* (1584, STC 17086).

Lyon, Tara L., 'Richard Jones, *Tamburlaine the Great*, and the Making (and Remaking) of a Serial Play Collection in the 1590s', in *Christopher Marlowe, Theatrical Commerce and the Booktrade*, ed. Kirk Melnikoff and Roslyn Knutson (Cambridge: Cambridge University Press, 2018), pp. 149–63.

McCord, David (ed.), *What Cheer* (Ann Arbor: University of Michigan Press, 1945).

McEnery, Tony, *Swearing in English: Bad Language, Purity and Power from 1586 to the Present* (Abingdon: Routledge, 2006).

McGann, Jerome, *The Textual Condition* (Princeton, NJ: Princeton University Press, 1991).

McKenzie, D. F., '*What's Past is Prologue*': *The Bibliographical Society and History of the Book*, The Bibliographical Society Centenary Lecture, 14 July 1992 (Munslow: Hearthstone Publications, 1993).

McKitterick, David, 'What is the Use of Books without Pictures: Empty Spaces in Some Early Printed Books', *La Bibliofilia* 116:1–3 (2014), 67–82.

McLeod, Randall [Random Cloud], 'Obliterature: Reading a Censored Text of Donne's "To his mistress going to bed" ', *English Manuscript Studies* 12 (2005), 83–138.

McLeod, Randall [Random Cloud], 'Shakespeare Babel', in *Reading Readings: Essays on Shakespeare Editing in the Eighteenth Century*, ed. Joanna Gondris (Newark, DE: Associated University Presses, 1997), pp. 1–70.

McMillin, Scott, *The Elizabethan Theatre and the Book of Sir Thomas More* (Ithaca, NY: Cornell University Press, 1987).

MacNally, Leonard, *Sentimental Excursions to Windsor and Other Places* (London, 1781).

McNeir, Waldo F., 'Robert Greene and *John of Bordeaux*', *Publications of the Modern Language Association* 66 (1951), 540–3.

Maguire, Laurie E., 'Classical and Commercial Drama in Print in Sixteenth-Century England', plenary talk, 'Academic Drama and the Popular Stage', University of St Andrews, June 2020.

Maguire, Laurie E., *Shakespearean Suspect Texts: The 'Bad' Quartos and their Contexts* (Cambridge: Cambridge University Press, 1996).

Mak, Bonnie, *How the Page Matters* (Toronto: University of Toronto Press, 2011).

Manly, John, and Helen Rickert, *The Text of the Canterbury Tales: Studied on the Basis of all Known Manuscripts*, vols V–VIII (Chicago: University of Chicago Press, *c*.1940).

Manningham, John, *Diary*, British Library Harley MS 5353.

Marlowe, Christopher, *The Complete Plays*, ed. Mark Thornton Burnett (London: J. M. Dent, 1999).

Marlowe, Christopher, *Doctor Faustus: A 1604-Version*, ed. Michael Keefer (Peterborough, ON: Broadview Press, 1991).

Marlowe, Christopher, *Dr Faustus* (1604, STC 17429).

Marlowe, Christopher, *Dr Faustus* (1616, STC 17432).

Marlowe, Christopher, *Dr Faustus A- and B- Texts*, ed. David Bevington and Eric Rasmussen (Revels; Manchester: Manchester University Press, 1993).

Marlowe, Christopher, *Dr Faustus: Based on the A-Text*, ed. Roma Gill (London: A. & C. Black, 1989).

Marlowe, Christopher, *Dr Faustus: The A-Text*, ed. David Ormerod and Christopher Wortham (Nedlands: University of Western Australia Press, 1985).

Marlowe, Christopher, *Edward II* (1594, STC 17437).

Marlowe, Christopher, *Hero and Leander* (1598, STC 17413).

Marlowe, Christopher, *The Jew of Malta* (1633, STC 17412).

Marlowe, Christopher, *Tamburlaine the Great* (1590, STC 17425).

Marston, John, *Antonio and Mellida* (1602, STC 17473).

Marston, John, *The Dutch Courtesan* (1605, STC 17475).

Marston, John, *Parasitaster, or, The Fawn* (1606, STC 17484).

Marston, John, *Histriomastix* (1610, STC 13529).

Marston, John, *The Malcontent* (1604, STC 17479).

Marston, John, *The Malcontent* (1604, STC 17480).

Marston, John, *The Malcontent*, ed. George K. Hunter (Revels; Manchester: Manchester University Press, 1999).

Marston, John, *The Metamorphosis of Pygmalion's Image*, in *Elizabethan Minor Epics*, ed. Elizabeth Story Donno (London: Routledge & Kegan Paul, 1963), pp. 244–52.

Marston, John, *What You Will* (1607, STC 17487).

Marston, John, and John Webster, *The Malcontent* (1604, STC 17481).

Martin, Demetri, *This is a Book* (London: Penguin, 2011).

Mascall, Leonard, *Art and Manner How to Plant and Graft All Sorts of Trees* (1572, STC 17574).

Mazzio, Carla, *The Inarticulate Renaissance* (Philadelphia: University of Pennsylvania Press, 2009).

Medwall, Henry, *Fulgens and Lucres* (1512–16, STC 17778).

Medwall, Henry, *Fulgens and Lucres*, ed. F. S. Boas and A. W. Reed (Oxford: Clarendon Press, 1926).

Melnikoff, Kirk, *Elizabethan Publishing and the Makings of Literary Culture* (Toronto: University of Toronto Press, 2018).

Melville, Herman, *Moby Dick*, ed. Tony Tanner (World's Classics; Oxford: Oxford University Press, 2008).

Mennis, Katie, 'Alice Oswald and Homer', unpublished dissertation (Oxford University, March 2018).

Meres, Francis, *Palladis Tamia* (1598, STC 17834).

Middleton, Thomas, *The Changeling* (1653, Wing M1980).

Middleton, Thomas, *A Chaste Maid in Cheapside* (1630, STC 17877).

Middleton, Thomas, *The Collected Works*, ed. Gary Taylor and John Lavagnino with MacDonald P. Jackson, John Jowett, Valerie Wayne, and Adrian Weiss (Oxford: Clarendon Press, 2007).

Middleton, Thomas, *Papistomastix* (1606, STC 17913).

Middleton, Thomas, *The Phoenix* (Q 1607, STC 17892).

Middleton, Thomas, *The Second Maiden's Tragedy*, ed. W. W. Greg (Malone Society Reprint; Oxford: Oxford University Press, 1909).

Middleton, Thomas, *Women Beware Women*, in *Two New Plays* (1657, Wing M1989).

Middleton, Thomas, and Thomas Dekker, *The Roaring Girl* (1611, STC 17908).

Milton, John, *The History of Britain* (1670, Wing M2119).

Milton, John, *Poems 1645* (Wing M2160).

Miola, Robert S., 'Ben Jonson, Catholic Poet', *Renaissance and Reformation/Renaissance et Réforme* 25:4 (2001), 101–15.

Mohr, Melissa, *Holy Shit: A Brief History of Swearing* (Oxford: Oxford University Press, 2013).

Montaigne, Michel de, *Essais* (Bordeaux, 1580).

Montaigne, Michel de, *Essais* (Rouen, n.d.).

Montaigne, Michel de, *The Essays*, trans. John Florio (London, 1603, STC 18041).

Montaigne, Michel de, 'On Educating Children', in *Michel de Montaigne, The Complete Essays*, ed. M. A. Screech (Harmondsworth: Penguin, 1991), pp. 163–99.

Moss, Ann, *Printed Commonplace-Books and the Structuring of Renaissance Thought* (Oxford: Clarendon Press, 1996).

Munday, Anthony, *Fedele and Fortunio* (1585, STC 19447).

Munday, Anthony, and Henry Chettle, revised by Henry Chettle, Thomas Dekker, Thomas Heywood, and William Shakespeare, *Sir Thomas More*, ed. John Jowett (Arden; London: A. & C. Black, 2011).

Munday, Anthony, and Henry Chettle, revised by Henry Chettle, Thomas Dekker, Thomas Heywood, and William Shakespeare, *Sir Thomas More*, BL MS Harley 7368.

Munday, Anthony, and Henry Chettle, revised by Henry Chettle, Thomas Dekker, Thomas Heywood, and William Shakespeare, *Sir Thomas More*, ed. W. W. Greg (Malone Society Reprint; Oxford: Oxford University Press, 1911).

Nashe, Thomas, *The Complete Works of Thomas Nashe*, vol. II, ed. A. B. Grosart (London: privately printed, 1883).

Nashe, Thomas, *An Epitome of the First Book . . . Written Against Puritans* (1588, STC 17454).

Nashe, Thomas, *Have With You to Saffron Walden* (1596, STC 18369).

Nashe, Thomas, *Nashe's Lenten Stuffe* (1599, STC 18370).

Nashe, Thomas, *Pierce Pennilesse* (1592, STC 18371).

Nashe, Thomas, *Pierce Pennilesse* (1592, STC 18372).

Nashe, Thomas, *Pierce Pennilesse* (1592, STC 18373).

Nashe, Thomas, *Pierce Pennilesse*, in *Illustrations of Early English Literature*, vol. II, ed. John Payne Collier (London: privately printed, 1867–70), bound independently as separate pamphlet.

Nashe, Thomas, *Pierce Pennilesse et al.*, ed. Stanley Wells (London: Edward Arnold, 1964).

Nashe, Thomas, *The Terrors of the Night* (1594, STC 18379).

Nashe, Thomas, *The Unfortunate Traveller* (1594, STC 18380).

Nashe, Thomas, *The Unfortunate Traveller and Other Works*, ed. J. B. Steane (Harmondsworth: Penguin, 1971).

Nashe, Thomas, *The Works of Thomas Nashe*, 5 vols, ed. R. B. McKerrow (London: Sidgwick & Jackson, 1910).

Nell, Victor, *Lost in a Book: The Psychology of Reading for Pleasure* (Ann Arbor: Michigan State University, 2005).

Nesbitt, E., *The Wouldbegoods* (London: Ernest Benn, 1958).

Newbould, M.-C., *Adaptations of Laurence Sterne's Fiction: Sterneana, 1760–1840* (London: Routledge, 2013).

Newman, Harry, *Impressive Shakespeare: Identity, Authority and the Imprint in Shakespearean Drama* (London: Routledge, 2019).

Newman, Harry, ' "[P]rophane fidlers": Medical Paratexts and Indecent Readers in Early Modern England', in *Medical Paratexts from Medieval to Modern: Dissecting the Page*, ed. Hanna C. Tweed and Diane G. Scott (Basingstoke: Palgrave Macmillan, 2018), pp. 15–41.

Nicholl, Charles, *A Cup of News: The Life of Thomas Nashe* (London: Routledge/Kegan Paul, 1984).

North, Marcy L., *The Anonymous Renaissance: Cultures of Discretion in Tudor-Stuart England* (Chicago: University of Chicago Press, 2003).

Ong, Walter, *Orality and Literacy: The Technologizing of the Word* (London and New York: Methuen, 1982).

Oswald, Alice, *Falling Awake* (London: Jonathan Cape, 2016).

Oswald, Alice, *Tithonus: 46 Minutes in the Life of the Dawn* (London: Letter Press, 2014).

Oswald, Alice, *Woods etc.* (London: Faber and Faber, 2008).

Palmer, Thomas, *The Sprite of Trees and Herbs*, British Library MS Add. 18040.

Paracelsus, *How to Cure the French Pox*, comp. Phillippus Hermanus, trans. John Hester (1590, STC 13215).

Paterson, Don, *God's Gift to Women* (London: Faber and Faber, 1977).

Paterson, Don, *Reading Shakespeare's Sonnets* (London: Faber and Faber, 2010).

Peele, George, *The Arraignment of Paris* (1584, STC 19530).

Peele, George, *The Love of King David and Fair Bethsabe* (1599, STC 19540).

Peele, George, *The Tale of Troy* (1589, STC 19537).

Peele, George, *Volume One: The Life and Minor Works of George Peele*, ed. D. H. Horne, in *The Life and Works of George Peele*, 3 vols, ed. C. T. Prouty (New Haven, CT: Yale University Press, 1952).

Perec, Georges, *Species of Spaces and Other Places*, trans. and ed. John Sturrock (Harmondsworth: Penguin, 1999).

Perry, Curtis, *Eros and Power in English Renaissance Drama: Five Plays by Marlowe, Davenant, Massinger, Ford and Shakespeare* (Jefferson, NC: McFarlane & Co., 2008).

Petrarch, Francesco, *Il Petrarca, con l'esposizione d'Alessandro Velutello* (Venice, 1552).

Petrarch, Francesco, *Il Petrarca, con nuove spositione* (Venice, 1586).

Petrarch, Francesco, *Il Petrarca, con nuove spositione* (Venice, 1595).

Pittenger, Elizabeth, 'Dispatch Quickly: The Mechanical Reproduction of Pages', *Shakespeare Quarterly* 42:4 (1991), 389–408.

Pope, Alexander, *The Dunciad in Four Books Printed According to the Complete Copy Found in the Year 1742 with the Prolegomena of Scriblerus and Notes Variorum*, vol. IV (London: M. Cooper, 1743).

Porter, Henry, *The Two Angry Women of Abingdon* (1599, STC 20121.5).

Porter, Henry, *The Two Angry Women of Abingdon* (1599, STC 20122).

Posselius, Johannes, *Dialogues Containing all the Most Useful Words of the Latin Tongue* (STC 20129).

Potter, Lois, 'The Plays and the Playwrights, 1500-1576', in *The Revels History of Drama in English*, vol. II: *1500–1576*, ed. T. W. Craik, Clifford Leech, and Lois Potter (London: Methuen, 1980), pp. 143–257.

Prescott, Lara, *We Were Never Here* (London: Hutchinson, 2019).

Price, Owen, *English Orthographie* (1670, Wing P3395A).

Puttenham, George, *The Arte of English Poesie* (1589, STC 20519.5).

Puttenham, George, *The Arte of English Poesie*, ed. Gladys Willcock and Alice Walker (Cambridge: Cambridge University Press, 1936).

Rabelais, François, *Gargantua and Pantagruel* (1653, Wing R105).

Rajan, Balachandra, *The Form of the Unfinished: English Poetics from Spenser to Pound* (Princeton, NJ: Princeton University Press, 1985).

Raleigh, Walter, *The Poems of Sir Walter Ralegh*, ed. Agnes M. C. Latham (Cambridge, MA: Harvard University Press, 1951).

Rastell, John, *Calisto and Melibea* (*c.*1525, STC 20721).

Rastell, John, *The Nature of the Four Elements* (*c.* 1520, STC 20722).

Rauschenberg, Robert, 'Erased de Kooning Drawing', Rauschenberg Research Project, July 2013. San Francisco Museum of Modern Art. Available at: <https://www.sfmoma.org/essay/erased-de-kooning-drawing/>.

Reza, Yasmina, *Art*, trans. Christopher Hampton (London: Faber and Faber, 1996).

Rhodes, Neil, 'Nashe, Rhetoric and Satire', in *Jacobean Poetry and Prose: Rhetoric, Representation and the Popular Imagination*, ed. Clive Bloom (Basingstoke: Macmillan, 1988), pp. 25–43.

Richards, I. A., 'How Does a Poem Know When It is Finished?', in *Parts and Wholes*, ed. Daniel Lerner (Glencoe, IL: Free Press, 1963), pp. 163–74.

Ricks, Christopher, 'William Wordsworth 1', in Christopher Ricks, *The Force of Poetry* (Oxford: Oxford University Press, 1997), pp. 89–116.

Roberts, Dunstan, 'The Expurgation of Traditional Prayer Books (*c.*1535–1600)', *Reformation* 15 (2010), 23–49.

Roberts, Sarah, 'White Painting'. Available at: <https://www.sfmoma.org/essay/white-painting-three-panel/>.

Ross, Trevor, *The Making of the English Literary Canon from the Middle Ages to the Late 18th Century* (Montreal and Kingston: McGill-Queen's University Press, 1998).

Rothenberg, Jerome (ed.), *Technicians of the Sacred*, 3rd edn (Los Angeles: University of California Press, 2017).

Rowley, William, Thomas Dekker, John Ford, &c., *The Witch of Edmonton* (Q 1658, Wing R2097).

Ryan, Marie-Laure, *Narrative as Virtual Reality: Immersion and Interactivity in Literature and Electronic Media* (Baltimore, MD: Johns Hopkins University Press, 2001).

S. S., *The Honest Lawyer* (1616, STC 21519).

Salomon, Linda Bradley, 'A Face in the Glasse: Gascoigne's *Glasse of Government* Re-Examined', *Studies in Philology* 71 (1974), 47–71.

Salzman, Paul (ed.), *An Anthology of Elizabethan Prose Fiction* (Oxford: Oxford University Press, 1987).

Saunders, George, *Lincoln in the Bardo* (London: Bloomsbury, 2017).

Sawday, Jonathan, *Print, Space, and Void* (in progress).

Schurink, Fred, 'Manuscript Commonplace Books, Literature, and Reading in Early Modern England', *Huntington Library Quarterly* 73:3 (2010), 453–69.

Scott, Alison V., 'Making a Virtue of Giddiness: Rethinking Troilus' (E)Motion', in *Shakespeare and Emotions: Inheritances, Enactments, Legacies*, ed. R. S. White, Mark Houlahan, and Katrina O'Loughlin (Basingstoke: Palgrave Macmillan, 2015), pp. 124–36.

Scott, Charlotte, *The Child in Shakespeare* (Oxford: Oxford University Press, 2019).

Scott-Warren, Jason, 'Reading Graffiti in the Early Modern Book', *Huntington Library Quarterly* 73:3 (2010), 363–81.

Seneca, Lucius Annaeus, *Thyestes* (1560, STC 22226).

Shakespeare, William, *1 Henry IV* (1598, STC 22280)

Shakespeare, William, *2 Henry IV* (1600, STC 22288).

Shakespeare, William, *The Complete Poems of Shakespeare*, ed. Cathy Shrank and Raphael Lyne (London: Routledge, 2018).

Shakespeare, William, *The Complete Sonnets and Poems*, ed. Colin Burrow (Oxford: Oxford University Press, 2002).

Shakespeare, William, *The Complete Works*, ed. Jonathan Bate and Eric Rasmussen (New York: Random House, 2007).

Shakespeare, William, *The Complete Works: Modern Critical Edition*, ed. Gary Taylor, John Jowett, Terry Bourus, and Gabriel Egan (Oxford: Oxford University Press, 2016).

Shakespeare, William, *The Complete Works of Shakespeare*, ed. David Bevington, 4th edn (New York: Longman, 1997).

Shakespeare, William, *The Norton Shakespeare based on the Oxford Edition*, ed. Stephen Greenblatt, Walter Cohen, Suzanne Gossett, Jean E. Howard, Katherine Eisaman Maus, and Gordon McMullan (New York: W. W. Norton, 1997).

Shakespeare, William, *Hamlet* (1603, STC 22275).

Shakespeare, William, *Hamlet* (1604, STC 22276).

Shakespeare, William, *Hamlet*, ed. Edward Hubler (Signet Classic; New York: New American Library, 1963).

Shakespeare, William, *Hamlet*, ed. Harold Jenkins (Arden 2; London: Methuen, 1982).

Shakespeare, William, *Hamlet* (*Q1 and F*), ed. Ann Thompson and Neil Taylor (Arden 3; London: Thomson Learning, 2006).

Shakespeare, William, *Hamlet* (*Q2*), ed. Ann Thompson and Neil Taylor (Arden 3; London: Thomson Learning, 2006).

Shakespeare, William, *Love's Labour's Lost* (1598, STC 22294).

Shakespeare, William, *Merchant of Venice* (1600, STC 22296).

Shakespeare, William, *Merchant of Venice* (1652, Wing S2938).

Shakespeare, William, *The Norton Folio Facsimile*, ed. Charlton Hinman (New York: W. W. Norton, 1968).

Shakespeare, William, *Othello* (1622, STC 22305).

Shakespeare, William, *The Rape of Lucrece* (1609, STC 13360).

Shakespeare, William, *Richard II* (1597, STC 22307).

Shakespeare, William, *The Riverside Shakespeare*, ed. G. Blakemore Evans with J. J. M. Tobin, 2nd edn (Boston, MA: Houghton Mifflin, 1997).

Shakespeare, William, *Romeo and Juliet* (1597, STC 22322).

Shakespeare, William, *Romeo and Juliet* (1599, STC 22323).

Shakespeare, William, *Romeo and Juliet*, ed. Brian Gibbons (Arden 2; London: A. & C. Black, 1990).

Shakespeare, William, *Romeo and Juliet*, ed. René Weis (Arden 3; London: Bloomsbury, 2012).

Shakespeare, William, *Shakespeare's Sonnets*, ed. Katherine Duncan-Jones (London: Thomson Learning, 1997).

Shakespeare, William, *Sonnets*, ed. G. Blakemore Evans with new intro. by Stephen Orgel (Cambridge: Cambridge University Press, 2006).

Shakespeare, William, *Sonnets*, ed. John Kerrigan (Harmondsworth: Penguin, 1986).

Shakespeare, William, *The Winter's Tale*, ed. Frank Kermode (New York: New American Library, 1963).

Shakespeare, William, *The Winter's Tale*, ed. John Pitcher (Arden 3; London: Methuen/A. & C. Black, 2010).

Shakespeare, William, and John Fletcher, *Two Noble Kinsmen* (1634, STC 11075).

Shaw, G. B., 'Letter to Ellen Terry, 5th January 1898', in *Ellen Terry and Bernard Shaw: A Correspondence*, ed. Christopher St. John (London: Reinhardt & Evans, 1949).

Sherman, William H., 'The Beginning of "The End": Terminal Paratext and the Birth of Print Culture', in *Renaissance Paratexts*, ed. Helen Smith and Louise Wilson (Cambridge: Cambridge University Press, 2011), pp. 65–87.

Sherman, William H., 'Early Modern Punctuation and Modern Editions: Shakespeare's Serial Colon', in *The Book in History, the Book as History: New Intersections of the Material Text*, ed. Heidi Brayman Hackel, Jesse M. Lander, and Zachary Lesser (New Haven, CT: Yale University Press, 2016), pp. 303–23.

Sherman, William H., *Used Books: Marking Readers in Renaissance England* (Philadelphia: University of Pennsylvania Press, 2008).

Shirley, Rodney W., *The Mapping of the World: Early Printed World Maps, 1472–1700* (Riverside, CA: Early World Press, 2001).

Sidney, Phillip, *Arcadia* (1590, STC 22539a).

Sidney, Phillip, *Arcadia* (1593, STC 22540).

Sidney, Phillip, *Astrophil and Stella* (1591, STC 22536).

Sidney, Phillip, *The Countess of Pembroke's Arcadia* (1593, STC 22540).

Skelton, John, *Magnyfycence* (*c.*1520, STC 22607).

Slights, William W. E., 'The Edifying Margins of Renaissance English Books', *Renaissance Quarterly* 42:4 (1989), 682–716.

Slights, William W. E., *Managing Readers: Printed Marginalia in English Renaissance Books* (Ann Arbor: University of Michigan Press, 2001).

Smith, Barbara Herrnstein, *In the Margins of Discourse* (Chicago: University of Chicago Press, 1978).

Smith, Emma, *This is Shakespeare* (Harmondsworth: Penguin/Random House, 2019).

Smith, Keri, *Finish This Book* (London: Penguin, 2011).

Smith, Keri, *This Is Not a Book* (London: Penguin, 2011).

Smith, Keri, *Wreck This Journal* (London: Penguin, 2013).

Smith, Peter J., 'Medlers and Meddlers: John Davies' *The Scourge of Folly* and Another Look at Rosaline's Open *Et Cetera*', *Cahiers Elisabéthains* 46 (1994), 71–3.

Smith, Zadie, *On Beauty* (London: Penguin, 2005).

Smyth, Adam, *Material Texts in Early Modern England* (Cambridge: Cambridge University Press, 2018).

Southwell, Anne, commonplace book, Folger Shakespeare Library MS V.b.198.

Spenser, Edmund, *Colin Clout's Come Home Again [and Other Minor Works]* (1611), FSL copy bound with *The Faerie Queene* (STC 23083.8).

Spenser, Edmund, *The Faerie Queene* (1590, STC 23080).

Spenser, Edmund, *The Faerie Queene* (1590, STC 23081).

Spenser, Edmund, *The Faerie Queene* (1590, STC 23081a).

Spenser, Edmund, *The Faerie Queene* (1590, STC 23083).

Spenser, Edmund, *The Faerie Queene*, ed. A. C. Hamilton (London: Longman, 1977).

Spenser, Edmund, *Shepherd's Calendar* (1611, STC 23093.5).

Spenser, Edmund, *Spenser: The Shorter Poems*, ed. Richard McCabe (Harmondsworth and New York: Penguin, 1999).

Spenser, Edmund, *Works* (1590, STC 23084).

Stallybrass, Peter, 'The Library and Material Texts', *Publications of the Modern Language Association* 119:5 (2004), 1347–52.

Stallybrass, Peter, ' "Little Jobs": Broadsides and the Printing Revolution', in *Agent of Change: Print Culture Studies after Elizabeth L. Eisenstein*, ed. Sabrina Alcorn Baron, Eric N. Lindquist, and Eleanor F. Shevlin (Amherst: University of Massachusetts Press, 2007), pp. 315–41.

Stallybrass, Peter, and Roger Chartier, 'Reading and Authorship: The Circulation of Shakespeare 1590–1619', in *A Concise Companion to Shakespeare and the Text*, ed. Andrew Murphy (Oxford: Blackwell, 2007), pp. 35–56.

Stayley, George, *Life and Opinions of an Actor* (Dublin: George Faulkner, 1762).

Steinberg, Leo, *Encounters with Rauschenberg* (Houston, TX: Menil Foundation, 2000).

Stenner, Rachel, *The Typographic Imaginary in Early Modern English Literature* (London: Routledge, 2019).

Stern, Tiffany, *Making Shakespeare: From Stage to Page* (London: Routledge, 2004).

Sterne, Laurence, *The Life and Opinions of Tristram Shandy*, vol. II (York: Ann Ward, 1759).

Sterne, Laurence, *The Life and Opinions of Tristram Shandy*, vol. III (Dublin: Henry Saunders, 1765).

Sterne, Laurence, *The Life and Opinions of Tristram Shandy*, vol. VI (London, 1759–67).

Sterne, Laurence, *The Life and Opinions of Tristram Shandy*, vol. IX (Dublin: Henry Saunders, 1779).

Sterne, Laurence, *The Life and Opinions of Tristram Shandy*, vol. IX (London: T. Becket & P. A. Dehondt, 1767).

Stoppard, Tom, *The Real Thing* (London: Faber and Faber, 1984).

Sturm, Johannes, *A Rich Storehouse or Treasurie for Nobility* (1570, STC 23408).

Sullivan, Hannah, *The Work of Revision* (Cambridge, MA: University of Harvard Press, 2013).

Swift, Jonathan, *Poems on Severall Occasions* (Dublin: George Faulkner, 1735).

Swift, Jonathan, *A Tale of a Tub and Other Satires*, ed. Kathleen Williams (London: J. M. Dent & Sons, 1975).

Swift, Jonathan, *Works*, vol. II (Dublin: George Faulkner, 1735).

Syme, Holger Schott, 'Unediting the Margin: Jonson, Marston, and the Theatrical Page', *English Literary Renaissance* 38:1 (2008), 142–71.

Tailor, Robert, *The Hog hath Lost his Pearl* (1614, STC 23658).

Taylor, Gary, and Michael Warren (eds.), *The Division of the Kingdoms* (Oxford: Clarendon Press, 1983).

Taylor, John, the Water Poet, *Works* (1630, STC 23725).

Taylor, Michael, ' "X" Marks the Spot: Petrarch's Censored Sonnets', blog post, 26 September 2016. Available at: <https://libguides.unm.edu/blog/x-marks-the-spot-petrarch-s-censored-sonnets>.

Terence, *Andria*, trans. Maurice Kyffin (1588, STC 23895).

Terence, *Works* (Venice, 1476).

Thwaites, Tony, 'Currency Exchanges: The Postmodern, Vattimo, Et Cetera, among Other Things (Et Cetera)', *Postmodern Culture: An Electronic Journal of Interdisciplinary Criticism* 7:2 (1997). DOI:101.1353/pmc.1997.0015.

Tomkis, Thomas, *Albumazar* (1615, STC 24101).

Tomkis, Thomas, *Lingua, or The Combat of the Tongue, and the Five Senses for Superiority* (1607, STC 24104).

Toner, Anne C., *Ellipsis in English Literature* (Cambridge: Cambridge University Press, 2015).

Tono, Yoshiaki, 'From a Gulliver's Point of View', *Art in America* 48:2 (1960), 54–9.

Tribble, Evelyn, *Margins and Marginality: The Printed Page in Early Modern England* (Charlottesville: University of Virginia Press, 1993).

Tudeau-Clayton, Margaret, ' "The Lady Shall Say her Mind Freely": Shakespeare and the S/Pace of Blank Verse', in *Shakespeare and Space: Theatrical Explorations of the Spatial Paradigm*, ed. Ina Habermann and Michelle Witen (London: Palgrave Macmillan, 2016), pp. 79–102.

Turberville, George, *Book of Hunting/Art of Venery* (1575, STC 24328).

Twycross, Meg, with Malcolm Jones and Alan Fetcher, 'Fart Pryke in Cul: The Pictures', *Medieval Theatre* 23 (2001), 11–121.

Vendler, Helen, *The Art of Shakespeare's Sonnets* (Cambridge, MA: Harvard University Press, 1997).

Vermeule, Blakey, *Why Do We Care about Literary Characters?* (Baltimore, MD: Johns Hopkins University Press, 2010).

Vickers, Brian, 'Bacon and Rhetoric', in *The Cambridge Companion to Bacon*, ed. Markku Peltonen (Cambridge: Cambridge University Press, 1996), pp. 200–31.

Vickers, Brian, *Shakespeare, Co-Author* (Oxford: Oxford University Press, 2004).

Vine, Angus, *In Defiance of Time: Antiquarian Writing in Early Modern England* (Oxford: Oxford University Press, 2010).

Vonnegut, Kurt, *Breakfast of Champions* (London: Jonathan Cape, 1973).

Voogd, Peter de, 'Sterne and Visual Culture', in *The Cambridge Companion to Laurence Sterne*, ed. Thomas Keymer (Cambridge: Cambridge University Press, 2009), pp. 110–59.

Wagstaff, Christopher, *The Life, Travels and Adventures of Christopher Wagstaff, Gentlemen, Grandfather to Tristram Shandy*, 2 vols (London, 1762).

Wakelin, Daniel, *Humanism, Reading, and English Literature 1430–1530* (Oxford: Oxford University Press, 2007), pp. 194–9.

Wakelin, Daniel, *Scribal Correction and Literary Craft: English Manuscripts 1375–1510* (Cambridge: Cambridge University Press, 2014).

Wakelin, Daniel, 'When Scribes Won't Write: Gaps in Middle English Books', *Studies in the Age of Chaucer* 36 (2014), 249–78.

Wakelin, Daniel, 'William Worcester Writes a History of his Reading', *New Medieval Literatures* 7 (2005), 53–71.

Water, Julia C. van de, 'The Bastard in *King John*', *Shakespeare Quarterly* 11 (1960), 137–46.

Webster, John, *Duchess of Malfi* (1623, STC 25176).

Webster, John, *The Duchess of Malfi*, ed. E. M. Brennan, 3rd rev. edn (New Mermaids; London: A. & C. Black, 1993).

Webster, John, and Thomas Dekker, *Northward Ho!* (1607, STC 6539).

Weedon, Margaret, 'An Uncancelled Copy of the First Collected Edition of Swift's Poems', *Library* 5th series 22 (1967), 44–56.

Weimann, Robert, *Author's Pen and Actor's Voice: Playing and Writing in Shakespeare's Theatre* (Cambridge: Cambridge University Press, 2000).

Wells, Stanley and Gary Taylor, with John Jowett and William Montgomery, *William Shakespeare: A Textual Companion* (Oxford: Clarendon Press, 1987).

Wheeler, Susan, *Meme* (Iowa City: University of Iowa Press, 2012).

Whetstone, George, *Promos and Cassandra* (1578, STC 25347).

Wiggins, Martin, with Catherine Richardson, *British Drama 1533–1642: A Catalogue*, vol. V: *1603–1608* (Oxford: Oxford University Press, 2015).

Wilkins, George, *The Miseries of Enforced Marriage* (1607, STC 25635).

Williams, Abigail, *The Social Life of Books: Reading Together in the 18th-Century Home* (New Haven, CT: Yale University Press, 2017).

Williams, Gordon, *A Dictionary of Sexual Language and Imagery in Shakespearean and Stuart Literature* (London: Athlone Press, 1994).

Wilmot, John, Earl of Rochester, *The Complete Poems of John Wilmot, Earl of Rochester*, ed. David M. Vieth (New Haven, CT: Yale University Press, 2002).

Wilmot, John, Earl of Rochester, *Poems on Several Occasions* (1680, Wing R1754A).

Wilson, Robert, *The Cobbler's Prophecy* (1594, STC 25781).

Wilson, Thomas, *The Art of Rhetoric* (1563, STC 25802).

Wittrock, Merlin C., 'Reading Comprehension', in *Neuropsychological and Cognitive Processes in Reading*, ed. Francis J. Pirozzolo and Merlin C. Wittrock (Oxford: Oxford University Press, 1981), pp. 229–60.

Wood, Anthony, *Athenae Oxonienses*, ed. P. Bliss (London: F. C. & J. Rivington et al., 1813).

Woodeson, Nicholas, 'King John', in *Players of Shakespeare 3*, ed. Russell Jackson and Robert Smallwood (Cambridge: Cambridge University Press, 1993), pp. 87–98.

Woods, Gillian, "Strange Discourse": The Controversial Subject of *Sir Thomas More*', *Renaissance Drama* 39 (2011), 3–35.

Woolf, Virginia, *Orlando: A Biography*, ed. Michael H. Whitworth (Oxford: Oxford University Press, 2015).

Woolf, Virginia, *Orlando: The Original Holograph Draft*, transcribed and ed. Stuart Nelson Clarke (London: S. N. Clarke, s).

Woolf, Virginia, *A Room of One's Own and Three Guineas*, ed. Anna Snaith (World's Classics; Oxford: Oxford University Press, 2015).

Worthen, W. B., 'The Imprint of Performance', in *Theorizing Practice: Redefining Theatre History*, ed. W. B. Worthen with Peter Holland (Basingstoke: Palgrave Macmillan, 2003), pp. 213–34.

Woudhuysen, H. R., 'The Dash—A Short but Quite Dramatic Account', paper delivered at 'The Jacobean Printed Book', Queen Mary College, University of London, September 2004.

Woudhuysen, H. R., 'Early Play Texts: Forms and Formes', in *In Arden: Editing Shakespeare*, ed. Ann Thompson and Gordon McMullan (London: Thomson, 2003), pp. 48–64.

Woudhuysen, H. R., *Sir Philip Sidney and the Circulation of Manuscripts 1558–1640* (Oxford: Clarendon Press, 1996).

Yarington, Robert, *Two Lamentable Tragedies* (1601, STC 26076).

Zunshine, Lisa, *Why We Read Fiction: Theory of Mind and the Novel* (Columbus: Ohio State University Press, 2006).

Index